MW00787006

The Children's Civil War

Ah, the children who came through the war. . . .
There are no monuments raised to them, no medals
struck in their honor.

   Grace King, *Memories of a*
   Southern Woman of Letters
   (1932)

Civil War America

Gary W. Gallagher, editor

The *Children's* Civil War

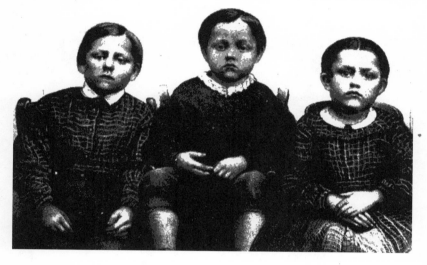

James Marten

The University of North Carolina Press

Chapel Hill and London

© 1998 The University

of North Carolina Press

All rights reserved

Designed by Richard Hendel

Set in Monotype Walbaum

by Tseng Information Systems

Manufactured in the United States of America

The paper in this book meets the guidelines for

permanence and durability of the Committee on

Production Guidelines for Book Longevity of the

Council on Library Resources.

Library of Congress

Cataloging-in-Publication Data

Marten, James Alan.

The children's Civil War / by James Marten.

    p.   cm. — (Civil War America)

Includes bibliographical references (p.   ) and index.

ISBN 0-8078-2425-9 (cloth: alk. paper)

ISBN 0-8078-4904-9 (pbk.: alk. paper)

    1. United States—History—Civil War, 1861–1865—Children.

I. Title.   II. Series.

E468.9.M125   1998

937.7'083—dc21   97-43647

    CIP

Portions of this work have been published previously,

in somewhat different form, as "Fatherhood in the Confederacy:

Southern Soldiers and Their Children," *Journal of Southern

History* 63 (May 1997), and "For the Good, the True, and

the Beautiful: Northern Children's Magazines and the Civil

War," *Civil War History* 41, no. 1 (March 1995), and are

reprinted here with permission, respectively, of the *Journal of

Southern History* and Kent State University Press.

04   03   02   01   00   7   6   5   4   3

For

Lauren Ruth Marten

and

Eli James Marten

Contents

Illustrations

Acknowledgments

What fun it has been to write this book! Old friends, acquaintances, and perfect strangers happily obliged requests for aid and advice. A number of scholars offered insights and citations through the mail or on the Internet, at conferences, or over beers, including Peter Bardaglio, William A. Blair, Jane Turner Censer, Stacy A. Cordery, Elizabeth Glade, Ted Karamanski, Karen Kehoe, John Leffler, Reid Mitchell, Paula Petrik, Patricia Richard, Ron Spiller, and William M. Tuttle Jr. Just before the final version of the manuscript was due in Chapel Hill, William H. Armstrong sent me a copy of his charming edition of Edward Parmelee Smith's letters to his daughter Gerty, which I gratefully incorporated into the book. Liam O'Brien photocopied the Newark High School *Atheneum* at the New Jersey Historical Society, while James C. Roach of the Gettysburg National Military Park and Robert K. Krick, chief historian at Fredericksburg-Spotsylvania National Military Park, sent me photocopies of hard-to-find documents. Mary Ruth Collins, Joel Jaecks, Dan Johnson, and John Y. Simon helped obtain illustrations. Research assistants provided by Marquette University made my job easier by, among other things, slogging through reels and reels of microfilm. They included James Bohl, Myrte Campbell, Annie Chenovick, Brian Faltinson, Frank Keeler, and Patricia Richard. Mary Cushing Smith and Dale Weisman provided room and board in Austin, while Violet Boyer put me up in Washington and humored me as we spent a Sunday visiting Virginia battlefields. T. Michael Parrish, George C. Rable, and Elliott West read the entire manuscript, and although I did not follow all of their advice, their friendly and encouraging and tough comments improved the manuscript immeasurably. It's a pleasure to join the long line of authors thanking Gary W. Gallagher, who "recruited" this book for the Civil War America series, gave me the opportunity to try out some of my ideas for a piece in the book he edited on the battle of Chancellorsville, and offered direct and helpful comments on the manuscript. Finally, it's an honor to be published by the University of North Carolina Press, where Kate

Douglas Torrey, David Perry, Ron Maner, and the entire team lived up to the press's reputation for professionalism and skill. Stephanie Wenzel's expert copyediting saved me from numerous errors and inconsistencies. Of course, I alone am responsible for any remaining errors of omission or commission.

My research was aided immeasurably by the typically stellar job of Julie Gores and Joan M. Sommer in the interlibrary loan office at Marquette University's Memorial Library. I'm proud to say that I'm one of their few customers with his own file, but not too proud to say that I'd be helpless without them. Even the best interlibrary loan department cannot get everything a historian needs, and I had the pleasure of visiting a number of archives and corresponding with archivists at many more. I was welcomed in person by the staffs at the American Antiquarian Society, the Center for American History at the University of Texas at Austin, the Perkins Library at Duke University, the Filson Club Historical Society in Louisville, the Library of Congress, the Maryland Historical Society, the Milwaukee County Historical Society, the New Hampshire Historical Society, the North Carolina Division of Archives and History, the Southern Historical Collection at the University of North Carolina at Chapel Hill, and the State Historical Society of Wisconsin. Librarians and archivists at the following institutions provided advice and photocopies: the Atlanta History Center, the Boston Public Library, the Historical Society of Pennsylvania, the Illinois Historical Survey at the University of Illinois at Urbana-Champaign, the J. Y. Joyner Library at East Carolina University, the Maine Historical Society, the Mississippi Department of Archives and History, the Museum of the Confederacy, the New Jersey Historical Society, the New York Public Library, the J. D. Phillips Library at the Peabody Essex Museum in Salem, Massachusetts, the Special Collections and Archives Division at the Rutgers University Library, and the Manuscript Department at the University of Virginia Library.

Travel to these scattered archives was funded by a Marquette University Regular Research Grant. MU also provided time to write with a Summer Faculty Fellowship and a semester-long sabbatical. Additional travel money and a summer stipend came from the Bradley Institute for Democracy and Public Values.

Parts of Chapters 2 and 3 first appeared as articles in *Civil War History* (vol. 41, March 1995) and the *Journal of Southern History* (vol. 63, May 1997), respectively, and are used with their editors' permission. Finally, I would like to acknowledge the following archives for permission to quote from their manuscript collections: the J. Y. Joyner Library at East Carolina State University, the Filson Club, the New Jersey Historical Society, the New York Public Library, and the Peabody Essex Museum.

During the years in which my professional life was occupied with Civil War children, my personal life was made richer and more meaningful by my wife, Linda, and our children, Lauren and Eli. Lauren seemed to be just a little girl when I started preliminary research; now she's a teenager. Eli was born early in the life of the project and sped through his infant, toddler, and "little boy" stages before it was finished. Lauren swallowed her embarrassment enough to let me talk to her class at school about Civil War kids; Eli took naps just often enough to let me get my work done. But those aren't the reasons I've dedicated the book to them. It has mattered a lot to me that, as I tried to piece together the lives of children born a generation before my great-grandparents even arrived in the United States, I had real-life children to watch over and worry about. I like to think that I know how the parents of Civil War children felt about their sons and daughters; I hope that my intimate knowledge of these two late twentieth-century kids gave me some insight into the responses of mid-nineteenth-century children to the danger and excitement they encountered during the Civil War. I don't pretend to completely understand these diverse and fascinating children from either century, but I've treasured my experiences with all of them.

The Children's Civil War

Introduction
Children of War

Children haunt our images of war. As victims and warriors, sources of heroic inspiration and tragic reflection, they appear in every conceivable medium. A blood-spattered Chinese baby
cries amid the wreckage of bombed-out Shanghai in a famous 1937
photograph, while over thirty years later a naked, napalm-seared
girl fleeing down a Vietnamese lane provides one of the most striking images of the Vietnam War. In print, Johnny Tremain fights
the American Revolution for millions of baby boomers, and Anne
Frank represents the depravity of the Holocaust. Motion pictures
bring to life the disruption of the Second World War: *Hope and
Glory* chronicles a boy's wonderful and frightening experiences
during the Battle of Britain, *Empire of the Sun* portrays another
boy coming of age in the grim confines of a Japanese prison camp,
and *Au Revoir, Les Enfants* presents the collision of youthful innocence with Nazi genocide in Vichy France. Television news broad-
casts feature the intersection of children and war with the riveting
stories of a young girl about the Iraqi murder of hundreds of Ku-
waitian babies; although apocryphal, her testimony helps propel
the United States into the Gulf War. The ethnic conflict in Bosnia
produces an international celebrity and a best-selling child's-eye
view in the person of Zlata Filipovic and her famous diary.[1]

But historians, surprisingly, have ignored those American children most affected by war. The men who fought the Civil War
have certainly had their stories told in increasingly sophisticated
and compelling ways.[2] Women—especially southern women—
have also been examined and reexamined by historians interested
in how their particular points of view were affected by the war.[3]

Numerous volumes describe the drama and hardships that characterized the strange wartime limbo between bondage and freedom for African Americans.[4] But virtually nothing has been published about children during the Civil War.

The Children's Civil War explains how the Civil War engaged northern and southern children.[5] Yet there are several things that I have not done. For example, this is not a comprehensive account of all children during the war or of their lives after the war. Most obviously, I chose not to look at underage soldiers or drummer boys. Although certainly children in a chronological sense, their military service made them de facto adults; their experiences resembled the exploits of the men with whom they served more than those of the children who stayed home.[6]

Asymmetrical sources pose another issue, which is perhaps inevitable in a study of northern and southern as well as black and white children. For instance, although I read virtually every children's periodical and novel published in the North and every schoolbook produced in the South during and just after the war, relatively little creative literature appeared in the Confederacy, and except for religious tracts and textbooks produced in the North, nothing was published for black children. In addition, although I was able to read hundreds of published and unpublished memoirs, autobiographies, reminiscences, and collections of correspondence of white Americans, I had to rely primarily on the famous, if problematical, multivolume collection of oral interviews from the 1930s with former slaves for information on African American children during the war. These sources reveal the incredible array of children's experiences during the Civil War, which often cut across regional, gender, and racial lines. Superficially, the war infiltrated the play of all children. But it also burdened them with greater responsibilities, opened them to greater autonomy and freedom, and politicized them.

Yet the war did not touch all children identically—especially in terms of material conditions, social mores, and the meanings children gave to the concept of liberty. To cite a few examples, girls and boys often played at war in different ways, neither southern nor northern white children experienced the same mixture of glorious release and tragic abuse as did young slaves, and few northern children had to cower in basements while enemy artillery destroyed their towns. Perhaps the greatest differences surfaced long after Appomattox, when as adults Civil War children sought meanings for the terror and excitement and heartbreak they had witnessed years before.

The Civil War, according to a northern woman who was only two when the war began, "made itself felt" even to the youngest children "from the words and looks of those about us; there was some struggle going on in the world which touched all life, brooded in faces, came out in phrases and exclamations and pitiful sights. . . . We knew, by the time we were four years old, what blue coats and brass buttons stood for." Of course, children learned far more about war than what color uniforms their side wore or how to read the moods on their worried parents' faces.[7]

The learning process followed several different tracks, each of which occupies a chapter in this book. Children first learned about the war—in its political and military manifestations—through the mass media. Newspapers and illustrated weeklies provided much daily information, but children also consumed war images at public performances and panoramas and from games and toys designed expressly for them. Other important sources of information were children's periodicals and novels and, especially for southern children, schoolbooks. Through these, children learned about the issues that sparked the war and about possible, even necessary, responses to the conflict. These rather abstract sources were amplified by letters from absent fathers, who provided firsthand information about the bloody war that had deprived them of their children's hugs as well as advice about how children could help their families get through the fiery trial. Finally, the horror and hardships and ferment and frenzy spawned by the war confronted children directly, as fathers and brothers were wounded or killed; as invaders bore down on plantations and farms, battles ravaged towns, and families fled their homes to places of relative safety; as blockades and poverty caused unprecedented hardships; and as patriotic excitement gripped northerners and southerners alike. I argue that this information and these experiences politicized children in the North and South and guided them to integrate the war into their everyday lives and to contribute in a myriad of ways to their countries' war efforts. I further suggest that the war affected, in striking ways, how they viewed the world, their country, their communities, and themselves.

In a demonstration of how the war touched the lives of children throughout the United and Confederate states, youngsters pose in front of a Confederate torpedo boat near Charleston in 1864. (Francis T. Miller, ed., *The Photographic History of the Civil War*, 10 vols. [New York: Review of Reviews, 1911], 6:267)

One of the unintended — although not necessarily surprising — discoveries that I made in writing this book is how much like modern Americans these long-dead people seem. Their prose may ring with Victorian cadences and their attitudes about race or gender relations may appear antique, but other facets of their personalities seem refreshingly familiar. For instance, we probably tend to think of the mid-nineteenth century as somewhat free of the commercialism that absolutely dominates the late twentieth century. But Civil War children saw all around them simplified, transient, and even exploitative images and notions about the war. More importantly, a modern reader will find common ground in the ways that children and parents interacted, if not in the exact language they used, at least in the attitudes and concerns and regrets their words expressed. Like parents in our own age, Civil War parents desperately wanted to tell their children that they would be safe always, that papa would come home soon, that enemies would stay away, and that the war — that harm in any guise — could not touch them. Through no fault of their own, many parents failed to keep those promises during the War between the States, but their children refused to blame them. This, perhaps, may be the most important evidence proving that children insisted on getting involved in the sectional conflict; they saw themselves not merely as appendages to their parents' experiences but as actors in their own right in the great national drama.

There are no images of Civil War children burned into our national memory like the stark photo of the terrified Vietnamese girl or the shyly smiling portrait of the doomed Anne Frank. But like previously unseen ghosts, children peer out from Civil War photographs taken in virtually every situation: they sit cross-legged outside a military hospital, picnic beside a primitive Confederate submarine, and gather before a U.S. Sanitary Commission warehouse. They muster to campaign for Lincoln in 1860 and to welcome home grizzled veterans in 1865. They appear as visitors to soldiers' quarters at Corinth, Petersburg, and City Point. There are no photographs of civilian children killed by stray bullets or by falling shells, although children were occasionally victims of the war's massive violence. But the following pages will provide many equally moving images of the war: the "Children of the Battlefield," a photograph of three youngsters, found in the death grip of a dead soldier at Gettysburg; the young Atlantan dodging shells to fetch milk for his baby brother; the sick and bewildered African American children huddled in leaky shacks in the mud of a Washington contraband camp. There may be no statues of these or any other children among the tens of thousands staring out over old battlefields, no tarnished medals on frayed ribbons lying in velvet-lined museum displays. But Civil War children will be remembered; their stories are their monuments.[8]

1 War Ain't Nuthin' but Hell on Dis Earth

Children, Society, and War

"One need not be a grown-up to imbibe the peculiar feeling that hangs over everything in time of war," wrote Hermon De-Long nearly fifty years after the war ended. "It was something like that sensation that goes about when a contagious disease suddenly breaks out in a peaceful community and the infected houses are placarded and streets barricaded. Young and old felt it weighing down like an incubus, and . . . our happy town seemed suddenly to grow grim and forbidding." Hermon was a northern boy who never heard a shot fired in anger, never feared invasion, and barely felt wartime hardships. But in his enthusiasm and participation in his country's war effort, he speaks for all Civil War children.

Although Hermon and his friends, tucked safely away in a small New York town, realized the magnitude of the crisis, they could be "just boys," taking pleasure from the excitement and drama of enlistment drives, the "awkward squads drilling on the public square," and the departure of recruits for the seat of war. Hermon fondly recalled war rallies, where bands played, "our most eloquent citizens" delivered "fervid speeches," and enlistment bounties crept higher as recruits "became more reluctant." At meetings of the local chapter of the U.S. Sanitary Commission, "young and old would meet and pick lint and sew bandages, singing at our work those sad old war songs such as 'Tenting Tonight,' 'Dear Mother, I've Come Home to Die,' '[The] Vacant Chair.' "

Hermon and his friends became avid politicians, "about equally divided between . . . Black Abolitionists and Copperheads." The latter wore Indian-head pins cut out of big copper cents, "while we Republicans had a big marching organization called the Wide-awakes, all fitted out with caps, capes, and torches." When war bulletins arrived at the local telegraph office, "we boys would read them to the eager crowd assembled" outside.

Even though Dansville never came within range of Rebel guns, the war did occasionally hit home. Northern children noticed the rising prices and declining quality of their snacks: "Peanuts were rare and wormy, and sticks of candy were reduced to the size of pipe stems." More seriously, Hermon remembered a friendly, older boy who was wounded; his "terrible suffering came very close to me, and I was glad when he got safely home." When another acquaintance died in battle, the dead youth's mother invited "we boys . . . to look at him, for in the midst of her grief there was a strong Spartan pride in the sacrifice she had made and she knew the lesson to us young Americans would be a good one."

Such occasions made for "solemn times," even in an isolated village, "and their influence was felt keenly by the boys through those long four years." Yet Hermon recognized that life went on, even in wartime: "People married and were given in marriage, business throve, and we boys kept right on with our tasks and sports. Our bodies and our minds developed with the passing years and all political differences were buried when we met on the ball field, at the swimming hole or at our homes."[1]

If war often meant reflective funerals and shoddy candy for northern children, it could mean blood and destruction for southern children. Fourteen-year-old Sue Chancellor described the extremes faced by Confederate children in a memoir published nearly sixty years after the war. Sue, her mother, and her six siblings lived in their ancestral home, the imposing brick house that had at one time served as an inn on the Plank Road between Fredericksburg and upcountry Virginia. From early in the war, Confederate pickets had frequently taken their meals at the Chancellor house, pausing to hear Sue's sisters play piano and to teach them card games. A number of Confederate generals visited, including J. E. B. Stuart, who presented Sue's sister Fannie with a gold dollar. Yankees also joined the Chancellor landscape early in the war. They would "come in a sweeping gallop up the big road with swords and sabres clashing," while servants hid meat under the front steps and Sue would "run and hide and pray . . . more and harder than ever in my life, before or since." Completing the wartime scenario in the Chancellor household were several refugees from Fredericksburg.

But nothing they had experienced so far prepared them for the cataclysm of the battle that would bear their name. Sue's account of the battle of Chancellorsville began with the arrival of Gen. George G. Meade and his staff, who established Gen. Joseph Hooker's headquarters in the house. The Chancellor women and their refugee friends had little idea of what was going on beyond their crossroads clearing, but they saw "couriers coming and going" and sensed that the Yankee officers "were very well satisfied with their position and seemed to be very confident of victory." Sue and her family and friends "got through Thursday and Friday as best we could." On Saturday—the day of Gen. Thomas "Stonewall" Jackson's famous march across the Union front—the firing grew nearer and the women took shelter in the basement. "There was firing, fighting, and bringing in the wounded all that day," Sue reported, and then, on Saturday afternoon, as Jackson launched his flank attack, the fighting took a sharp turn for the worse.

The Chancellor house quickly filled with wounded, screaming men, and surgeons turned the piano on which the girls had entertained Confederate officers into an amputating table. As Jackson's corps crashed into the Federal right flank, the situation worsened. "Such cannonading on all sides, such shrieks and groans, such commotion of all kinds!" Sue exclaimed. "We thought that we were frightened before, but this was far beyond everything, and it kept up until long after dark." When the bloodshed resumed the next morning, the Chancellor house caught fire, thrusting the Chancellors into the most harrowing portion of their trial.

Union general Joseph Dickinson, Hooker's adjutant, led the frightened women and children out of the cellar and through their battered home. "As this terrified band of women and children came stumbling out of the cellar," they saw amputated limbs spilling from an open window and "rows and rows of dead bodies covered with canvas" littering the yard. The little band followed Dickinson through the bombardment. "The woods around the house were a sheet of fire," wrote Sue, "the air was filled with shot and shell; horses were running, rearing, and screaming; the men were amass with confusion, moaning, cursing, and praying." Ducking "missiles of death" and gingerly treading among "the bleeding bodies of the dead and wounded," the Chancellors joined the Union exodus. "At our last look, our old home was completely enveloped in flames." The Chancellors found General Dickinson to be an honorable and steadfast guard. As he led his little group of southerners through the chaos, Dickinson again and again proved his gallantry by obtaining a horse for Sue's ill sister and shielding them from less chivalrous Yankees. Other Federals also aided them. A kind chaplain escorted them across the "wobbly" pontoon bridge that spanned the Rappahannock, and a jovial Yankee guard promised "to write my mother and tell her what a good time I have had with these rebel ladies." On another occasion a "little drummer boy" scrounged up some ice and a lemon for Sue's sister. Although the Chancellor girls were at first "very cool" toward their Federal guards, Sue remembered that "after a while they relaxed and relieved the irksomeness of our confinement by talking, playing cards, and music." In retrospect Sue even believed "that there were some flirtations going on." After their release, the family sat out the rest of the war in Charlottesville, where Sue attended school and Mrs. Chancellor worked as a hospital matron.[2]

A third version of the children's war comes from the oral reminiscence of Hammett Dell, who experienced the war as a young slave near Murfreesboro, Tennessee. Hammett remembered his master, "Mars White," as a kindly man who fed his single family of five slaves well and never, as far as Hammett could remember, sold one off the plantation. In fact, the years before the war were "the happiest in all my life." But about the time the fighting began, his mother died; shortly after, apparently, his father ran off to join the Union army. Hammett was aware of the war because he heard his white folks talking about moving away. "I didn't lack [like] the talk but I didn't know what 'war' was," he recalled.

Hammett would find out about war soon enough, however. When the great Union and Confederate armies clashed at Murfreesboro, "it was a continual roar. The tin pans in the cubbard rattle all time. . . . The house shakin' all time. . . . The earth quivered. It sound like the judgment." Even after the fighting was over, "nobody felt good" because both armies ranged through the country, "foragin' one bad as the other, hungry, gittin' everything you put way to live on." By the time the soldiers were through, "there couldn't be a chicken nor a goose nor a year of corn to be found bout our place." It seemed to Hammett that "we couldn't make a scratch on the ground nowhere the soldiers couldn't find it." Soldiers carried off all the salt on the plantation, forcing the residents to salvage what they could from the dirt floor of the smokehouse. After a Yankee cavalry company rounded up every horse on the place, they set the house on fire. "We all got busy then, white folks and darkies both carryin' water ter put it out." They succeeded in dousing the fire, but Hammett was so angry that he later burst a hornets' nest with a well-thrown rock just as a Yankee squad rode underneath it. He boasted to his master about his stunt, but Mars White scolded the boy and ordered him never to do anything like it again. The Yankees, White warned, "would [have] killed you right on the spot" if they had found him. "That's 'war,'" Hammett declared emphatically as an old man. "I found out all bout what it was. Lady it ain't nuthin' but hell on dis earth."[5]

These three narratives highlight many of the facets of the children's Civil War, showing how children in both sections, white and black, played roles in the war. There were significant differences, however. Northern children generally watched the conflict from afar, while southern children were much more likely to be slapped by the hard hand of war. White children passionately supported their sections' war efforts, while black children distrusted soldiers of both armies and, especially when they enjoyed civil relationships with their masters, often remained loyal to them. As the spectrum of experiences described by Hermon DeLong, Sue Chancellor, and Hammett Dell show, children missed little of what the war had to offer, from the pageantry and the excitement to the hardships and the tragedy.

Children as Symbols and as Consumers

Children who lived through the war assigned it a central place in their memories and attributed many of their political, social, and personal characteristics to their wartime experiences. Subsequent chapters show just how exposed they were to the war and how thoroughly involved they became. But contemporaries also seemed to recognize the importance — as actors and as symbols — of the children of war. Children comprised a much larger portion of the population in 1860 than in the late twentieth-century, making up well over a third of the population in 1860 (compared with less than 22 percent in 1988).⁴ They could hardly be avoided, and the sketch artists of the great weekly magazines such as *Harper's* or *Frank Leslie's* rightly placed them in nearly every off-the-battlefield scene. When artists portrayed troops marching past cheering throngs, the giant Sanitary Fairs of 1864 and 1865, southern refugees or "contrabands," and besieged residents of Vicksburg or Petersburg, they frequently included children. In their pictures, cap-waving boys run beside troops, girls comfort broken-hearted mothers, and babies are threatened by foul-looking Missouri guerillas. Youngsters appeared as heroes in illustrations such as the maudlin "The Drummer-Boy's Burial" and wearing zouave uniforms, firing cannon, and riding in howitzer-shaped baby carriages in the satiric cartoon "After the War: Everything and Everybody *en militaire.*" Children in wartime illustrations tearfully hugged soldiers goodbye, saw them off at train stations, appeared in their dreams, prayed for their safe return, visited them in hospitals, and listened intently as they related war stories in front of roaring fires. They even showed up as hyena-like draft rioters in at least one illustration.⁵ Painters sprinkled children into scenes of refugees warming themselves before a wintry fire outside Fredericksburg and in the famous evocation of southern piety and patriotism, *The Burial of Latane.* Others offered warlike children brandishing toy guns, swords, and pikes; celebrating news of battlefield victories; playing nurse; writing letters to absent fathers; and knitting socks for soldiers.⁶

In addition to these sometimes fanciful impressions of children's participation in the war, contemporaries often invoked children to explain why or how the war should be fought. Soldiers who tried to explain what motivated them frequently wrote that they had their children's best interests in mind. They naturally hoped to save the Union or the Confederacy for the sake of their children's futures, but they more frequently referred to the importance they placed on their own and their children's honor as defenders of their nations. An Alabama cavalryman clearly missed his seven young children when he wrote his wife shortly after joining the army that "I would bee glad to see little ginny and give her a kiss and see the rest of the children frolic around and play on my lap and see babe suck his thum." Yet his duty to his country and to his family kept him in the field; if not for "the love I have for them and my country I would have been ther now." Nearly two years later

War Spirit at Home, by Lilly Martin Spencer (1866). Spencer's painting of a family celebrating news of the Union capture of Vicksburg—modeled after herself and her children—shows the enthusiasm with which northern children embraced the war effort. (Newark Museum)

he assured his wife that he would not give up the cause. "I dont want it throwed up to my children after I am dead and gone that I was a deserter from the confederate army." Marcus Spiegel, an Ohio colonel, told his wife during the Vicksburg campaign "that my fighting in this War will leave an inheritance to my beloved children of more value than all the Gold in India." Even death would not be too high a price to pay. A Georgian frequently asked his wife not to grieve for him if he died in the line of duty, for "if I fall I will fall like a man and leave no stigma on my darling boy." Another Georgian, in one of the first letters he had written in his life, assured his wife that he longed to see their two-year-old boy, but if he came home "in that way . . . it would be a scandle to me as long as I live and to my sweet Willie after I was dead and gone."[7]

Just as Civil War soldiers projected their own loyalty and service onto the futures of their children, adult slaves took great pleasure in the knowledge that their children would grow up to be free men and women. Annie Burton's mother literally had to kidnap her three children from a master who refused to admit that his bondservants were free. When the hired slave of an Austin, Texas, woman learned that slavery had ended, she scooped up her little daughter, threw her into the air, and cried, "Tamar, you're free! You're free." Her employer, normally quite typical in her racial assumptions, recorded perceptively in her diary that, to this mother, "freedom was for her child; she looked in its face, at its hands, at its feet. It was a new baby to her—a free baby."[8]

Children clearly inspired soldiers to risk their lives and slaves to welcome their emancipation. Children also became central to the war effort in a somewhat different way, especially in the South, where the proper political education of children became a home front war aim. North Carolina teachers meeting in Raleigh early in the war issued an "Address to the People of North Carolina" that stressed the importance of maintaining their public school system despite the pressures and excitement of war. The struggle against the North, they declared, must be carried not only through "legislative acts" and "force of arms," but also "in the school room, at the fireside, and by all those moral agencies which preserve society, and which prepare a people to be a free and self-governing nationality." The common schools of North Carolina comprised a "nursery of popular intelligence and patriotism," the interruption of which would be a serious blow to liberty in the South. A primary weapon in this intellectual war was the publication of textbooks that would correct the "erroneous opinions" of the South and of slavery promulgated by northern propagandists. "Distinguished by a peculiar social system, and one obnoxious to the phariseeism of the world," the Confederate states "are especially called on to think in such things for themselves, and to see that their children are instructed out of their own writing."[9]

Two years later, educators met in Columbia, South Carolina, to establish the Educational Association for the Confederate States of America. In addition to writing a constitution and discussing curricular issues, the delegates formed a number of committees, including one on "educational interests and text-books." The committee's report declared that southern children "must be able to appreciate the greatness of the trusts committed to their hands" by the Confederate cause. One way of ensuring this, of course, was to publish and distribute textbooks reflecting Confederate interests. The crash publishing program of Confederate schoolbooks produced scores of primers, spellers, and other publications, many of which did contain material with a distinctly southern point of view.[10]

One of the most effective rhetorical uses of Civil War children came in the public discussion of how to care for the orphans of men killed in battle. Fatherless children proved to be potent symbols and poignant reminders of the sacrifice of hundreds of thousands of good men in the name of the Union or the Confederacy. Soldiers' orphans frequently reminded Americans of their obligation to follow through on the promise they had collectively made to the soldiers going off to war. In the famous concluding paragraph of his second inaugural address, Abraham Lincoln accepted on behalf of the government responsibility "to care for him who shall have borne the battles, and for his widow, and his orphan." As a director of the New Jersey Soldiers' Children's Home reminded the state legislature just after the war, these children's "homes were desolated and broken up to save ours." "Oh!" he wrote melodramatically, "we wish their father[s] could have known how kindly his children would be cared for . . . ; would it not have thrown a ray of brightness even over Libby and Andersonville?"[11]

Even before the war ended, the plight of war orphans and half-orphans and the country's duty to provide for them as a kind of memorial to their dead fathers had inspired patriotic rhetoric. A *Harper's Weekly* cartoon in August 1862 had portrayed a beneficent Uncle Sam, waving with a crowd of women and youngsters at departing soldiers, urging the men, "Go ahead, Boys: I'll take care of the Wives and Babies." Although Congress passed a two-dollar-per-month pension for the children of deceased soldiers late in the war, most of the efforts to secure homes and education for soldiers' orphans came at the local and, especially, state levels. Soon after the war began, the *Chicago Tribune* used the death of a local officer to promote the responsibility of society to "honor the brave departed soldier" by supporting his widow and orphans, not "as a charity, nor a grudged dole, but as . . . a debt discharged from which the community will not shrink." A few schools appeared even before Appomattox. The Institute of Reward for Orphans of Patriots began raising money for scholarships and other educational programs in 1862, while New Yorkers established a trio of schools: the New York State Volunteer Institute, a military school for male orphans; the Union Home School for the Children of Volunteers; and the Patriot Orphan Home, which eventually relocated with several score children to Flushing. A temporary school for the children of Iowa orphans opened in 1864, at least partly funded by donations from soldiers in Iowa regiments.[12]

Southerners employed the same rhetoric of responsibility. A circular published by C. K. Marshall, a Georgian, in 1864 promoted a scheme to found an "Orphan's League" to raise money to pay for the tuition, books, and, if necessary, room and board of orphans and the children of disabled veterans. Little came of the plan, but Marshall reminded readers that "the debt of gratitude due for the self-sacrificing and heroic conduct of their fallen, or disabled and suffering parents, can only be appropriately discharged by bestowing its highest testimonials upon their dependent offspring."[13]

Children played important roles in the rhetoric of war, but the extent to which they were considered members of their society-at-arms can also be measured in less high-minded ways. Like their parents, even when they could ignore the grim casualty lists and woefully inaccurate newspaper reports, or when the latest letters from friends and relatives in the army avoided the pathos and gore of the war, they were besieged with commercialized images of the conflict. Publishers, entertainers, philanthropic societies, and other individuals and organizations sought to cash in on northerners' and southerners' natural interest in the war. Children participated in this culture of war as consumers, readers, and audiences alongside their parents and, in some cases, were specifically targeted by the producers of war-related fare. Due to the booming economy, the dense population, and the greater wealth of artistic talent and entrepreneurial ambition in the North, children in that section could draw on a far richer popular culture than the Confederacy offered. Yet even young Rebels could relish the wide variety of spectacles and articles that, in some cases, purported to explain the war but, in others, merely used the war as a source of entertaining or patriotic images.

These toys and public performances served as patriotic primers for white youngsters in both sections. Mixing patriotism with opportunism, they set out in broad strokes the vital "facts" of the war, drummed into consumers' minds its salient issues, and rallied them to the cause of the North or the South. The ideas thus presented targeted the lowest common political and moral denominators, but they did introduce Civil War children to the war aims and experiences of both the Union and the Confederacy, beginning the process of mobilization that would culminate in the politicization of a generation of children.

Although the American commercial game and toy industry was in its infancy in the 1860s, many entrepreneurs—especially in the North—also eagerly exploited the children's market with playthings that drew on images of war. Unlike popular mid-century board games such as Milton Bradley's *Checkered Game of Life,* most games based on the Civil War eschewed any attempt to instill the virtues of hard work or moral improvement. Some had fairly serious, even realistic approaches to the war, but many sought only to offer mildly informative pastimes. If they also encouraged a certain amount of patriotism, so much the better.[14]

For instance, the game *Visit to Camp* offered a lighthearted look at army life in which players took the parts of caricatures such as a rather foppish captain; a hard-drinking sutler; a zouave; a bewhiskered colonel; a surgeon (shown taking the pulse of a rather worried patient); a cross-eyed, fat musician; and a vivandier (in a feminized zouave uniform). In decks of cards, eagles, shields, stars, and flags substituted for the traditional suits, and colonels replaced kings, the Goddess of Liberty replaced queens, and majors replaced jacks. Pictures of prominent generals and politicians appeared on the cards of a game resembling "slapjack," while trivia games tested players' knowledge of battles and generals. Children could also "run the blockade" through a simple maze drawn on a two-foot-square sheet of paper printed with colorful nautical and naval obstacles. Other war-related toys included such unique pieces as the "Walking Zouave" and jigsaw puzzles depicting a recruiting scene in Boston or Lee's surrender. An unusually political-minded object was an automated "sand toy"—sand trickling over a wheel triggered the mechanism—presenting Abraham Lincoln as an organ grinder with a fiddle-playing monkey who bore more than a passing resemblance to Gideon Welles, the secretary of the navy.[15]

Children also took in photographic displays, plays, concerts, "magic lantern" shows, and a wide variety of martial exhibits and performances. They posed for photographs with guns and swords and in front of military camps painted on studio backdrops. They collected envelopes and stationery imprinted with political and military images and cartoons and bought war-inspired valentines and patriotic song sheets. The selection of entertainment options and ostensibly educational objects imparting some sort of knowledge about the war was unlimited, especially for northern children.[16]

An even more spectacular method of reaching mass audiences was the panorama, which had been popular in the United States since the late eighteenth century. Showmen in both the North and the South eagerly adapted the latest in theatrical gimmicks to this popular prewar form of public entertainment to present up-to-date images of the war.[17] Children could take advantage of reduced prices or special matinees—Lipp's Place in Philadelphia offered free admission to its *Grand Panorama of the War*—to see northern presentations such as *Banvard's Painting of the Mississippi and the Historical Section of the War on Its Banks*; *Pearson's Polyrama of the War*; *Norton's Great Panorama of Recent Battles*; *Clapp, Stemley and Company's Diorama and Polopticomarama of the War*; *The Mirror of the Rebellion*; and *A Cosmorama of Battles of the Civil War*. The leading southern spectacles were Burton's *Southern Moving Dioramic Panorama*, which swung through Atlanta, Savannah, and Charleston in the spring of 1862, and Lee Mallory's *Pantechnoptemon*, which evolved throughout the course of the war, as its proprietor added battles and scenes as events dictated. Most major cities enjoyed long runs of at least one and perhaps several different shows. Philadelphians could attend at least five separate panoramas during the course of the war. Charlestonians could view not only Mallory's exhibit during at least two extended runs but also the *Grand Panoramic Mirror of the War* and, a year after the war's end, the *Dissolving Views of the Binoptric Lantern* that featured the Holy Land as well as scenes of "the late war."[18]

The wildly varying names of the displays obscured their basic similarities. Exhibitors no doubt believed that a convoluted, original name would lead the public to believe that a program was even more dramatic, technologically advanced, and entertaining than its competitors. Perhaps the most extreme application of this principle appeared in a show traveling the South in the spring of 1862, *The Grand Panopticon Magicale of the War and Automaton Dramatique*. The basic technology for the exhibits remained the panorama, a series of paintings on a canvas hundreds of feet long and several yards high that slowly scrolled from one reel to another. Most included a spoken narration, while many were also accompanied by music. For instance, Stanley & Conant's *Polemorama* featured "Excellent and Appropriate Music" in which could be heard "the Rattle of Musketry — the Booming of Cannon, mingled with the tumultuous noise of the deadly conflict." While the overall goal of these displays seems to have been to provide a factual but patriotic chronology of the war, certain stock images of pathos and heroism did appear. Many featured moonlit scenes of sleeping armies or of ruined battlescapes, while more than one offered sentimental tableaux such as "the DYING OFFICER AND HIS FAITHFUL STEED."[19]

Other effects heightened the drama. Fixed and moving figures of soldiers and ships — some life sized, others built to scale — stood or lay before the moving pictures; theatrical explosions and smoke lent authenticity to simulated battles; shifting from front- to back-lighting magically changed scenes from night to day or from bucolic prebattle vignettes to postbattle wreckage before the audience's eyes. Advertisements for these exhibits not surprisingly emphasized their spectacular and expensive effects. La Rue's *Great War Show, the Wonderful Stratopateticon, or Walking Army* claimed to have 90,000 "Moving and Acting figures." Mallory's *Pantechnoptemon* featured a "Magnificent Scenic and Automatic Spectacle" with 500,000 drawn figures and pyrotechnic displays. *Cutting's National Polyrama*, the "*Ne Plus Ultra* of Scenic Reflections," had fifty scenes that utilized "intricate Marching, Chemical Lights, Colored Fires, &c," while *Pearson's Historic Mirror of the Present War*—"the only work of its kind"—presented "the most interesting objects and incidents connected with the Rise and Progress of the War, illustrated with startling Dioramic Accompaniments, entirely new and on a scale of magnificence never before attempted." In the fight between the *Monitor* and the *Merrimac*, as portrayed by Goodwin & Wilder's *Polyrama*, the vessels, "heave[d] majestically to and fro, pouring volley after volley of iron hail into each other's sides."[20]

Panoramas offered flashy and exciting images that thrilled huge audiences. But youngsters could also imbibe the war spirit by simply browsing in their favorite shops and stores. Many towns could duplicate the report by the *Philadelphia Ledger and Transcript* that "most" of the city's shops were prominently displaying "articles, either useful or ornamental, growing out of the Union feeling of the war," including soldiers' equipment, hats and caps, and neckties and collars decorated with stars and stripes, as well as military books and manuals. Cedar Falls, Iowa, residents could purchase silver, star-shaped pins engraved "Constitution and Union" for twenty-five cents, and at least one local wedding boasted a cake bearing the inscription "The Union Forever." Early in the war the United States Flag Company in Chicago advertised "Four Sizes of Toy Flags from One to Four Feet in Length," while at least twelve advertisements appeared in the *Savannah Morning News* for military manuals such as the *Volunteer's Handbook* and the *Skirmisher's Drill and Bayonet Exercise*, as well as tents, "army clothing," "military buttons," and the "Cheapest and Best Map of the Seat of War."[21]

Amateur soldiers and ambitious young officers obviously needed these items, but an advertisement on the back cover of a children's book revealed that many were also directed toward young military enthusiasts. It promoted "Fifty Lithographed Games and Twenty Four Lithographed Picture Books" for the 1863–64 winter season. The ad offered paper soldiers; the "Eastern Army Guide" and the "General Army Guide of southern territory"; the "Glorious Union Packet" (for just two bits); bird's-eye maps of southern territory and battlefields; "Grand Battle Tableaux" of Gettysburg, Pea Ridge, and Second Manassas; and pictures of camps and hospitals, as well as illustrated note paper and envelopes for two cents each.[22]

Children were also drawn to the Sanitary Fairs held around the United States between the fall of 1863 and the summer of 1865 on behalf of the U.S. Sanitary Commission. All told, local branches of the Sanitary Commission raised $4.3 million at fairs held in cities all over the East and Midwest and in towns stretching from Damariscotta, Maine, to Dubuque, Iowa, and all the way to California. Hundreds of thousands of Americans paid the minimal entrance fee, wandered the crowded aisles, packed into the booths sponsored by communities and organizations, attended concerts, and shelled out cash for souvenirs, homemade pastries and clothing, toys, and other goods donated by businessmen, church groups, and individuals. Among the fairs' enticements were "New England Kitchens," where young women served hot food and desserts to hungry visitors; historical artifacts and war-related relics from the American Revolution as well as the current "Rebellion"; and appearances by political and military luminaries such as Edward Everett, Abraham Lincoln, and General Grant and his family.[23]

Although they were not aimed solely, or even chiefly, at children, fair organizers obviously believed that children could become potent consumers of the patriotism the fairs promoted. Authorities closed the Chicago public schools so students could attend the fairs held there in 1863 and 1865. Newspaper descriptions show why children flocked by the thousands to the fairs. The Great Central Fair in Philadelphia offered automaton rope dancers, stereoptican views, magic shows, ventriloquists, and (foreshadowing a marketing device in late twentieth-century fast-food franchises) an indoor playground adjacent to the sprawling restaurant. The Children's Department of New York's Metropolitan Fair, according to *Leslie's Illustrated Newspaper*, was "a treasury of useful articles, toys and knick-knacks, almost realising the fables of fairyland." Youngsters in Albany could cluster around the "very remarkable animal called the Gorilla" at the "Gipsey tent" and the "life picture" of Indian life—complete with a canoe, baskets, and ladies dressed in Native American costumes—at the "Wigwam." Boys elbowed through crowds sometimes "so immense that locomotion was well nigh impossible" to get into the 1,800-square-foot "Military Department." There they admired a musket fired at the battle of Bunker Hill, a Cornwallis pistol captured at Yorktown, and Lafayette's camp kettle. Even more interesting were such items as the clothes worn by Elmer Ellsworth when he was killed, as well as the gun that killed him and the soldier who avenged him; scores of firearms; fragments from a shell fired into Fort Sumter; the battle flags of seventy New York regiments; and a number of captured Rebel banners. The "Trophy Room" offered more captured Confederate battle flags as well as metal splinters from the Confederate ironclad *Virginia* and an iron plate from a Union monitor. Children at the Brooklyn Fair cast a quick glance at William Bradford's china, George Washington's punch bowl, and Miles Standish's hoe in the "Art and Curiosity Museum" but probably devoted more attention to the "Rebel war memorials"—"muskets, pistols, sabres, pikes, swords, and Arkansas tooth picks"—and a hook from the Confederate gunboat *Atlanta*.[24]

Childhood at Mid-Century

Even if they wanted to, children could not ignore the war. Of course, those living in the Confederacy often experienced hardships and dangers unimagined by northerners, children in both sections suffered anxiety over and the loss of fathers and brothers fighting in the armies, and slave children were affected in many sublime and dangerous ways. These experiences, and the inclusion of children in wartime entertainment and rhetoric, show that they were clearly seen as important members of the societies waging war in the 1860s. They participated in virtually all of the war's off-battlefield events, provided inspiration for soldiers and politicians, and represented the cost of the war as well as the responsibility it laid on its survivors. But these examples of children's participation in the war show them in fairly passive terms, as spectators or as objects of patriotic pity. They were far more than that, as subsequent chapters show. As the nation slid toward war in the 1850s, at least two aspects of the lives of mid-century children conditioned them to respond to the war: an increasingly child-oriented, nurturing style of child rearing and a burgeoning literature written expressly for children.

Historians have shown that mothers gained preeminence in the raising of children early in the nineteenth century, as women sought rewarding and vital roles in the New Republic, as the "cult of domesticity" and numerous child-rearing guides assigned primary responsibility for child care to mothers, and as stern colonial assumptions about child development gave way to a less rigid, more empathetic style that stressed the importance of affection over rigid discipline. A complementary development was the Victorian belief — especially among northerners and urban dwellers — that the family was an institution threatened by the modern age. It became a haven from stress, a conduit of moral values, and a prominent component of what their descendants would call "quality of life" whose disruption was to be avoided at all costs. In addition, even as children became less important as contributors to household economies (in a slaveholding family, they would never have been considered as economic assets), they became more important as sources of emotional, even sentimental, satisfaction. Although in 1861 industrialization and urbanization had made few inroads in the South and in large swaths of the North, the separation and stress of war created similar, even exaggerated, conditions for fathers from rural backgrounds. For them the hazards and uncertainties of the war, rather than hectic urban lives, caused stress, while military service, rather than factory or office work, removed fathers — sometimes permanently — from their families.[25]

Even outside the urban North, the child-centered families that supposedly developed under the pressures of industrialization and urbanization had surfaced as early as the American Revolution. Eighteenth-century Chesapeake planters sought to instill self-sufficiency and strength in their children through affection and autonomy. Children were not annoying objects to grimly mold and shape but centers of familial emotion and well-being. Virginians in the early nineteenth century expended so much emotional energy on their children that they created standards to which those children, as grateful adults, could never measure up. Although historians have argued that fathers detached themselves from the daily rituals and chores of child rearing, this assumption may not be entirely correct.[26] For example, during the war Unionist Thomas H. DuVal of Austin, Texas, used his enforced idleness as a Federal judge without a bench to share with his wife Laura the care of their fourteen- and twelve-year-old daughters and infant son. DuVal administered medicines, took the girls swimming and fishing in a nearby creek, played his flute for birthday parties, and spent long afternoons and evenings "dry nursing" the "little melon," as he and his wife affectionately called their youngest child. It may well be that antebellum fathers continued their colonial practice of taking charge of child rearing, especially of boys, soon after the children were weaned — exerting discipline, guiding children toward careers or marriages, and even feeding them and putting them to bed.[27]

Simply put, by the 1850s, even as their nation became a "house divided," for many Americans the relationships between parents and children in their own homes had become more important than they had been during colonial times. Families, especially among the urban middle class, grew smaller.[28] Parents celebrated their offsprings' birthdays, purchased growing numbers of commercially manufactured books and toys, and generally became more affectionate. Adults also enthusiastically embraced reforms directed at the moral development of children. Public schools and

Sunday schools, asylums and refuges, and published guidebooks and state laws pointed parents and children in the right direction. With the heightened interest in children of the mid-nineteenth century, it is not surprising that they became such important parts of the war efforts and rhetoric of the North and the South. These antebellum assumptions about the value of family meant that when war came to the United States, the emotional and material preservation of families became, in a sense, a war aim of soldiers in both armies. In addition, soldiers and their families would be confronted with long-term separations and nearly disabling worries about one another, which not only caused them to reflect on what family already meant to them, but also led to an enhanced appreciation for their parental and filial roles and responsibilities.[29]

Other mid-century developments left Civil War children poised to respond to or be acted upon by the experiences and information brought to them by the war. Increased access to public schools, for instance, made them likely vehicles for the transmission of patriotic ideas. In addition, the Civil War toys mentioned earlier tapped into a growing market for store-bought playthings that accompanied the rise after the 1820s of a relatively affluent, urban, and child-oriented middle class. Antebellum children, taking advantage of the nurturing environment in which they were being raised, explored styles of play that liberated them from dour expectations of rural duty and obedience, even as they played at being soldiers and slaveowners and mimicked other aspects of adult life. Slave children also incorporated their own experiences —even slave auctions and whippings—into their play before the Civil War.[30]

Children's literature reflected and encouraged these developments. Secular as well as denominational magazines had long undergirded the moral and social assumptions of common child-rearing practices. They promoted the principles of hard work, obedience, generosity, humility, and piety; provided moral guidance and examples of the benefits of family cohesion and the consequences of its absence; and furnished mild adventure stories, innocent entertainment, and instruction. Works of fiction and nonfiction alike stressed character and framed the world in moral terms. Authors of stories and novels as well as schoolbooks for children combined a faith in virtue with a confidence in the American political and economic systems. Patriotism and good deeds and hard work and unselfishness together would guarantee individual success and national honor.[31]

The relentless moralizing in children's literature between 1820 and 1860 tended to focus on individual self-improvement — especially temperance — and on pacifism rather than on politics. The always controversial debate over slavery rarely appeared in juvenile books in the 1850s because publishers feared alienating potential customers. For the same reasons, pamphlets and books distributed by the American Sunday School Union avoided the issue of slavery. When Jacob Abbott and others featured African Americans in their stories and novels, they burdened even the most sympathetic characters with stereotypes and the condescension and patronizing attitudes of the clearly more intelligent white characters. Although many of the same ideas and themes would appear in wartime children's literature, the magazines and novels written for children would broaden their content to include politics and scathing critiques of slavery — and, somewhat less effectively, racism — and to promote a vigorous prosecution of the Union war effort. Wartime writing for children would retain familiar ideas and forms but would apply them to new issues and needs.[32]

Little Politicians

Antebellum assumptions about children and child rearing, the development of a morally charged but still-evolving children's literature, and even the development of material affluence for many Americans became channels through which the war entered the lives of children. Their responses ranged from terror to stoic acceptance to enthusiastic patriotism. However they experienced or responded to the war, they became politicized by it. The political effects of the Civil War on children have never really been examined, but studies of children living in other war zones suggest fruitful approaches to the politicization of Civil War children. Political scientists have discovered that sometime between the ages of six and thirteen, children have already had experiences that will shape their political values for the rest of their lives, and that by age ten, children's political sensibilities have become sophisticated enough to allow them to perceive disagreements over issues and, in many cases, to choose political parties. Moreover, they have also learned that conflict is a part of the political world. In fact, young children rather easily understand war and other forms of political strife, because their own games and stories revolve around violence and competition. Richard M. Merelman posits that conflict can have a strong impact on children's political learning. When they live in a situation where their government is a "contested regime," children tend to see issues in black and white, good and evil, and to identify strongly with the group that they believe is good and to develop negative impressions of the opposition.[33]

Growing up in wartime does not cause children to become politicized against their wills; youngsters seem eager to enter the political world. Children idealize their political leaders in the process of acquiring the values of the political system under which they live and affiliate themselves with political parties or causes in order to demonstrate family solidarity and loyalty. Fred Greenstein points out that children begin adopting their future political roles very early in their lives, "through processes which neither they nor those who instruct them are especially conscious of." Exposure to political events and to politicians comes from direct experience, but mostly "through the conversations of adults and peers, and through the mass media." When political controversy develops into armed conflict, young children—especially boys of six to eight years—tend to accept war, or at least the idea of war, more readily than their older brothers and sisters. If, as Robert Coles argues, personal contact with government agencies or policies creates strong political opinions, then the experiences of Civil War children must have fostered a rather intense engagement with the political system.[34]

Most studies on the politicization of children have examined urban children who lived a century after the Civil War, yet it stands to reason that children living in the far more politically violent 1860s would experience at least as much identification with parties and political ideas as children living in the relative peace of post–World War II America. Evidence suggests that children living in places where, according to Thomas Davey, "serious political and moral struggles are part of the child's daily fare" grapple with political issues at an earlier age than children living in politically calm areas.[35] Young Yankees and Rebels grew up in an atmosphere of spiraling sectional conflict and violence; they received their political educations by reading magazines and novels and attending popular entertainments, by observing the actions and listening to the words of parents and other adults, and by directly confronting political and military events.

A Confirmable Past

The politicization of children can be measured not only by their actions during the war but also through the memoirs and auto-biographies they wrote years later. As the grown-up children of war attempted to attach meanings to it, they often drew on values and assumptions that predated the war or were formed by their experiences during the war: their attitudes about slavery, for in-stance, or their contacts with enemy soldiers or the hardships they had personally endured. Their reminiscences, memoirs, and auto-biographies, published and in manuscript, belong to old narrative traditions that historians have long relied on in their attempts to understand the beliefs and attitudes and experiences of past gen-erations. Although the years that passed between the memoirists' decisions to write about their lives and the events they described may have clouded the memories of some, they also served, accord-ing to a historian of pioneer women, "to deepen the insight and heighten the perspective of the writers." The intervening years had given Civil War children the chance to work out what the Civil War meant to them and how specific events and ideas of the war had fit into their lives. Not unlike the unpublished autobiog-raphies of nineteenth-century English men and women compiled by John Burnett, the typical memoir of a Civil War era child— especially if he or she was a southerner—"enabled the author to give himself identity, to place himself in the context of history, geography and social change, and so to make a kind of sense out of an existence which might otherwise seem meaningless." Auto-biographers tend to focus on events or ideas that marked their discovery of a sense of self or brought forth emotions or attitudes distinct from those of their parents. Most feature early memories that are unhappy or traumatic, events that delineate a transition from a happy time to a less happy, more challenging, even tragic period of their young lives. Similarly, diarists were also more likely to record their feelings and concerns during times of crisis or of dramatic personal changes.[36]

Historians are obviously aware that reminiscences written long after the circumstances they relate present certain problems: sometimes the facts are wrong, for instance. But more important are the tendencies by their authors to shape their memories to fit the values and needs of the present. David Lowenthal has shown that the powerful desire to transform the past into more noble, interesting, or merely palatable stories than the cold, hard "truth" can seduce individuals and societies as well as scholars and museum curators. People spread happy memories like a quilt of nostalgia over the past and difficult or even horrifying recollections to support their perceptions of themselves as tough survivors. In either case, individuals hunger to link their personal experiences and memories to those of fellow countrymen and to confirm what they believed happened. One historian has referred to western children's stories of triumph over adversity as "personal myths" that "justify and validate" the lives of homesteaders who beat the odds and endured the vagaries of the Great Plains. A psychologist calls these life stories "personal fables," which develop through the stages of growth from the simple and often inaccurate facts collected by very young children to the adolescent need to create a personal history and set of values. There are two sides to these memoirs: they reveal their authors' uniqueness but also reflect a "universal significance." The information memoirs and autobiographies provide may be less than emotionally truthful and may obscure the difficulties and disillusionment met by their authors. Yet these sources do provide the authors' assessments of the progression of their lives and the meanings they gleaned from their experiences. A similar phenomenon seems to be at work in the writings of southerners, especially, who were children during the Civil War. They may well put what to modern eyes are unreasonably—indeed, immorally—positive glosses on the nature of slavery. Yet their selection of events and lessons communicates how the war affected their and their society's shared mindset.[37]

Similar limitations and opportunities arise in the available sources on African American children. Since the genre of published autobiographies of slaves, its poignance and propaganda value declining with the end of slavery, had died out by the 1860s, the bulk of the information on slave children in wartime comes from the famous interviews with former slaves conducted by the Works Progress Administration in the 1930s and published decades later as *The American Slave: A Composite Autobiography.*[38] Although race and class inhibited completely open exchanges between the elderly former slaves and mostly white interviewers, although some questions were avoided and some answers ignored, and although age and depression and decades of racial oppression intruded on the memories of the freedmen and freedwomen, the interviews, if carefully used, remain important windows into the lives of the black children of war. Despite their weaknesses and idiosyncrasies—the thick dialects that can make for difficult reading were sometimes imposed on the subjects' actual speaking styles—they reveal what slave children deemed important, expose how the war altered their lives, and suggest how the liberated African Americans gave meaning to their childhood experiences.[39]

Civil War children, like people in any time and place, built memories of personal experiences, of stories they heard second- or third-hand, of commemorations that happened long after the events they noted, and of family lore and popular expressions in entertainment or art. The Civil War was a central event—for some, *the* central event—in the history of the United States and, it goes without saying, in the lives of the people of all ages who experienced it. As a result, its memory has been subject to the force of myth and celebration and political manipulation more than, perhaps, any other event in American history.

Before we despair of ever getting at the "truth"—at least the truth about the children's Civil War—we must remember that participants' memories can be at least partly confirmed through other sources and, in the case of Civil War children, other events. Historians and their readers share an elusive goal: to reach a point in their study of a certain time or place or person at which they can understand and appreciate the interplay of emotional and psychological and physical evidence. This search for a palpable contact with the past is hardly ever completely successful; we are rarely able to achieve that level of descriptive and analytical comprehension and elegance. One problem shared by historians of all but the most recent historical periods is that our sources are unable to respond to the precise questions we want answered. Although the last Civil War veteran died in the 1950s, he no doubt outlived most Civil War children. All but a dwindling handful of even our oldest neighbors and relatives were born in the twentieth century.[40]

Yet there is still a way to tap into this more-than-a-century-old past. Millions of Americans who lived through the Second World War as children are still available to share their stories and the lessons they learned. Their experiences were hardly identical to those of Civil War children, of course: invasion was only a nightmare, not an actual danger; shortages rarely caused great hardship; and a much lower percentage of men left the private sector for the military, and fewer came back crippled or in caskets. Their wars were different, but the Civil War and the "Good War" challenged children in similar — if not precisely the same — ways.

In a sense, we can begin to understand in pretty concrete ways the wartime lives of the children of the Civil War through the events and circumstances experienced by the children of the Second World War. For example, a book on child development published in 1946 included a brief appendix of "growth gradients" for children from the age of eighteen months through nine years in a number of categories, including "war." Although the technology referred to is obviously different, the survey reveals that the levels of comprehension about war in 1860s and 1940s children were remarkably similar. At 2½ years, for instance, children might say that a soldier "marches." A year later they might know that sailors "shoot the Japanese" and "teach the WACS to be Coastguards." At four years they might add that when sailors were not on boats, "They're walking with girls." By age six, boys and girls in the mid-1940s had developed anger toward Japanese, Germans, and especially Hitler, and some had begun following the war on maps or globes, while seven year olds began having nightmares about the war. They also began thinking in terms of contributing to the war effort by collecting scrap paper and buying defense stamps; many, especially boys, became interested in movies and comic books about the war. Eight year olds could ponder the causes of the war and the conflicting ideologies of the major belligerents but also continued to construct more elaborate "war play," an activity begun before age six, when it had already assumed much detail and ranged from flying planes to shooting guns to drilling and marching. Finally, by age nine, children took an "almost adult interest" in the war, were able to comprehend important issues and events, willingly helped with "war work," and showed "surprisingly little" aggression toward the enemy.[41]

Civil War children were not subjected to psychological testing or public opinion polls, but the Second World War does provide a well-studied example of the ways that children can be mobilized for war. Although virtually no American children were physically threatened by the Germans or the Japanese, William M. Tuttle Jr. has shown that they shared almost every other experience faced by their ancestors. They lost fathers and brothers and found themselves alienated from them when they returned from war; they drilled and formed clubs and received military rank for good grades at school; they worked out their fears in their play; they filled movie theaters to see the latest Nazi thriller and eagerly bought up comic books and pulp war fiction; they took on greater responsibilities and put off educations for the good of their families; and they carried emotional scars and political beliefs out of childhood and into their adult lives. To push the comparison even further, the experiences of southern children might be fruitfully compared to those of French and English children during the Second World War. The children of Vichy France were exposed to foreign ideas and organizations in much the same way that children in occupied New Orleans or Memphis were forced to modify their Confederate sympathies. The terror and dislocation experienced by hundreds of thousands of English children during the famous "Blitz" and other crises were shared by many southern children exposed to northern armies crashing through the Confederacy. Specific comparisons with German and Russian and even Japanese children might also be useful. But the point is that, for modern reference points for the experiences of children during the nineteenth century's greatest conflagration, one need only look to the twentieth century's greatest conflict.[42]

2

Fighting against Wrong, and for the Good, the True, and the Beautiful

The War in Children's Literature and Schoolbooks

Gerald Norcross was only seven and just over the mumps when the Civil War began. For nearly two years he barely mentioned the conflict in the terse paragraphs of his daily diary. But he did record the titles of the books he read, and as the volume of war news in his journal grew after the beginning of 1863, so did his catalog of books and stories about the war. Gerald particularly liked travelogues and the famous "Rollo" books by Jacob Abbott — *Rollo at Play*, *Rollo at School*, *Rollo's Vacation*, *Rollo's Museum*, *Rollo's Travels* — but in May 1863 he read *The Little Drummer*, the first of the many war-related pieces he consumed. Subsequent books included forgettable "dime novels" such as *War Trails*, *Vicksburg Spy*, and *Old Hal Williams; or the Spy of Atlanta* as well as better-known factual narratives such as *Life and Campaigns of Gen. McClellan*, *Days and Nights on the Battlefield*, *Following the Flag*, and all of Oliver Optic's popular wartime adventure tales: *Sailor Boy*, *The Yankee Middy*, *The Brave Old Salt*, *Soldier Boy*, *The Young Lieutenant*, and *Fighting Joe*. Gerald loaned his copies of the Optic trilogies to a number of friends and relatives and happily accepted a Christmas subscription to *Our Young Folks*, a popular juvenile periodical that published numerous stories, poems, and articles on the war.[1]

Since Gerald lived far from the fighting and had no close relatives in the army, war literature became one of his major sources of information about the events, issues, and personalities of the conflict. This preoccupation with the war sped the evolution of children's magazines from an overriding concern with religious conversion to an interest in presenting wholesome entertainment, a transition evident in Gerald Norcross's reading list. Yet the children's magazines and books produced in the 1860s also continued to embrace many of the assumptions that had shaped children's literature for decades, providing models of moral behavior and of youths dutifully obeying their parents, working hard, and accepting their lots in life with humility and gratitude. But they also changed in significant ways, not only by providing accounts of battles and of life in the army, short biographies of leading generals and politicians, and war-related trivia and statistics, but also by encouraging children to take part in the northern war effort. They explained the causes and history of the war in its political and moral contexts, inspired children with tales of bravery and patriotism, and showed them how they could contribute to Union victory.[2]

Novels naturally offered larger casts of characters and more expansive settings than the short stories appearing in the juvenile magazines. The war was an adventure, to be sure, and some authors focused almost solely on its drama and heroism. Yet most writers — even authors of fast-paced action stories — also presented the war as a challenge to the patriotism as well as the virtue of Americans, who clearly were supposed to be fighting the war as both a political and a moral crusade. In these books the conflict provided an opportunity for individuals, many of whom were very young men or even children, to prove themselves physically and spiritually. Highly individualistic efforts to overcome fear, resist temptation, escape from treacherous Rebels, or prove one's loyalty drove the plots of the children's novels published during and just after the war. At the same time, the characters learned how their individual efforts contributed to the survival of a larger whole, whether it was their family, their community, or their nation. Camp life and African Americans were all but ignored, while the battle scenes were usually just vehicles for describing the individual heroism of "minor officers experiencing sudden and unrealistic success," in the words of one critic.[3]

Southern publishers, plagued by shortages of ink, paper, and skilled printers, focused less on publishing magazines and books and more on instructional literature, including over two dozen catechisms and hymnals. Nearly three-fourths of the children's books published in the Confederacy were schoolbooks, ranging from Latin grammars to alphabets. Although many of these books avoided politics entirely, this sudden and determined outpouring of Confederate textbooks was designed to meet the same challenges and opportunities as wartime juvenile magazines and novels in the North: to make children aware of the issues that caused the war and to muster southern youngsters' support for the Confederate war effort. In fact, the need to instill southern nationalism in their children and pupils, to free the South from the grip of perverted northern textbooks, spawned the Confederacy's most important literary tradition: primers, spellers, and readers at least partly devoted to the political socialization of the Confederacy's children. Cranking out books with names such as *The Dixie Primer*, *The Confederate Spelling Book*, and *A New Southern Grammar*, publishers explained the war and promoted southern values and institutions. As in the creative literature produced for northern children, antebellum forms and assumptions loomed large in Confederate textbooks; yet in defending slavery and condemning the North, schoolbooks also departed sharply from the products of Yankee houses.[4]

Finally, a minor genre of books and journals for African Americans also appeared during the war. Focusing on the transition of freedpeople from slavery to liberty, tracts, textbooks, and the journal *The Freedman* duplicated the efforts to explain the war to northern children. Relentlessly moralistic and oozing paternalism, they often did not specifically target black children over black adults. But their authors featured themes, styles, and concerns familiar to any reader of children's creative and educational writing, and evidence suggests that black children were exposed to them by their northern white teachers.

There's a War On

Leading northern children's magazines such as *The Student and Schoolmate*, *The Little Pilgrim*, *Our Young Folks*, *The Little Corporal*, *Forrester's Playmate*, and *Merry's Museum* offered information, opinions, or war-related trivia in virtually every type of feature: short stories, nature sketches, travel articles, and "declamation" pieces. Even games and songs offered political propaganda, like the "enigma" that declared, "Negro slavery is an institution the South did prize, Now dead and buried forever it lies." *The Little Corporal* contained elaborate rebuses, called "picture

William T. Adams, the prolific children's author and editor better known as Oliver Optic. (Frontispiece from *The Student and Schoolmate*)

stories," that often went on for several verses. One devoted half of its six stanzas to the Civil War and challenged readers to deduce the following: "They fall upon the falling South, / American eagle at the cannon's mouth; they rush upon the last redoubt. / The eagle grasps the flag about, / For Union and for victory!" Songs printed on the last page of each issue of *The Student and Schoolmate* often heralded the United States as God's handpicked home for freedom. In an 1860s version of "Kids Say the Darndest Things," *The Little Pilgrim* produced a section called "Anecdotes and Sayings of Children," which included comments by the very young on the war. A little girl who had skinned her head, knees, and arms in a fall said sadly to her mother, "Oh dear! what dreadful times these war times are!" Another, revealing a small cut on her hand, explained, "I been to war, and fell down on a bullet, and it bleeded." [5]

In 1863 Oliver Optic, editor of *The Student and Schoolmate*, berated the "cheap patriotism" of drum beating and flag waving early in the war and applauded the deeper, more confident, and more sustained patriotism of both the army and the public. This seriousness was reflected in the scores of stories and articles that presented in a rather matter-of-fact way the nuts and bolts of life in the army and provided other war-related information of interest to their readers. Biographies of generals and descriptions of military insignia and armaments appeared very early in the war. Optic published a series of "Letters from the Army" showing the daily life of soldiers in camp and, two years later, another series called "Campaigning," which discussed the organization of armies and their deployment in battle. Even a Boston Sabbath School paper published a homey and very frank series of letters from Edward Parmelee Smith, a Congregational minister who worked for the United States Christian Commission. A book-length version of the "life in the army" genre was Col. Charles C. Nott's *Sketches of the War*, which described the campaigns in western Tennessee through letters written to the North Moore Street School in New York City. Nott, a graduate and trustee of the school, had originally intended the letters to be read aloud or passed around among the students. Nott focused in his letters not on great battles but on "the details of military life," such as setting up camp and performing picket duty, scouting and foraging, and dealing with surly secessionists and grateful southern Unionists. Like many soldiers, Nott constantly contrasted the rural South with the urban North: there were poor roads and "thriftless"-looking houses, bad food and quaint speaking habits, pipe-smoking women, and unruly horses.[6]

Like the best of the personal narratives, a few novels offered at least glimpses of the real war. For instance, the title character of J. T. Trowbridge's *Frank Manly, the Drummer Boy* temporarily succumbs to the soldierly temptations of gambling and liquor, while in the midst of relentless moralizing about a young paragon of virtue, *The Little Helper* reported that only 24 of the 101 men in a local military company returned home. In an even rarer recognition of the reality of war, the hero of *Frank on a Gun-Boat* witnesses an explosion in an ironclad turret that left "the deck . . . slippery with blood and the turret . . . completely covered with it. The shrieks and groans of the wounded and dying were awful." "For a moment, the young hero was so sick he could scarcely stand."[7]

Dead Drummer Boys and Little Prisoners

The juvenile press went far beyond providing minutiae about the war. Although it would be too much to argue that children's writers in the North actually encouraged underage boys to join the army, many stories threw their protagonists—often twelve years old or younger—into battles and prisons. Stock characters included courageous drummers; kindly, grizzled veterans; honorable officers; and oily Confederates. Characters represented the very best in patriotic, compassionate, and pious northern youth and the worst in mean, impulsive southerners. In "The Little Prisoner," young James is finally allowed by his widowed mother to become drummer boy of an Ohio regiment. He proves his mettle at the battle of the Wilderness, where he is also bayoneted by a Rebel intent on robbing a dead Yankee. A kindly black woman takes him to an abandoned plantation, where she nurses him back to health, reads the Bible with him, and mourns her long-lost son, who had been "sold South" years before. The son miraculously appears just as James is captured by John Mosby's raiders. The author describes the famous partisan as "manly" but cautions that the "stormy, unbridled passions, and . . . cruel, inflexible disposition" ingrained in this slaveholder made him an oppressive commander and an unworthy enemy. Nevertheless, Mosby eventually releases James, who returns home to his mother. His safe passage revealed how "God dealt with a little boy who trusted in and prayed to him." [8]

Most children did not, of course, have to face down lowly Confederates, but they did act out their more violent patriotic impulses by forming their own "boy" companies behind the lines. They also found ways to support the troops or the families of soldiers and took on heavy responsibilities at home. All of these activities were represented in wartime children's literature. Although authors depicted boys and girls alike packing boxes for soldiers, raising money for hospitals or the Sanitary Commission, or taking on additional chores, some differences in their roles did emerge. Contrary to real life, in literature only boys organize companies of play-soldiers; young ladies express their enthusiasm for the war in gender-appropriate ways as spectators or, like their mothers and sisters, as nurses.

Sometimes the only enemies the boy soldiers have to contend with are the little girls giggling at their maneuvers, but in a humorous "Dialogue" in *The Student and Schoolmate*, they encounter actual Confederates. In this brief playlet the "Union Boys in Kentucky" don their uniforms and march to Confederate general Braxton Bragg's headquarters to protest successfully his soldiers' destruction of their playground and wooden rafts. Fictional girls never had the opportunity to strike the foe directly. They might, however, express their patriotism in more appropriate, nurturing ways. One girl named Nelly, inspired by her convalescent brother's stories of the U.S. Sanitary Commission, resolves to create a hospital—she is the nurse, while the gardener's son is the surgeon—for wounded animals she finds in her yard. She builds a tiny ambulance with the Sanitary Commission emblem on the side and proceeds to treat a fly trapped in a spider's web—she calls it "a black contraband"—and a gray snake, even though it is obviously a "rebel." Her efforts cheer her brother to recovery and shame neighborhood boys into forsaking their sport of throwing rocks at innocent animals. Gender differences appear more subtly in "A Box for the Soldier" when a family of children carefully choose the presents they send to their father. One son sends his favorite knife, while another sends a crudely whittled gun, sword, and cannon. In keeping with their roles as women-in-training, the older daughters knit mittens and socks, while the youngest sews a sleeping cap "to keep his precious head from the frosty ground."[9]

Stories not only encouraged children to support the war directly but also taught humility and generosity, two cherished values in prewar literature. The spoiled children in Lydia Maria Child's "The Two Christmas Evenings" learn the true spirit of the holiday but also raise money for a local orphan asylum and for books and toys for black children in South Carolina with a yearlong series of tableaux, speeches on liberty and patriotism, and sales of handicrafts. A girl in another story gives the money she had hoarded to spend at a Sanitary Fair to a poor soldier's orphan, while Gertie, "the Discontented Girl," finally does her share for the soldiers after her older brother calls her a "rebel" for her lazy refusal to get to work. In stories such as these, readers learned the valuable lessons that fictional characters had been demonstrating for years. Even the war effort had to include life lessons applicable to peacetime.[10]

As many readers already knew, and as every child needed to be aware of, one prominent feature of life on the children's home front was the loss of loved ones. The deaths of fathers and brothers brought emotional and material burdens and often forced children to take on responsibilities normally filled by adults. "The Soldier's Little Boy" appeared in August 1863, just after the unprecedented bloodletting at Chancellorsville and Gettysburg, and depicted "little Willie" dying of an unnamed disease. "Who will care for you now, mother," he asks. The "pain of leaving you here alone / Is the sharpest pain I have; / For I know you will never smile again, / And no little boy will be nigh / To wipe the tears on your cheek away, / And whisper — 'Dear mother, don't cry!'" Since his father's death at Antietam, "I did what I could. . . . But my hands were young and weak." Despite his sorrow at leaving his mother alone, like a good Victorian Christian boy he was "not afraid to die. . . . / For the fear of death is past; / But mother — oh, mother, you must not grieve, / We'll meet again by and by — . / Where every tear shall be wiped away — / Father, you, and I."[11]

Willie's death deprived his mother of his help and comfort. In addition to its standard religious message, the poem implied that Willie had been worn down by the burden of replacing his father. Luckily, however, most fictional youngsters who took on expanded responsibilities survived. "The House That Johnny Rented" was serialized in *The Little Corporal* during the first summer after the war. It told the story of the White family, whose minister father goes off to become a chaplain in the Union army, leaving his invalid wife and several children, including twelve-year-old Johnny, to fend for themselves. With his family forced out of the parsonage in which they had lived for many years, Johnny locates a smaller but equally pleasant cottage to rent. There the children raise a garden, help their mother, fret about their father, and help teach a contraband boy to read. The children are obedient and cheerful, they patriotically bad-mouth Confederate generals, and they discover that racial differences are less important than they previously thought.[12]

For Gertie, Willie, and Johnny the war provides a challenging backdrop to their lives. Louisa May Alcott showed her famous heroines enduring genteel poverty and puberty while their father serves as an army chaplain and their mother busies herself on behalf of the Sanitary Commission. Although *Little Women* is, of course, one of the best-known novels of the period, many books dealt with the moral challenges of life on the northern home front. *Frank's Campaign*, an early effort by Horatio Alger that contains many elements of his more famous postwar books, exemplifies how the war made it possible for a determined, honest boy to get ahead. Its hero, Frank, wins a school contest with a composition on what boys can do to help win the war and gets a chance to put theory into practice when his father enlists. His prowar and antislavery letters from camp provide the book's primary political tone. Meanwhile, Frank is immersed in several subplots dealing with Squire Haynes, a war profiteer who tries to foreclose the mortgage on Frank's father's farm; a family of refugee blacks befriended by Frank's family; and a mysterious stranger looking for the man who had years before cheated his father in a business transaction (the villain, of course, turns out to be the shady army contractor). Everything turns out well in the end: Haynes is ruined, the mortgage is paid, and Frank's new friend—the man who has successfully exposed Squire Haynes's larceny—promises to pay for Frank's education.[13]

Children could match the patriotism of soldiers, even if they never strode onto a battlefield. In some cases family responsibilities and moral prerogatives loomed larger than the war itself; of course, if the moral threads of the American society were not sustained during the war, the country would unravel even if the military effort was unsuccessful. The main character in *Kathie's Soldiers*, a virginal teenager, fulfills her duty to her country by working for the local Sanitary Fair and watching over the motherless daughter of a soldier. But she also performs her moral duty by refusing to engage in the constant gossiping and backbiting among the fashionable girls at her school and by persevering against the condescending daughter of yet another dishonest army contractor. Her uncle and her brother discover that their duty is at home, not in the army; the former hires a substitute so he can remain at home to support his widowed sister and her family, and the latter submits to going off to boarding school rather than becoming a drummer. Even Kathie's little brother Freddie does his duty by staying out of trouble and by eagerly supporting the war effort in his miniature soldier's uniform. As a young lieutenant tells the troubled hero of *Battles at Home*, "Our battles must be just where we are put to fight them." He dissuades Bob from running away to the army to escape the wrath of his beloved but straitlaced grandfather. "You think it would be doing something—something brave—to go off in this way—do you?" he asks. "Now I call it turning one's back on what one is called to suffer, and saying, weakly, 'I can't bear it'!"[14]

Like the wise lieutenant, many authors cast the war as a metaphor for the struggle within everyone between good and evil. For the children in this genre of wartime story—a number of examples of which were published by the American Sunday School Union and the American Tract Society—the war between the states gave them an opportunity to test their good intentions and Sunday School training in the crucible of wartime pressures.[15] After his father is reported killed, a little boy is haunted by his last words before leaving for the army: "Always obey your mother"; a teenaged emigrant to "Bleeding Kansas" links her country's honor to her piety, insisting that "to rally for its defence is not less a duty of religion than of patriotism"; for Andy Hall, his steadfast service in the Union army is the culmination of his reformation and redemption after a life of poverty and petty crime. Other books showed young drummer boys converting grizzled soldiers or inspiring adults with their pious deaths.[16]

Rebellion in Such a Country as This

Although the moral lessons that could be gleaned from the war were obviously important, children's books and magazines made the political meaning of the war an even higher priority. They sought to instill a resolute patriotism in their readers by defining northern war aims, establishing the centrality of slavery as a cause of the war, and recognizing the humanity of the former slaves. The Uncle Rodman who narrated J. T. Trowbridge's "The Turning of the Leaf" summarized this political dogma: "In a word, children, slavery was the cause of the war; and God permitted the war in order that slavery might be destroyed." He goes on to stress the intolerance of southern slaveowners, who had "grown arrogant, conceited, overbearing . . . determined to destroy the government they could not control." Obviously, according to Uncle Rodman and dozens of other politically knowledgeable characters in children's stories, "the rebellion was a stupendous piece of folly, as well as stupendous wickedness." The benefits of the American political system, argued *Merry's Museum*, made "rebellion in such a country as this . . . the highest of crimes." No author hesitated to blame the South. Fearful that their power was slipping away, southerners "became proud, insolent, domineering, and ambitious," sparking the sectional conflict and pushing the nation into crisis. Even southern children had become contemptuous of honest labor.[17]

Exploiting the Victorian rage for drawing-room theatricals, *The Student and Schoolmate* published brief "Dialogues," many of which dealt with patriotic and war themes. Set in the "Union Seminary" for girls, the main characters of the satiric "The Comedy of Secession" included "Madame Columbia," the principal; "Madame Britannia, a neutral old Lady, fond of giving advice"; "La Belle France, fascinating, but cautious"; the "Goddess of Liberty, a popular belle"; and a bevy of students with names such as "Georgiana," "Mary Land," "Vermont," "Little Rhody," and "K. Tucky." The scene opens with Madame Columbia complaining about the behavior of a half-dozen young ladies who "have become exceedingly rebellious, and threaten to leave—secede, they call it—without reason or justice, and contrary to the wishes of their fathers and mothers." Throughout the play Madame Columbia lectures the wayward young ladies on their irresponsibility, the advantages of seminary life, and the shame they will bring to the memories of their ancestors. Nevertheless, the girls begin planning the "Confederate Seminary," where "J. Davis" will be principal; "Beauregard," dancing master; and "Wigfall," chaplain. The Rebels are interrupted in their plotting by Goddess Liberty, whom Miss Caroline tries to convince to come over to the upstart school. When the former asks why they are deserting the seminary, the latter replies, "Because our rights have been trampled upon," to which Liberty retorts, "Nonsense! You mean if you cannot be the greatest toad in the puddle, you will set the river on fire." Accusations fly, Madame Britannia and La Belle France try to pick a fight with Madame Columbia, and the "northern" girls rally around their principal. Although eleven young ladies eventually exit in a huff, "Miss Tennie" returns after a severe "whipping," and the company closes by singing the "Star-Spangled Banner."[18]

A basic tenet of the gospel according to northern children's magazines was that the South had gone to war at the instigation and in the best interests of only a few aristocratic slaveholders. The assumption that a "slave power conspiracy" gripped the South had sustained northerners during the long secession winter and helped shape the policies of the early Lincoln administration, but juvenile magazines stressed the idea throughout the war, even after alternative beliefs and policies emerged. Trowbridge's "The Turning of the Leaf" characterized Rebel leaders as "confident that they could override Northern freemen as they had so long overridden their black slaves," deceiving and misleading "the ignorant masses" into going to war under the banner of secession.[19]

Trowbridge played variations on his theme in a series of travelogues that appeared in *Our Young Folks* during the last months of the war and the year that followed. The articles generally featured sites and battlefields in the South, but he first visited Camp Douglas, the Union prisoner-of-war camp in Chicago. Rather blithely ignoring the disease, discontent, and mismanagement that characterized the real Camp Douglas, Trowbridge described a clean, orderly, well-managed camp, the proficient guards, and good-natured and healthy inmates. The most important political point is that most of the men in the prison are delighted to be safely away from the war. They are well treated and many have taken the loyalty oath to the United States. In fact, most are actually very much like northerners, "differing . . . only as they are warped by slavery or crushed by slaveholders." Subsequent trips south showed that generally good-hearted southerners had been led by a tiny coterie of slaveowners into a war few of them favored. Others offered accounts of Confederate cruelty toward Yankees and southern Unionists combined with the realization that many — perhaps most — southerners had only reluctantly supported the Confederacy.[20]

If the Confederacy described for young northerners had only a thin veneer of unity, slavery was its corrupt center. Several authors and correspondents added a humanitarian aspect to these political truths by describing the conditions and needs of refugee blacks. Although condescending and even racist to modern sensibilities, these letters and stories, however clumsily, strove to tear down the barriers between black and white children. Many of the thousands of freedpeople crowding Norfolk, Virginia, in the spring of 1864, G. N. Coan wrote, "are as white as any of you are, with blue eyes and straight hair, or pretty auburn ringlets." Yet the African blood in their veins had doomed them to suffer the cruelty of "the auction block," where "mothers and children [were] torn asunder by their cruel masters." The little ones among the freedpeople loved school and learned quickly. "Could you see their eyes sparkle and their faces shine with delight, as they sing their little songs (such as you sing), and hear them answer questions from the Bible, I am sure you would be delighted, and think they were anything but stupid." The letter concludes with a request that readers "send them some of your old dresses, quilts, sacks, or shoes, so that they may be able to go to school, and learn to read the word of God, and thus become good men and women." Another appeal for aid assured readers that former slave children "love [*The Little Pilgrim*] and his pretty stories, very much," but also stressed that many of the recently freed blacks "are ignorant and debased." They needed help in the form of clothes, schools, and books. The correspondent urged children to "whisper a sweet, pleading whisper in the ear of each and every dear friend . . . to send all they can spare," to convince affluent parents or uncles or aunts to send money, and to contribute toy and candy money to the cause of the freed children.[21]

Such charitable efforts were encouraged in children's fiction. But in keeping with their application of civic responsibility and moral correctness to wartime exigencies, authors showed that there were wrong and right ways of helping the less fortunate. In Christie Pearl's "The Contraband," the half-dozen children of a solidly upper middle-class family treat the call for aid for freed slaves flippantly, eagerly casting off clothes that are too small, too ugly, or too impractical to keep. Along the way they laugh at improbable images of the contrabands wearing the "dickeys" and bracelets and old hats they plan to pack into the barrel and rejoice that after discarding their unwanted clothing they can buy new wardrobes. Their father interrupts the fun with "a loud 'Ahem!'" and asks sternly, "Are there any things there that you want or need?" When they reply that there is not, he lectures them, "Then you have not given properly. Your clothes may keep the 'contrabands' warm, but they will bring no additional warmth to your own hearts. You must make sacrifices in order to reap the benefit of giving." Promptly and properly chagrined, the children repack the aid barrel with some of their favorite clothes and toys.[22]

While most references to African Americans were to the unfortunate but worthy contrabands, a story appearing in *Forrester's Playmate* in early 1864 related an incident between the narrator and a free black living in the North. One evening while playing, the narrator and several of his "playfellows" begin harassing Jim Dick, a young black boy playing with them, by calling him "'negro,' 'blackamoor,' and other ill names." Jim leaves the group, "very much hurt at our conduct." Nevertheless, when the narrator asks to borrow Jim's ice skates a few days later, Jim lends them willingly. When the white boy returns the skates, he finds Jim reading his Bible "with tears in his eyes." He then "kindly and meekly" says, "Do not call me blackamoor again." Although the incident had taken place a number of years before the war, the narrator remembers that "these words went to my heart; I burst into tears, and from that time I resolved I would never again be guilty of abusing a poor black." Many lessons could be learned from this little parable. Do not use insulting names or mock others; keep a forgiving spirit and control your anger; and "do not undervalue any for the color of skin, or the shape of their bodies, or the poverty of their condition, for we are as God made us." [23]

While few stories offered full-fledged black characters, several novels did. Despite the stereotypes of African Americans that frequently slipped into their characterizations, authors generally sympathized with the slaves. Surprisingly, the otherwise quite typical dime novel *Old Peggy Boggs; or, The Old Dominion, Inside Out*, offered sobering images of slavery. One subplot portrays a black man named Pompey searching for his wife, who was sold away from him; another scene shows a slaveowner betting—and losing—a little slave girl in a poker game. Antebellum writers of juvenile fiction had rarely risen above easy generalizations about blacks, even when they attacked the institution of slavery, and wartime writers were no different. For instance, Pic, the only black to appear in the adventure book *Dora Darling*, speaks in a barely intelligible dialect. He is devoted to Dora, who returns his affection while retaining her sense of maternal and racial superiority. The distance that remained between blacks and even the most sympathetic whites leaps from the pages of an American Tract Society book issued shortly after the war. Its author, a former nurse, gingerly describes her work at a hospital near New York. She also provides an account of a black church service where her "own sense of the ludicrous caused me to smile." Yet the chanting and foot-stamping and swaying and singing also sadden her, and she asks herself, "Will not the Saviour accept the feeble attempts of these darkened minds at worship, and sometime lead them into the higher and purer light of his love?" [24]

Blacks—as slaves, as freedpeople, and as objects of sympathy—were clearly central to the political lessons in wartime writing for children. Even so, they were hardly presented as political, economic, or intellectual equals to whites. Although the heroic free black Pompey is arguably the most intelligent and self-assured character in J. T. Trowbridge's *The Three Scouts*, most authors, and perhaps their readers, could not quite leave behind old assumptions and stereotypes about African Americans. They could, at best, imagine them as rather helpless, pitiable beings. *The Little Pilgrim* once quoted a little girl's prayer about poor black refugee children. "Oh God, you have made these poor children black," she pleaded, "and now will you please make white people kind to them." African Americans may have served as models of stoic suffering and symbols of what the northern armies were fighting for, but the images of blacks appearing in children's magazines and books encouraged little more than pity.[25]

Young Heroes

Of course, some authors focused more on the adventure than the politics of war. Although the famous dime novels of Beadle and Adams continued to draw on the frontier for most of their stories, between 1863 and 1865 nearly twenty titles of the hundred-page novellas featured Civil War themes. They focused almost exclusively on individual loyalty and courage, particularly by southern Unionists fighting overwhelming odds to save the Union, to preserve their fortunes, and, in nearly every book, to marry a beautiful woman — or, in some, a handsome Union officer. The improbable coincidences and startling plot twists indigenous to the genre lent themselves especially to stories of espionage and secret societies. In addition to providing eye-popping adventures, these cheaply made books showed that most southerners, when push came to shove, would stay true to themselves and to their country.[26]

Slightly more respectable was Oliver Optic (William T. Adams), the prolific editor of *The Student and Schoolmate*, whose "Army and Navy Stories" chronicled the adventures of twin brothers Tom and Jack Somers and set the standard for exciting and patriotic war fiction. The boys, seventeen when the war began, represented the common soldiers and sailors in the Union military effort (although each becomes an officer before the war ends). Optic introduced *The Soldier Boy*, the first in the set of books about Tom, as "a narrative of personal adventure, delineating the birth and growth of pure patriotism in the soul of the hero," and as a portrait of a "true soldier, one who loves his country, and fights for her because he loves her; but, at the same time, one who is true to himself and his God."[27]

Optic's books followed a strict formula. Each presented elements of military life and tradition, introduced a squad of loyal sidekicks and dangerous enemies, and allowed Jack or Tom to demonstrate their martial skill and bravery in a large unit action. Then they set the hero free to operate deep behind enemy lines, where he experienced a round of captures and escapes, met sympathetic southern Unionists, finished his mission, and made his way back to safety, where he received a promotion that led him to similar adventures in the sequel. The Somers boys operate more or less alone, relying on their own skills, only a few close friends, their courage and patriotism, and their virtue — qualities found in nearly every story and novel for children during the middle third of the nineteenth century. A fairly typical plot drives *The Yankee Middy*. In this second volume about Jack, the naval recruit, he stumbles into a conspiracy to divert captured contraband goods to the Confederacy. His foe, a Confederate spy named Phil Kennedy, is also Jack's competitor for the lovely Kate, a Union commodore's daughter. While attempting to foil the plot, Jack is captured but escapes; his pursuit of his military and romantic rival ends in a rousing hand-to-hand struggle between the crews of Kennedy's and Jack's gunboats. Jack mortally wounds Kennedy, and his crew overcomes the Confederates. Afterward, Jack reads the Bible to the Rebel spy, who then peacefully and gratefully drifts into death.[28]

A female version of Oliver Optic's youthful heroes was the title character of Jane Goodwin Austin's *Dora Darling*. Dora is the twelve-year-old daughter of a drunken southern farmer and a Unionist mother. After Dora and her mother help a wounded Union soldier — "Captain Carl" — to escape, her father is upset. When her mother dies, two older brothers sell the farm and join the Confederate army, and Dora goes to live with a cruel aunt. She soon runs away and, in the first of a series of amazing coincidences, is reunited with Picter, the loyal slave who had earlier been sent away with the Union officer. Dora, who hopes to join her mother's sister in the North, is adopted by the regiment to which Captain Carl belongs as a sort of vivandiere. Although her character goes against the usual portrayal of girls fighting their wars behind the lines, her gender is protected when she takes on the roles of nurse, chaplain's assistant, and all-around civilizing influence for the regiment. "It was a strange life for a little girl," wrote the author with dazzling understatement, "but a very comfortable and happy one." Dora performs her duties efficiently, prevents a wounded Union soldier (another southern Unionist) from settling an old feud by murdering an injured Confederate, finds herself on the run behind Confederate lines, is captured and then escapes from the Rebels, saves the life of Captain Carl (who was about to be shot by her brother Tom), and later helps her brother escape (after he promises never again to fight against the Union). The chaplain, the colonel, and Captain Carl all vie for the chance to adopt her. When she finally decides to go to live for a time with Carl's mother, she discovers the aunt she had been hoping to find in the first place and learns that Carl is her cousin.[29]

Young America Reports the War

The chords struck in children's stories and novels sounded in children's own voices. One way to measure the extent to which northern children absorbed wartime messages and lessons is to read their wartime writings, which frequently offered the same combination of humor, sentimental poetry, and human interest stories found in juvenile magazines. Although the heyday of "amateur newspapers" would not come until the invention several years after the war of a cheap, easy-to-use miniature printing press, children had been producing their own papers for years. Some were professionally printed, ran for several years, and were distributed to hundreds of child and adult readers, while others were hand-printed, lived for only an issue or two, and were shown only to parents and a few best friends. Yet the editors of these juvenile newspapers replicated the great political and social debates of the day, using the arguments and styles of "adult" newspapers as well as juvenile magazines. Almost every genre published in children's magazines appeared in the amateurs: adventure stories, fire-breathing editorials, correspondence, serials, poetry, and jokes.[30]

Even though the child publishers lived relatively privileged lives, the war intruded even on them, and on their newspapers. The editor of the Providence *Sunbeam* acknowledged that while he and his siblings "are made comfortable and happy" at the school they attended in their own home, "thousands of children are deprived of friends and homes, by this cruel war. We do not forget them, but often wish we could do something for their comfort." The New Year's editorial for 1864 gratefully reported that "health, and happiness have been bestowed upon us: the lives of our friends have been spared, and each day has seemed to bring some new source of comfort and enjoyment." However, "How different the lot of many about us. This cruel war has brought sorrow and sadness into many homes. Fathers and brothers have been taken, and many children, who, at the commencement of the last year, were as happy as we, are now left orphans." Other pieces provided the mixture of trivia and pathos common to periodicals such as *Our Young Folks* and its competitors. Writers described a visit to Fort Adams at Newport, where they saw Confederate prisoners in balls and chains and "caught a glimpse of Maj. Anderson, the hero of Fort Sumter"; contrasted the "gay sight" of soldiers on parade with the "not . . . very pleasant" life of a soldier in the field; and submitted a loving obituary of a young relative, who was "a good son, a kind brother, a faithful friend, and a brave officer. His end was peaceful, for his hope was in Jesus."[31]

Other editors kept their readers informed as well as entertained. A young Pawtucket, Rhode Island, editor named Edward Dix offered political commentary at the outbreak of the war. Although caught a little off guard by the secession of the South — "That is Young America, we are a fast community" — Dix warmed to the crisis, assuring his readers that "we are able to carry on the war without the assistance of foreign aid" and approvingly reporting that a regiment of men from every county in the state of New York was forming to avenge the death of the martyred Elmer Ellsworth. Like the juvenile magazines these editors were no doubt emulating, their occasional forays into humor depended on wordplay and on the foibles of amateur soldiers. *The Union* quoted the *Charleston Mercury* as calling "the Yankee troops now threatening the south 'tin pedlars' " and agreed that "it is true that the Yankees have generally in their visits South peddled tin, but we guess they mean to peddle lead this time." The handwritten Worcester *Monthly Chronicle* printed a genial account of an inexperienced commander who, "exhibiting less recollection of 'the tactics,' " deployed his unit as skirmishers by yelling, "Get up there on the hill, & scatter out as you did yesterday."[32]

The longest-running wartime amateur newspaper was published by the boys attending Newark High School. Their *Athenaeum*, a handwritten monthly, offered stories, poems, and essays originally composed as class assignments. They ranged from a two-part narrative of a classmate's hair-raising escape from the

1863 sack of Lawrence, Kansas, to an editorial arguing that the moral courage of patriots had to match their physical courage, and to the humorous story "Uncle Zeke at the Fair," where an old "down easter" battled crowds and high prices at the local Sanitary Fair. A number of authors submitted pleas to remember the soldiers and to overlook their shortcomings. "It becomes us not to censure the soldier who has enlisted under the banner we love," wrote J. M. Quinlan, "to keep it sacred from vile traitorous hands, or give his life as an alternative!" One curious piece traced the "career" of a leather boot, from the slaughterhouse and tannery through bloody campaigns, Libby Prison, and a dramatic escape, to its final resting place as a war "momento" in its wearer's closet.[33]

A few editors included patriotic poetry that portrayed the soldiers' sacrifices, called on God to help save the Union, and attempted to heighten the patriotism of their readers. Much less sanguinary was "The Little Soldier," which appeared in the *Monthly Chronicle*. It confronted the loss and grief spawned by the war with a unique pacifism. A little boy surrenders the trumpet, gun, and sword his mother gave him, explaining sadly, "I shall choose some other play." The erstwhile soldier explains, "Mother! I have just been reading / What a soldiers' life must be. / And of fearful scenes of carnage / He on battlefields must see." Forsaking his heretofore favorite pastime — "I would not a soldier be! / Scenes of blood are not for me" — he dedicates his life to "labors . . . of love and mercy."[34]

This antiwar message seems as out of place in a children's newspaper as it would have in *The Little Pilgrim* or *The Student and Schoolmate*. Their choice of topics, as well as their faithful recreation of the themes and styles of children's magazines, indicate the extent to which these child editors and writers had taken in the forms and attitudes of the commercial magazines. There is no way of determining how many of these children subscribed to or even read one of the numerous journals published for them, but it is clear that the middle-class child culture of the North was certainly infused by their rhetorical examples and editorial stances.

Most of the stories or novels for children written during the Civil War became war-flavored artifacts rather than notable and lasting pieces of literature. In an essay published early in 1866, Thomas Wentworth Higginson — himself an occasional writer for children — devoted a few pages to the children's books inspired by the war. He particularly liked Coffin's pair of books, which he called "more interesting than fiction." He dismissed Oliver Optic's books as "spirited and correct enough" but hastily written and filled with caricatures of women. Higginson also criticized novelists who, when their characters encountered African Americans, resorted to the predictable and unfortunate "retribution on the negro race" of colorful but confusing, inaccurate, and racist dialects.[35]

Despite the shortcomings mentioned by Higginson, untold thousands of northern boys and girls read the periodical literature and novels inspired by the Civil War. From these stories and editorials, games and illustrations, and adventures and parables they could piece together the causes and ramifications of the conflict and their roles in it. They continued to stress the age-old values that had been promoted in children's antebellum literature and which would remain a bedrock of writing for children for decades after the war. In a sense, northern children learned through their reading that those very assumptions were being challenged by the slaveholding, aristocratic, backward-looking South. Their rebellion threatened the notions on which northerners had based their comfortable social and moral systems. Piety and humility, a strict work ethic, and all the other treasured values inculcated in Yankee children were now joined by an aggressive patriotism. Assuring their readers that their country's course was correct, that the war could be won if northerners demonstrated the necessary piety, determination, and willingness to sacrifice, and that no contribution to the war effort was too small, authors during and immediately after the war politicized and inspired young Yankees to act on their loyalty.

For the Children of the Southern Confederacy

Very similar themes shaped southern literature for children during the Civil War; in fact, their similarities attest to the tenacity of Victorian ideas and attitudes, at least as they appeared in children's literature. Yet far fewer children's magazines and books appeared in the Confederacy than in the Union. Sparse resources and a deteriorating economy forced southern publishers to prioritize their publishing efforts. As a result only a few issued juvenile literature in magazine or book-length formats. Those that appeared did, however, present patriotic narratives and images. Samuel Boykin's *Child's Index*, a hard-shell Baptist Sunday school paper, and the North Carolina Institution for the Deaf and Dumb and the Blind's *Deaf Mute Casket* were the longest-running Confederate juveniles. The Presbyterian *Children's Friend* and the Methodist *Children's Guide* each lasted for about two years. Shorter lived was *The Child's Banner*, another religious publication out of Salisbury, North Carolina. Although far more theologically oriented than typical northern magazines, they, too, explained the war to children and encouraged their involvement. As a Confederate newspaper declared in announcing the publication of *The Child's Banner*, these papers would meet "as nearly as possible . . . the wants of the children in these days of evil."[56]

Themes of sacrifice, loss, and pious patriotism shaped southern writing for children. The first issue of the *Child's Index* — actually a sample sent to prospective subscribers in churches and Sunday schools — described some of the hardships faced by Confederate soldiers in the field and the "suffering and sorrow and distress" it caused. Readers "ought all to pray for peace" but also to take comfort from the knowledge "that we are fighting . . . to drive wicked invaders from our land." Articles urged children to mind their mothers while fathers were absent, described the admirable religious spirit in the Macon military hospital, compared the Confederacy's struggle favorably with the American Revolution, and "proved" biblical support for slavery. Southern fiction echoed northern approaches to the duty of children. In one story a little girl converts her soldier-father on his sickbed, while in another a boy, despite his enthusiasm for joining the Confederate army, stays home to help his mother upon learning of his father's death in battle. The account of a valiant drummer and advice to girls to study hard so they would be prepared to educate the next generation of southerners appeared in the *Deaf Mute Casket*.[37]

A few of the handful of book-length imprints produced during the war did attempt to explain the conflict.[58] *For the Little Ones*, a book of verse "Dedicated to the Little Girls and Boys of the Southern Confederacy," included "Dickie—The Boy Soldier," which offered a mother's description of her two year old playing soldier. Another piece, "Willie's Political Alphabet," provided rhymes inspired by Confederate words and names. For instance, "A's for the Army—now don't you forget— / And B's for the Banner, the 'flag of the free,' / For Beauregard, Bartow, Bethel, and

Bee!" Other phrases representing letters were Hampton's Legion, "King Cotton," Lincoln ("oh, woe to his crown"), Union ("a *wreck on the sea*"), and Washington ("soon to be won").[39]

Uncle Buddy's Gift Book contained several items designed to inspire devotion to the cause. "The Young Confederate Soldier" was a straightforward story of a fourteen-year-old Confederate capturing a squad of Yankees, while "A Mother's Prayer" asked God to sustain a young recruit through danger and hardship. Finally, the pocket-sized *Boys and Girls Stories of the War* contained several pieces on various aspects of the conflict. "Story of a Refugee" painted a bleak picture of the plight of a refugee woman and her two young children, who had been burned out of their Shenandoah Valley home. At the point in the story when the heroic Stonewall Jackson finally throws Union general Banks back across the Potomac River, the author asks his readers to "raise your little hands and swing them around your head every time I do, and cry, 'Huzza, for Stonewall.'" Subsequent stories displayed old, loyal "Uncle Ned," a slave who hates the Yankees and helps guide Stonewall's troops through the mountains; related a wounded Rebel prisoner's experiences in New Orleans, where he saw the famous midgets "Commodore Foote" and "Tom Thumb"; and applauded the courage of a Confederate editor who remained in the midst of the fighting at Chancellorsville despite the "whistling balls and shrieking shells" and the "really frightful . . . dead and dying strewn thick upon the ground."[40]

Carrying the Fight into the Schoolroom

Few southern children read such stirring scenes, and the Confederacy never really established a literary tradition while the war raged. But in their attempt to break what one Tennesseean called "our vassalage to the North," southerners undertook a crash program of publishing textbooks for schoolchildren in the Confederacy.[41] Scores of primers, readers, and arithmetics emerged from southern presses, as southern educators acted on their conviction that their revolution would be complete only if they established their own educational institutions and publishing houses. They based this belief on a somewhat exaggerated but widely held perception of northern textbooks' antisouthern biases.

In fact only a few antebellum publications specifically attacked slavery, and they were all published prior to 1830. A few school histories provided factual information, limited mainly to laws and compromises related to the institution. Although slavery was virtually never mentioned as a sectional issue, schoolbooks increasingly provided examples and excerpts that highlighted the intrinsic value of the Union. Spellers used sentences such as "Stand by the Union!" and "In union there is strength," while readers offered stories that showed the benefits of union and emphasized the institutions and customs common to all of the United States. Other themes that could be characterized as "northern" were the ubiquitous assumption that temperance was a virtue upon which the very survival of the republic depended and the tendency among schoolbook compilers to decry war and promote the rather vague antebellum crusade for peace. The best-known readers of the period, of course, were *McGuffey's*, whose prewar editions avoided controversial issues like slavery in order to attract the southern trade. Even the 1862 and 1866 revisions of the famous "blue" reader, which did include stories and poems that showed the hardships and destruction associated with the war, did not condemn slavery or specifically promote the Union cause. Yet a North Carolina teacher bitterly complained that northern textbooks' ignorance and misperceptions had created a condescending "egotism" in the North. "I shudder to think," he wrote, "how deep a hold their insidious doctrines had taken even upon the southern mind."[42]

The schoolbooks rolling off southern presses originated in part from the efforts of a number of prominent southern educators to create a coherent approach to the education of Confederate children. Throughout most of the Confederacy—North Carolina was a modest exception—public and private schools fell victim to tightened budgets, invading Union armies, and patriotic teachers deserting classrooms for battlefields. Hundreds of schools closed, some for good; terms were shortened; attendance declined precipitously; and women and elderly men increasingly took over as instructors.[43] Despite the difficulties that schools faced, as states, communities, and families strapped for cash shifted money normally reserved for school budgets or tuition, some farsighted southerners urged their countrymen to maintain southern schools. As early as October 1861 the *Atlanta Daily Intelligencer* bemoaned the fact that war excitement had distracted teachers, parents, and pupils. "Our schools have suffered an interruption during the present year," it admitted, "let it not grow into their suspension. . . . The opportunity for instruction, if now lost by the boys and girls who are soon to be our men and women, will be irrevocably lost." The South stood "on the threshold of a new civilization," argued a Virginian promoting a female normal school, requiring "agencies of moral as well as intellectual influence . . . both to resist at once the immediate demoralizing effects of the war upon the young" and to satisfy "the multiplied intellectual and moral wants of this new country."[44]

Although most of their efforts to save southern schools proved futile, southern educators and publishers rather incredibly managed in a very short time to establish a Confederate tradition in pedagogical literature. Southern presses in cities from Richmond to Mobile to Galveston produced nearly 100 schoolbooks for both patriotic and economic reasons. The Reverend Robert Fleming combined both motivations. The war, he noted in the preface to his speller, was caused by "protected, unjust and oppressive Federal legislation"; the blockade — "the offspring of an unjustifiable and tyrannical war" — had interrupted the importation of books into the Confederacy. His volume, published in Atlanta, would help ease the shortage. The publisher of *The New Texas Series*, newspaperman E. H. Cushing, characterized himself as a sort of Confederate hero; other publishers hesitated to involve themselves in such an "uncertain" and difficult business due to chronic shortages of newsprint and other supplies. Yet Cushing decried the "evil" of children being "deprived of the advantage of school, for the want of suitable books." The crisis was actually a force for good in the lives of impressionable youngsters. "In former times," wrote the publisher of *Chaudron's Spelling Book*, "the country was overrun with an endless number of competition school books in every line of instruction. The present condition of the country has delivered us from this evil."[45]

Authors pointedly criticized prewar schoolbooks, virtually all published in the northern states, and welcomed the chance to overcome the misconceptions presented in such books. John H. Rice appended a nearly full-page subtitle to his *System of Modern Geography*, which promised that the "Political and Physical Condition of the States composing the Confederate States of America are fully treated of, and their progress in Commerce, Education, Agriculture, Internal Improvements and Mechanic Arts, prominently set forth." His volume, "compiled by a Southern man, published upon our own soil," would correct "every *yankee* work" that had "studiously concealed" the "actual conditions and resources" of the South. Similar southern credentials were presented by Allen M. Scott, who boasted that "for the first time in the history of our beloved South, a new Grammar, written by one of her own sons, [is being] printed by a Southern house in a Southern city." [46]

Commentators generally applauded these works. "We hope the day is past," a Columbia, South Carolina, newspaper declared, "for the importation of books for our children from our enemies, who never omitted an opportunity . . . to inculcate their fanatical teachings against our institutions." In a notice for *Chaudron's First Reader* and *The Second Reader* two-and-a-half years later, the *Charleston Mercury* agreed. "We must exclude from our schools all those productions of Yankee pretension and superficiality." Another southern editor was relieved that Confederate publications freed "the moral judgment" as well as "taste of our people" from "the mercy of a people as oblique in their morals as they have been defective in taste." [47]

Obviously, Confederate authors did not reject their traditional responsibility to inculcate morality and good behavior; they merely added Confederate values to those values readily accepted by most Americans. Richard Sterling chose selections for his reader based on their "simplicity of style," "good sense," and "pure Bible morality," while the compiler of *The Child's First Book* hoped to "present to the impressible mind of the child sound instruction in morality and true religion." Another compiler selected the pieces for his reader on the basis of their ability "to interest and instruct the pupils . . . to elevate their ideas, form correct tastes, and instill proper sentiments." [48]

Despite the glee with which many southern educators and publishers declared their independence from northern texts, not every schoolbook published in the Confederacy launched pedagogical offensives against Yankees. Some — even those with titles proclaiming Confederate patriotism — ignored sectional issues and the war entirely. [49] Others acknowledged it only superficially by appending a few paragraphs of Confederate history, engravings of Confederate flags, lists of Confederate states and territories, and isolated allusions to individual battles and generals. [50] Adelaide De

Vendel Chaudron's *Second Reader* referred only to the soldier-play of a little boy, while tucked among the homey examples drawn from everyday life and the Bible stories of *The First Reader, for Southern Schools* was lesson twenty-nine, which explained the usages of words such as "arm," "cut," "sad," and "war": "The man's arm has been cut off. It was shot by a gun. Oh! What a sad thing war is!" Finally, the most extensive borrowing of incidental wartime situations and celebrities appeared in Levi Branson's *First Book in Composition*, in which the names of famous Confederates and snide comments about northern generals and politicians appeared in nearly every section.[51]

An unusual attempt to provide guidance to match the specific needs of southern children appeared in *Chaudron's Third Reader.* Although generally ignoring the war itself, it did offer a series of lessons completely absent from prewar northern texts: instruction on pronunciation and enunciation problems peculiar to southerners. For instance, "poor" must not be pronounced "pooah," and it was "matter," not "mattuh"; "sorrow," not "sorruh"; and "children," not "childrun." Students must be careful not to drop "ed" from the ends of words and should refrain from using "Africanisms" like substituting "d" or "f" for "th" ("deeze" for "these" or "bofe" for "both"). Other common problems included saying "neck'ed" for "naked," "stomp" for "stamp," and "git" for "get."[52]

Even these brief mentions of Confederate or southern institutions, values, or leaders promoted the Rebel cause. They confirmed common assumptions about slavery, about the sacrifices of Confederate soldiers, and about the strengths of southern and the weaknesses of northern culture. These asides and suggestions helped Confederate children fit comfortably into their new country by creating links between it and the familiar prewar past. A similar normalization of the war and assumption of the superiority of southerners appeared in Confederate arithmetics. Students had to work out problems about rations at Fort Sumter, servants picking cotton, the productivity and cost of slaves, the area of the Confederate States, and casualty rates in unnamed battles.[53] The most imaginative use of war images in a Confederate arithmetic appeared in L. Johnson's text for beginners. This brief volume featured long lists of story problems and examples featuring a number of war situations. In one a Confederate cavalry captain buys a horse and a gun, while in another a merchant sells salt to a soldier's wife. Students were asked to imagine rolling cannonballs out of their bedrooms, to divide Confederate soldiers into squads and companies, and to figure out how to use Confederate currency. Johnson also included such famous problems as "A Confederate soldier captured 8 Yankees each day for 9 successive days; how many did he capture in all?"; "If one Confederate soldier kill [sic] 90 yankees, how many yankees can 10 Confederate soldiers kill?"; and "If one Confederate soldier can whip 7 yankees, how many soldiers can whip 49 yankees?"[54]

The prolific Mrs. M. B. Moore produced several children's texts that featured the war. Her *Dixie Speller* pursued a prosouthern but uniquely antiwar point of view. Lesson thirty-seven described "War" as "a sad thing, and those who bring it about will have much to answer for." It is quite clear who is to blame for this specific war. "If the rulers in the United States had been good Christian men, the present war would not have come upon us." The moral for her readers was "Let every boy learn this lesson, and when he is a man, let him not vote for a bad man to fill an office of trust." Expanding on her theme of the horror of war, Moore offered a child's excruciating first-person narrative of war weariness with a rather fatalistic patriotism underlying its sheen of Christian hope. "This sad war is a bad thing," it began. "My papa went, and died in the army. My big brother went too, and got shot. A bomb shell took off his head. My aunt had three sons, and all have died in the army." Needless to say, the narrator hoped "we will have peace by the time [I] am old enough to go to war." He noted that when "little boys fight, old folks whip them for it; but when men fight, they say 'how brave!' " If he were a grown-up, "I would not have any war, if I could help it." However, if forced to go to war, "I would not run away like some do. . . . I would sooner die at my post than desert." If his father had "run away, and been shot for it, how sad I must have felt all my life!" The fictional boy concluded in a striking mixture of weary worldliness and bland Christianity: "This is a sad world at best. But if we pray to God to help us, and try to do the best we can, it is not so bad at last. I will pray God to help me to do well, that I may grow up to be a good and a wise man."[55]

Moore's grim patriotism may have depressed rather than inspired young scholars, some of whom doubtless identified with the sense of loss and hopelessness presented in the boy's narrative.

But several ardent Confederate educators used their schoolbooks to promote the southern cause in much more positive ways, developing the reasons that the South had been forced into war by the North, justifying slavery, and glorifying Confederate heroes. John Neely clearly sought to promote southern political values as well as an awareness of the war's gravity in his original speller and reader. A number of examples pointed out the dangers of warfare and the hardships of the soldier's life: "Of all that left the en-camp-ment to take part in the en-gage-ment, not more than one hun-dred sur-vived." Others castigated Yankees: "Troops who enter a state with hos-tile purpose, are in-va-ders. Let all who are able, take up arms to drive them back." Confederate slackers were also taken to task: "It is dis-grace-ful for a man to be dis-loy-al to his coun-try." Neely demonstrated the beneficence of slavery in a passage describing slaves picking cotton: "Hark! how merrily they sing. . . . These negroes are well fed, and well clad, and well cared for when they are sick." The Reverend Robert Fleming offered more than a half-dozen biblical passages supporting the institution of slavery and applauded the American form of representative government, at least as practiced in the Confederate States. "In free governments," he wrote, "like the government of the Confederate States of America, the people choose their legislators." On the other hand, "A despotism is a tyrannical, oppressive government. The administration of Abraham Lincoln is a despotism."[56]

Two geography texts offered extensive commentary on the institutions and politics of both the Confederacy and the United States in explaining the causes of the present war. John Rice insisted that, contrary to the information provided in northern books, Africans lived "in a most degraded and savage condition" from which enslavement and Christianization had saved them. Rice implied that slaves—or at least the slaves' souls—were, in fact, better off than white northerners, whose "infidelity and a reckless puritanical fanaticism" were "fast robbing the people of all enobling traits of character." He promoted the stereotype of Yankees as "keen, thrifty . . . money-loving and money-making" people who conducted their business "without much restraint as to means, success being the all absorbing object." Finally, the old Constitution, sagging under the weight of these moral infractions, "has been overthrown, and despotism reigns supreme in the hands of a political anti-slavery party." Southerners were well rid of their association with northern backsliders and hypocrites. In the Confederacy, where slavery "is the corner stone of her governmental fabric" and "an indomitable spirit of self-reliance" regulates men's behavior, "a career of greatness" has "just commenced." Mrs. M. B. Moore also criticized the now abbreviated United States in her *Geographical Reader.* "Once the most prosperous country in the world," the United States had been ripped apart after northerners found slavery unprofitable in their region, when they began "to preach, to lecture, and to write about the sin of slavery." This hypocritical fanaticism and the election of a Republican president had led to armed conflict; since Lincoln "declared war" on the Confederate States, the "earth has been drenched with blood."[57]

On the other end of the Confederacy from Moore's North Carolina, E. H. Cushing issued *The New Texas Reader* as a part of his New Texas Series. Barely touching on the sad realities of war, the newspaperman selected his topics "with the view of inspiring our youth with a love of Texas, and an admiration of Texan heroes." Although he included fairly brief sections on Native Americans, religion, and natural history, his primary focus was on the history of the Lone Star State. After highlighting Texas's pre–Civil War history in about forty pages, Cushing spent well over half of his text on the prominent role played by Texans in the conflict, as well as several miscellaneous topics relating to the larger history of the Confederacy — not necessarily in chronological order. He featured the battles for Galveston, the stunning upset of the Federals at Sabine Pass, the heroics of Hood's Texas Brigade at Gaines's Mill, the Texan Tom Green's victory at Fordoche in Louisiana, and the role of Texans such as the late General Ben McCulloch at Elkhorn Tavern. Non-Texas topics included the CSS *Virginia*, the hotelier who killed Elmer Ellsworth, and a long hagiography of Stonewall Jackson.[58]

If the war had been decided in the schoolbooks rather than on the battlefield, Cushing and his colleagues would have routed their Yankee counterparts. Most northern texts published between 1861 and 1865 were based on earlier editions and left out the war entirely or treated it superficially. A few grammars included military and political terms in their exercises, some arithmetic texts incorporated the war into scattered story problems, and several readers featured stories, documents, or excerpts from patriotic speeches, songs, and poems.[59] The only mention of the conflict in

The Union ABC—published in Boston in 1864 and printed in red, white, and blue—incorporated the war into reading exercises for even the youngest northern children.

Hillard's *Third Reader* represented a fairly common genre in war literature—the story of a faithful drummer boy—with a difference: although he is mortally wounded by a Rebel cannonball at Wilson's Creek, Confederates try in vain to save his life.[60]

Two of the northern educational publications most interested in the war came at opposite ends of the instructional spectrum. The *Union ABC*, colored red, white, and blue, offered illustrations and verse full of military and patriotic images to preschool or early grammar school children. With two letters and pictures on each page, the booklet began with "A is America, land of the free," and ended, inevitably, with "Z is Zouave, who charged on the foe." In between were such obvious images as a captain; a flag; a "Drummer Boy, called little Ben"; Union; and knapsack. Others included "H is for Hardtack, you scarcely can gnaw"; "J is for Jig, which the Contrabands dance"; and "T is a Traitor, that was hung on a tree."[61]

The Patriotic Speaker provided patriotic word images for much older students. It was, in a sense, a book-length version of the declamation pieces published in *The Student and Schoolmate*. Its elaborate subtitle explained its contents as "Specimens of Modern Eloquence, together with Poetical Extracts Adapted for Recitation, and Dramatic Pieces for Exhibitions." In order to bring young orators into the "all-absorbing present," the compiler had chosen a number of speech extracts and dialogues produced during the three years prior to its 1864 publication date. Charles Sumner's long speech on the Kansas question provided a number of selections, while other prominent speakers represented in the book were Henry Clay, the abolitionist Owen Lovejoy, and William Seward. Selections from the secession crisis and after came from Joseph Holt, Edward Everett, and William Lloyd Garrison. Although a few southerners were included, most examples stressed the importance of maintaining the Union more than the necessity of eradicating slavery. Despite its title, however, more than half of the book was devoted to essays and poetry from Europe.[62]

Free to Be a Good and Noble Man

Publishers produced relatively little reading material specifically for African Americans, although a third genre of Civil War literature appeared late in the war: newspapers and books for the tens of thousands of freedpeople crowding into schools through-out the South. Many black students—adults as well as children—learned from traditional northern textbooks such as *McGuffey's*, but at least some had access to publications written expressly for freedmen and freedwomen. The American Tract Society brought out the most complete set of instructional materials, including a pamphlet called *First Lessons*; the *United States Primer*, which provided "elementary educational" information along with "scriptural instruction"; *The Ten Commandments Illustrated*; two dozen short *Tracts for Beginners* printed in large type; and several sets of "cards" printed on heavy paper or cardboard and featuring the alphabet, the Ten Commandments, short sentences, and other lessons in grammar and spelling. One set of cards, designed so they could be seen by the huge classes meeting in southern barns and churches, measured three feet by four feet, with short words and sentences, borrowed primarily from the *Bible*, printed in huge letters. The society reported that in 1864 300 sets of these cards were in use and that 20,000 copies of *First Lessons* and 24,000 copies of the *United States Primer* had been sent to freedmen's schools.[63]

Better known, perhaps, were the tract society's Educational Series published in 1864 and 1865: *The Freedman's Spelling Book*, *The Freedman's Primer*, *The Freedman's Second Reader*, and *The Freedman's Third Reader*. For the most part, these books were modeled after antebellum spellers, primers, and readers, but they also contained material directed specifically at former slaves. Abraham Lincoln loomed large as the great emancipator. Black heroes and heroines such as Paul Cuffe, Toussaint L'Ouverture, Frederick Douglass, and Phillis Wheatley furnished examples not only of a rather predictable piety but also of humility, hard work, and temperate behavior. Poems and stories about African American soldiers highlighted their bravery and patriotism. Not surprisingly, spelling and grammar lessons drew heavily on scripture and on the moral platitudes common to prewar northern textbooks: work hard, mind your manners, know your place. The society approached the subject of equality more gingerly, applauding emancipation but avoiding any overt political statements regarding voting or civil rights. *The Freedman's Spelling Book* devoted several sections to pronunciation; one featured a series of tongue twisters for freedpeople to rehearse.[64]

Another American Tract Society publication, *The Freedman*, appeared in January 1864 and ran until early 1869. It was widely distributed, with 648,000 copies produced in 1865–66 alone. The four-page monthly featured the typical society formula of straightforward language instruction presented in an overwhelmingly moralistic tone. Although the publication was aimed at adults— one story featured black soldiers eagerly studying their copies of the little paper—the editors suggested that when the grown-ups were finished, the paper "may be given to the children as a reward for diligence and good conduct, and thus become doubly useful." Indeed, letters from teachers in the South indicated that their adult students did exactly that. Others requested copies specifically for their younger students. The format of the paper resembled that of a juvenile periodical or Sabbath school paper: brief vignettes, writing drills, simple reading and arithmetic lessons, poems, prayers, and general information about geography, nature, and history. The Ten Commandments appeared in every issue, along with the occasional exegesis of a selected commandment. Articles, stories, and exercises hammered home the importance of middle-class values such as thrift, hard work, forethought, temperance, honesty, and perseverance. The freedmen may have gained their liberty, but that freedom also carried responsibilities. As a writing example intoned, "But what is it to be free? . . . I am free to be a good and noble man, and not an idle, bad, worthless fellow."[65]

Many of these stories contained no reference to race and could have appeared in any of the many periodicals for children published in the North and South during this period. In fact, the first illustration featuring black characters in the masthead as other than Africans or students did not appear until the sixteenth issue. Yet several characteristics differentiated *The Freedman* from publications aimed at white audiences. Information about Africa, though rather vague, and about African Americans sought to educate the freedpeople about their common heritage and to create a community of black men and women in America. "A Scene in Africa" painted a rosy picture of their homeland, "a beautiful land, where the sun shines very brightly, and many fine trees and fruits grow which we do not have." Yet, as the illustration accompanying the story indicated, white invaders had long threatened this verdant place. In the picture, white slave traders chase down African toddlers, who are "carried off, and stowed away in the dark hold of the vessel, to be . . . sold into wearisome bondage." [66]

Many of the paragraph-long articles in the "Intelligence" section of the paper boasted of the large number of black men joining the Union army and of their soldierly behavior and battlefield exploits. The men of the First Alabama, for instance, were models of teetotaling, refused to use profanity, maintained extraordinarily healthy camps, and eagerly attended the schools established in every company in the regiment. During the Overland Campaign in 1864 virtually no black soldiers had fallen out of the line of march, although nearly half of the white soldiers had become stragglers. A front-page article featured a short history of black soldiers in the American Revolution, particularly at the battle of Bunker Hill, and commented that in the present war, the black soldier "is proving himself a patriot and a hero, and preparing by education to be a true man, and a worthy citizen." Black troops in one company of the U.S. Colored Troops transcended the proslavery stereotype of thriftlessness by saving $2,000 of their meager pay. In a twist on Confederate arithmetics, students were asked, "If the freedmen should kill, or take prisoners, 394 of the rebels who numbered 462, how many would be left to run away after the battle?" [67]

Northern children's magazines had frequently cast African Americans as beneficiaries of northern philanthropy, and articles in both *The Freedman* and *The Freedman's Spelling Book* invoked a sense of obligation toward northern whites, who had contributed money, established schools, and supported the effort to emancipate the slaves with their lives. The caption for an engraving of a white soldier hugging a little girl explained, "How glad he is to see his little Mary!" Although "it was sad to see men die in battle[,] . . . it was to make us free." More to the point was a *Freedman* article headed by an engraving of a white woman rocking her baby to sleep, which reminded readers of the sacrifices made by the wives and children of the soldiers fighting to save the Union and to free the slaves. "The love and sympathy of your friends at the North, and the prayers and blood given so freely in your behalf by your white comrades," *The Freedman* pointedly remarked, "should be a strong motive for you to exert yourselves to the utmost that you may prove worthy of it all." Northerners had contributed to the welfare of black Americans off the battlefield, too. Little Meta, a four-year-old white girl living in the North, had "loved to hear about the freed children" and enthusiastically sent clothes to contraband camps. Sadly, she died, but the money she left behind was sent to a freedmen's school, where it was used to purchase classroom maps. "Of Books and Societies" applauded the devotion and contributions of the United States Christian Commission, the American Tract Society, and the American Missionary Association and of northern abolitionists and freedmen's aid societies. Union heroes such as Gen. Benjamin Butler, who first applied the concept of "contraband" to runaway slaves, were presented as friends to the freedmen deserving the respect and gratitude of blacks throughout the South.[68]

Focusing primarily on biographical sketches and including the writings of blacks such as Phillis Wheatley, slaves named "Mingo" and George Horton, and Harriet Jacobs, Lydia Maria Child's *The Freedman's Book* offered examples of African Americans seeking and achieving intellectual and spiritual equality with whites. Child certainly encouraged freedpeople to become thrifty, moral, and hard-working, yet the role models she held up before them included the astronomer Benjamin Banneker, the poet Wheatley, the revolutionary Toussaint L'Ouverture, and the editor, reformer, and statesman Frederick Douglass. These men and women frequently appeared in freedmen's publications as notable African Americans, but Child emphasized their independence and achievements over their acquisition of white middle-class values. In addition to abolitionist speeches and essays and the Emancipation Proclamation, Child also offered a polite yet defiant letter from a former slave to his former master. Child clearly meant her selections to show African American readers that freedom meant more than the opportunity to become servants and laborers for white folks.[69]

Despite their good intentions, American Tract Society publications relegated the former slaves to a status inferior to that of northern whites. This is especially true when they are considered as instructional material for adults and when *The Freedman* is compared with the more politically oriented *Freedmen's Torchlight*, published by the African Civilization Society after the war. By ignoring politics and emphasizing obedience and piety, *The Freedman* and the schoolbooks produced specifically for freed blacks undercut their hard-won freedom.[70]

Although it is entirely unclear whether the freedpeople and their children perceived the racist socialization contained in American Tract Society materials, African American adults must have detected the extraordinary condescension that emerged from many of the articles. An extended paragraph in *The Freedman* in June 1865, for example, explained to its readers that the earth was round. Despite their shortcomings, when freedmen's publications are considered as children's literature, they clearly resemble in important ways the standard texts to which white children in both the North and the South were exposed before and during the Civil War. They promoted most of the same values, used the same formats, and offered stories that with only a few exceptions could have fit into northern juvenile magazines. Yet there were important differences. In their emphasis, however condescending, on the basic humanity of African Americans; in their attempts, however stilted, to show freedpeople of all ages their common history and contributions to the Union war effort; and in their urging, however biased by middle-class assumptions, of the freedmen to meet high standards of behavior, these books and papers provided a counterpoint to the racial ideas of southern whites.[71]

The Civil War penetrated, invigorated, and politicized educational as well as creative writing for children. War literature did not reject prior assumptions and forms as much as it adapted them to the national emergency. The motto of *The Little Corporal*, "Fighting Against Wrong, and for The Good, The True, and The Beautiful," combined perfectly the moral and patriotic urgency of publishers' campaigns to educate and mobilize northern and southern children. Books and magazines became, for children, a part of the process of discovery and analysis of the causes and progress of the war, providing a blueprint for their responses and contributions. Although occasional antiwar messages provided alternatives to the calls to duty and loyalty found elsewhere, stories, articles, novels, and schoolbooks overwhelmingly supported the Union or Confederate causes. Even northern potboilers, in which plot and adventure nearly drown out any meaningful war message, vague notions of patriotism and sectional pride and ennobling courage and good-natured camaraderie emerge from stories of Yankees working together to defeat a common foe.

It is impossible, of course, to trace directly the effects of juvenile magazines, novels, and schoolbooks on the political development of Civil War era children. Subscription lists have vanished, and virtually no memoirist mentions reading any of the periodicals referred to above. Although Gerald Norcross of Boston apparently read dozens of famous and obscure books, few other children were as systematic in reporting their reading habits. It is even more rare to find mention of a specific text in their diaries or reminiscences. Newspapers occasionally advertised Confederate schoolbooks and noted their adoption by public school systems, and distribution estimates of books for freedmen did appear in the American Tract Society's annual reports.[72] Yet thousands of youngsters did read these books and magazines and, if political scientists who study the politicization of children are correct, they internalized at least some of the values and ideas that were promoted in the stories and poems and games and editorials of their youth. John Morton Blum suggests that *Our Young Folks* — and, by extension, other children's periodicals — "gave direction and possibly also courage to children, whatever their place of residence, who did their reading in New England's lingering twilight."[73] Magazines, juvenile books, and texts not only complemented the formal education of American children but also incorporated their readers into a world wrought by civil war. Applying familiar themes and formulas to exciting and frightening new situations, they helped explain the war — its causes, its conduct, and its ultimate meaning — to the sons and daughters and nieces and nephews and brothers and sisters of the soldiers fighting it.

3

When I Come Home Again, I Won't Go Away Any More

Fathers, Brothers, and Children

Surgeon Edward Pye lightened the dreariness of a Confederate hospital in Houston with a cozy vision of home. "Stand aside little ones & let me edge in to your *bright fire* this dark, cold, dismal night," he wrote gently. "Ma need'nt move & *Charley & Bud* can find a *place on each knee*—so now—how cheerful & pleasant to be amongst you all again! Now how Natural it seems to me—and how glad you all seem!—So You had not got used to doing without 'Pa' all these long *long weary days*! Nor have I, Dear ones, got used to doing without you." Breaking the spell, the forlorn doctor explained, "This is the way I beguile the *lonely hours*—by my *solitary* fireside—I imagine myself among you—I fancy I see your dear faces & feel your *good-night kiss.*" A much younger Confederate drew on similar images to sustain himself. "This is the sort of day I always liked to be at home," nineteen-year-old Fred Fleet wrote his little sister on a chilly fall day in Virginia, "where we could all be sitting around a large fire in the chamber, some reading, others talking, and the little ones playing." Alas, he sighed, "I am afraid those happy days are past for me now." Norman Riley, a black soldier posted in Nashville, also longed to see his family. "I want to see you and the children very bad," he wrote to his wife just after the war ended, "and my love for you and the children is as great to day as it ever was."[1]

Countless other fathers and brothers warmed themselves with memories of inviting family circles, of tousled heads peeping out of cribs, and of husbands and wives "eating and talking to each other as hapy as too kings." Daytime musings yielded nocturnal visitations, as children invaded the dreams of Confederate and

Union soldiers. Although he had been away only a few weeks, Winston Stephens described for his wife "a regular soldiers dream" in which he "had returned home" and "Rosa called Pa Pa & smacked her lips for a kiss." Dreams seemed more real than the nightmare of war, "so life-like & natural," according to a one Confederate, "that I could hardly realize that I was not *at home* when I awoke in the morning. I seemed not only to see *your faces* — loving faces — but I heard & distinguished the voices. . . . I saw & heard you all *so plainly*!" In a Texas conscript's frequent dreams, "it appears to me just as natural to be talking to you & Priscilla." When he inevitably woke up, "it nearley kills me for to think it ain't so."[2]

Of course, night visions such as these were real, at least to the extent that they reflected soldiers' earnest desires to be with their wives and children. The scenes of domesticity that they repeatedly turned to in their subconscious also appeared in their correspondence. Confederate and Union fathers filled their letters with reminiscences and vignettes of time spent with their wives and children — of chats and playtimes, rowdy suppers, and cozy winter evenings — that clearly suggested that when at home, they interacted intimately and wholeheartedly with their children and that they found extended separation from them intolerable.

But the soldiers' responses to the separation wrought by the Civil War did not merely showcase the prewar stirrings of "nurturing" child-rearing habits. Correspondence between soldiers and their families suggests that wartime absences prompted more intense relationships among family members. High postal rates and an unreliable delivery system turned letters between southern husbands, wives, and children into precious emotional commodities. Although northern soldiers may have enjoyed better mail service, communications from their families remained high points of their dreary, terrifying lives. George C. Rable has suggested that, for Confederate husbands and wives, "separation often reawakened dormant emotion." Despite occasionally falling back on the "conventional, stiff, and syrupy Victorian formulas of mutual worship," sincerity broke through the wishful thinking and sentiment. Letters among family members forced apart by the war, even when they flew into rhetorical clichés or lapsed into redundant recitations of detail, could expose the sorts of inner feelings and hopes for the future that emerged from Victorian courtship correspondence. As Bell I. Wiley pointed out many years ago, no subject was too mundane, sensitive, or childish to include in Civil War era letters between soldiers and wives. The same can be said about soldiers' correspondence with their children. Charged with fear, amplified by patriotism, and haunted by economic hardships and danger, the letters exchanged by Civil War fathers, mothers, and children reveal deeply felt notions of familial affection and responsibility.[3]

Although focusing on Union and Confederate fathers may seem to turn the spotlight away from Civil War children, it actually explores a basic facet of their lives: their relationships with their fathers. The war's most immediate impact on the lives of children was to rip apart their families, separating them for years or forever. And the most common experience of Civil War children, one that cut across sectional, gender, and even class and racial lines, occurred when their fathers marched off with their Union and Confederate regiments. But their absence gave fathers the chance to articulate their concerns and affection, to put their love in writing. The overwhelming loneliness and longing of fathers and children, heartbreaking as it was, revealed the contours of the relationships between nineteenth-century children and fathers in ways that may not have been as clear if the war had not intervened.

Civil War fathers displayed at least three separate conceptions of fatherhood in their correspondence. The first and simplest related to the daily care of children, which they could only enjoy in their dreams or remember in nostalgic letters with which many modern fathers can easily identify. The second, the notion that their duty to their country and to uphold their families' honor superseded the mundane emotional and material support of their families, actually deprived them of the physical closeness to which they were accustomed. The third, a paternal insistence on providing wide-ranging guidance and instruction, reflected their attempt to reconcile the former with the latter. Duty and honor may have torn them from the arms of wives and children, but distance alone could not cause them to forsake their responsibilities completely. As a result, Civil War fathers desperately sought to project their authority and love through the erratic mails, remaining fathers in function as well as in name.

An early scene in *Little Women* portrays Mrs. March and her four daughters huddling near a fire for the ceremonial reading of a letter from Mr. March, a chaplain in the Union army. "Very few letters written in those hard times were not touching, especially those which fathers sent home," wrote Alcott. This one, which touched all the issues and subjects in actual letters from the front, was "a cheerful, hopeful letter, full of lively descriptions of camp life, marches, and military news." Mr. March closed by asking his wife to greet and kiss all of the girls. "Tell them I think of them by day, pray for them by night, and find my best comfort in their affection at all times." The kindly patriarch expressed his confidence that "they will remember all I said to them, that they will be loving children to you, will do their duty faithfully, fight their bosom enemies bravely, and conquer themselves so beautifully, that when I come back to them I may be fonder and prouder than ever of my little women."[4]

The real-life counterparts of Mr. March poured concern and affection into their letters to their own little women and little men, offered rewards for acceptable behavior and chastisement for offenses, spun tales of adventure and bravery and parables of hardship and sorrow, tried to inculcate correct political ideas, argued for the necessity of education and of earning a living, and provided advice on a wide range of moral issues. Southern fathers, as well as many northerners, invoked honor as an ideal to which their sons must subscribe, while Yankees, and a number of southerners, stressed the value of hard work and duty. Aside from obvious differences in political points of view, northern and southern fathers differed very little in the ways they communicated with their children. Men from both sections penned affectionate attempts to comfort and inform their sons and daughters. But more importantly, their missives from camp and field instructed their children about beliefs and behavior and assumptions that they believed carried more weight when propelled by paternal authority.[5] Although fewer letters from children to soldiers survive, children seem to have been enthusiastic correspondents, willing pupils, and loyal offspring. They wrote what their fathers wanted to hear: things were going all right, they had been good boys and girls, and when could papa come home?

I Cannot Sleep for Studying about Home

A three year old once asked his mother what his soldier-father could be thinking about in his far-off camp. "About you," she assured him. "Then tell him to think *big*," pleaded the toddler, "so I can hear." Soldiers did, in fact, think *big* about their boys and girls, and their letters were most affecting in their expressions of concern for the physical and mental well-being of their children. They hated the powerlessness imposed on them by separation and military duty. Most would have loved to read, like one Iowa soldier did, that baby Charlie "has no fever and runs around. he is a caution for fun." Yet most could not be assured of such benign and happy news. When four-year-old Corry Thompson was struck on the head with a windlass, her father could only offer long-distance comfort. "Tell her," Thompson wrote in his last letter home before being killed by Confederate guerillas in Tennessee, "that her Pa recollects very distinctly of getting just such a rap on the head very much in the same way" when he was twelve. After learning of his newborn daughter's crippled hand, a Mississippi cavalryman anxiously scolded his wife for failing to tell him everything. "My imagination has given wings to my anxiety," he exclaimed, "until my sleep has been disturbed and my waking hours rendered gloomy in consequence of all kind of vague suppositions."[6]

Even without injury or disease to worry about, military fathers felt great stress at the absence of news from home. The distance from home and the inevitable paucity of information "seems to me . . . more than I can stand," complained one father. "I cannot sleep for studdying a bout home and the hard ships that you have to go under." Even the pronounced formality of the letters of Confederate engineer Jedediah Hotchkiss could not obscure his pain at being away during his daughter's critical illness. "I read with streaming eyes by the camp fire . . . your two letters," he wrote his wife. Obviously trying to take on his share of the parental burden, he reported that he had been spending "sleepless nights . . . thinking of her and your sorrowing condition." The crisis passed in a few days, and more than a week after he had received the first word of his daughter's sickness, he got a letter containing a violet from her. "I was very happy to think my little daughter was reviving and getting new life again just as the sweet flowers are opening under the influence of the vernal sun."[7]

The birth of a son or daughter obviously inspired elation tempered by dismay at the miles separating father from newborn. When Lt. Col. James Williams, commanding the garrison of Fort Morgan near Mobile, heard of the birth of his son George in May

1863, he wrote his wife, "It is well that I have some control of my very restive and excitable nerves or they might have led me into extravagancies . . . that would ill accord with the dignity of the post commander." When he tried to work, his "wife and the black haired babe charge into my thoughts — break my lines of battle — harass my columns and demolish my squares in four ranks in a manner unknown before to military art." He managed a summer furlough but was still distracted in August. He would try to put pen to paper but would be diverted by "pictures of Master George asleep and awake, in bed and perched like a bird in his mother's arm." A South Carolinian was so happy to hear of the safe arrival of a new daughter that he gladly endured some good-natured and slightly risqué ribbing. "I know it is pretty if it looks like me," he wrote his wife, although a friend had suggested that "it looks like Mr. Taylor. I expect you fooled me this time but never mind."[8]

The death of a child caused equally strong, if opposite, emotions. The importance placed by Victorians on infant nurture and on the family, combined with the less harsh Protestantism of the Second Great Awakening, put bereaved parents through a series of ritualized responses in which fathers in the army could participate only through aching letters to their wives.[9] During the month after Edwin Fay's oldest son, William Edwin, died at age five, the despondent sergeant issued a stream of self-pitying letters to his wife. "My heart is bursting," Fay cried, "I almost fear I shall go crazy — I don't see how I can stand it." Drunk with misery, he blamed his wife, who negligently allowed the boy to run outdoors too often and to eat too much fruit; the Yankees, whose "accursed villainy took me away from my family"; and himself. If only he had not joined the Confederate army, perhaps he could have prevented Will Ed's death. He could at least have "been at home to see him die." He pleaded with his wife to "take care of our last one, do not let it die," then almost hysterically closed, "My heart is broken — I dont deserve or crave to live. . . . My heart is bursting, my brain on fire." Drained and heartbroken, Fay seemed to retreat from this kind of emotional investment in his surviving son, for he rarely mentioned Thornwell in his letters during the remainder of the war. Henry Ankeny of the Fourth Iowa expressed the same mixture of pain and remorse when his daughter died a few months after he entered the Union army. "Oh Tina," he mourned, "I know where I ought to have been in this great trial of yours, and would to God I had never left you to bear so heavy a load of grief and sorrow alone." A death could even blunt a soldier's longing to return to his family. An Alabaman mourned his little daughter's passing but dreaded "to come home for I no I shall miss her so much she will not be there to fondle on me nees." [10]

The fragility of life in the nineteenth century—of their own, as soldiers, and of their children, who were vulnerable to untold diseases and accidents—led soldiers to relish encounters with other children when the latter visited camps or when units were posted near towns or farms, even for only a night or two. In fact a Lamar County, Texas, woman reported to her husband that their little boy Eddy "shed tears when he heard that you could find no little boys to hug you around the neck." A nine year old in North Carolina could understand exactly how much his father missed his company when he read in a letter that his father "would give as much to see a little boy or a baby as you would give to see Genl. Beauregard." Even unmarried men missed the sight of children. A member of the Seventh Pennsylvania Reserves complained about the absence of youngsters along his regiment's line of march. "Nothing would do me more good than to see a half-dozen bright little girls at play," he wrote his younger sister. Of course, admitted the twenty-something bachelor, "it would do me as *much* good to see one or two big ones." The northerner Elijah Cavins enjoyed a "romp" with southern children whenever the opportunity presented itself, while even the stern Stonewall Jackson delighted in the afternoon visits of little Janie Corbin to his headquarters near Fredericksburg during the spring of 1863. Separated from his own infant daughter, Jackson visited for hours with the five year old and cut the gilt band from his army cap and arranged it on her curly locks. When she died of scarlet fever shortly after the general moved his headquarters to another location, a staff officer remembered that Jackson "was much moved and wept freely." [11]

It became a cliché in wartime stories and novels for children that the presence of drummer boys and other youngsters could soften gruff soldiers and inspire them to live up to the moral and social expectations of the times. Even in real life, if Col. Thomas Wentworth Higginson can be believed, a single child could brighten the mood of an entire regiment. When Higginson's quartermaster brought his wife and six-month-old baby daughter into the regiment's winter quarters on Port Royal Island, "the new recruit" became a valued member of the regiment. Her African American nurse frequently strolled her about the encampment, and according to Higginson, the baby nearly always attended the daily drills and dress parades. Officers-of-the-day reported to her for "orders" every morning, drummer boys entertained her, and the sergeant major would sometimes wrap her up in the folds of the lowered flag at retreat "like a new-born Goddess of Liberty." Higginson "never saw an inspecting officer, old or young, who did not look pleased at the sudden appearance of the little, fresh, smiling creature,—a flower in the midst of war." Even the childless Higginson seemed happily distracted. He remarked in his memoirs at his surprise that he had not shouted, "Shoulder babies," rather than "Shoulder arms," since he never failed to notice the little girl out of the corner of his eye. Annie left camp in the spring and, in fact, died shortly after returning to the North. Yet Higginson devoted an entire chapter of his famous memoir to her short stay. "I know . . . that her little life, short as it seemed, was a blessing to us all, giving a perpetual image of serenity and sweetness, recalling the lovely atmosphere of far-off homes, and holding us by unsuspected ties to whatsoever things were pure."[12]

Of course, the satisfaction gained from playing with the children of strangers or even comrades paled when soldiers returned to their lonely tents. A child's cry or the strains of a popular song could conjure up tearful memories. As David Coon sat in his tent munching a dessert he had concocted out of stewed dried apples, milk, sugar, and hardtack, he began thinking of home. "I don't know why," he wrote to his wife, "but I thought how Johnny [their four-year-old son] would enjoy it if he would sit down with Pa and help eat it." Similarly, as a lonely Texan stared up at the stars that shone down on his cold encampment and his Waco home one night, he thought of "the children's favorite, 'Twinkle, twinkle, little star,'" and wondered "if Stark has taught it to Mary yet." The comforting thought gave way to a deeper fear expressed in the next sentence: "I want to see them grow up and love each other."[13]

Fathers in blue and gray typically had to work through their instinctive worries about the health and activities of their children from hundreds or thousands of miles away. In addition, like men fighting any war, they feared that their small children would forget them. Furloughs facilitated joyous reunions but could also remind soldiers how fragile were the memories of the very young, as a Georgian found out when his daughter "looked so strange at me." Indeed, one Confederate's fear that his five-year-old daughter might forget him took on special urgency because, lacking photographs of his wife and child, he worried that he might actually "forget how you & priscilla looked." Most fathers attempted to demonstrate through their own letters that their boys and girls remained paramount in their thoughts. Soldiers assured their children that they frequently gazed at their pictures or kept locks of hair or other mementos with them at all times. Capt. Joseph Adams described surrounding himself with photographs of his several children while he wrote them a letter outside Vicksburg.[14]

Yet the fear that they would fade out of their children's lives burdened many soldiers. Future president James Garfield left a one-year-old daughter when he marched off with the Forty-second Ohio. In one of his first letters he asked his wife "not to let her memory of 'papa, papa' fade away. Have her say it, so that when I come she may know to call me." Dorsey Pender had two sons — Turner, age two, and the infant Dorsey — when the war began. "Don't let Turner forget me," the young colonel urged his wife Fanny, "Make him talk of papa" even "if he is too litle to know anything about [me]." In a dramatic letter to his wife, Shephard Pryor accepted whatever fate awaited him on the battlefield but pleaded, "Oh, don't let them forget that they had a father and [to] my dear boy speak of me frequently and learn him to love me, though I may be dead to this world." Even with constant reminders, however, fathers might grow dim in their children's consciousness. A veteran Yankee sergeant articulated a fear that many men may have shared, that his children would not only forget him but would not understand his paternal role. He asked his wife if their youngest son actually knew that he had a father; perhaps he thought that she was "his only protector." At least one father, however, actually discouraged his wife from tutoring their two children about him. "If I return," wrote Joshua Chamberlain, "they will soon relearn to love me. If not, so much is spared them."[15]

Soldiers agreed that the best way to defeat misery-producing worry was to hear about the "sports & tricks" of their children. "Nothing is better calculated to shed light & smiles over my face," wrote Texan Theophilus Perry, "and to lift a great load from my heart." Accordingly, wives tried their best to keep husbands up to date on the newest words and latest pranks that may have been funnier to tell than to clean up after. "Bam" Gordon of Georgia, for instance, had scooped ashes out of the stove into a tub of water and tried to pour the mixture into a tea kettle. "You can judge for yourself," his mother wrote to his father, "how he looked when I came in. He is a great rogue," she complained, "he is no sooner stopped from one piece of mischief, before he does something else equally as bad." Mothers dutifully reported on the comings and goings and social and academic and moral development of their offspring, hoping to bridge the distance between soldiers and their children. Julia Davidson wrote of her children's study habits and assured her husband John that although their sons "have heard a great deal of Swearing," they "have not taken it up." Many mothers focused on academic achievements, while others chronicled persistent, if entertaining, lapses of discipline by their children. The mother of a toddler wished her husband back in Maine "to make the little image behave, for I'm too lazy."[16]

More importantly, wives and mothers insisted that children had certainly not forgotten their fathers and provided minute details of the ways children kept the memories of their fathers alive. At least one told her husband (who had actually gone west to avoid conscription and was working in a mine in Nevada) that "you must not rite for the children not to forget you it hurts their feelings they say pa nead not think that they will forget him." Laura DuVal, wife of a Texan Unionist who fled the Lone Star State late in 1863, assured him about three months after his departure that their toddler son Johnny "has not forgotten you in the least." She did not speak of her absent husband often, for "it makes me too sad," but when she asked Johnny "what I must tell his Papa— He says 'Tell him come here & pay the fute [flute].'" Little Laura Peddy "runs to the door and looks for a long time for you, then turns away with a disappointed look on her face," while a three-year-old daughter of a member of the Richmond home guards told her mother to "tell Papa I love him ten thousand dollars." A young Texan named Willy Bryan "showed his feelings" toward his father, according to his mother, by naming his new pig after him.[17]

Harriet Perry of Marshall, Texas, filled letters to her husband Theophilus with the doings of their daughter to assure him that little Mattie had not forgotten him. One day Mattie convinced herself that her father was coming; "I never heard her laugh out so loud or seem so delighted as she was." Other times she held her doll up to the window to look for "Papa," and one day she donned her bonnet and headed out the door to find him. Harriet reported that little Mattie "talks of you every day, particularly at meals." On at least one occasion she kissed the page on which her mother was writing; Harriett circled the spot and labeled it "daughter kissed here." She apparently found describing Mattie's play for Theophilus therapeutic. "She is the sweetest little creature in the world," she wrote in the fall of 1862. "I could not live without her. . . . I seldom let her go out of my sight; she is a great deal of company for me — in fact all I have & I cant bear for her to be away from me. . . . I shall almost fill my letter about our little darling but I know that is more interesting to you than any thing I could write." [18]

A chilling incident on a South Texas farm showed how deeply some children worried about their fathers. Although Lizzie Simons's two-year-old daughter remembered her father in all the usual ways — she made him a hat out of a palmetto leaf, used a pin to scratch out a "letter" to him, and saved him a piece of her birthday cake — she was also deeply affected by her mother's fears for her husband and brother, both of whom were fighting in Mississippi. During a buggy ride late in October 1862, the little girl jerked awake from a nap and sat still for a few minutes. Then she said calmly to her mother, who recorded the incident in her diary, " 'Mama, Papas dead.' I was startled & said 'what' & she repeated Papa's dead & then said as if plagued at what she had said, 'Papa gone a war.' " The premonition — apparently false — nevertheless "mad me feel strong all day & Ive thought a great deal about it since." Children worried a lot about their fathers, of course. At least one little boy took his fear a step further. Blair Lee's mother reported that he "seems to fear that I'll go away too," completing the disintegration of their little family. [19]

Even better than affection and concern filtered through wives' correspondence were the letters of children, even those, like little Julia Jackson's, "dictated" to mothers or grandmothers, who often wrote in a child's giant letters. The last letter of Leander Stem, a Yankee who died at Murfreesboro, encouraged his wife to write letters on behalf of the children containing "their childish thoughts about themselves, papa and mama and all other subjects that enter their little brains." In some cases the children's letters were the first they ever attempted. "As this is the first time I hav ever wrote a letter," sixteen-year-old Mary Lewis wrote to her soldier-father soon after his departure for the army, "I cant find one more worthey than my one dear Papa." Childish thoughts tumbled over one another: "Billy says 'send' him a 'cannon ball' Bob says write to him some. Buddy walter says send him some candey Kate says howdy," wrote Mary Neblett of Texas. In a subsequent letter Mary contrasted her longing to see her father with the astonishing—to her—fact that cousins living nearby never wrote to their soldier-father. Even worse, they did not even wake up when he came home during the night. She assured Will that she and her brothers would certainly wake up if he suddenly arrived. "Ma would raise sutch a noise that the whole place would be aroused and the chickens would commence crowing," and "we all would break our necks [scrambling] over the chairs."[20]

Like travelers from all times and places, soldiers in both armies attempted to keep themselves fresh in the memories of their children and younger siblings with presents and souvenirs. In fact, at least some children expected such indulgences. A family of children in Rusk County, Texas, "stood by with a wishful eye" when a cousin returned home with a saddlebag full of presents for his own children. Even when an African American mother in Missouri wrote her husband pleading for money—"me and my child are almost naked"—she also asked him to "Sind our little girl a string of beads in your next letter to remember you by."[21]

Most fathers did not have to be asked; they seem to have been constantly on the lookout for little trinkets and mementos. Some, especially those in the Confederate army, tried to make sure their children were kept in shoes. But less practical gifts caught the eyes of most soldiers: song sheets of the latest patriotic airs, books, dolls, money for candy, or toys such as the "little tin cup and a confederate knife and fork," just the right size for the "little hands" of George Peddy's daughter.[22]

Even the simplest gift could spark children's imaginations. Will Neblett sent home a bean he had found in his shoe and some seashells, which his children loved—at least according to his wife—"as much as if it cost $20." The baby played with the bean contentedly until the bean disappeared. At the other extreme from Neblett's profoundly simple approach to gift giving was George Denison, a U.S. Treasury agent in occupied New Orleans, who outdid most northerners in his penchant for sending home goods and relics of the rebellion to his young son, mother, and assorted

Writing to Father, by Jonathan Eastman Johnson (1863). Letters from home helped soldiers and their children maintain relationships interrupted by the war. (Museum of Fine Arts, Boston)

siblings. Taking advantage of low prices and of opportunities presented in his job at the customhouse, Denison shipped home crates of furniture, barrels of oranges and sugar, works of art, books, clocks, Confederate treasury notes, and clothing, as well as enough Confederate flags and firearms to fill the "grand Museum of rebel Curiosities & relics" he planned to organize after the war.[23]

Joshua Chamberlain apologized for the only presents he could find to send home: stale candy and bits of exploded shells. He need not have worried, for the most eagerly awaited souvenirs came from battlefields. Elijah Cavins sent home the sword and sash he had worn in numerous battles of the Army of the Potomac, "a very pretty glass globe" he found on the ruined streets of Fredericksburg, and a spent bullet that struck him on the chest during that horrific battle. His son Sammy received the "blue Trefoil" badge worn by the Third Division, Second Corps, so he could join the "great many boys [who] will wear the badges that their fathers wear." Many soldiers sent home spent and even live ammunition that had struck trees or breastworks near their positions, Confederate flags, pictures of heroes such as the martyred Elmer Ellsworth, army commissions, and parts of Confederate or Yankee uniforms. Matilda Lamb treasured a Bible inscribed, "To my little sister" from her brother John, who later died at Petersburg, as well as a cross made of iron from the USS *Merrimack* and a ring carved from a button by one of John's men. An Illinois officer shipped home a Confederate cartridge box and a double-barreled shotgun fired at him by a Confederate soldier during the attack on Fort Donelson. At least two Union officers sent home ponies from the South for their children, while Silas Browning offered his youngest daughter the choice of an exotic southern bird or a "little black boy" about her age who had been hanging around his regimental hospital.[24]

Good Soldiers

Early in the war Sarah Watkins of Winona, Mississippi, announced to her son-in-law William Walton of Austin, Texas, that she and her husband thought Walton should enlist in the Confederate army. "I would dislike for it to be thrown up to my grandchildren that their father did not fight for his country." She went on to assure him that his family would be cared for; "Give yourself no uneasiness about your family . . . in case of your death." Walton may not have appreciated the unsolicited advice and may even have resented his in-laws' ready acceptance of his possible death. Yet many fathers did believe that their paternal roles demanded playing an active part in the war. This clashed with the more domestic side of fatherhood, where they acted as sources of comfort and affection. Children had been accustomed before the war to a wide range of intimate connections with their fathers, many of whom tucked them in, chatted easily about daily concerns, and provided companionship and humor. But the war added another dimension to this instinctive, natural response to their children: being a good and loyal soldier was now one of the duties of being a good father. Their belief that patriotic sacrifices were necessary to maintain their families' good names overcame sentimental attachments. In effect, they were saying that the love they felt for their families mandated their continued absence in Confederate or Union service. The difficulty of their decisions to leave wives and youngsters in exposed and potentially dangerous situations—and the guilt it must have created—inspired many to attach great significance to their actions. Southerners often remarked on their determination literally to defend their homes and families from invading Yankees. Contrary, perhaps, to the recent discussion about the nature of "Southern" honor, soldiers on both sides stressed the honor that their loyal service would bring to the family and the shame their descendants would suffer if they shirked their duty. Men on both sides seemed to believe that such a blot of dishonor would be particularly damaging to their sons' futures.[25]

Some men composed quite formal justifications for leaving hearth and kin that directly linked parental to patriotic responsibilities. Their fervor suggests that they were trying to convince themselves as much as their wives that they were doing the right thing. Many women complained—some bitterly—about the domestic duty erased by service in the army, sparking arch rejoinders from husbands that Confederate and Union wives must not forget their duty to support their country's war effort. Henry Hitchcock's wife asked him to explain why he had accepted a commission as a staff officer to Gen. William T. Sherman late in the war, ostensibly so "you could have it to show to our boy, from his father, hereafter." His letter took the form of a transcript of a conversation with Sherman, who asked him why he had come to the army. "The reason I wished to enter the service," Hitchcock had said, "was simply that I could not stay at home and let other men do the fighting & run the risks while I was safely making money & enjoying the fruit of their toils." When he finally joined the army, "I was very sure that I should hereafter be able to respect myself for at least having tried to do my duty."[26]

Similar sentiments animated men across the ranks. "We shall

try it again soon," Joshua Chamberlain wrote his children after a Union defeat, "and see if we cannot make those Rebels behave better, and stop their wicked works in trying to spoil our country and making us all so unhappy." Less charming but equally determined were the words of an Indiana sergeant. "It may be . . . my unfortunate lot to fall," he reminded his family in a letter he wrote before his unit shipped out to the South. "If so I desire that we may so live that we will Meete in a better Land Where there is no Rebbels nor traitors to mare the peace of the inhabitants." He had left his home and family "for pure motives to sustain . . . The Goverment of our fore Father. But if it should be that I do not Return I wish you to instruct My little Boy that I die a Marter to my country, without any simpathy for traitors." [27]

Soldiers hoped their families would understand, and often couched their arguments in familial imagery. Josiah Patterson of Georgia explained to his sons that a soldier had "many hard, disagreeable duties to perform," but the true soldier does not grumble and complain but does all that his country's service demands willingly and cheerfully like a "good little boy that obeys his father and mother for the love he bears them and the kindness he has received from them." He loved his "little ones . . . too dearly to permit the ruthless footsteps of the invader to crush out your liberty while I am enjoying an inglorious inactivity or ease at home." Nor should children forget the duty and responsibility they shared with their fathers. "It is a glorious country," wrote a Yankee from a Rhode Island training camp, "and *must* be preserved to our children." The previous generation had given it "to *us entire*, and *we* must give it to you, entire and you must give it as you receive it, to those who come after you." [28]

Confederate and Union fathers clearly believed that part of their paternal duty would be fulfilled if they served their country well. They also sought to educate their children about the southern and northern crusades. While some intended their comments as political statements, most simply hoped to open sympathetic lines of communication with their children, allowing them to draw closer, at least at a vicarious level, to their faraway fathers. Although a man's duty to his country might have more bearing on the future of his sons than that of his daughters, most Civil War soldiers did not distinguish between boys and girls in the information they provided about the war. Geared to the maturity or interests of individual children, the soldiers' stories ranged from humorous incidents and camp scenes to tales of hard marches and sickness to vivid descriptions of bloody battles.

Younger children frequently received fairly simple descriptions of the everyday lives of their father-soldiers, while older children tended to receive grittier accounts of army life and combat. For example, James Hall, a widower whose two daughters lived with his parents while he rose to the rank of captain in a Tennessee regiment, filled his first letter home with mundane details about his tentmates, the rations, and the boxcars on which his company had ridden. "We have a great deal of noise in camp at night," he wrote, "some of the boys sing some holler some bark like dogs, some crow like chickens and one whistles so much like a mocking bird that you would think it was a bird indeed." Nearly three years later, with his daughters older and, perhaps, inured to war stories, Hall described a battle at Marietta, where the Federals "were repulsed with terrible slaughter. I have never seen so many killed in so short a time. The ground in front of our works in some places seemed almost covered with them."[29]

Men often focused on the minutiae of military life, the daily trials and tribulations and experiences of common soldiers. Children could take comfort in knowing the simple routines of their fathers' lives; fathers could comfort themselves with the idea that their boys and girls would not be too worried about them. Henry Hitchcock described camp life for "my darling boy" in a letter to his wife Mary, who was to tell the child that "I wear the 'soldier cap' that he liked, all the time; and that I have a nice dark brown horse, who is pretty gay, and whose name is 'Button'; — that we live in tents and build our fires . . . on the ground in front of them." A year before his death at Vicksburg, a Wisconsin captain promised his three-year-old son that after the war they would build themselves a tent and "camp in it and be soldiers and [he] will see how it is." In his frequent letters to his six younger sisters, a young surgeon in the 105th Pennsylvania related his adventures on the picket line and described the camp guard, his office, his three orderlies, and a drummer boy named Dixie. Inevitably, many letters resembled travelogues, as soldiers wished to share unusual experiences in, to them, exotic sections of the country.[30]

Students in Laura W. Stebbins's school in Springfield, Massachusetts, learned about the war from several former, slightly older classmates in the Forty-sixth Massachusetts, whose letters from New Bern, North Carolina, were read aloud by Stebbins. Addressed to "Dear Teacher and friends" or to "Dear Teacher and family," they were filled with information that the boys apparently believed their friends would enjoy. They noted the high prices they paid for apples in Boston, their seasickness on the voyage south, and army life and routines and assured Stebbins that they would soon join a Bible class. The boys were particularly struck — and decidedly unimpressed — by the African American laborers they met. Reuben Currier described the regiments of contrabands working nearby as "the most black greasy and forlorn looking things that I ever saw, the women don't wear any hoops and the men go bear foot." However, he admitted, "for all of this they seem to live happy." C. J. Lakin unblushingly expressed his desire to "see a fine looking white lady for I have got sick of niggers they look so black but they cannot help it." Interestingly, he had earlier confessed to having pasted Stebbins's photograph in his Bible.[31]

Most soldiers eventually felt compelled to write about the bloody business of war. Some only sprinkled a few references or incidents into their letters. A Pennsylvanian described the bones and debris littering the old battlefield at Manassas, while a Mississippian, in an otherwise lighthearted letter to his young niece during the war's first summer, reported the execution of a soldier for disobedience and the death of another "in a drunken spree in a house of ill fame." A Yankee officer titillated his eight-year-old son in a letter to the boy's mother: "Tell Hamlin that he must be a good Son and I will tell him all about the big fight; how I seen a Shoe with a foot in, shot off by a Cannon Ball and lots more."[32]

Less gory but no less honest were the letters of a Congregational minister working for the Christian Commission to his four-year-old daughter, which frequently — and with a gentle but insistent touch of Puritan directness — broached the subject of death. Edward Parmelee Smith handed out Bibles and tracts to soldiers but also visited hospitals and front lines, where he confronted the deadly side of war. He described his visit with "a soldier boy who is going to die," a battlefield still littered with the carcasses of horses and bodies of men, and the soldiers' funerals he presided over, and assured little Gerty that he prayed for the "little children who will never see their father again till they all go home to die no more."[33]

Far more detailed accounts show how unprotected children

were from the realities of war. Soldiers not only reported on the sights and sounds of bloody battlefields, but some also went so far as to reveal exactly how close their children had come to being orphans. An extraordinarily realistic battle narrative came from Texan John West, who wrote a somber birthday letter to his four-year-old son during the Army of Northern Virginia's painful retreat from Gettysburg. "I thought you would like for papa to write you a letter and tell you something about the war and the poor soldiers," he began. "God has been very good to me since I wrote to mamma." He went on to describe the great battle he had just survived, "when many thousands of good men" were "slain all around me." West participated in the attack through Devil's Den on July 2, during which "one poor fellow had his head knocked off in a few foot of me, and I felt all the time as if I would never see you and little sister again." He told about his own near miss, when a bullet cut through his beard and struck a rock a half-inch from his head. He was lucky, though. Passing a hospital, he saw many "mangled and bruised" men, "some with their eyes shot out, some with their arms, or hands, or fingers, or feet or legs shot off, and all seeming to suffer a great deal." West hoped his son would save the letter for posterity; "I wanted to write my little man a letter, which he could read when he was a big boy."[34]

Two other graphic depictions of war were written a week apart from opposite sides of the bloody battleground at Shiloh. A Union soldier breathlessly described a battlefield "strewn with dead men and horses." "Some lay in heaps of four & five some with there heads arms and legs torne of, it is one of the most horrible sights, there is no one can give A description of it." Shortly after the fight, a Confederate cataloged the carnage behind the Confederate line, where "the wounded passed all the time and I saw men pass that was shot from the top of their head to the bottom of their feet Some with one eye shot out, nose shot off mouth shot off side of their face shot off shot in the arms hand & legs feet Some brought dead in waggons." Still shaken, he tenderly asked his wife to tell their children that "I would like to have holt of them awhile certain."[35]

The Best Keepsake I Could Wish to Remember You By

Although such grisly information was an implicit part of fatherly attempts to educate their children, most fathers and a number of brothers also engaged in more overt instruction that covered the whole gamut of issues important to the proper development of a boy or girl in the mid-nineteenth century. They offered far-ranging advice on schooling and careers, morality and ethics, and behavior and etiquette. These lessons might have been spread out over several years and been delivered in a variety of subtle ways in normal times. The war, however, forced men to exert their paternal and fraternal authority through the formal medium of the written word and encouraged them to concentrate their advice because combat soldiers did not, of course, know how many more chances they had. Although they grimly accepted the need to do their political and military duty for their country, they also believed in a higher duty to guide and counsel their off-spring and siblings. Some perceived the heightened emotions and urgency sparked by the war as a unique opportunity for getting their children's attention and teaching them a lesson. A Confederate surgeon emphasized that "these are times such as one *sees only once* — when we are all dead & gone many lifetimes hence — they will be spoken of as the *'bloody age'* — the times of horror — of famine — misery — wretchedness." Yet a lesson could be learned from such misery. He wanted his children to imagine the diseased, cold, hungry, blighted soldiers living and dying in "*camps* all over the land" and to "*resolve* never to *complain* of the little difficulties & troubles that come in your way."[36]

Hardships like these gave fathers leverage to induce good behavior by inspiring guilt. They recognized the fathering possibilities opened by the sacrifices they were making for the sake of their country and their children. Their authority would be unassailable when projected from the high moral ground they attained through patriotism and courage. David Coon encouraged his nine children to work hard to behave well, for if he could "hear a good report" from home, "it will be the best keepsake I could wish to remember you by." Yet he did not shrink from spicing his encouragement with a little shame. Coon ended a long description of the hardships and dangers he had faced with a lecture to his fourteen-year-old daughter Emma on minding her stepmother. "Oh, my dear daughter," he wrote, "your father may be lying dead on the field of battle and you may not know it. . . . O, Emma, Emma! How can you have the heart to go to dancing parties, against your kind mother's wishes and advice and your own conscience and judgment? How can you add to my grief and trouble by such a course?" He punctuated his jeremiad with an apology highlighting the importance of what he had written: "I am sorry I can't write with ink, as I perhaps may never write to you again." Theodore Montfort of Georgia also expected his tribulations to inspire his children. In a letter written early in the war, he detailed the difficult conditions in which he lived. "While you are all at home where you can keep dry with a good room, fire and bed to sleep in," he pointedly remarked, they "should feel grateful . . . your Father is undergoing these hardships and dangers that you might remain at home and be comfortable as you are."[37]

Just as they expected their children to meet the crisis of war with helpful, respectful, and obedient demeanors, soldiers saw their paternal responsibilities heightened, even as the war threatened their ability to fulfill them. Franklin Gaillard wrote his son in South Carolina in the fall of 1861 that he "never thinks of going into battle and being shot, but right off he thinks of his little David being left without him to impress upon [him] those principles which he would like to have govern and guide him when he grows to be a man." Although his younger sister would be advised by the aunt with whom they were both staying, young David would have to mature without paternal influence. Gaillard, a widower, summarized his advice in a few sentences: He wanted his son "to be always obedient and grateful," "kind and polite to all, study hard at school, tell the truth always," and "make no friends with mean and untruthful boys." In addition, "he must always be brave" and "never do wrong to anyone — nor let others do wrong to him." If he followed that advice, "when he grows up to be a man, if war should come again . . . he will make a good and faithful soldier." David and Maria Gaillard were orphaned when their father fell during the battle of the Wilderness.[38]

Many soldiers shared Gaillard's assumption of a special relationship between father and son. Men of the southern planter and northern middle classes had long taught their boys about career, racial and sexual relationships, and public responsibilities, beginning at age six or seven in the South or just before puberty in the North. Even in urban areas, by mid-century, as mothers became identified as the primary caregivers for young children and mentors for teenaged daughters, fathers retained their duties as their sons' instructors and guides to a moral life, productive work habits, self-reliance, and healthy ambition.[39]

Fathers in the northern and southern armies extended the same types of advice to boys and girls — be good, mind your mother, do your schoolwork — but they rearranged emphases for boys and girls. Just as his war record would mean more to his son's future than his daughter's, one of the chief concerns of a Confederate or Yankee father was for his son to develop an honorable character and a respected name. For instance, Joseph Young of Indiana wanted his daughter Mary to mind her mother and to "learn her Book" and extended affectionate greetings to Martha Ann and to Willey — "God bless her little Rosey cheecks." But he instructed his wife "to take good care of Little Jake for [I] have a great deal of confidence in him if he has the proper Raising he will make a man that will make his mark in the world." Kentuckian Willis Jones worried to his wife that sixteen-year-old Willis, Jr., was "just at the age when my supervision of him is indispensable" and asked her to tell their son "how much I think of him and if I ever live to see him, that I hope to find him an educated, modest, accomplished gentleman."[40]

Some soldiers ignored their daughters almost entirely. James Goodnow left three sons in Jefferson County, Indiana, when he enlisted in the Union army late in 1862. He immediately began a correspondence that continued until his resignation as lieutenant colonel two years later. Although his oldest, the teenager Sam, received the longest and most detailed letters, James often enclosed separate notes for Daniel, who must have been eight or nine years old, and for Johnny, who was perhaps three or four. Yet Goodnow never included his youngest child, Belle, in his frequent missives. At one point he assured his wife Nancy that he would not advise her on how to raise Belle, because "I don't pretend to understand a girl or a woman."[41]

Despite his apparently limited interest in his only daughter, Goodnow's letters to his sons provide one of the most comprehensive examples of a father's concern for his children. "I want that you and I should be regular correspondents during my absence," he wrote Sam in his first letter home. He later urged him to "tell your mind freely," in weekly letters, to "tell me all about what you are doing—and all about your cares and troubles—and you may be Sure I will always feel an interest in whatever interests or affects you." Sam and Daniel both wrote frequent notes to their father, which he deeply appreciated. Goodnow matched his responses to the interests and needs of each son. As the oldest, Sam received most of the general news about Goodnow's unit, including information about their travels in Alabama and other parts of the western theater, speculations about military strategy, and a detailed description of the only engagement in which Goodnow reported fighting. More important, however, were the pieces of fatherly advice and compassion and affection that Goodnow carefully extended to his sons. His letters to Sam frequently, if gently, nudged him toward adulthood. "It will not be long before you will have to go out in the world to make your own way," he wrote in that first letter, "and you will then be too busy to study." He naturally urged him to work hard at school, for "your success and usefulness will altogether depend on the way you employ your time now." Sam was also to "remember always that your Mother has a right to your help" and that he could "never do too much for her."[42]

The senior Goodnow returned to the subjects of preparing for the future and being responsive to the needs of the boys' mother in many of his letters. On one occasion he was uncharacteristically stern when he blamed Nancy Goodnow's poor health at least partly on the fact that "you have made her do too much work." Sam must realize how hard she had labored to care for him over the years and out of "common gratitude make up to her for what She has done for you." He and his brothers were to carry all the wood, make all the fires, milk the cow, work in the garden, help with the wash, and generally "take all work off her hands that you can do." Variations on these typical themes abounded. Although he expressed surprise that Sam had been temporarily suspended from school—he could not "believe you were deserving of such harsh treatment"—he advised him to go to the teacher, apologize, and promise to obey him in the future. "If he is a reasonable man that will be enough." As he approached manhood, Sam must learn to value the "habits of industry and also to . . . not be ashamed of honest labor." Apparently the young man was working at least part time while he attended school, which pleased his father, who commented that even if Sam did not care for the job, he could at least have "the Satisfaction of knowing that you are earning your own livelihood."[43]

Younger sons received similar but also unique messages. Goodnow's first extant letter to "Master Daniel Goodnow" began with chitchat about Christmas and St. Nicholas, but he quickly moved to more exciting information regarding his army experiences. "Well Dan," he wrote intimately, "you ought to be out here and See our big armies." He described their march out of Memphis and their encampment. "If you would have been there you would have thought there was going to be a battle there was So much noise. The men Cheered and yelled and the mules brayed loud enough to make you jump out of your boots." Nevertheless, Goodnow was very glad that his boys were not with him, "for wherever the large armies go here they drive the people away from home and take all they have to eat and all their corn and then burn their houses and fields — and a great many little boys down here do not have enough to Eat and often have no home." Dan also received advice, but of a sort very different from Sam's. Whenever he felt like quarreling or crying, suggested Goodnow, "just run out into the wood Shed and Saw a few Sticks of wood and See if you don't get in a good humor before you get done." Even Johnny, whose mother had to read his letters to him, got advice. "I have been wanting to See you for a long time," wrote James, "but I am too far away to go home often." He promised that when he returned, "we will have a big talk." In the meantime, "I want you to be the best little boy. . . . I dont want you to Say any bad words — or cry much — I want you to be a man." Dan and Johnny later received a joint letter that assured them that "although you are little fellows I think as much of you as I do of Sam" and emphasized their importance to maintaining the household. "I want you to play and enjoy yourselves as much as you can," wrote their father, "but you must not forget to be at home when your Mother wants you." Johnny could care for their little sister, while Dan could fetch wood, wash dishes, feed the cow, and "do a hundred little things that wont be much trouble to him, but will Save mother from getting tired."[44]

The boys frequently received congratulations from their father for their good behavior. Colonel Goodnow was happy to hear that they were behaving themselves at school and at home. "I have always had confidence in you, knowing that you would do right when you reflected on your duty, and I am proud indeed to know that my confidence is well founded." To Dan, Goodnow wrote how much he appreciated the little boy's "very good letters"; "if you will only learn to write a little plainer, you will Soon do first rate." He was also immensely pleased when Nancy reported that Dan sawed and split all the wood. "I don't say go in lemons," he wrote—in a long-forgotten phrase apparently meaning "don't let it go to your head"—"but I do say there are not many boys of your age can do that much."[45]

Goodnow's letters reveal many of the concerns Civil War soldiers had for their children and are important because of their writer's attention to the differing developmental stages of his boys, but they do not represent every style of correspondence. Most men, for instance, did not leave their daughters so completely out of their letters, while other soldiers were less comprehensive, limiting their advice to brief lists with specific instructions addressed to each child. Some fathers offered terse but pithy jewels of advice. A black soldier wrote from a hospital in St. Louis that he had not forgotten his children, who were still slaves, and that they must be "contented with whatever may be your lots [in] life." Thomas Brady's last letter home before he was killed in April 1865 offered homely counsel to his only son: "I want him to be a good boy, and . . . not go too close to the Horses & Mules." The Hall sisters, staying with their father's parents, were instructed to "take plenty of exercise in the open air," carry chips for their aunt, be "obedient to Grandma," and "talk loud to Grandpa." Capt. Luther Cowan urged his little boy to treat his sisters well and not to "cry much it will make your face ugly." Few pieces of advice were so direct as M. A. McMurtrey's, a Georgian who warned his four-year-old son twice in less than a week to "be a good boy or the bad man will get him and burn him."[46]

Many fathers were obviously stricken with what they could only fear would be their last chance to impress upon their children their own core values. Southerners seemed more likely to instruct their children on the fine points of getting along in the world and becoming a respected member of society, which, of course, had different meanings for boys and girls. For instance, Col. John L. Bridgers Sr. of Tarboro, North Carolina, issued stern orders to thirteen-year-old John, Jr., who was attending boarding school. From something John, Jr., had said in a recent letter, the colonel had identified "Restless[ness] and dissatisfaction" as "the weak points in your character." He must strive to overcome or at least to "endure" difficulties; "son I appeal to you to become firm and to throw away that feeble determination of yours." Subsequent letters addressed young John's animosity toward teasing classmates ("Such a wholesale hatred would be more worthy of [a] Yankee than my son"). The elder Bridgers pointedly announced that a cousin was "the most popular boy at Dr. Nelson's School," which "renders his father so proud and happy." Of course, that was not the case with John. "You do not know what that idea causes your mother and myself to feel, to have raised a son the hated object of school." In another letter he reminded his son that "I never had the pleasure of receiving a letter from a father as you are *now* doing." [47]

In contrast to the Bridgers' hard-edged correspondence were the long, loving letters exchanged by Edgeworth Bird and his Georgian family. His detailed and sympathetic counsel to his teen-aged daughter Saida steered her toward personal goals entirely different from the businesslike, almost political ambitions urged upon young John Bridgers. Bird wrote Saida that, as she entered her " 'teens,' . . . it behooves you to begin to prepare yourself in earnest to face the stern realities of life." She would soon have to depend less on other people's advice and direction and more on her "own sound judgement and good conduct." He praised the "twin sisters" of truth and virtue and urged her to be cheerful but not giddy, studious, patient, humble, and dutiful. These characteristics "will bear you up and o'er every wave of trouble, and hurl back every billow of misfortune that Satan's rage or a world's envy may cast at you." Although he apologized for producing in this instance "more a lecture than a letter," later communications encouraged Saida to "avail yourself of any means of improving your mind." She was to be "truthful under all circumstances" and to "Study, study, study," for "an enlightened, well polished mind, well regulated and stored with useful knowledge, is the greatest blessing you could prepare for yourself, after a true piety." [48]

Direct Them as Reasonable Beings

In keeping with the paternal ideal that, at least for Civil War fathers, seemed to flourish in both the North and the South, many soldiers amplified their fatherly advice with husbandly directives. One wife was only half-teasing when she scolded her husband for "thinking no one could take care of the baby like yourself." The extent to which men considered fatherhood to be central to their self-images can be measured at least partly by the intensity of their efforts to instruct their wives about child rearing. Many put incredible pressures on the mothers of their children. "Out from under a father's protection," according to William Whatley, his and his wife Nannie's children "can only look to you . . . for training." Doubtless already anxious about having to raise four youngsters on her own, Nannie nevertheless had to read that William "would rather bury them in infancy than to see them act as some people do." A like-minded Virginia mother assured her husband that he "need not be uneasy about me neglecting my duty with the children." Although she would rather have him home to help guide them down the right paths, "I had rather bury all three of our children to morrow than for them to act in disgrace to themselves & Parrents." Children must have understood how their behavior mattered to their parents. Perhaps they even understood that the war, while it did not change these expectations, sparked an urgency that might not have existed before.[49]

Absent Confederates and Yankees naturally focused on the moral health of their children, but they also offered practical advice on their physical health. Referring to his two-year-old son, Dorsey Pender ordered his wife to "let his body develop more, and his mind less." William Nugent advised his wife Nellie to wean their year-old daughter, for "if your system becomes enfeebled your milk may be an injury to her," while an officer from Florida cautioned his wife not to wait too long before she opened their teething daughter's gums to prevent fever; later he sent home the makings for smallpox vaccinations. On campaign in the South, James Garfield warned his wife against letting their two-year-old Eliza become "a house plant." "The half-naked, half-starved children of this valley are rarely sick," he wrote from Kentucky, because they were so active and spent so much time outdoors.[50]

The advice they felt compelled to give as husbands dovetailed perfectly with the advice they handed out as fathers. Unable to raise sons and daughters themselves, soldiers tried to make sure that their wives understood what was at stake. A formula of strictness and affection, many argued, would produce children they

could be proud of. Pender advised his wife to stand firm in her attempts to prevent his parents, with whom she was staying, from
spoiling their young son. He also assured her that he had "told
them they must not interfere in your whipping affairs either." An
occasional use of the rod was necessary for effective discipline,
but one father predicted that "a soft word may often touch the
heart, make an impression, which years can never wipe out." An
Arkansas captain wanted his wife to "direct" their only child, a
three-year-old son, "as a reasonable beeing, capable of seeing and
judging the rights and wrongs of things." Different children required different approaches. James Goodnow urged his wife to recognize, as he did in his correspondence with them, the differences
in their three sons. Sam, he wrote, "should be treated as a reasonable being — You must command yourself before you can command him. Dan is different — being impulsive and excitable and
needs firm but gentle management. Johnny needs nothing for two
or three years but just breaking in." He also asked her to "above
all try to be even tempered. Don't for any sake give way to anger,
when things go wrong with you." His last comment may explain
why he waited until he left home to impart this advice: "And don't
be angry with me for telling you plain truths."[51]

Older brothers rarely ventured to instruct their mothers about
child rearing, but their words of love and advice to younger brothers and sisters showed their self-conscious sense of responsibility
and burgeoning paternalism. Henry Abbott, for instance, wrote
loving and witty letters to his several young siblings, in which
he offered playful affection to the two youngest and more serious
guidance to the oldest brother. He assured five-year-old Grafton
that "I should like to get home & give you a hug & have your
little hands round my neck" and complained that the kiss sent by
eight-year-old Arthur via a friend returning to Henry's regiment
remained undelivered. The friend "wouldn't do it," he explained,
"because I hadn't shaved for two or three days & he was afraid
of getting scratched." Although he generally restricted his broth-
erly advice to Grafton and Arthur to wishes for good behavior, the
Harvard alumnus had more interesting things to say to seventeen-
year-old Samuel, a sophomore in Cambridge. Despite the fact that
"there is nothing very wicked about hazeing the faculty[,] . . . getting drunk, gambling & whoring are bad"; Samuel should drink
and smoke only in moderation.[52]

Less racy but equally engaging was the advice from Willie Sivley, himself a child when he joined the Confederate army at age seventeen, to his younger sister Jane, attending a girls' school in Alabama. A passage beginning, "now will you take advice from me who, loves you so dearly," showed that Willie believed that his role as a defender of the Confederacy and, by extension, of his family gave him the right—the responsibility—to lend her the benefit of his knowledge and experience. Jane should "apply your self to your studies & not think about home & the Texas scouts" camped nearby. "For my sake & your own," the young soldier pleaded, do not "think about . . . boys" at the expense of her studies. Like those fathers who tried to ease the fears of their families with lighthearted anecdotes, an Illinois drummer boy sprinkled funny stories and cocky banter into letters he wrote his younger siblings. While other soldiers complained about the maggots in their "crackers," "I don't look for them," he boasted. "All I have to say is if they get between my teeth they will get hurt." Several months later he reported the unfortunate addition to the regimental band of a bass drummer who, in addition to being unable to keep time, had ruptured the drum head. He also complained about the southern ladies in Mississippi, some of whom were "nice looking girls" but, unfortunately, chewed tobacco.[53]

More worldly intimacies were shared by Pvt. Jasper Barrett and his teenaged brother Marion, who remained on the farm back in Illinois. One can easily imagine the Barrett boys talking through evening chores or smirking in the back bench at church about the sorts of topics now relegated to letters. Jasper painted a jolly picture of a regimental Christmas with "plenty" of "long range" whiskey. He teased his brother about girls; a friend had told Jasper that Marion "came around a mong the girls with your ears pricked up like mice in a bag of pumpkinseads." The senior brother admitted, however, that "I cant say that I blame you for that for I should like to see some of the loving creatures myself." Just before the end of the war, Jasper wrote from a New Orleans hospital urging Marion not to enlist. Soldiering was all right "while a fellow has a good health but let him get sick and see where he is. . . . he haint got mother to make tea for him and wait on him."[54]

Although brothers could sometimes avoid the grim details of war, fathers were less able to ignore the question of their own mortality. The grave tone of the advice extended by Civil War fathers sometimes evolved into a fatalistic doubt they would ever see their families again. In the summer of 1864 Sgt. Marion Fitzpatrick wrote his wife that he desperately wanted to see their young son. "But it seems doubtful now about ever seeing him again," he admitted. "Men are killed and wounded around me nearly every day and I know not how soon my time may come." He died a few weeks later at Petersburg. A German immigrant serving in a Wisconsin regiment rejoiced at the birth of his sixth child but wondered whether the little one would be "allowed to get to know his Father." Another fear was the future of his oldest son, who, if the father was killed, "would become so unmanageable that it will be hard to make anything of him." He died a year later at Andersonville. Volney Ellis hoped that "God will again restore me to you" and their two children, neither of whom was more than three years old, but prayed that "God be a father to my little ones. I cannot brook the idea of dying away from home."[55]

The sense of loss and even despair in soldiers' writings about their children can be interpreted in several ways. Some men's ideas about fatherhood typified strict gender values and relationships. William Nugent, the commander of a Mississippi cavalry company, found time during the Atlanta campaign to expound on the joys of parenthood and the importance of children in sustaining a marriage. "I never have believed a woman's entire character and individuality could be developed until she became a mother," he wrote to his wife Nellie. But parenthood also changed the position of the father. The birth of a child gave both parents "a common object upon which they can lavish their affection; a daily, living exemplification of . . . spiritual unity. . . . It is only when the innocent child is prattling around their knees that they feel that oneness so indeterminate before." Other soldiers, such as South Carolinian C. L. Burckmyer, commented wistfully on the heartbreak of separation and on the lost years spent away from his only child. Shortly after his daughter's twelfth birthday, he complained that "I cannot bear the idea . . . of Mary's growing to be so large. I like to fancy her still a little child with all her childish simplicity and innocence." Despite the differences in how Nugent and Burckmyer articulated the meaning of fatherhood, both clearly show the ways children made their lives whole.[56]

How Careful We Must Be

A few years before the Civil War the editor of *The Knicker-bocker* reprinted an article he had published some time before. In it he told of a father whose eight-year-old son, normally a kind, obedient child, had apparently gone swimming on the way home from school against his parents' explicit instructions. Refusing to listen to young Henry's explanation, the father sent him to bed without supper. By the next morning the boy was critically ill; in two days he was dead. When a playmate confessed that Henry had gotten wet when he jumped into the water to save another boy, guilt overwhelmed the father's grief. In a letter to his friend — the author of *The Knickerbocker* piece — he wrote that everywhere he went, he found reminders of Henry: sketches he had drawn for his little brother, the still muddy boots he had worn on the day he had risked his life to save another, and the field in which he had played. All of these called to mind happy scenes, yet, he admitted, "I *cannot* recall any other expression of the dear boy's face than that mute, mournful one with which he turned from me on the night I so harshly repulsed him." "Oh!" cried the repentant father, "how careful should we all be that in our daily conduct toward those little beings sent us by a kind Providence, we are not laying up for ourselves the sources of many a future bitter tear!" The lessons to be learned, of course, were for parents — perhaps fathers in particular — to recall the intensity of childish feelings and tragedies, to appreciate and listen to children, and to avoid lashing out with words that can never be taken back.[57]

The Civil War occurred just as economic, demographic, and social currents were shuffling priorities and changing the nature of relationships between parents and their children. Although northern and southern soldiers may have arrived at their assumptions about parenting by different routes, the separation and anxiety generated by the war no doubt amplified soldiers' commitment to and affection for their children. Their letters reveal that, whether or not they had ever read Clark's sentimental account of parental angst, they instinctively sought to guide, nurture, and love the children that they desperately longed to see. Yet accompanying the sense of loss and even despair in soldiers' correspondence was a less obvious realization that the war had provided them with an opportunity to enhance their roles as fathers.

Although even when they were at home they may not have spent much time changing diapers or nursing sick children, these letters clearly show an emotional attachment to and deep interest in their children's well-being and physical and mental development. Separation became a lens that helped fathers focus more completely on their progeny, inspiring them to extend advice and counsel— as well as love and humor—to the youngsters behind the lines. The affection that leaps out of their letters to their children transcends Victorian rhetoric and indicates how important to their self-images were their roles as fathers.

It may be oddly pleasing, if slightly maudlin, to think that advice appearing in the correspondence of doomed fathers or brothers carried more weight than advice offered in letters that, in later years, would be merely interesting souvenirs rather than reverenced artifacts from martyred heroes. Col. Charles Blacknall's last letter home, which he sent a few weeks before his death in the Shenandoah Valley, warned his twelve-year-old son Oscar—who he addressed as "Captain"—that "it is now, while you are a boy, that you have to form a character to last you during life, & if you are idle, vicious & insurbordinate, you will surely grow up to be a worthless & corrupt man, instead of being an honor to your family & to your country." He concluded his advice with a vote of confidence: "I know that you have sense enough to know what is right & that you will act accordingly." A Mississippian wrote from the Army of Northern Virginia early in Lee's drive into Pennsylvania that "this maybee the last time i ever write to [you] for wee . . . [are] expecting a great fight an wil hav one no doubt. an i may get killed." He urged two of his sisters to go to work as teachers, advising one to "assume a vury solid way an spek with arthority." In addition, he told his oldest sister, she must "improve yourself" and "i[n]fluence an advise your younger sisters and impress it upon their minds." The twenty-one-year-old veteran lost a leg in Pickett's charge and died a month later.[58]

The children reading, treasuring, and preserving these tender letters of hope and guidance—even those whose fathers made it home—learned much about the bloody reality and noble causes of the war that had interrupted their lives and robbed them of at least part of their childhoods. They also learned much about the men they called father and through their examples learned the nature of sacrifice and the profound costs of patriotism. They gleaned important lessons about life and death from the notes and letters and epistles written with pencil nubs and dull pens on scrap paper while their lonely authors rested after dusty marches, tedious picket duty, or numbing combat. Children probably expected the advice they received. More important to them, perhaps, was realizing that their fathers still loved them. The glow of these soldiers' sacrifices illuminated the Confederate and Union causes for their children, inspiring many to dedicate their young lives to support the same causes their fathers served. Many of those children, especially in the South, would, like their fathers, confront their own dangers and take in experiences that would in far less tender but no less crucial ways continue their education in politics and war.

4 We Lived Years in As Many Days
The War Comes to Children

The war seared images of glory and of tragedy into the memories of Richard Yates Jr., a future governor and congressman from Illinois. He was a well-traveled toddler, for his father served as Illinois's war governor and went to the U.S. Senate in 1865. Snatches of music lodged in Richard Jr.'s earliest recollections: a military band, a bugler trumpeting cavalry calls, the refrain "Glory, Glory, Halleluiah!" The first ships he ever saw were gunboats and monitors in the Washington Navy Yard, the first prison he ever saw was the infamous Libby in Richmond, and the first graves he ever saw were in the brand-new cemetery on the grounds of Robert E. Lee's Arlington.[1]

Grief rather than nostalgia framed other children's remembrances, especially in the South. George Donaghey, another future governor whose father spent part of the war in a Union prison camp, claimed that "starvation is one of the sharpest memories of my childhood." The Arkansan recalled going barefoot, even in winter, and wrote that "by the time I was seven or eight years old, I had to work almost like a man, helping mother to keep life in myself and my younger sisters and brothers." For eight-year-old Annie P. Marmion, wartime life in Harpers Ferry was a nightmare in which "the great objects in life were to procure something to eat and to keep yourself out of light by day and your lamps . . . hidden by night" so as not to draw the fire of Union pickets. Life could be cheap in a town that changed hands numerous times during the war. During one siege a shell fragment killed an infant in its mother's arms, and a black woman venturing out for water was shot and lay in the street all day.[2]

The death of the anonymous slave woman indicates how tightly African Americans were bound up in the conflict. Since they clung to the bottom rung of the southern socioeconomic ladder, the war had severe ramifications on the lives of enslaved and free blacks living in the South. Their already stark diet dwindled, thousands endured squalid contraband camps, and hundreds perished from exposure and violence. Yet no other group of war children enjoyed the exhilarating sense of freedom gained by African Americans.[3]

The personal experiences of children during the Civil War ranged from community celebrations to community destruction, from reading war stories to living war adventures. The infinite variety of experiences can be categorized into uniquely northern and southern episodes and circumstances. Early in the war, youngsters shared their parents' rather innocent perception of the conflict as a glamorous adventure. Even as the war turned bloodier, most northern children had to rely on sobering reports from friends and relatives or the stirring accounts in children's magazines and newspapers. Some would learn the hard realities of war through the loss of fathers and brothers. Many southerners — and a few northerners — witnessed battles or their bloody aftermaths and submitted to terrifying and sometimes deadly encounters with invading armies. Slave children endured many of the same conditions as southern whites, but with unique demands and opportunities. Despite the vast differences in the ways that the war affected northern and southern children, those thrills and tragedies and hardships led youngsters in both sections to respond to the war in very similar ways — as participants, not as bystanders.

Seeing the Elephant

Inspired, perhaps, by exciting tales from children's books or magazines, intrigued by lively letters from brothers and fathers, or merely curious about the noise and commotion created by the huge armies tramping across their land, children all over the United States and the Confederate States dreamt of getting into the action. Although southern children obviously had more opportunities to snoop around army camps and gape at the great and terrible battlefields, whenever Yankee children got the chance, they, too, inched as close to the "real" war as they could. Civil War youngsters explored battlefields and, as soon as army units from either side set up camp near their homes, struck up conversations, grabbed souvenirs, or earned a little money peddling food to soldiers. Living in a war zone, even temporarily, seemed to free children, especially boys, from prewar restraints on their behavior and limits on their imaginations. Young males in the mid-nineteenth century were anxious to prove their worthiness to their peers, through taking risks and demonstrating their mastery of the environment by hunting or riding or proving themselves in individual combat. Just as boys had joined in the riotous political campaigns of the 1850s as ways of emulating adult men, they sought to make themselves a part of the drama when fighting broke out near their homes.⁴

The most famous children to come under fire belonged to the president and the commanding general of the United States. Only three when the war began, one of Jesse Grant's earliest recollections was the shelling of the steamboat he and his mother and siblings were taking to join their father in Vicksburg. Another of his most prominent memories occurred at City Point, Virginia, when while reviewing troops with his father, the president, and Tad Lincoln, the latter's horse bolted, and the general and the president galloped off in hot pursuit. The commotion alerted the Confederates, who began to lob shells toward the Union lines. Once Tad's pony was brought under control, the party took cover in a crowded bombproof.⁵

Jesse and Tad relished this brush with danger. Opie Read showed the same boyish adventurousness when he bribed a Confederate bugler with brandy to let him ride with him into a skirmish with Union cavalrymen. "On a beautiful morning," with "shouts and songs of discordant loudness we rode forth to battle." As the long lines of horsemen crossed sabers, "it was beauty and not horror" that impressed Opie; he "saw an iron weed bend its purple head beneath the touch of a lark, . . . saw a man with his skull split open, fall to the ground." As the sword fight developed into a decidedly less romantic fire fight, Opie's bugler friend stiffened and leaned back against the boy, nearly unseating him. "I moved to one side, reached around and took hold of the horn of the saddle. Blood spurted from the bugler's breast." Letting the dead Confederate slide to the ground, Opie rode off the battlefield, dismounted, and ran home.⁶

Less romantic than Read's experiences were those of Cornelia

Children enthusiastically edged as close to the action as possible, as these Virginia children do at Sudley Ford on Bull Run in 1862. Note the military-style caps worn by the two boys. (Library of Congress)

McDonald's two oldest sons, who successfully begged to investigate a battle being fought near their home at Winchester. Later, as she sat surrounded by her five younger children listening to the not-so-distant sounds of battle, Cornelia bitterly regretted her decision. At nightfall, after the battle had ended, the boys finally came home, "very grave and sad looking." To their mother, "they seemed not like the same boys . . . though there was no sign of fright or of excitement, they were very grave and sorrowful." They described the battle and their disappointment after the Confederates retreated. At one point they sat on a fence watching the fighting until a human head rolled by and they moved to less exposed ground. The MacDonalds showed how well children and their parents could adapt to even the worst situations. More than a year later, during another nearby battle, Mrs. MacDonald let even the little ones play in the yard. She later calmly wrote that they "seemed to forget the shells," turning the battlefield into a playground. As retreating Confederate soldiers limped past their yard or collapsed to rest for a moment, the children were "running and catching the men as they passed, saying, 'I take you prisoner.'"[7]

On those few occasions when the shooting war moved into their section, young northerners also dashed into the fray. Residents of northern border towns had, of course, heard rumors of "battles, of town-burnings, or horrible massacres, of treacherous surrenders," according to fifteen-year-old James Sullivan. But it was not until the Army of Northern Virginia invaded Carlisle, Pennsylvania, that James and his friends got a taste of the real war. A few days later, as the Confederates moved into Gettysburg, Charles McCurdy followed Confederate soldiers into the town square, where they showed him "the feeling of protective comradeship that nice men show to little boys." Swallowing their fears, Yankee youths clustered around as Rebel soldiers cooked their suppers, chatting about peace, the causes of the war, and army life. They were surprised to find that these dreaded enemies were "touchingly like our own boys." Others had different images. When Jubal Early's Confederate division stormed into Gettysburg, one ten year old peeked through shutters and thought of a "wild west show."[8]

Once the fighting started, boys scrambled for the best vantage points. Charles McCurdy's parents inexplicably placed "no restriction . . . on my goings and comings." Neither did Billy Bayly's. He roamed all over the battlefield, watching Federal troops arrive and then climbing Seminary Ridge with his younger brother and a few other friends to pick blackberries. Momentarily forgetting about the imminent bloodletting, the boys were stunned by the concussion of a cannon and a volley of rifle fire, then redeployed to a fence rail near a blacksmith shop. Despite his fright, Billy wrote years later, "to me as a boy it was glorious!" When the main body of Confederates advanced to within a few hundred yards of their position, the boys finally withdrew, "not riotously or in confusion, but decorously and in order." During the battle a group of

Gettysburg teenagers forsook their homes, spending a night sleeping fitfully in a storeroom above a shop, listening to Confederate sentries and trying to learn how the battle was going.[9]

Albertus McCreary and a group of friends tagged along after the Eleventh and Twelfth Corps as they formed a line of battle on Seminary Ridge on July 1, but the boys returned home when shells began exploding nearby. The next couple of days were a blur of exciting images: ladling water from huge buckets for sweat-drenched Yankees as they retired through the town, an apparently overburdened drummer boy asking him to keep his drum for him, and shadows of "men rushing back and forth . . . fill[ing] us with horror" when the family retreated to the cellar on July 1. As the Confederates settled into the town, Albertus talked with many of them, and the soldiers taught him to distinguish between the sound of minié balls and musket balls and between the various kinds of artillery projectiles. After the battle finally ended, the McCreary household was occupied by wounded Union soldiers for weeks. Albertus and his brothers slept on the floor and ate at the Sanitary Commission headquarters. Dead bodies were everywhere, of course, and "the stench from the battle-field after the fight was so bad that every one went about with a bottle of pennyroyal or peppermint oil." Albertus remembered for the rest of his life vast areas strewn with abandoned and broken equipment, bloated horse carcasses, and wrecked fences. From his perch on the back fence he spent hours watching surgeons operating on wounded soldiers. "I must say," he wrote forty years later, "I got pretty well hardened to such sights." Gettysburg children maintained their enthusiasm even after the armies left, eagerly scooping up souvenirs such as rifles, swords, haversacks, cartridges and cartridge boxes, clothing, books, letters, and photographs that littered their streets. Entrepreneurial boys also hunted for bullets to sell for scrap and for keepsakes and sold guidebooks to tourists for years afterward.[10]

Few of these boys seem to have gotten into trouble for flirting with such terrible and unpredictable danger. Perhaps the adults were so relieved when their sons reached home that they suspended their judgment. The reaction of Opie Read's father offered another possibility. Opie Reid's horror at the death of his bugler friend was eclipsed by his fear of what his father—who had explicitly ordered him to stay home—might do to him. "My only hope was to thrill him with my story," and for the first time in his life he "made a clean confession." It worked. His father seemed proud of Opie's courage and the honor it brought to the family name. As if his father acknowledged that the war had changed the ground rules for preadolescent behavior, the whipping Opie received for disobeying an order "fell upon me with gentleness."[11]

Other parents may have simply felt powerless to prevent their children from flexing their independence. When a skirmish broke out near the Fremaux house, Leon decided to capture a horse in the confusion. Spotting a Yankee major shot out of his saddle, he dashed into the melee, grabbed the bridle, and retreated to cover. When the firing stopped and the children were ordered to bed, Leon slipped out a window and back to the battlefield, where he spent most of the night and the next day. Although he came home "looking worn and sad" and refused to answer any questions about his nocturnal activities, it was clear to his little sister that he "was getting out of Ma's jurisdiction."[12]

Children did not have to travel to Virginia or Louisiana to witness the violence of war. Many children lived through the draft riots that plagued several northern cities in the summer of 1863. The bloodiest, of course, erupted in New York City, where groups of small boys joined the rioters by throwing stones through the windows of the homes of black residents to "mark" them for future attacks. Mobs looting carriages and burning the Colored Orphans Asylum elicited a "mixture of terror and pleasurable excitement" in a boy watching from the roof of his family's home. His most vivid memory was of "a hag with straggling gray hair, howling and brandishing a pitchfork." Eleven-year-old John Bach McMaster saw a black man chased down by a mob and "beaten to death," while Eddie Foy and several friends ventured into the "large colored settlement" near his home, where they also spotted a black lynching victim. "The sight almost turned me sick," he remembered years later, "yet it had a terrible fascination for me," and he repeatedly went back to view the horrible, curious scene.[13]

When children, particularly boys, lived too far from the fighting to actually witness a battle, they avidly toured military camps, battlefields, and capital cities, relishing the martial flavor of life in their war-torn land. For some, trips to Richmond or to other centers of activity were rites of passage that they remembered fondly all of their lives. Jacob Michaux, a twelve-year-old country boy from Powhatan County, Virginia, toured besieged Petersburg and Richmond in August 1864 with his two cousins. The boys were fascinated by everything they saw, from brand new cannon barrels just out of the foundry to the tidy rows of unpainted sheds housing thousands of sick and wounded Confederates at Chimborazo Hospital to fences peppered with bullets, one of which Jacob pried out for a souvenir. The boys also saw Union prisoners peering out the windows of Libby Prison, a column of marching soldiers they assumed to be "a rather full regiment" that turned out to be a much-depleted brigade, and the forts from which Rebels had driven away Gen. Benjamin Butler's failed attack on the city a few months before. They particularly enjoyed their brief trip to an army encampment, where friendly Confederates teased them— one young aide pretended to be the great General Beauregard— and where they could see Gen. Robert E. Lee working with his staff near his headquarters tent. The most memorable part of the trip, however, was actually coming under fire from Federal artillery and joining scores of men, women, and children on a hillside, watching Federal shells arch over the lines and into the city. After a few days, "with our boyish heads and hearts full of the sights of the war, and full of compassion for those incomparable 'boys' who fought and suffered," they boarded a James River packet boat for the trip home.[14]

Of course, many children who did not seek out the war nevertheless came into harm's way. William Wallace of the Third Wisconsin reported that during the Atlanta campaign he saw a woman with two small children dodging shell fire. At each explosion, "she would jump up and the children cling to her dress crying and looking up most pitifully in her face, imploring help from their frightened parent." He also witnessed the Confederates' shelling of Williamsport, Maryland, where "women and children were running screaming and hollering, women barefooted and bareheaded running with their babes in their arms. . . . The soldiers running over every baby that came in their way." Not all children could escape the battles that boiled up and over their lives. Sarah Morgan Dawson reported that during the exodus from Baton Rouge in May 1862, at least two small children drowned, while after a battle in East Louisiana, one former slave remembered that the bodies of little slave children littered the road near a plantation caught in the crossfire.[15]

Children living in or near Vicksburg suffered particularly harsh and dangerous conditions. The Lanier children, for example, had to subsist for three days on the sugar spilled on the floor after marauding Yankees stripped their farm clean. Many slept or even lived for weeks in caves scooped out of the hills in the town and endured the bombardment from Yankee artillery and gunboats. Arching shells made terrible and beautiful displays during the nightly artillery duels. "Shells were plainly seen," a girl wrote years later, "with their tiny flames of light shooting through the air, making that peculiar scream that the old darkies used to say meant, 'whar is you? Whar is you?' and when they exploded 'Dar you is.'" Of course, the shells posed a mortal danger to the children of Vicksburg as well as their parents and defenders. Mrs. W. W. Lord described the "horrible shells roaring and bursting all around" her family and neighbors, "the concussion making our heads feel like they would burst." Her own four children were quite young; one of the women with whom she shared a cave had a ten-day-old baby. She proudly reported that her "children bear themselves like little heroes." Every night, "when the balls begin to fly like pigeons over our tent and I call them to run to the cave, they spring up . . . like soldiers, slip on their shoes without a word and run up the hill." [16]

And like soldiers, they frequently became casualties. In an extreme example of making the best of a bad situation, after a little girl was struck in the arm by a minié ball, a convalescing Rebel fashioned the soft lead into a tiny set of knives and forks. Most injuries left worse scars. A Unionist woman recorded that a slave child belonging to a neighbor lost an arm and that her own cook's daughter was struck on the forehead by shrapnel. Another Vicksburg mother reported the broken arm of a little boy and the deaths of a white and a black child during the bombardment. A series of letters from her sisters to a woman living in San Antonio provided excruciating details of the misery experienced by the besieged residents of Vicksburg, including the diphtheria deaths of four of her youngest siblings just over two months before the city fell to Union forces. The letters reported that at least three women had been decapitated by Union shells, that a little boy had died in a cave, and that the young son of an Irish couple living nearby was killed during the shelling. A neighbor had "heard screams down [in the kitchen] one morning and ran down there. A piece of shell had passed through the bed where the child was laying cutting it in two and its legs were sticking out of the wall where the shell had driven them and still kicking." The horrifying scene had "killed" the sick mother, "and the Father rushed all about town screaming and going on terribly."[17]

The rain of death moved to Atlanta just over a year later. Julia Davidson certainly did not ease her husband's worries when she informed him of a soldier dying in a nearby yard and two wagoneers losing their lives on a street not far from their home. Worse, Davidson wrote her husband, "a little child was killed in its mothers arms," and a week later a shell passed through "the white house on the corner," killing a man and "his little daughter Lizzie whom you have seen at our house" as they lay in their beds. Before the Union army had converged on Atlanta, nearly the entire family of a Confederate soldier, including his two children, died even as he defended his own house, when Federal artillery fired at the Confederate flag his wife hung from an upstairs window.[18]

Ann Banister detailed her life during yet another protracted campaign against a Confederate city — Petersburg — in matter-of-fact tones that belied the tragedies her family endured. Her father was killed and her sixteen-year-old brother died of disease while serving with the home guard, and two other brothers fought with Lee. The Banister home was in an exposed part of town, so for the last year of the war they lived in a two-room basement of a large house in a different neighborhood. Ann described the explosion at the Crater that shattered their windows and wrote of her brother Blair's visit home the night after the battle, his clothes stained with blood from the hand-to-hand fighting. By the fall of 1864, children in the neighborhood could identify the kinds of shells they spotted soaring overhead, while young and old alike would, at night, "go out . . . to watch the mortar shells. They were like arches of fire, and very beautiful." The highlight of the war for Ann was Gen. Robert E. Lee's frequent visits to her house and his open invitation for Ann and her playmates to visit his headquarters, where they could play in safety.[19]

The war brought calamity even to children living outside war zones. Nineteen children at St. Mary's Orphan Home in Natchez died after they contracted smallpox and measles from Union soldiers encamped nearby. All over the United States and the Confederate States, children were killed and wounded in accidental shootings and attacks by soldiers. On one occasion, shells accidentally exploded in Charleston, killing two white and two black boys, while in another incident, a little girl fell into a water-filled entrenchment near Mobile and drowned. Careless soldiers discharged weapons that wounded hapless children, while, inevitably, others were seriously hurt or killed while playing with weapons brought home by furloughed fathers or relatives. According to Albertus McCreary, two Gettysburg boys died when they detonated shells while trying to salvage fuses and powder. Soldiers killed or seriously hurt young boys over the price of a glass of lemonade or for refusing to "hurrah" for Jeff Davis. In a rare instance a black soldier stationed near Baltimore killed a thirteen-year-old black girl. Sometimes the tables were turned. A fifteen-year-old Atlanta lad, miffed when a soldier failed to pay a gambling debt, killed him with a rock.[20]

Given a chance, children would eagerly jump into dangerous situations to get close to the fighting. This willingness to take chances, to sate their curiosity, seemed to be shared equally by northern and southern youngsters. In actuality, however, their experiences were hardly symmetrical. The descent of armies on a town or village could prove devastating to the children and families living there, and these hardships were far more likely to be endured by southern than northern families. For the boys of Gettysburg, the clash of great armies in their town was an aberration, an exciting, if dangerous, lark. For boys and girls in Virginia or Tennessee or Georgia, however, the presence of large numbers of troops from both sides and the destruction they inevitably caused could often become a disagreeable, even deadly fact of everyday life.

War Casts a Gloom over Everything

Experiencing or even witnessing combat could exhilarate even as it disturbed the sensibilities of children. But the war placed other hard-to-measure pressures on children. One of the most important was the sometimes debilitating fear, loneliness, and weariness that plagued many soldiers' wives, depriving northern and southern children of their attention and guidance and good cheer. Some women lost weight from the worry, but more damaging to children were those who fretted over where to take their children after their husbands' departures, who argued with in-laws over everything and nothing, and who succumbed to the depression that forced them to withdraw from the children, to become physically ill, or to crave sleep. Even if they accepted the "culture of resignation" Joan Cashin has described for southern women, the pessimism and detachment this entailed were hardly likely to relieve war-induced stress in themselves or their children.[21]

As a classic study of British children during World War II pointed out, the children who stood the best chance of sustaining their emotional health in the face of fear and uncertainty were those whose parents, especially mothers, could manage their own anxiety. However, beset with worry over their husbands' well-being, scrambling to overcome food shortages that reduced their families' status and quality of life, and overcome with feelings of defenselessness and alienation as the war dragged on, many mothers, especially in the South, feared the effects on their children. An Alabama woman knew that her own state of mind affected the young granddaughter who was living with her while her husband and two sons were in the army. In a letter to her husband, she reported that, as usual, she was unhappy and sickly. "Caldonia," she fretted, "ses that the hissteria is what ales me about you and I no when I miss geting a letter I feel worse." A difficult pregnancy and a long-standing feud with her landlady sharpened a Texas woman's obsession with her husband's absence; her sad diary barely mentioned their children.[22]

The war could knock an entire household off kilter, especially if the mother in charge was having a hard time grappling with the challenges of war. Even though she maintained a life of relative comfort, Lizzie Neblett, a Grimes County, Texas, plantation wife, was one of the most distraught mothers in the Confederacy. Although her husband Will's post on the Texas coast kept him out of combat, a house full of children, increasingly independent slaves, and a growing sense of despondency about the future nearly overwhelmed her. In long, sometimes angry, and always emotionally demanding letters to Will, she betrayed a deep unhappiness that her children could hardly have missed. Just a month after Will left for the army, Lizzie, whose fifth baby was nearly due, complained, "I do feel so utterly wretched & hopeless at times, when I think that you may never return and my being left a widow with five little helpless dependent children, to raise & educate." She confessed that "if it was not for them, I might end my own life." When her new daughter proved to be a handful, she reported shedding "bitter tears, over the work of last August," the month in which the baby had been conceived. She could "take no pleasure" in little Bettie, "the very sight of her is a pain to me," and "I can't help feeling that her death would be a blessing, to me & her." Lizzie eventually gave in to the infant's charms and described her antics for the father who had never seen her, but at times she still succumbed to dark moods. Six months after Bettie's birth, whenever the baby cried or fussed, Lizzie immediately fell into "a bad humor . . . for the first thought that comes up is, if I had not been the biggest fool in the world that child would never have been here, to molest me as she does." Will rarely responded directly to Lizzie's complaints, although in one letter he asked Lizzie to "kiss the children for me—particularly my Bettie. Poor thing she has no friend but me."[23]

Bettie may have instinctively detected her mother's at least temporary estrangement, but older children could feel psychological demands more directly. Young boys felt constant pressure from worried parents to take advantage of their youth, to learn their lessons quickly, to prepare themselves to fill the gaping holes in society left by the thousands of men lying dead on battlefields around the South. A southern grandmother encouraged her grandchildren to "be diligent in their studies and gain all they can for it is not likely there will be much left to live upon if the war lasts long, and you may all *have to work* for your living." Some parents stressed that the next generation would have to come of age quickly. "The hope of our country for educated men is from boys who are now of your age," wrote Anna Burwell to her twelve-year-old son Edmund. "If this horrid war does not cease all the men who are young & from whom our country expects great things will be killed & you young ones that are coming on must be qualified to take their places." Burwell buried two of her sons during the war—both died in Confederate service—and she wrote Edmund to study hard now, "for if the Yankees come here & our darkies leave . . . you will have to come home to help us work." His education might have to be sacrificed; "you boys that are left will have to do more, will have your part & theirs too to perform in life— be a man 'be of good courage' in *every thing*, do with your might what your hands find to do."[24]

If young southerners had to prepare for a shortened childhood, it was also very apparent that in future they would enjoy fewer resources. Indeed, the war straitened the circumstances of most southerners, sowing doubt and uncertainty in the minds of many children. Middle- and upper-class children saw, perhaps for the first time in their lives, their parents worry about financial matters. When one girl imagined aloud what she would do with $100 in the fall of 1864, her father—frustrated because his work as railroad superintendent in Georgia kept him from the army—bitterly handed her a Confederate $100 bill and said, "There! Take it down the street and see if you can buy a stick of candy." Another Confederate father, renowned chemist Joseph Le Conte, lapsed into a deep depression late in the war. His oldest daughter, Emma, described a scene in early 1865. "Poor father! He had Carrie in his arms just now, but her innocent joy and laughter so grated upon him that he had to send her away. It seems dreadful to see anyone smile." After Gen. William T. Sherman ordered the inhabitants of Atlanta to leave the city, "every one," wrote Carrie Berry, including her parents, "seems sad. . . . Mama seems so troubled and she can't do any thing. Papa says he don't know where on earth to go." Among the southerners crowding into the Confederate capital were a number of desperate mothers, many of whom were recently widowed by the war, who applied for jobs in the Confederate Treasury Department. Mrs. F. C. Jones explained in a letter requesting help that "I do not know what will become of us unless some kind friend will lend a helping hand. Certainly," she hoped, "there are some generous hearts in this City, that would not let the widow & orphans of a deceased Chaplain suffer if they knew it." [25]

Northern children were not generally exposed to all of the same pressures and hardships as southern children. But they could also detect a change in their mothers, especially when sons and husbands went away. When little Jeannette Gilder and her sisters dashed into their mother's room to tell her about watching the regiment to which their brother and father belonged march off to war, she "looked at us without seeing us." Mrs. Gilder had shut the windows and closed the shutters to block out the sounds of the regiment's farewell. "The words that were on our lips were unspoken," Jeannette remembered, "we turned and went silently down stairs, leaving her alone with her grief." Gilder's father and brother survived the war, but many others were not so lucky. "The war cast a gloom" over McClean County, Illinois, wrote Phoebe Morrison, who clearly recalled the uneasiness and sadness that settled over her farm community when new calls for volunteers came out, when bad news arrived at the tiny local post office, or in the case of her own family, when word of her brother's and cousin's deaths arrived. "Wherever we went or whoever came to our house we heard dreadful things talked about." George Norris, the future senator from Nebraska, was only three when his father and brother both died in the army. Brother John had entered the army against his mother's wishes—in fact, he had broken a promise not to enlist—but she tied up his treasured letters with expensive red ribbon. It seemed to George that, when word arrived of John's death, the spirit went out of his mother. He wrote that he "never heard a song upon the lips of my mother. I never even heard her hum a tune. . . . The war ended, and the young men came back, but John slept in a soldier's grave in the blackened southern countryside. There were times when it seemed that her heartache over her son never would pass."[26]

But for most women the anxiety and despair did soften, and many mothers steeled themselves to the hardships and disappointment and projected an image of relative calm—or at least the absence of panic—to their children. This could take the form of dealing with their grief and worry quietly. Genie Spalding wrote his father that "Mother has your photograph in her trunk where she can see it every time she goes to it and she kisses it and talks to it just as if you could hear every word she says." The little boy innocently reported his mother's habit as something of a curiosity; it was, of course, her private coping mechanism. Such fortitude in the face of adversity no doubt helped the boy face his own fears. Emma Balfour, who with her five children under age thirteen endured the siege of Vicksburg, at times felt the danger and stress living in one of the city's caves. One day the artillery fire and the "sense of suffocation from being underground" briefly created "the certainty that there was no way of escape." She felt "hemmed in, caged:—for one moment my heart seemed to stand still—then my faith and courage rose to meet the emergency, and I have felt prepared ever since and cheerful." Others recognized her strength in the face of extraordinary difficulties. A chaplain once asked her to take in a badly wounded and "highly excited" lieutenant because he had heard "I was the coolest lady in town, never discomposed by the shelling." "I could but laugh," she wrote, "but I told him I would take him with a great deal of pleasure and do my best for him." A similar comforting toughness characterized the mother of a future governor of West Virginia, who clearly developed a worshipful admiration of his strong, steadfast mother, who had been widowed early in the war. She "supported . . . privation like a Roman matron," he boasted many years later. Going hungry so her three little children could eat, she finally moved them into a nearby town, garrisoned by Union troops, and opened a millinery store to eke out her family's subsistence. Through it all, "she valiantly worked . . . without one complaint" to make a bare living. "I shall never forget her heroic attitude."[27]

Another psychological burden carried by thousands of children was, of course, the guilt and sorrow they felt when fathers or brothers died in battle. A few soldiers put unbearable pressure on their children and siblings when, in what can only be described as shortsighted attempts to comfort as well as to influence children, they associated their survival on the battlefield with the youngsters' behavior at home. "A great many little girls like you, have lost their father in this battle," Col. Hans Heg once wrote his daughter Hilga, who probably did not have to be reminded about the dangers her father faced. Late in 1862 Heg wrote, "When I get into Battle I might get shot, but if you are a good girl and Edmund is a good boy, God will take care of me for you." Marcus Spiegel was a little more subtle when he mentioned that he had recently been in a battle with "the Cannon Balls . . . flying over my head but none hurt me; the good Lord preserved me from any harm and if you will only be right good Children, mind well and pray to the good Lord, I trust soon to see you all well and hearty." Henry Abbott suggested a similar link between his survival and the behavior of his favorite brother, five-year-old Grafton: "Now you must be good all the time & remember, when you get mad & begin to cry, it makes the rebel bullets come a good deal nearer to me." Hilga and Edmund Heg, the three Spiegel children, and Grafton Abbott no doubt appreciated their role in keeping their fathers and brother alive; unfortunately, they may have paid a huge psychic price when Colonel Heg was killed at Chickamauga, Colonel Spiegel died in a Confederate ambush in May 1864, and twenty-two-year-old Major Abbott died in the Wilderness at about the same time.[28]

We Lived Years in As Many Days

Northern and southern children shared not only an earnest desire to "see the elephant" but also the psychological burdens created by the war. These were important elements of their common experiences. Yet in several significant ways children in the United States and the Confederacy lived very different wars. Northerners—at least most of them, most of the time—could see the conflict as a distant crisis: exciting, perhaps, but something to be experienced through newspapers, panoramas, and parades. Many could report, like Henrietta Dana, that even as the war deepened, "we children soon fell back into the gentle tenor of our pleasant school life" at Craigie House, the manse of poet Henry Wadsworth Longfellow in Cambridge. There, an English tutor showed little interest in the war, and the aging poet "wished to keep its shadows from darkening his children's minds." Henrietta and her classmates, the Longfellow children, did not ignore the war, but they could focus on its less sanguinary side (although they had a scare when their older brother, Charlie, was wounded while serving in the Union cavalry).[29]

Other northern children caught the spirit of the fight to preserve the Union, but as adults they called up mainly colorful, even glamorous images of the war. A St. Louis boy recalled Nellie Grant, the commanding general's daughter, portraying "the old woman who lived in a shoe" at the St. Louis Sanitary Fair and "depositing" a $10 Confederate bill into his first checking account with the help of an amused grandfather. In a perhaps too-predictable early memory, John Philip Sousa, the son of a Marine bandsman, recalled relishing the countless military bands in wartime Washington, while a girl in her early teens also painted a rather romantic picture of life in the wartime capital, where she frequently visited the Senate gallery and met Abraham Lincoln at a White House levee. The excitement made it seem "that we lived years in as many days," she wrote a lifetime later. Addie Hibbard Gregory of Chicago remembered as a little girl the Ellsworth Zouaves "in their picturesque uniforms" marching past her Michigan Avenue house, accompanying her mother when she called on officers' wives at Camp Douglas, and seeing the "beautiful Miss Mattie Hill, serving lemonade as 'Rebecca at the Well,'" and "Old

Abe, the War Eagle" at the last great Sanitary Fair in the summer of 1865.[30]

"Went to school had a good many lessons to make up. Rode both ways. There was a surprise at P.C. Could not go on account of cough. Had a grand time. The band was out. Richmond is taken." That terse entry by a New England schoolboy named A. B. Morong suggests how lightly the war weighed on the lives of many child diarists in the North. A. B. gave Lee's surrender roughly equal billing with a local funeral on April 10, although A. B. devoted the next day's entire entry of seventeen words to the celebration of the end of the war. His remarks on the fifteenth did lead off with President Lincoln's assassination and the not-quite-accurate statement, "the rascals have been caught," but it also referred to his father's business trip, a family visitor, and the weather. A twelve-year-old farmboy in upstate New York ignored the first year of the war completely but provided detailed accounts of his chores, weather, schooldays, and visiting peddlers, while a sixteen-year-old Brooklynite found fit to include only a brief mention of her parents' attendance at a Union meeting amidst her diary's descriptions of numerous ice skating parties. Fifteen-year-old Sarah Cook Williamson, a diarist at Troy Female Seminary, included a cursory remark on the election of 1864 but otherwise managed to ignore the last autumn and winter of the war entirely.[31]

Yet most of these protected children eventually took an interest in the war. It grew in their imaginations like nightmares — or at least ripping good yarns. The diary of a seventeen-year-old schoolgirl from Concord, New Hampshire, illustrated how the war gradually infiltrated the lives of many middle-class northerners. Lizzie H. Corning usually wrote about school, visits with and letters from friends, church affairs, the weather, her family's new house, and other normal adolescent concerns, but as the war entered its second year, she began to record her attendance at political speeches, a "panorama of the present war," a local officer's funeral procession, her participation in local fund-raising efforts, an "emancipation party" on January 1, 1863, and numerous visits to a nearby army camp. By April 1862 she had also begun noting the anniversaries of incidents such as the Baltimore riot, the secession of several southern states, and the fall of Fort Donelson. Another girl about Lizzie's age, Alice Hawks of Goshen, Indiana, casually remarked on troops training at a nearby camp and on their departure for the front, related romantic dances with officers and a "farewell [hand]shake and a kiss" from a sergeant passing through with his company, and reported her attendance at a local soldier's funeral. She also made rifle cartridges at least once and, in one of her extremely rare political statements, commented on January 1, 1863, that the new year, in addition to "war and rumors of war . . . brings freedom to a poor oppressed nation for this day the slaves become free."[32]

Despite their distance from the fighting, northern children enthusiastically tracked wartime developments. Children joined adults in the holiday atmosphere whirling around the muster days of local military companies and in the calmer reverence shown to wounded veterans. Cape Cod resident Mary Eliza Starbuck would lie on the floor, chin in hands, "just absorbed in worship" of a colored lithograph of the North's first martyr, Elmer Ellsworth. When she went with her mother to pick lint and make bandages with other village women, she deeply admired those older girls whose "young men were at the front." One of them proudly sported her beau's silver trefoil, the badge of the Army of the Potomac's Second Corps. She also remembered crowds gathering at the Nantucket pier, eager for the newspapers from the mainland that the "town crier" would read to the assembled Yankees.[33]

Children like Mary Starbuck could experience the war as a distant echo in weeks-old letters and days-old newspapers, but boys and girls in those parts of the South swept by clashing armies did not, of course, have the luxury of deciding for themselves whether or not to pay attention to the epic fight. John Steele (age eight when the war began) and his sister Sarah (age ten) kept a joint diary of daily life in the no-man's-land between the Union and Confederate forces in northern Virginia during much of 1863. They tersely recorded family news—their father and younger sister died during the war—and chores but also included the comings and goings of northern and southern forces. Wounded men from both armies frequently stayed in their house or stopped for meals, while thousands of Federal prisoners marched past on their way to camps in the South. They also witnessed a skirmish and the death of a Confederate officer nearly on their porch steps. John mentioned having "battle class" at school and "playing soldier" with other boys. Their diaries tell of a conflict that, despite its apparent aimlessness, nevertheless overran the lives of the civilians and children it touched.[34]

The material differences in the wartime lives of northern and southern children were brought into high relief at Christmastime. The Steele children mentioned eating cake, fried doughnuts, and pies (brought by Federal soldiers); serving eggnog to a friendly Confederate officer; and attending an exhibition of some sort on Christmas Day 1863; but not presents. Even in the North, where material conditions were relatively unchanged, children found Christmas invested with new meanings. A sampling of *Harper's Weekly* Christmas illustrations suggests some of these changes: fathers coming home on furlough, their shy children holding back from the near-strangers; Santa Claus sporting patriotic garb; the stark contrast between the prosperous North and the devastated South. The *New York Herald* featured an irate Santa complaining that the blockade prevented his visits to southern children. Those youngsters did, indeed, have much more to complain about than their northern peers. By the second year of the war, most Confederate children were eating less and plainer food, enjoying fewer luxuries on birthdays and holidays, and sometimes going hungry due to the blockade, the inadequate Confederate transportation system, or inflated prices. Southern shortages became especially apparent at Christmas, when the expensive toys and plentiful dinners that formerly cluttered the parlors and dining rooms of even modestly affluent southerners were only prewar memories. A gloominess settled over the Confederacy; country roads that in peacetime would have been filled with Christmas revelers were deserted. Although celebrations often taxed their resources and emotions, most families tried to carry on old traditions. For some, it seems, celebrating an even drastically scaled-back Christmas was one way of supporting the Confederate war effort.[35]

Most southern children seem to have endured austere wartime holidays as patriotic gestures. Adults often tried to explain why the toys and goodies that usually appeared might be lacking. The *Richmond Examiner* played Scrooge when it called Santa Claus "a dutch toy-monger, an immigrant from England, a transflated scrub into New York and New England," who "has no more to do with genuine Virginia hospitality and Christmas merry makings than a Hottentot." A crotchety slave told the Howell Cobb children not to expect a visit from St. Nick because the Yankees had shot him, while other parents offered more sensitive explanations. As a Yankee, Santa would be held up by Confederate pickets, or perhaps Union blockading vessels had interrupted his journey.[56]

Whatever the reason for Santa's failure to scuffle down southern chimneys, Confederate children saw their piles of presents dwindle as the war dragged on. The Thomas children of North Carolina received mountains of dolls and books and games in 1862, but a year later, with Santa Claus "gone to the war," the children found only cakes and coins in their stockings. In 1864 their mother's only mention of celebrating on a "dull, gloomy, and cloudy" Christmas day was attending church. Most mothers settled for what one woman called "homely Confederate presents": popcorn balls, ginger cakes, fruit, and a few pennies. Eighteen-year-old Susan Bradford, her mother, and a number of aunts busied themselves making presents for younger siblings and nieces and nephews. They bound small books; fashioned toy animals out of scraps of material, ginseed cotton, and watermelon seeds; and stitched rag dolls dressed as babies, nurses, Confederate soldiers, and "fine ladies in hoopskirts." Even the Jefferson Davis children settled happily for flannel toys and makeshift treats. Hard times and high prices in Richmond made for a rather sparse holiday in 1864, but in typical fashion the John B. Jones family made scarcity into a virtue. They welcomed the celebratory pies and cakes that Mrs. Jones baked as well as a few scrawny remnants from their vegetable cellar. In addition, the Joneses had sworn among themselves that "no unpleasant word" would mar the day. No presents were forthcoming either, but the parents and children spent the afternoon happily rummaging through an old chest containing clothes, toys from Mrs. Jones's childhood, and other long-forgotten items. The large family seemed "content with this Christmas diversion" and "oblivious to the calamaties which have befallen the country." [37]

Of course, the war deprived some children of even the simplest Christmas. The children and slaves of a Unionist family in Nashville, according to an older sister, "received money enough all around to feel that it was Christmas tho', of course, all the usual toys, fire crackers, and merry makings were dispensed with." Laetitia Nutt, who had three children under age six, complained in her diary about how sadly unique the Christmas of 1863 was:

"not a stocking hung . . . no Santa Claus for happy, expectant children, no toys, no raisins or nuts, not even a cake or a piece of candy." Dolly Sumner Lunt's nine-year-old daughter hung a stocking expectantly, but after leaping out of bed the next morning to see what Santa had brought, she was shocked to find nothing. Heartbroken, she broke her mother's heart by crawling back into bed, pulling the covers over her head, and sobbing into her pillow. Mrs. Lunt's slave children soon came to the door for their traditional Christmas gifts; of course they, too, were disappointed. Too young to recall prewar Christmases, Robert Martin, only three when the war began, "tired of the war" at least partly because "Santa Claus forgot to come to the Shenandoah Valley."[38]

However tragic the sparse Christmas presents and dreary holidays seemed to Confederate children, many had to face much worse challenges and hardships. Even the most determined Santa Claus could not protect southern children from the war. As Union pressure on the Confederate homeland mounted, untold thousands of southerners fled their homes. The population of Augusta, Georgia, doubled during the war, in large measure because of refugees from the path of Sherman's armies. Many newcomers joined longtime residents in war-induced poverty; by early 1865, 1,500 families lived on the pittance provided by local relief agencies. Confederate sources described the pitiful cabins and shelters in which Fredericksburg women and their children shivered during the late winter of 1862, while a large proportion of their more affluent neighbors arriving in Petersburg a few weeks later were reportedly children. After Atlanta fell, perhaps 200 families with 1,000 children fled to Macon, where they lived in railroad cars and clustered at the mayor's office to beg for food. In Nashville in the summer of 1864, hundreds of women and children languished in stark, filthy refugee camps, suffering and dying from typhoid and other diseases. Administrators of orphanages in Charleston and Natchez scrambled to find refuge for their young charges. Over 130 orphans received absolution from the bishop under a Yankee bombardment before escaping to a rat-infested, abandoned plantation house outside Natchez. At least some of the women and children among the 400 mill workers expelled from Roswell, Georgia, by Gen. William T. Sherman ended up in a Louisville military prison or in an Indiana refugee camp. The *Baltimore Daily Gazette* reported indignantly that some of them had been hired out as servants in Louisville.[39]

Of course, statistics can obscure the human face of the refugee epidemic that made untold thousands of children homeless. A correspondent for the *Charleston Daily Courier* described a family of refugees leaving Corinth after they were driven from their homes by Federal artillery in the spring of 1862. A mother, baby, and toddler clung to a "miserable horse," while six other children all under age ten followed on foot, with the oldest carrying yet another baby. "It's a hard lot, gentlemen," she said tearfully to the newspaperman, "to have to leave your house in this way and look for another among strangers."[40]

Children who moved to other parts of the Confederacy often faced problems typical of uprooted youngsters living in strange places. The war merely provided a dramatic backdrop for the age-old problem faced by the "new kids in town." The Stones, an aristocratic plantation family who had been forced from their home near Vicksburg in early 1863, eventually settled in East Texas, where they were called "renegades" and lived uneasily in a small colony of refugees among the poorer and, at least to diarist Kate Stone, less sophisticated Texans. "The more we see of the people, the less we like them," she wrote soon after their arrival near Tyler. Without a trace of self-consciousness, she blamed local prejudice against refugees on "just pure envy. The refugees are a nicer and more refined people than most of those they meet, and they see and resent the difference." In the face of such arrogance the locals, not surprisingly, took out their own feelings about the refugees on the children. Jimmy and Johnny Stone, sixteen and fifteen, respectively, attended school in Tyler and almost immediately ran into problems. Their older sister reported that local boys unfairly accused them of putting on airs by " 'wearing gold watch chains and black broadcloth' — a slender little strand of gold and a second-hand suit of clothes." They tormented the newcomers by sticking pins in them during prayers and picking fights with them. After the Stone boys armed themselves, but before anyone was seriously hurt, Mrs. Stone withdrew them from school.[41]

Families separated by flight or by military service naturally complained about the distance and dangers that kept them apart. Little Georgia Ashley's grandmother and young aunts missed the toddler desperately when she left with her parents for a posting in South Carolina. "I am almost dead to see her," wrote Mary Jane Lucas, "I do not see how I can stand it." Her seventeen-year-old daughter, Georgia's youngest aunt, was "greatly distressed. . . . She takes her little gown & walks it about like she did her." The house seemed deserted; "every child I hear cry I think it is her," sighed the lonely grandmother.[42]

Separation could be hard on entire families, but for a select class of Confederate girls, boarding schools provided comfortable refuges. Although schools for boys regularly closed during the war, enrollment at girls' schools grew, as parents believed their daughters would be safer at institutions located behind Confederate lines. Even well-to-do Cherokee and Creek parents in far off Indian Territory sent their children to schools removed from the vicious fighting in that theater. A large Moravian academy in Raleigh, North Carolina, according to one of its students, "was a haven for girls of the over run sections of the South." The three hundred girls and three dozen instructors formed "a happy contented family." The southern girls attending St. Cecilia Academy in Nashville were similarly cut off from their homes and forced to remain with their school "family" when the Tennessee capital was evacuated by Confederate forces early in the war.[43]

As it seems to have been for at least a few of these stranded students, for some children, refugeeing was more of an adventure than a trial. When Lucy Hull, the daughter of a railroad superintendent, finally left Atlanta during the Confederate evacuation, her sorrow melted as the chilly morning gave way to a warm, sunny day. "I enjoyed the journey and novelty of the freight car with furniture in it, beds and chairs and bureaus to play on." Best of all, their temporary home would be the large, lavish, Georgia plantation owned by her beloved "Gran'pa." Years later she remembered, "The happiest memories of my childhood cling to that great red brick house" and the graceful, Old South lifestyle lived inside it, with colorful house servants, including a century-old African-born slave. A very different adventure awaited Charles Nagel in his flight into Mexico with his father and other Unionists escaping Texas. He delighted in the rough South Texas desert, thrilled to see the sites of Zachary Taylor's victories in the Mexican War, and enjoyed the exotic food and Catholic churches and bullfights and gamblers in Monterey. Even more exciting was his first shift standing guard. "True, I had never used a six shooter, but I carried one now; and what more would a boy of fourteen want out there in that strange land, where there might be Indians any time."[44]

Compared with the plight of child refugees in the South, the hardships of those few northerners who became refugees were quite minimal. Their time away from home tended to be of short duration, and they rarely faced life-altering choices or dangers. An exception was the 1,800 free blacks and contrabands who crowded into Harrisburg, Pennsylvania, in 1863, correctly fearing that if Robert E. Lee's invading army caught up with them, they would be sent into slavery. But whites also fled before the Confederates. A teenager in Carlisle, Pennsylvania, recalled many years after the war the forlorn white refugees who preceded the Rebels into town, perched unhappily on worn buggies and covered wagons holding most of their rather pitiful possessions. Just before the battle of Gettysburg, the caravans formed a "nearly continuous procession" past his family's home. "The men and boys pegged along like tramps," while the "women and children, peering from their poor vehicles, seemed frightened dumb." Townspeople looked on, and the refugees stared back at them silently; "the small children neither laughed nor cried," bewildered beyond comprehension. According to a student at Rosedale Seminary in Chambersburg, the rumors preceding the Rebel invasion of the Keystone State filled the road leading out of town with a "grotesque procession" of "men, women, and children, carrying all sorts of bundles" in a motley parade of "horses, wagons, carts and carriages." A similar flight occurred a year later when Confederates burned much of the town as well as the seminary.[45]

A World Turned Upside Down

An orphaned free black named Jim Limber lived the last year of the war with the Jefferson Davis family. He participated in family outings and holidays, became an inseparable playmate of Joe and Jeff Davis Jr., joined the little boys' gang that clambered through the neighborhood near the Confederate White House, and accompanied the Davises when they fled Richmond. He was eventually taken from them and sent, almost literally kicking and screaming, into Union lines by the soldiers who captured the Confederacy's first family in Georgia.[46]

Jim Limber shared his white benefactors' fortunes and disasters. Yet black children generally experienced a war very different from that known by white northern and even southern children, facing the most dramatic changes, as well as the most difficult conditions, confronted by Civil War children. They were exposed to soldiers and other northern whites, who treated them differently from, if not always better than, their masters. Those who became refugees — contrabands, in wartime lingo — were thrust into unnerving, harsh, deadly situations. By the same token, the upheaval opened new worlds of education and opportunity that they could not possibly have anticipated.

The war saturated the lives of many slave children, who like their white counterparts, eagerly sought news about the progress of the war or about the well-being of family members living near the fighting and of masters or masters' sons serving in the Confederate army. Many young blacks watched the drills and maneuvers of southern militias and army units and overheard war news from the gossiping soldiers. Booker T. Washington, who was only nine when the war ended, often fanned the flies away from his master's family during mealtime. "Naturally," he wrote in his famous memoir, "much of the conversation of the white people turned upon the subject of freedom and the war." The little boy "absorbed a good deal of it" and no doubt reported it to his elders back in the quarters. Even the youngest slaves on his Virginia farm knew what was at stake in the great war. As a result, "every success of the Federal armies and every defeat of the Confederate forces was watched with the keenest and most intense interest." Washington believed that slaves often acquired the latest intelligence before the whites, usually from slaves who fetched the mail for their unsuspecting owners. As a slave who frequently worked in the big house, young Booker was part of what he called the "grape-vine telegraph" that alerted slaves to events and incidents of the war.[47]

But the most basic experience for southern black children was hunger. Supplies of clothing and shoes declined quickly in the South, and when salt reserves disappeared, so did meat from the diets of masters and slaves. As southern whites found themselves tightening their own belts, their much-vaunted paternalism withered, causing shortages and hardships to be passed on to slaves already living on the margin of survival. The war "sho' did mess us up," said one former slave, as the food and clothing and shoes they would normally have received went instead to the army. Slaves substituted parched potatoes for coffee and poke berries for greens and went without salt and sugar. Even a prewar staple like peas vanished from one South Carolina plantation, where the slaves ate only "corn-bread, mush, 'taters and buttermilk." After Union troops had swept through the neighboring countryside, burning or confiscating any foodstuffs they found, George King and his six siblings had to "search 'round the barns" hoping to find kernels of corn in the manure left in abandoned livestock pens. According to former slaves, many children and older people starved during the war.[48]

Other facts of life also changed. Slave children learned to fear the beefed-up slave patrols as well as deserters from either army, who, according to Booker T. Washington, would cut off the ears of any "Negro boy" they found in the woods. When fugitives near Magnolia Springs, Texas, found black children near their hiding places, they would "ketch dem an' whip dem an' scare dem an' sen' dem home so dey wouldn' come back no mo!" Other young blacks were afraid of being kidnapped by strangers roaming the countryside looking for slave children to steal and sell.[49]

Slaveowners reserved particularly harsh treatment for the families of African American men who ran away to join the Union army. Angry masters took out their frustration in physical abuse, deprived them of food and clothing, or sold them off to plantations far from husbands and fathers. Other planters simply drove the families of African American soldiers away, condemning them to destitution and homelessness. Black soldiers bitterly resented the abuse their families endured. A white colonel testified to the American Freedmen's Inquiry Commission that one of his African American soldiers had enlisted for the sole purpose of freeing his wife and three children; he paid the ultimate price for their freedom at the battle of Pascagoula. Another insisted that the colonel retrieve his children from his former mistress. "I am in your service," he declared, "I wear military clothes; I have been in three battles; I was in the assault at Port Hudson; *I want those children.*" In some parts of Kentucky, according to a Freedmen's Bureau agent, family members of black soldiers could not be buried.

"Only this day," he wrote just after the war, "a colored woman walked . . . six miles, bringing in her arms the *body of her dead child* because the chivalry . . . refused it burial." [50]

The impressment of male slaves by the Confederate government to work on fortifications and of slave women to work in hospitals and factories separated thousands of families and forced children into adult jobs. Even within Union lines, as black men went into the Federal army, their wives and sons and daughters had to take over the work on the small farms the army gave them to manage. A more dramatic uprooting of slave children occurred when masters hustled their bondsmen and -women out of the paths of advancing Union armies or when their own parents exploited the chaos of invasion to flee. At least 30,000 and perhaps more than 100,000 slaves ended up in the relative safety of Texas, working on rented plantations or hired out to other whites. Masters left some of the youngest and least valuable slaves behind. When Union troops threatened Rosa Green's East Louisiana plantation, her owner collected his best slaves and headed for Texas. He "lef us little ones; say de Yankees could git us effen dey wan' to." Allen Manning was only a child when his master packed up his Mississippi plantation and moved to Louisiana, where after only a year he relocated once again to Texas. "About that time it look like everybody in the world was going to Texas," Allen remembered. He and his siblings often had to get off the road to let wagons "all loaded with folks going to Texas" pass by. Allen and the other slaves moved at least twice more in Texas before the end of the war finally freed them. [51]

Many other slaves freed themselves when Union forces approached, sometimes at the cost of breaking up their families. *Douglass' Monthly* told of a contraband named John Parker, who while working on Confederate fortifications, survived a Federal assault and escaped to Union lines. Although his wife had also planned to run away, their reunion fell through. At the time of his interview Parker was en route to New York, hoping his wife and two daughters would soon join him. Their two sons were elsewhere: one with his Confederate master, the other in Louisiana. Many other families were split up as Federal forces swept through the South. Slaves deserting the farms and plantations near Holly Springs, Mississippi, in late 1862 lined the roads leading toward the Federal encampment. Just after the end of the siege at Vicksburg, an Iowa infantryman reported freed slaves, mostly women and children, "pouring in by the hundreds from every direction." When Gen. William T. Sherman executed his famous march through Georgia and the Carolinas, thousands of slaves took advantage of the disrupted southern heartland to follow the Union armies to freedom. They formed their own column to the rear of the army, traveling in ragtag wagons, riding broken-down mules, or walking. Although they foraged for their own food, they also scavenged in the supplies and rations cast off by Sherman's men.[52]

Like their white counterparts, refugee slave children faced unfamiliar scenes, encountered white people different from any they had ever known, and endured greater hardships than they probably expected. Children comprised a significant percentage of refugee blacks. In the "contraband camps" that sprang up wherever Union armies established posts, women and children dominated the population because so many men were absent as workers or soldiers. Army posts and occupied territories naturally became magnets for African American refugees, with over 10,000 streaming into the lower four counties of the Virginia peninsula. Fifteen thousand sheltered on South Carolina's Sea Islands even before the arrival of the additional thousands trailing Sherman's troops in the spring of 1865, and over 50,000 refugees lived in enclaves along the Mississippi River from Cairo all the way south past Vicksburg. Nearly half of the 2,000 residents of a camp near Murfreesboro, Tennessee, were children, while 2,500 women and children—the families of a regiment of black soldiers—clustered around Clarksville, Tennessee. President's Island, near Memphis, held over 5,600 women, children, and old men in 1864, while out of just under 2,000 contrabands in a camp near Helena, Arkansas, about 800 were school-age children.[53]

Some of the camps took on the aspect of rustic villages, with schools, churches, and shops lining bustling streets. A former slave who spent part of his childhood on a "government farm" in wartime Alabama remembered that "dey treated us all mighty good. We had plenty of good food and clothes." However, most occupants of the camps bore severe deprivations, caused at least partly by army quartermasters who sold their rations and supplies on the black market. Medical care in the camps was sporadic at best, and in 1864 Congress eliminated funds for treatment of contrabands, leaving overworked and undertrained army surgeons with woefully inadequate resources to care for the seriously ill. The "contraband hospital" in Washington was only a collection of "rough wooden barracks" planted "in an open, muddy mire." A white nurse reported that dozens of refugees arrived daily suffering from malnutrition, exposure, smallpox, frozen limbs, hernias, and injuries sustained on their hard journeys to freedom. Cornelia Hancock reported that two little boys each lost a leg after falling from the wagon transporting them to the hospital. Sometimes grinding poverty forced parents to give up their children; on another occasion a weary, desperate freedwoman turned her children over to Hancock because she could not feed them.[54]

The quality of housing in the camps varied greatly, although many refugees lived in primitive conditions. As military governor of Tennessee, Andrew Johnson refused even to issue tents to contrabands during the winter of 1863, claiming that it would make them too dependent on the government. The number of refugees in Tennessee that winter grew to about 9,000, with many living in unauthorized camps set up by commanders of military posts around the state. Other freedmen, -women, and -children occupied old packing crates, tobacco barns, sod huts, and if they were lucky, abandoned houses. In some places single rooms housed six families. The crowding took a heavy toll, particularly on children. Even those youngsters who survived witnessed heartrending and health-breaking conditions that rivaled and probably exceeded anything they had experienced before. Of the 4,000 black refugees living in Helena, Arkansas in 1863–64, about 1,100 died. In Memphis, 1,200 of the 4,000 contrabands died in only three months, while the camp at Natchez, also holding 4,000 refugees, suffered a nearly 50 percent mortality rate in 1863. Many of the children living near Memphis had no shoes or "suitable underclothing" during an abnormally cold winter in which five soldiers had frozen to death. At another camp, 600 or 700 "poor creatures" huddled in tents and leaky, smoke-filled cabins. One report from Vicksburg in the summer of 1863 called the camp at Young's Point "a vast charnel house" with "thousands of people dying without well ones enough to inter the dead." According to one horrified visitor the extraordinary hardships had crushed the energy and motivation of the freedmen. "They had become so completely broken down in spirit through suffering," wrote a Yankee minister, "that it was almost impossible to arouse them." A white nurse in Arkansas wrote that the freedmen were so demoralized by the squalor of their lives that "any idea of change for the better seems utterly impossible" to them. To make matters worse, Confederate guerillas frequently attacked isolated and defenseless contraband settlements, sometimes kidnapping and selling men, women, and children, who fetched $100 each on the slave market.[55]

As is so often the case, children bore the brunt of the hardships faced by the contrabands. A missionary reported that because of their parents' destitution, 200 children had left school in Nashville so they could "be hired out for their food" or because they literally had no clothes to wear. A visitor to the freedpeople in Washington in the spring of 1865 described the helplessness and degradation of families without food and babies without diapers or clothes. A nine-year-old girl supported her mother and younger siblings by selling rags. The dozen freedpeople huddled in a stable on Capitol Hill included a young girl with consumption, a motherless boy with pneumonia, and an infant dying of malnutrition, while another group of six children ranging in age from one to twelve lived in a shed in a sea of mud with no fire or food and wearing only "shreds of garments." An agent for the Cincinnati Contraband Relief Commission described the "degradation" at Davis Bend, Mississippi, in early spring 1864, where in an open cattle shed he found thirty-five "poor wretched helpless negros [sic]." The band consisted of a nearly blind man, five women, and twenty-nine children all under age twelve. The appalled northerner went on to detail unimaginable poverty and horror:

One of the Women had the small pox, her face a perfect mass of Scabs, her children were left uncared for except for what they accidentally rec[eive]d. Another woman was nursing a little boy about 7 whose earthly life was fast ebbing away, she could pay but little attention to the rest of her family. Another was scarcely able to crawl about. They had no bedding. Two old quilts and a soldiers old worn out blanket comprised the whole for 35 human beings. I enquired how they slept, they collect together to keep one another warm and then throw the quilts over them. There is no wood for them nearer than half a mile which these poor children have to toat [sic] . . . hence they have a poor supply, and the same with Water. . . . the only vessel they had to carry it in was a heavy 2 gallon stone jug, a load for a child when empty. . . . They were filthy and will all probably have the small pox and a number of them likely [will] die.

Life must have seemed cheap to these sad and blighted individuals, perhaps as cheap as it was in New Orleans, where a newspaper reported during the war that "a negro child has been lying dead at No. 81 Perdido Street . . . three days. Warm weather is coming on and it ought to be removed."[56]

Children who managed to live through such brutal conditions faced other challenges. Although many thousands did attend the scores of schools established throughout the occupied South, they, like their parents, were also treated as commodities. Federal authorities expected contrabands of all ages to work in return for the security, rations, and housing the army provided. As the plantation superintendent at St. Helena Island, South Carolina, happily reported, the men, women, and children under his control were all "swinging . . . heavy hoes." By age ten or twelve, as they had as slaves, freedchildren took their places alongside older African Americans in the fields. A treasury agent coldly reported that of the 9,050 contrabands on the 189 plantations on the Sea Islands, 3,619 were children "not useful for field labor," while another 335 — boys about age twelve — were considered one-quarter hands. Paid half-wages or less, women and children comprised well over half the workers engaged on confiscated plantations near Vicksburg and Skipworth Landing, Arkansas, in the spring of 1864. At the very least, children worked as caretakers for their younger brothers and sisters while their mothers labored in the fields. Young girls brought babies and toddlers with them to school, leaving them to snooze on the porch while they studied inside.[57]

But most black refugee children did manage to spend at least some of their time in school. On the Sea Islands they worked in the morning and attended class in the afternoon, while in at least one district in Virginia the routine was reversed. Scores of freedmen's aid societies as well as individuals, missionary associations, the army, and others established or supported schools throughout the occupied South by raising money or recruiting teachers; over 1,400 were teaching in 975 schools in the year after the war ended. Some of the contrabands descending on Hampton in the summer of 1861 attended schools, including one organized by an escaped slave in the early fall of that year. Two years later there were 21 teachers in 11 schools with 3,000 day and night students of all ages. African Americans opened the first schools for contrabands in the Tennessee towns of Nashville, Columbia, Springfield, and Pulaski. Other schools ranged in size from a few girls attending a school organized by the nine-year-old daughter of a Union army surgeon on the veranda of a Corinth hotel to the 1,422 children in public schools run by the U.S. Army in New Orleans and more than 14,000 in schools operated in rural parishes in Louisiana. Just after the surrender of Lee's army, Lucy Chase opened a school in Richmond's First African Church, in which she taught over 1,000 pupils—alone. Later the most advanced students became assistant teachers.[58]

Obviously, since very few southern slaves could read or write before the war, the most unusual aspect of black children's school experiences was their discovery of new worlds of learning and skills denied them under slavery. Some teachers had to start with basics such as the names of the days and months, counting, cleanliness, and sewing. But the three "Rs" remained central to the teachers' mission. A report from the Sea Islands in mid-1863 revealed advanced students mastering Hillard's and Willson's second readers and younger students working on short sentences. Others were learning arithmetic, geography, and writing. At least one Sea Islands teacher taught his pupils elocution, while the *New Orleans Times* approvingly noted the special attention given by teachers of black students to the "correct vocalization of the elementary sounds . . . creditable to Saxon voices."[59]

Their teachers became the first white people many former slave children knew outside the master-slave relationship. Teachers in Louisiana were often native southerners, but most came from the North. Their experiences were mixed, as the northern men and women who ventured South applied preconceptions and prejudices, as well as unusual notions about education, discipline, and religion, to their young charges. William L. Coan, who administered the schools in Norfolk, refused to whip unruly students but tied pairs of them together, face to face, by their ears; forced misbehavers to stand on one foot; and shamed children into good behavior by calling them Rebels. Mary Ames had to stamp her feet and shout to get the attention of the scores of students crowded into her classroom; sometimes she could quiet them by singing.

Elizabeth Botume seemed to have an easier time. Although her students were, indeed, restless and noisy and not always attentive, she found that the best way to encourage acceptable behavior was to let well-behaved children ring her brand-new school bell.[60]

Despite northerners' idiosyncrasies, young contrabands were fascinated by them. Their relationship was not based on economics; these were the first whites the freedchildren had ever known who valued the former slaves' interests over their former masters' interests. But these facts, which the children may not have consciously understood, did not automatically make them fast friends. Early in Laura Towne's long stay in the Sea Islands, when she and three other white women rode onto a plantation, "the children screamed and ran to hide at the sight of white faces." Only later did the youngsters each claim "a favorite 'missus,'" whose dresses they clung to while singing over and over "*my* missus." A similar scene greeted Elizabeth Hyde Botume when she arrived at her first school in Beaufort, South Carolina. Although the piazza had been "crowded with children, all screaming and chattering like a flock of jays and blackbirds in a quarrel," when the children spotted her, "they all gave a whoop and a bound and disappeared." After several attempts she finally captured "one small urchin, who howled vociferously, 'O Lord! O Lord!,'" which brought out the other children. Eventually she got them seated, and over the next few months they came to trust her.[61]

Even after teachers and students became better acquainted, rough spots in their relationships sometimes surfaced. Part of the problem stemmed from the northerners' perceptions of race and class. Most teachers hired freedmen as servants, rarely socialized with African Americans, and distrusted the emotion-charged religion of the black churches. Some exhibited much more extreme racism. When a young black girl said "good mornin'" to Miss Pope, who worked with Laura Towne, the teacher snapped, "'I slap your mouth for your impudence, you nigger.'" Another teacher rarely held classes and paid little attention to her students when she did, simply declaring that they could do whatever they pleased. Communication could cause problems, especially with South Carolina slaves who spoke the Gullah dialect. Even in Texas, far from the exotic Sea Islands, a former slave recalled how his northern teacher "didn't talk like folks here and didn't understan' our talk." Children also acted like children, playing the kinds of timeless pranks reserved for new teachers: they switched their names from day to day or made up new ones — like Stonewall Jackson — much to the dismay of the confused teachers.[62]

Eventually, at least according to the teachers, the Yankees and freedchildren overcame the massive differences in their cultures and assumptions and learned to get along. They "would fain worship us, the little things," reported a teacher in Norfolk, whose students "like to handle us, to pull at our hoops, and hang about us." Mary Ames noted that a close bond formed between the white women and their black students. One night one of her favorite little boys seemed uneasy. When she asked him what was wrong, "he whispered, 'Is the reason you don't kiss me 'cause I'm black?'" His question melted the heart of the young teacher, who had maintained a fairly detached attitude toward the African Americans surrounding her during her first two months on the island. She took him into her lap until he fell asleep. By Christmas 1864, after a year and a half in the Sea Islands, Laura Towne felt less lonely, at least partly because of her relationship with the black children to whom she would devote twenty years of her life. She and her partner baked gingercakes for all the children in their care, and at their Christmas party they gave them pocketbooks, sewing kits (for the girls), and combs and knives (for the boys). After teaching in a New Bern, North Carolina, school for several months after the end of the war, Nellie Stearns exclaimed, rather enigmatically, "I declare I never think but I am black too when I am with my scholars."[63]

Although few sources reveal specific points of view, freedchildren no doubt admired and respected their white teachers. Yet northerners must have remained rather distant role models. A few children, however, mainly in Virginia, North Carolina, and Washington, found themselves in the classrooms of African American teachers filling roles inconceivable to the young former slaves. A number of blacks opened small, short-lived schools wherever slavery had crumbled, but more formal schools were also established by the American Missionary Association, which employed more than two dozen black teachers during the war (and scores more during Reconstruction). In fact, the association's first school opened under the leadership of Mary Smith Peake, the free daughter of a white man and a mulatto woman, in Norfolk. The school Peake operated in Brown Cottage would later become Hampton

Institute. Other black teachers traveled from the North. Edmonia Highgate of Syracuse, New York, had lectured and raised money for the missionary society before the war and had taught in the Binghamton public schools; she became a teacher and principal in Norfolk during the war. Her colleague Sara G. Stanley came from Cleveland via Oberlin College. A teacher at the American Missionary Association school at Camp Barker in Washington was a former slave but had been an educator and writer in Brooklyn for twenty years before joining the association. A handful of freedmen came from the South, such as "Uncle" Cyrus White, a local black man who taught school in Beaufort for several months in 1863, and William D. Harris, a plasterer, and his assistant, Amos Wilson, who taught in Grosport, North Carolina. These men and women opened the eyes of the children who came into contact with them, exposing them to the possibilities of a world where race mattered less than merit.[64]

Whether they learned from white or black teachers, slave children expected their education to make a difference in their lives. Teachers commonly remarked on their black students' fidgety, restless behavior and erratic discipline but also welcomed their enthusiasm for learning and their quick minds. A New England Freedmen's Aid Society teacher in North Carolina interrupted a group of black children playing raucously on a church pew. Irritated, she asked them, "What good does it do you to come to school?" They stopped playing, and "one of the most roguish . . . replied, 'If we are *educated*, they can't make slaves of us again.'" At least one teacher believed the children attached an almost spiritual significance to education. When her class formed a ring around the grave of another child, they began singing their ABCs over and over. Each held "his schoolbook or picture-book — another proof that they consider their lessons as some sort of religious exercise."[65]

Friends and Enemies, Liberators and Oppressors

The proximity of southern children to the fighting obviously differentiated their war from that of northern children. Shortages of food and clothing, the necessity — or opportunity — to flee from war zones, the potential danger of nearby clashes, and the liberation and destruction brought by blue- and gray-clad armies alike were all experiences limited almost entirely to the South. So, too, was the opportunity — or curse — to form intense relationships with Confederates stationed nearby or with Yankees occupying conquered areas of the Confederacy. These contacts humanized the combatants in both armies. On the positive side, meeting Confederates made the soldiers' sacrifices more concrete to their young white admirers, while getting to know invading Yankees actually eased some of their deepest fears. Few African American children mentioned their encounters with Confederate soldiers, but many described extremely ambiguous relationships with northerners.

Very young slaves heard all the talk about the war in general and Yankees in particular, especially as Union armies drove deep into the Confederacy. Masters frequently told their slaves that Union soldiers would kill them or sell them abroad, to Cuba perhaps. Apocryphal newspaper articles accused northern troops of killing twenty slave children near Meridian, Mississippi, just "to get them out of the way." Accustomed to an abusive slave system, young children could actually imagine such cruelty in these unknown white northerners. "I didn't know if they was varmints or folks," recalled Alice Johnson many years later. Other slave children, even if they were unaware of the political ramifications of the invasion of the South, awaited the appearance of Union troops anxiously. On a Georgia plantation, white and black children alike longed for the northerners to show up. "We wanted 'em to come," said one former slave, "we knowed 'twould be fun to see 'em." When Union troops did appear, some of the smallest slave children, whose masters had said all manner of bad things about the approaching army, were surprised to see men. Other young African Americans were attracted to the bright uniforms and polished buttons of the invaders and to the blaring brass and sounding drums of their bands.[66]

Many northern soldiers took an interest in the little slaves who clustered around them. Some handed out sugar or candy and struck up conversations. After begging for a uniform button from every Yankee she saw, Sarah Anne Green finally got one from a man fascinated by her pretty blue eyes — proof to him, perhaps, of the abolitionists' assertion of masters' sexual congress with their slaves. Caroline Richardson, who was about ten when the war ended, was interviewed by a member of one of the Union regiments passing by her North Carolina home. He asked her how many shoes she received each year and what she wore during the summer. "When I tells him dat I ain't wear nothin' but a shirt, an' dat I goes barefooted in de summer," she remembered, "he cusses awful an' he damns my marster." Other soldiers seemed to enjoy their roles as agents of freedom. One instructed Thomas Lewis to tell his mistress to buy him a cap "or I'll come back and kill the whole family." Another ordered a young girl to never let anyone call her a "nigger" again. "You tell 'em dat you is a Negro and your name is Miss Liza Mixon." Later, when her master asked her, "What you doin' nigger?" she said "real pert like, 'I ain't no nigger, I'se a negro and I'm Miss Liza Mixon.'" Her master took after her with a switch, and when she sought refuge in her grandmother's cabin and told her what had happened, the old woman gave her a whipping for her impertinence. Other relationships bore no political connotations. Slave boys went for rides on Union cavalry horses, earned money fetching water for companies camped near plantations, and showed soldiers where caches of money and liquor were hidden. Foraging parties sometimes gave the clothes and even the food they looted from plantations to the slaves. One Yankee told Minnie Ross and her sister, "Little Negroes you are free there are no more masters and mistresses" and ordered them to help themselves to their owners' property, which they did.[67]

Yet this kindly, if rather ignorant, response of Union soldiers to their encounters with black children revealed only one of a wide range of attitudes. Although many former slave children remembered the invading Yankees in benign, even friendly terms, their most coherent memories of northerners were negative. Black children were able to separate in their own minds the freedom the war achieved for them and the Yankees who did the fighting. Many remembered their liberators as bullies and bandits who left pillaged plantations and hungry slaves in their wakes. They seemed little different from the marauding bands of Confederates that often competed with northerners to strip the countryside of food and livestock. "A holy war, they called it," complained a South Carolina freedman, "but they and [infamous Confederate general Joseph] Wheeler's men was a holy terror to dis part of de world." Striking examples of harassment and brutality emerge from the oral histories of black men and women who were children during the war and from the writings of the soldiers themselves.[68]

A letter appearing in the *Christian Recorder*, the African Methodist Episcopal Church newspaper published in Philadelphia, detailed with quiet perception a parable of black-white relations during the war. Written by a black soldier serving in Florida, it showed the whimsical nature of Yankees' treatment of the African Americans they met. The letter told the story of a little black boy who had escaped slavery and accompanied the Twenty-fifth Pennsylvania back to Philadelphia. He began working for the white officers of the Twenty-fifth U.S. Colored Troops when they were in training at Camp William Penn and went with the unit into the deep South. Once there, he got into some kind of trouble and lost his job. Now, wrote the soldier, he went from company to company begging food. "You know how it is with some of our white friends," the correspondent wrote bitterly, "they will pretend to think a great deal of you, but they carry two faces under one hat." They quickly turn against a black "friend" at "the least improper thing you do." [69]

Most victims' encounters with Yankees were brief and unthinking. Yankees blithely wrote about locking terrified black youngsters in a dark room, laughing when a pan of burned beans scalded a hungry boy's mouth, and repeatedly dunking a small child headfirst into a barrel of molasses. A squad of soldiers kept telling little Charlie McClendon that they would give him a pistol if he came back tomorrow. "They had me runnin' back there every day and I never did get one," he complained years later. Apparently taking their cue from the minstrel shows popular throughout the North, when the invaders took over a plantation, they would often herd the slaves, including the children, together and force them to sing and dance. When one boy refused to dance, "dey puts him barefooted on a hot piece of tin an' believe me he did dance." Others threatened black children when they refused to show them where jewelry and other valuables were hidden. Union troops repeatedly came onto the plantation where Nelly Gray lived. They would often "pint the gun at me jest to hear me holler and cry." They whipped Louise Prayer's grandmother, forced Charlie Rigger's older brother to go with them, apparently as a servant, and kidnapped Mandy Leslie's mother, leaving the young girl crying along the side of the road. Eager for plunder, soldiers rarely worried about what would happen after they continued on their march. On one plantation a young girl finally told her inquisitors where her mistress's valuables were hidden. When he discovered this betrayal, her master hanged her for disloyalty.[70]

Although most of these incidents were committed by individuals or small squads of soldiers detached from the main bodies of northern troops, one of the worst atrocities committed by Union troops against black southerners occurred during the famous March to the Sea. Sherman's men frequently stole the property and shot the livestock of the African Americans they encountered, but hundreds of black refugees, including numerous children, nevertheless attached themselves to the army. When the Fourteenth Corps crossed Ebenezer Creek between Augusta and Savannah, its commander, the aptly named Gen. Jefferson C. Davis, ordered the pontoon bridge taken up immediately, before the column of contrabands could cross. This doomed them to recapture or death. Many drowned trying to swim the creek, while others were killed by Joe Wheeler's Confederate cavalry or by southern guerillas. Union troops abandoned hundreds of contrabands when redeployment mandated the evacuation of Rome, Georgia; the wives and children of black troops, many of whom were members of the Fourth U.S. Colored Troops who had been captured and put in Confederate prisons or work camps, were left to fend for themselves. Some staggered back to their former masters, ragged and hungry. Buffeted by abuse and betrayal, even at the hands of their liberators, it is not surprising that many slave children feared Union troops. Even black soldiers inspired terror among some young slaves. Jane Osbrook described a visit to her Arkansas plantation of a regiment of U.S. Colored Troops who, she recalled, were "so tall and so black and had red eyes. . . . I never was so scared in my life." Other former slave children remembered Yankees more rationally, but with feelings of contempt. Hannah Irwin remembered seventy years after the war that a Yankee had asked her "what wuz dem white flowers in de fiel'? You'd think," she said to an interviewer disgustedly, "dat a gentmen wid all dem decorations on hisself woulda knowed a fiel' of cotton." "I suppose," she sighed, "dem Yankees wuz all right in dere place, but dey neber belong in the South."[71]

Incidents such as these demonstrate the power of race in nineteenth-century America. The truism that many northern soldiers were not, in their own minds, fighting to destroy the institution of slavery has an equally well known corollary: many northern soldiers felt no sympathy for the African Americans they came across while campaigning in the South. They cared little for the child victims of slavery and conducted themselves accordingly. However, they tended to strike up very different relationships with the white children of their avowed enemies.

Southern children who grew up to become memoirists commonly described their encounters with northern soldiers. They naturally feared their first contact with the invaders. The terrifying stories of children captured by stereotypically "savage" Native Americans in Peter Parley's widely read *Child's History* shaped the fears of one southern girl. "My hair 'stood on end,' " remembered Sallie Hunt, "when I thought of the Yankees tying the children up in bags and knocking their brains out against a tree." As northern armies approached New Orleans, Grace King shuddered when she thought of the "pictures of captured cities of the Bible where men and women were cut through with spears and swords, and children were dashed into walls." First encounters with the invaders could be a bit of a letdown, even for children expecting the worst; a young Missourian was amazed to find that the Yankees he spotted were men, for she had expected them to "be some dreadful kind of animals!"[72]

Even after it became apparent that the mass murder of children was not Federal policy, southern children still resented the Yankee occupation of the South and showed remarkable loyalty to a Confederate government that had failed to protect them. Yet the occupiers and the occupied could not deny forever a common language, a shared ethnicity, and human nature, and they often formed workable, if ambiguous, relationships. Southern children, leading with their hearts rather than their heads, demonstrated the same mixture of feelings as their mothers and fathers, but their normal curiosity and natural thirst for attention left them vulnerable to kindly Yankees.[73]

As Emmie Sublett of Richmond admitted in a letter to a friend, she had "expected the Yanks would treat us so much worse than they really did." The well-dressed and orderly Union soldiers setting up camp outside Gallatin, Tennessee, greeted Opie Read and his playmates "with good humor." A Wisconsin soldier told Opie about killing a bear, and the young Rebel smuggled him a piece of peach pie; he heard a Yankee sergeant reciting a line Opie recognized from *McGuffey's Reader* as a Shakespearean quote and gave him an old hen for supper. A pair of adolescent sisters in Chapel Hill, North Carolina, had for some time had "great fun" planning what they "would do and say to them" if Yankees appeared in their town. "We decided we'd sing our most patriotic songs, letting them know there was life in the old land yet and patriotism in the hearts of her daughters." When Federal forces did arrive, however, "our tune changed and a deathly pallor settled upon our young faces." A friendly guard soon asked them to perform for him, "which we took as our opportunity to carry out our plans." Their "rebel concert" included "The Southern Girl," "The Homespun," and their entire "repertoire of songs." Although the performance was originally planned as an act of defiance, the northern soldier "was charmed with the sentiment as he never had heard the songs before and did not know how dearly the Southern girls loved their Dixie land." He proved to be a "faithful protector" by sharing his rations with the family. Other Yankees gave hard-pressed families wounded horses, which could be nursed back to health and sold for much-needed cash.[74]

As northern soldiers and southern children mingled, they often became fast friends, although the youngsters made it clear that they remained ardent Confederates. When asked if they were afraid of the Yankees, they might, like one Alabama girl, respond smartly, "No sir, not when they talk right." After Union troops reached Savannah, Georgia, late in 1864, a one-armed officer on Gen. William T. Sherman's staff took three-year-old Juliette Low, future founder of the Girls Scouts of America, on his knee. She asked how he had lost his arm. " 'Got it shot off by a Rebel!' " was the laconic explanation. " 'I s'pose my father did it,' " Juliette artlessly exclaimed, " 'he shot lots of Yankees.' "[75]

The readiness with which "enemy" soldiers attached themselves to children was directly related to their loneliness for their own young ones. When Federal forces occupied Front Royal, Virginia, in May 1862, the Buck children, "although freely declaring their rebellious inclinations," nevertheless "made themselves great favorites with their new acquaintances." The soldiers freely handed out candy and oranges, while the officers, according to the oldest Buck daughter, "seem glad to be in the midst of little children again." Cold shoulders soon melted in the face of earnest friendliness. Dosia Williams's aloofness collapsed when the commander of the troops occupying the Williams plantation offered to show her the picture in a gold locket in return for a kiss. "I must have descended from Pandora," wrote Dosia years later, "for I could not stand it." She pecked him on the cheek and he showed her a "miniature of a lovely little girl about my age." Dosia's older sister refused the offer because, as she said, her father "told me not to kiss Yankees!" The "colonel's eyes twinkled. 'And don't you ever do it!'" he exclaimed. "'You stand by what your Pere tells you.'" "After that," he and the Williams girls became "great friends, and his aides brought us candy and made much of us." After learning how much the soldiers "wanted to see their children back up North," the Williams girls "excepted these particular Yankees from our fear and hatred."[76]

Most children seemed to be able to reconcile their loyalty to the cause with their unexpectedly cordial relationships with soldiers fighting to destroy that cause. Yet as the poignant reaction of a five-year-old Floridian shows, fraternizing with the enemy sometimes smacked of treason. Little Eddie Bradford eagerly clambered into the lap of an officer who asked him to "come and talk to me awhile, I have a little son at home just your size." They chatted pleasantly until the youngster asked him, "Don't you hate Yankees?" When his new friend admitted that he was a Yankee, little Eddie burst into tears and ran to his grandfather. "I sat in his lap and just a month ago they killed my . . . dear uncle Mack," he sobbed. "Do you think, grandpa, that this Yankee killed him?" At first giving in to his childish curiosity, Eddie's brief visit and his intimate friendliness — "I sat in his lap" — with a man who might have been the cause of so much family sorrow, seemed to be the worst kind of betrayal.[77]

As Eddie's experience shows, ambivalence characterized the encounters between southern children and northern soldiers, who demonstrated both cruelty and compassion. As Union troops swarmed into Columbia, South Carolina, a small girl played with her puppy on the front steps of her home. A passing Union soldier brained the dog with the butt of his rifle, and the child naturally burst into tears. Moments later another soldier stopped, consoled her, converted a cigar box into a tiny coffin, and dug a grave for the martyred pet.[78]

On a few occasions military discipline collapsed, and Confederate children were viciously attacked by northern soldiers. Rumors flew around the South of alleged atrocities, some involving children. An unverified newspaper story claimed Union troops had murdered a toddler because he was named for a noted Confederate general; a Confederate officer in Florida passed along a story that three Yankees had taken a ten-year-old girl into "the scrub & ravesed her"; and a Louisiana woman reported that soldiers raped and beat a girl so badly that she never regained her sanity. A chilling description of the near rape of a Virginia teenager shows how violence could strike any southern child. When men that Maria Fleet believed to be Yankee deserters and stragglers raided Green Mount plantation in June 1864, two of them locked themselves in a room with her thirteen-year-old daughter. The girl escaped unharmed after she offered to show her attackers where the family's valuables were hidden. On another occasion a drunken Federal guard in Lexington, Virginia, seized the four-year-old brother of Rose Page Pendleton and threatened to shoot him. The boy cried to his mother, "Mother, won't you save me?" but the soldier threatened to kill her, too. A passing Yankee colonel managed to end the standoff.[79]

These incidents show in stark relief the complex nature of the relationship between northern soldiers and southern children. Most men and most children avoided the worst conflicts; in fact, many were able to avoid one another altogether throughout the war. But when they did meet, when battle-hardened veterans ran across helpless children, sometimes conflicting instincts and behaviors collided. Robert Jay Lifton highlights exactly this kind of tension in GIs serving in Vietnam. Lifton describes an almost unfathomable course of events after the massacre at My Lai, when the same men who had murdered dozens of children and their parents in cold blood offered young survivors food and other aid almost immediately afterward. Lifton explains the unexplainable by arguing that, in this case, children acted as "resensitizing agents," reawakening in jaded soldiers "parental-nurturing impulses" buried under the stress of war. Children often seemed to have had the same effect on soldiers during the Civil War.[80]

Despite the excitement and drama and tragedy children encountered whenever the war came near, they exhibited a remarkable determination to maintain a sense of normality in their lives. They held taffy pulls, concocted mudpies, and made paper dolls out of pictures in ragged magazines even as they crouched in the caves of Vicksburg. During the siege of Atlanta, ten-year-old Carrie Berry tried to sustain her usual routines, including keeping a cheerful diary, but found it difficult in between sprints for the bombproof. She frequently wished that school and church would begin again and quietly reported on her tenth birthday that "I did not have a cake times were too hard so I celebrated with ironing." A good day was a day with little or no shelling or a treat like the bunch of "nice grapes" her aunt somehow scrounged. When the siege ended with the evacuation of the city by the Confederates, Carrie welcomed the quiet and shrugged off the suggestion that everyone would have to move, happy to have a chance to play with a friend for the first time in six weeks. For all intents and purposes, even though her father was briefly in trouble with Confederate authorities because he was among the handful of residents who did not leave Atlanta, Carrie picked up her normal girl's life after the siege ended, doing chores, sewing frocks for her dolls, and welcoming the chance to return to school and church.[81]

Of course, it is important to remember that even as children agonized over the fates of brothers and fathers fighting in Virginia or Tennessee or Louisiana, awaited apprehensively the approach of invading Yankees, or worried about where their next meal would come from, they also had to face normal—and some not so normal—childhood crises. They fretted about school and toys and boys and girls. Cora Warren Beck, around eight when the war started, endured her brother's enlistment in the Confederate army and occupation of her North Carolina home by Federal troops, yet one of her primary concerns was the increasing abusiveness of her stepmother. Matters came to a head when she severely beat Cora's sister. After Cora revealed the attack to her father, he exploded, restricted his second wife's authority over his children, and insisted that they "go to [him] when we want anything." As a result, "The Step Mother keeps closer to her own room, and we are left to our father and the servants." At least until this climax in the Beck family drama, the war remained only a backdrop to this story of child abuse.[82]

In one of the surreal threads of Ambrose Bierce's nightmarish tapestry of the Civil War, a six-year-old boy strays into the woods surrounding his southern farm. Armed with a crude wooden sword, he routs his imaginary foes and pursues them into the forest and across a stream. He soon loses his way and, after a frightening encounter with a rabbit, takes refuge between two large rocks. "Still grasping his toy sword," the little boy "sobbed himself to sleep." In the distance rumbles "a strange muffled thunder," while back home his family and their slaves search miserably for the missing warrior.

The nightmare begins when the lost boy awakens and tries to find his way home. He—and the reader—are unaware that while he slept a great battle swept over and around him. As he makes his way through the tangled undergrowth, now darkening in the misty twilight, he comes upon a small army of shattered men, crawling, creeping, dragging themselves toward the creek. Unknowing, the boy happily moves "among them freely, going from one to another and peering into their faces with childish curiosity." He laughs merrily at these seeming clowns, until one of them pushes him to the ground and rears up, revealing, instead of a lower jaw, "a great red gap fringed with hanging shreds of flesh and splinters of bone."

Sobered, the boy assumes the leadership of this sad and unnatural company. They make their way to the creek, where a fire raging somewhere on the far side attracts him and he splashes ahead of his men. Discovering a building blazing wildly, he gleefully feeds the fire with his sword and plays in its dancing shadows. Then he begins to recognize the outbuildings dotting the clearing. "Stupefied by the power of revelation," he realizes that this is—was—his home. He staggers around the ravaged homestead and stumbles across the body of a woman, half her head blown away. "The child," whom the reader now knows to be a deaf-mute, "moved his little hands, making wild uncertain gestures" and "uttered a series of inarticulate and indescribable cries" before standing "motionless, with quivering lips, looking down upon the wreck" of his dead mother.[83]

In another fictional Confederate home, three young creole girls wait impatiently on a Louisiana bayou for the war to come to them. Their French governess, the granddaughter of a captain in Napoleon's army, had filled their heads with images of glorious combat. "When a war broke out in their own country," wrote Grace King, who as a girl had left occupied New Orleans for just such an isolated place, "they could hardly credit their good fortune." Patriotism completes their childish perception of war, and they quickly learn about "State rights, Federal limits, monitors and fortresses, proclamations, Presidents, recognitions, and declarations." Yet when they evacuate their threatened city for the country, the war slips beyond the horizon, they are forced to subsist on old, unreliable war news, and they feel hopelessly left out of the excitement. Sadly, "there was an absence of the simplest requirements for war."

Romantic adventure finally arrives in the form of a squad of blue-coated soldiers, who lock three scruffy Confederates in the smokehouse and whose appearance encourages most of the slaves on the small plantation to slip away. Angry and enchanted and terrified, the two older girls, grown to teenagers on this peaceful backwater, fulfill their martial dreams, free the captives, and nurse the wounded Yankee captain when he faints from the loss of blood. The oldest girl even makes a cherished souvenir of a secret kiss from one of the released heroes.

The bubble bursts when the girls discover a series of muddled identities worthy of Shakespeare. The wounded "Yankee" is actually a shirttail cousin of theirs, a Confederate partisan with a dangerous, if local, reputation. The escaped "Rebels" are actually Union soldiers. The cousin fails to elaborate on the ill-fated ruse but announces even worse news: Lee has surrendered; the war is over.[84]

Although both of these stories are set in the South, they represent many of the experiences of Civil War children. Some faced the sharp edge of war; others confronted it as refugees and laborers, as friends and enemies of Union and Confederate soldiers, or as consumers of war news and war literature. Some were merely romantic patriots who barely participated in the real-life drama. Although most children were not so absolutely crushed as Bierce's nameless protagonist, some were; like the passionate girls on King's Louisiana bayou, their innocence was challenged and their naïveté blasted. But the war also freed them from ignorance and shoved them into the world of their parents. These personal experiences varied sharply, depending on one's race and allegiance. But, together with children's books and stories and their correspondence with fathers and brothers in the armies of the competing nations, those formative episodes politicized children and pointed them toward a wide range of responses to the Civil War.

5
Rabid Partisans among Their Playmates
Children Respond to the Civil War

Personal experiences of all kinds, from the lethal to the trivial, shaped children's loyalties and political participation, and their responses varied from the rhetorical to the violent. Girls of all ages claimed, as grown women, to have been swept off their feet by handsome patriots. Little Maggie Campbell had a memorable love-at-first-sight encounter with a Union drummer boy on a Pittsburgh streetcar; she promptly proposed. Twelve-year-old Elizabeth Preston fell head-over-heels for a secessionist cousin visiting her family in Lexington, Virginia. Four-year-old Nannie Belle Maury turned down a Union soldier's offer of candy, saying, "No, thank you; Yankee candy would choke me!" By her third birthday in October 1863, a young New Englander could sing "We Will Rally round the Flag, Boys" and "Johnny Comes Marching Home"; when Lee surrendered two years later, she breathlessly witnessed the celebration and, according to her mother, "marched around expressing all the joy she could." Howard Pyle, the future illustrator, began his career at age eight with a watercolor of a "bandy-legged zouave" waving a flag and threatening a "wretched Confederate" with a sword. The smoky background blazed with explosions, and the patriotic caption screamed, "Ded! Ded! Ded is the [se]cesioner!"[1]

The behavior of these Civil War children indicates the extent to which they breathed the politically charged atmosphere of wartime America. Despite the vast differences in how northern and southern, as well as black and white, children experienced the war, they were united in their responses to the crisis. Magazines, novels, and schoolbooks offered children examples of how they could honorably and usefully support their country. From them they learned to identify good and evil, Yankee and Rebel, and the right and wrong ways to act. Children always had to learn that hard work and prayer and loyalty and obedience were important, but the war now transformed those qualities into patriotic necessities. If children's reading matter awakened young patriots, letters from their fathers, which also educated and directed children's actions, energized them. As children strove to match the expectations raised by stories and books and to perform the duties set forth by fathers, they became a part of the struggle, not just as victims or spectators but as politicians and home-front warriors.

Obviously, the political choices made by children could sometimes be haphazard, even whimsical. But not all children depended on fate or on chance encounters with handsome soldiers to confirm their loyalty to one side or the other. In fact, geography and family loyalty limited most children to a single option. But all Civil War children had at least one unique experience: the moment they became aware that they had an "enemy," and that they were part of a larger community fighting that enemy. It could happen on streetcars or on street corners; sometimes it happened because parents took it upon themselves to give their children a political education. Fifteen-year-old Susan Bradford's father took her to see "history in the making" at the Florida secession convention in January 1861, where she proudly wore a Palmetto cockade, heard the fire-eater Edmund Ruffin of Virginia, and watched the final vote and the signing of Florida's ordinance of secession. After a long evening spent crouching in a corner while his Unionist father debated a secessionist colleague, a young Mississippian dreamt of exploding Yankee gunboats, "with flying smokestacks and timbers, and mutilated Yankees." Next morning, now a confirmed Confederate, he woke up "in a new world." His parents' decision to let him stay up long past his bedtime became a turning point in his life; he believed that by witnessing this national debate in microcosm, by choosing for the first time in his life a political position, the eleven year old "became a man."[2]

His political coming of age gave this young Mississippi Rebel confidence, but many children were made to feel unsure, picking their way through the political minefields laid by the conflicting loyalties of their families and communities. In the divided border state of Maryland, the mixed allegiances of neighbors and

relatives instilled a dangerous confusion. Surrounded by Unionist families in an area near Baltimore where few people owned
slaves, Lizette Woodworth's mother hid a portrait of Beauregard in
a closet, and her cousin wore red and white "Confederate" under-
wear. "Always," remembered Lizette, "our elders kept on whispering, whispering." Their isolation and the conspiratorial atmosphere in which they lived frightened Lizette and her younger
sister so much that sometimes they "were afraid to go to bed at
night."[3]

Another house divided belonged to the Egans of Philadelphia.
All of his life Maurice, who turned nine the year the war began,
had watched his father and mother argue politics. By 1860 his
father favored Abraham Lincoln and his mother, Stephen A.
Douglas; throughout the war Mrs. Egan was more Copperhead
than Unionist. Both parents tried to influence young Maurice by
reading newspapers aloud at the breakfast table, although Mrs.
Egan would wait until Mr. Egan left for work to read the controversial speeches of Clement Vallandigham from the *Congressional
Record*. Even during the war, southern friends taught the children songs like "The Bonnie Blue Flag." Despite his schizophrenic
upbringing, Maurice seemed to relish the politically inspired tension in his boyhood home, and he generally, with other boys his
age, cheered for Union victories and mourned the assassination of
Abraham Lincoln.[4]

Nurseries of Patriotism

Political scientists have discovered that parents' political attitudes deeply influence the politicization of children, a fact born
out by the development of opinions in Civil War children.[5] Adults
also propagated their political gospel in the schools, where northern and southern students participated in numerous patriotic ceremonies. The chief form by which "patriotism was pumped into"
the students at one New York City school was through daily re-
hearsals of a vast repertoire of war songs, ranging from "The
Star-Spangled Banner" and the "Battle Hymn of the Republic" to
"In My Prison Cell I Sit" and "Marching through Georgia." Early
in the war, public and private schools sponsored public flag rais-
ings, which included speeches by local dignitaries and patriotic
airs sung by students. Early in 1862 students in the Rockland,

Delaware, public schools staged a pageant in which thirteen girls representing the original thirteen states sang the national anthem, while a squad of boys performed the military drills they practiced every day at school.[6]

Displays of patriotism were not relegated to special occasions. Students in some schools had weekly "speaking days," when they delivered compositions such as "War sometimes a duty" and "Who says we have failed?" in addition to well-known poems such as "Barbara Frietchie," "Sheridan's Ride," and the tearjerker "Home News in Battle-Time." The closing exercises at Philadelphia's Girls' High and Normal School included performances of "The Soldier's Letter" and "The Crisis," while southern students worked their patriotism into end-of-the-year college "albums" in the form of original compositions, essays, poems, and stories.[7]

Of course, children from Democratic families might not appreciate the enforced patriotism; for others, simple schoolboy orneriness sometimes turned speaking days into farces. The diary of Charles Stratton, a student at the Boston Public Latin School, suggests that, at least for this teenaged, Democratic smart aleck, the constant bombardment of patriotic sentiment could easily become a joke. In June 1862 the boys taking part in a declamatory exercise performed "old worn-out pieces" halfheartedly and for laughs rather than sober reflection. By the time the last speaker closed with the rather solemn "Glory, Glory, Hallelujah," according to Stratton, "the fellows were laughing . . . and having a good time."[8]

Perhaps the songs and speeches meant more to African American children, who may have sensed the war's potential effects on their lives. Black students in both the North and the occupied South also performed songs and dramas with war themes. A concert by African American schoolchildren in New York City closed with their rendition of "The Song of the Contrabands, 'Oh let my people go,' " while according to a newspaper report of a school exhibition, black students "kept the house in a roar of laughter" with the dialogue "Bluster and Fuster, or ups and downs of Dixie." Northern "schoolmarms" on the Sea Islands indoctrinated their black students into a sort of "Father Abraham" cult. Laura Towne's Sea Island students entertained a July 4 gathering of freedmen and army officers with the "Star-Spangled Banner," while students in other schools sang famous war songs, including the northern children's favorite, "We'll Hang Jeff Davis on a Sour

Apple Tree" (sung to the tune of "John Brown's Body"). Teachers frequently offered politically charged material through songs and stories about Lincoln, the great emancipator; Brown, the martyred Yankee; and Toussaint, the Caribbean hero. They instructed their black pupils about their own history and the history of slavery, including the somewhat misleading fact that Virginians brought slaves to America in the same year that the Pilgrims arrived in Plymouth without slaves. Students at the Cairo, Illinois, contraband camp were drilled to answer partisan questions such as who the president was and why he should be reelected.[9]

The political assumptions displayed in such carefully choreographed events did not go unchallenged, and schools in both the North and the South became battlegrounds for opposing viewpoints among students, administrators, and parents. These rather innocent and usually adult-directed activities became more controversial when political or military authorities got involved. After Union troops occupied New Orleans, a running fight ensued between Gens. Benjamin Butler and Nathaniel Banks and the parents and teachers in the New Orleans public school system. The military government reopened the schools and established loyalty requirements for teachers and for course content and, on occasions such as the 1864 inauguration of a Unionist government, drafted hundreds of schoolchildren to take part in the ceremonies. Throughout the period of occupation, teachers and parents of unrepentant Rebels fought these plans. The Federal anthems only slowly replaced southern songs, and U.S. history only gradually subsumed "Confederate" history. Some teachers taught their students to call the invaders "Yankee scum" and, according to the Unionist newspaper the *Daily Delta*, "repeated . . . every idle tale that could feed the hopes of rebellion." Administrators of the school system also continued to pay the salaries of teachers serving in the Confederate army. In a case that attracted much attention in the local press, officials expelled five children whose parents refused to let them participate in the inaugural concert.[10]

Federal authorities in the Crescent City also attempted to purge rebellion from the private schools, many of which carried on as though the city had never been captured. At Madame Locquet's school, for instance, students wore mourning ribbons on the first anniversary of the city's fall. A student named Martha Moore bitterly reported the surprise inspection by "two coarse looking men, whom, I should think from their appearance had not been washed or combed in six weeks." They were Yankees come to inspect Madame Locquet's school for "secession emblems, flags, or anything treasonable." The men ripped a few pages out of books and cast several threatening looks toward Martha, then stomped out. She had drawn a small Confederate flag on a composition, and another girl sat through the ordeal "hugging" a book with a flag on it, declaring that she would not give it up. Although the intrusion was meant "to restore the Union feeling," it had, of course, just the opposite effect. Afterward, Martha "hate[d] the Northerners with a deeper, and more lasting hatred, than ever before."[11]

Far to the North similar struggles consumed the small city of Dayton, Ohio, dissenter Clement Vallandigham's hometown, where "Union Leaguers" wore Union army uniform buttons to school while "Butternuts" sported halved walnut shells. This sparked confrontations among adults as well as children, particularly in the high school, where the conflict escalated into fistfights and rock throwing by the spring of 1863. "Loyal" adolescents joined Union League clubs and sought to eliminate the "butternut charm" from their school. Efforts by administrators to end the violence by eliminating the wearing of all insignias sparked criticism from both sides, but especially among the more numerous Union parents in the city. The partisan battle raged through schoolyards and the columns of local newspapers and became embroiled in the rioting that followed the arrest of Vallandigham in May. Eventually the issue died down with the demise of strident antiwar feeling. Political violence also broke out in Chicago's high school, where the appearance of several Copperhead badges led to a brief but bloody brawl among the boys, after which "black eyes, scratched faces, and bloody noses, were quite plentiful."[12]

Schools were obviously not havens for freedom of speech and political dissent in either section. Predictably, at St. Anthony's Orphanage in politically divided Baltimore, the "warlike spirit" that possessed the children led Unionists and secessionists to bicker and wrestle at every recess. The children of southern Unionists, in particular, faced considerable antagonism because of their parents' choices. A Nashville diarist reported that her twelve-year-old sister Lettie was the only "Union girl in the whole school" but held "her own bravely." Opie Read, the son of a strident East Tennessee Unionist, did more than hold his own in the face of attacks by "secesh" bullies; he got even by ambushing his enemies separately and defeating them in detail. Even in some parts of the North, Unionists were in the minority. Southern sympathizers among the schoolboys at the Burlington, New Jersey, school attended by U. S. Grant's sons gave the general's boys "a disconcerting amount of . . . hostile attention." Fred, who was about thirteen, took it upon himself to battle every challenger and, at least according to his admiring little brother Jesse, won every fight.[13]

These sometimes violent outbursts suggest that children were not merely acting out their parents' politics or responding to the policies of school or military officials. More evidence of the political independence of schoolchildren surfaced at Missouri's Danville Female Academy. The students came from both Union and Confederate families, but politics took a back seat to the community formed at the school. When Confederate troops occupied the town early in the war, both "Union" and "Secessionist" girls entertained the soldiers for most of an evening. When an approaching Union column was spotted, the Rebels quickly evacuated the town, followed by the Union girls' gleeful cries of "skedaddle" and by the southern girls' angry tears. However, when a gang of Bill Anderson's guerillas sacked Danville in 1864, members of both political factions at the school successfully united to plead for the life of one of their favorite teachers, a Union man.[14]

The Spirit of the Times

Although many children obviously chose political sides based on juvenile crushes, emotionally charged incidents, or their parents' response to the sectional conflict, others were more thoughtful. Personal tragedy or loss could change the political orientation of mature children. James Sullivan had relished the Democratic parades and "boys' electioneering by fisticuffs" during the election of 1860 and remembered wondering how a local minister rumored to be a "Nabbo-Lisha-Ness" by his friends could consider wanting to "marry his daughter to a nigger." During the war, however, his Democratic loyalty crumbled. James had initially supported Gen. George B. McClellan for president because his beloved older brother Tom, a lieutenant killed at South Mountain, had been a loyal follower of "Little Mac." But during the 1864 campaign the Democrats' argument that the war had been a failure shook James to his bones. How could he admit that his brother's death had been meaningless? "Tom had died for the Union," he decided, "and it must be preserved." Torn between party and country, Sullivan "was continually in a fever of uncertainty as to my political duty," even though he would not be able to vote for several more years.[15]

Ambiguity rarely characterized Civil War children's responses to the war, however. Typical of the steadfastness of youngsters' loyalty was the attitude displayed by a sixteen-year-old school-girl in Gallatin, Tennessee, whose two older brothers were in the Confederate army. After Union troops occupied the town, Alice Williamson filled her diary with calumny against the Yankees, de-tailing alleged atrocities—the shooting of wounded Confederate prisoners, for instance—and reviling the local Union commander. "O, the horrible wretches!" exclaimed a Richmond girl in a letter to a friend soon after the occupation of the city by Union forces. "I can't think of a name dreadful enough to call them." Even the youngest children refused to back down from their south-ern patriotism. When northern troops threatened Warrenton, Vir-ginia, a five year old prayed for Jesus to "send your angels down to bring me to Heaven for I don't want to stay here if this is *Yankee-land*."[16]

Such examples of childish loyalty amply show how deeply chil-dren immersed themselves in Civil War politics. Georgian Andrew Miller remembered that "the small boy" became a politician, "as unflinching and uncompromising in his imaginary convictions" as his father. His principles were "imbibed at home," from where he went "forth a most rabid partisan among his playmates." So did the girls, of course, and very young children of both sexes pro-jected their politics through name-calling and playground bicker-ing. A Minnesotan remembered that she and her playmates knew nothing of "the tragedy and sorrow" of the war but believed they were "unquestionably more violent and unrestrained" than their parents. "Epithets such as 'Rebel,' 'Copperhead,' 'Black Republi-can,' and 'Mudsill' were flung about with the utmost freedom by the children," she recalled, "and the certainty of being able at any minute to stir up a fight simply by marching up and down aggres-sively and singing 'We'll hang Jeff Davis on a sour apple tree' filled one with a sense of power that was indescribable."[17]

The war absolutely dominated the thoughts of a thirteen-year-old boy living in southern Virginia. Even as he battled schoolboy

Latin, Archer Vaughan reflected long and hard on the secession crisis. He filled his diary with politics, war news, and his own confident opinions. He was an active member of the local slave patrol and, when the war first began, led an apparently bona fide militia company called the "Young Guard." He occasionally devoted an entire entry to his often violent opinions about the war. On May 5, 1861, for instance, he predicted that "a *bloody War* is inevitable." Consequently he believed many of the slaves were "ripe for open rebelion [*sic*]" and attacked the Republicans' "false philanthropy" as "revolting to the christian religion" because its purpose was specifically to incite just such a rebellion. A month later he declared that only "the bayonet" could settle the issue. His obsession with the war aged Archer, whose diary entries sounded like those of an adult fire-eater. On Easter Sunday 1862 he admitted that his "worst forebodings as to our fate were being realized." He pointed to the "imbecility of the government," "corruption in high places," and confusion in the army as the causes of the disastrous defeats "we constantly meet with." No doubt inspired by the holy day on which he wrote, he feared that "the enormity of our national sins has called forth the awful fist of Almighty God." [18]

After taking a political stand, northern and southern children acted on their convictions in ways ranging from the trivial to the martial. On a national fast day in April 1863 a Louisville secessionist and schoolgirl defiantly recorded in her diary that she had eaten "an uncommonly hearty dinner," while other girls gave up sleigh rides with handsome Yankee officers, pleaded with Confederate soldiers for souvenir uniform buttons, collected Confederate flags, and avoided even walking near the hated Yankees occupying southern cities. When the Confederates passed by the College of St. James, a boys' prep school near Hagerstown, Maryland, a number of youths ran away to join the army, although most sheepishly returned in a day or two. Well-known diarist and War Department clerk John B. Jones insisted that despite the steep decline in his family's standard of living, his children remained "more enthusiastic for independence than ever. Daily I hear them say they would gladly embrace death rather than the rule of the Yankee." Although they might have been well-coached by their determined father, they did sacrifice their traditional Christmas celebrations, and on one occasion Jones's youngest daughter sold her earrings in order to buy shoes.[19]

"My sweet heart is gone to war," wrote an Alabama schoolgirl, "& if he never comes back I am determined to die an old maid for I would not marry a coward." Although she was well under the age of consent, she showed that one of the favorite ways to demonstrate loyalty was to demand a high standard of patriotism in everyone. Indeed, many young Rebels saved their most vitriolic diatribes for disloyal southerners. Young ladies in occupied Natchez were quick to slight classmates spied walking with Union soldiers. Cora Owens frequently commented on the appearances and political persuasions of her classmates. At the beginning of the 1863 winter term she seemed surprised that "Mollie Parker, Union as she is, looked sweet & even pretty to me," perhaps because she heard Mollie singing "The Bonnie Blue Flag." Cora disapproved when another girl primped for visiting Federal officers. Nannie Haskins, a teenaged Tennesseean, endured the Federal occupation of her hometown with gritted teeth, sprinkling her diary with a hard-shell patriotism that few adults could match. She complained about the arrogance and cruelty of Federal officers and wartime fraternization by some of her schoolmates with the occupiers but fell especially hard on those who failed to do their duty. Early in 1862 she attended a party at which the only "young gentlemen" were "fireside rangers"—men who had evaded military duty— "and I had almost *as soon* see so many Yankees."[20]

Of course, northern children were exposed to fewer situations in which their loyalty and perseverance could be tested and exhibited so directly, but one form of political discourse reserved almost entirely to young Yankees was the newspapers they published for the enjoyment and edification of themselves, their families, and their hometowns. Mixing parody with politics and news with commentary, child journalists professed their political creeds in the confident, purple rhetoric of nineteenth-century editors. Overwhelmingly pro-Union, pro-Lincoln, and antislavery, these amateur papers reflected the ideas and attitudes of most children's magazines. "Don't give up the ship, boys!" urged the young editors of the Concord, Massachusetts, *Observor* early in the fall of 1862. "Stand by her to the last hour. . . . War must become the daily vocation of us all," lest "we . . . be conquered and forever kept beneath the foot of Slavery and Oppression." The Worcester *Once a Fortnight* threw its support behind the Lincoln administration during the 1864 campaign, arguing that only Lincoln's reelection would secure "an honorable peace, the restoration of the Union, and the abolition of Slavery."[21]

The Newark High School *Athenaeum* closely followed wartime politics. Its motto — United We Stand, Divided We Fall — broadcast the political principles of its student editors, who covered the election of 1864 with two extended pieces. One was a fairly straightforward description of rowdy electioneering in Newark, while another turned the canvass into a biblical parody. "Now it came to pass in the third year of the reign of Abraham the president," it began, "in the eleventh month on the third day of the month, that all the people on the north of the line, even the great line of Mason Dixon, gathered themselves together . . . to elect men who should go in and out before them, and who should speak for them." It went on to describe "Unionists," the "part adhered to Abraham," and "Copperheads," the "part adhered to him not," and the former's victory over the latter, after which "they had no more courage with which to contend against Abraham and his people." In a more serious vein the editors attacked slavery's "long catalogue of crime and blood-shed on the one side and of helpless suffering on the other." In a fashion reminiscent of the pamphlet-sized political speeches, one writer explained the long history of slavery in North America and blasted the South "for the course it has pursued in raising the traitors' hand against the Government." Complementing the articles on wartime politics were the sketches featured on the last page of each issue. Typical pictures included a band of angels unfurling a scroll that read, "In Memory of Our Soldiers and Sailors who on Land or at Sea Have Fallen for Liberty and Law"; a Union cavalryman plunging his sword through the breast of a Confederate opponent over the caption, "A Blow for the Flag"; and under the title "Fidelity," Union dead on a wooded battleground with a small dog lingering over the body of his master.[22]

Playgrounds into Parade Grounds

While few Civil War era children could proclaim their loyalty in print, most did insist on incorporating the conflict into their everyday lives. One of their most basic responses to the politically charged and sometimes dangerous war environment was to mimic the responses of their elders. They mustered their own military companies, learned the manual of arms, fought imaginary battles, and played "hospital." This universal behavior—imitating whatever they see or hear their parents do or say—is a basic step in the socialization of children. Play is a safe way to assimilate information, practice social skills, and take moral and emotional risks. It allows youngsters to achieve maturity, if only temporarily; to wreak vengeance, if only symbolically; and to master anxiety over stressful experiences, if only in simulation. In their play worlds, children can feel freedom as well as control, reliving pleasant experiences and reducing painful incidents to meaningful and bearable lessons and memories. In some cases, particularly in "dramatic play," happy endings can be invented, emotional release achieved, and frustrations and disappointments tempered.[23]

Children easily adapt war into their play and development because they accept it as just another trauma among childhood's normal stresses and strains. Dangers and fears spawned by war may replace traditional childhood fears of storms, the dark, and bogeymen. Since very young children are already in a "destructive" psychological phase, the destruction of war may not necessarily frighten them but spark what psychologists call a "primitive excitement" that leads them to destructive forms of play, or at least play that mimics destructive behavior. Youngsters seem to understand war more instinctively than peace; the former acquires concrete images almost naturally, while peace remains an abstract idea reflecting an inner state rather than relationships among groups. Children in even the most excruciating conditions have worked war into their play. Desensitized perhaps to the violence that surrounded them—literally or figuratively—Berlin children played "Border Patrol" and Irish children played "soldiers and terrorists." Incredibly, even child victims of the Holocaust attempted to rationalize the horror around them by playing games such as "Roll Call," "Gas Chamber," and "Returning the Clothing of the Dead."[24]

Nowhere were the social and psychological functions of play more apparent in the uncertain lives of Civil War children than in the ways even the youngest among them applied their experiences and fears to their games and pastimes. One of the most ubiquitous forms of play for American boys in the mid-nineteenth century was forming their own mock militia units and playing army. Antebellum artists had often posed young boys with military toys

Little boys — black and white — join in the martial festivities when a Woodstock, Virginia, company marches off to join the army. (Library of Congress)

and props, and wartime illustrators frequently showed boys and a few girls brandishing swords, wearing kepis at jaunty angles, and banging on miniature drums.[25] When military companies drilled and held parades, children naturally gravitated toward the excitement. According to the *Richmond Examiner*, after a home guard company finished drilling in the Confederate capital, several companies of little boys immediately took over the field. Boys in Culpeper County formed a sort of shadow company that practiced alongside their local heroes, the Little Fork Rangers, while in the first months of the conflict the older girls at Wesleyan Female College in Macon formed their own student company. Younger girls could also be enthusiastic little soldiers. The half-dozen sons and daughters of Rev. William Ward grabbed broomsticks and fire pokers and joined the eager young men he collected in his study to teach the rudiments of drill. "We could shoulder arms, carry arms, right-about face, guide right, and guide left, right wheel, left wheel, march, double-quick," and "keep step beautifully," according to his daughter Evelyn. Favoring such activities over more peaceful pastimes, Celine Fremaux and her brothers became so adept at the manual of arms that they gathered at a nearby field to heckle green recruits as they stumbled through their maneuvers.[26]

Enthused by martial sights and sounds, even African American children got into the act. Madison Brinn of Kentucky longed to be a soldier. "I didn't care what side," he remembered as an old man. "I jis' wants a gun and a hoss and be a sojer." Slave children excitedly watched local companies drill and tried to reproduce the military bearing of masters with officers' commissions. Yankee prisoners of war in Charleston witnessed an unusual performance in the war's first autumn when, according to the *Mercury*, "a band of woolly headed juvenile darkies . . . kept up a lively marching and counter-marching under their windows, to the jolly strains of Dixie Land." Whenever the white children on the Ward plantation drilled, so did the black children, who served as privates to the white "officers." On another plantation white boys threatened their black playmates with dire consequences if they refused the parts of despised Yankee soldiers. Slave children's mimickry of Confederate soldiers—one North Carolina slave remembered beating tin pans and marching to the tune of "Wheeler's Cavalry"—was often misconstrued as loyalty to their masters and to the South. "Shucks," recalled Emma Stone, "we . . . care nothin' 'bout Wheeler 'cept what we hyar, an that ain't so good."[27]

Yankee children were at least as likely as southerners to catch war fever. According to an early history of the war in Illinois, after Fort Sumter, "each school had its play-ground transformed into a parade-ground, while small drums, miniature cannon and harmless small arms were the playthings of the nursery." This was certainly true in Galena, where Julia Dent Grant reported that even as "the men were holding meetings and calling for volunteers," the "boys were playing at war, wearing military caps, beating small drums, guarding the crossings, and demanding countersigns." Early in the war many boys skipped school and household chores, hoping to get in on the excitement. The Ann Arbor, Michigan, *Argus* complained that too many boys were running loose in the streets. "They are not wanted as soldiers, and it can do them no good, but injury only to hang around armories, hotels, and street corners." Although Confederates failed to capture the capital, the White House was nevertheless the scene of many battles, as Tad and Willie Lincoln organized "Mrs. Lincoln's Zouaves"—reviewed on at least one occasion by the commander in chief himself—mounted a log cannon on the White House roof, and frequently court-martialed a zouave doll, which they would then execute and bury with full military honors.[28]

As the militant behavior of Evelyn Ward and Celine Fremaux showed, boys were not alone in casting themselves as heroes in the national drama. A young Yonkers, New York, "tomboy" so admired her brother's colorful Zouave uniform that she tried to convince him to take her along. He just laughed, but, undaunted, she obtained a soldiers' cap, canteen, and drum and practiced beating it as she marched "up and down the path in front of our house . . . until every head in the street must have ached." When she believed herself proficient in the military arts, she traveled alone by ferry and train all the way into New York City to talk her brother's colonel into taking her as the "daughter of the regiment." He declined her offer, and when she returned home, her parents sent her off to bed. "But I made a tent of my sheets, and with a broom for a musket, drilled myself till I was so tired that I fell asleep."[29]

Enterprising young soldiers moved beyond mere drill, graduating from pretend weapons made out of planks or broomsticks to real ones. A group of Cincinnati boys somehow obtained discarded flintlocks from the local militia armory and promptly formed firing squads to "shoot" helpless little boys forced to act the parts of "spies" and "deserters." They also pounded little mud and wood Fort Sumters to bits with cannon made of old brass pistols and blew up Jeff Davis effigies made of potatoes. Southern boys snatched up abandoned muskets and cartridges from deserted army camps. Tom Ashby would "practice target shooting by the hour, thinking I would some day have to practice shooting at the enemy if the war continued a few years longer." He also enjoyed shooting off a miniature brass cannon that could fire minié balls a few hundred yards and, with three or four friends, played "cavalrymen" on their old farm horses.[30]

Other companies actually marched into battles—of a sort. A few months before Baltimore authorities cracked down against Confederate flags and decorations, several dozen boys celebrated the Fourth of July by constructing a crepe-paper Confederate banner, donning red shirts and caps, and staging a protest march around a Federal encampment. Less than a year later an Ohio soldier wrote his young son from Kentucky bemusedly describing local boy militia companies who mustered near his unit's camp with "their officers & swords & pistols & guns." Forming lines of battle, they charged the Yankees, apparently hoping to capture a supply of crackers. "We always give them some," the Ohioan told his own little boy.[31]

Southern boys, closer to the actual fighting than northerners, reared perhaps in a more violent society, and with fewer fathers or other adult men around to dampen their martial enthusiasm, sometimes took the very short step from relatively harmless boys' companies to street gangs. The boys of Wytheville, Virginia, took names like the "Baconsoles" and the "Pinchguts" and carried on a war one newcomer thought was "too much like the big war that had been going on so long." They blasted away at one another with "cannons" made of sawed-off musket barrels mounted in small carriages and, like guards in many prison camps, rifled the pockets of captured foes. Similar gangs appeared in Richmond, where according to B. H. Wilkins, the boys of the Confederate capital formed "as many clans as the seven hills" on which the city was built. "They had all caught the fighting spirit, just like the new soldier boys. Their battles were like Second Manassas or Antietam with rocks and had to be broken up by policemen."[32]

One of the most elaborate and potentially dangerous examples of boys mimicking their martial elders occurred in tiny Rutherfordton, North Carolina, when a band of boys ranging in age from six to twelve organized a militia company under the command of "Captain Phip Flaxen." Their target was a watermelon patch whose owner, "Old Sam Calahan," had unexpectedly and unilaterally broken with community tradition and banned poachers, especially young boys. Borrowing their parents' states' rights ideals, the boys immediately determined that Calahan had violated their "watermelon rights." The company of just over a dozen boys assembled late one evening, loaded their shotguns with rock-hard peas, stole a boat, and mounted an amphibious attack from Chinquapin Creek. Phip sent a detail to steal the five biggest watermelons and formed the rest of his men into a line of battle along the creek bank. Hearing the boys' Rebel yell, Calahan and his son obligingly charged into the patch armed with shotguns. When old Sam's gun went off, sounding "like a cannon" to the boys, Phip cried, "Fire!" and the stinging but harmless vegetable pellets pep-

pered the Calahans and their dog, who quickly spun about in igno-
minious retreat. Their "natural" rights successfully defended, the
boys retired to feast on the contraband watermelon.[33]

The line between play and politics disintegrated even more de-
cisively for one boy in the spring of 1861. Ernest Wardwell, an
experienced practitioner of faux battles and the leader of a prewar
boys' company, joined his classmates and other Baltimore residents in attacking the Sixth Massachusetts as it marched through
the city on its way to Washington. Although his father came
from the North, Ernest was a southerner by birth and at first
taunted the Yankee soldiers. Later, however, impressed with "their
gallant bearing" and perhaps succumbing to his true political heritage, he braved the brickbats and curses and volunteered to carry
a Massachusetts sergeant's rifle. Swept along with the regiment
as it was attacked and then returned fire, the teenager ended up
enlisting and rising to the rank of captain. Even more striking
was the sudden enlistment of a Boston friend of Gerald Norcross.
The boys had spent many happy days fighting extended battles
and conducting "foraging" expeditions with armies of paper soldiers, whom they named for officers in prominent Boston-area
regiments. Gerald's somewhat older playmate crossed the line between imaginary and actual war when he lied about his age in
mid-1864 and joined a "100 day" regiment. He returned unharmed
and picked up where he and Gerald had left off in playing "soldier," no doubt with an enhanced understanding of the reality they
mimicked.[34]

Children acted out other aspects of the war as well. The Rogers
children of Tama County, Iowa, for instance, accompanied their
father to war meetings and then re-created the speeches and songs
for their mother when they returned home. Willie Kingsbury constructed a child's version of those prototypical moving pictures
called panoramas by coloring illustrations from *Harper's Weekly*
and pasting them together. As he rolled the series of war scenes
from one wooden spool to another, he narrated the events they portrayed to his audience of young neighbors and relatives. Charlie
Skinner, a budding theatrical manager, produced epic tragedies
with the help of family members and playmates that featured soldiers and sailors as well as slaves and planters and overseers, in
settings that ranged from southern plantations to Libby Prison
to Seminary Ridge to gunboat decks. Southern children could be

more subtly influenced by the circumstances in which they played. Like Nannie Belle Maury, they mimicked the women they had watched deal with various wartime situations. One day, "playing ladies" with a little friend, Nannie Belle responded to a query about her health by remarking, "I don't feel very well this morning. All my niggers have run away and left me." On another occasion her mother overheard her declare, " 'Upon my word an' honour, Sir, there are no letters and papers in this trunk at all' " — the exact words of protest her mother had uttered to a Federal guard on the way out of Fredericksburg some weeks before.[35]

Children immersed themselves in the events that dominated newspapers, pulpits, and dinner conversation, and parents understandably worried as the war infiltrated their children's every waking thought. "Almost their entire set of plays have reference to a state of war," wrote concerned Virginian Margaret Junkin Preston. Her five-year-old son George staged marches and battles with paper soldiers, took prisoners, built hospitals with blocks and corncobs, made ambulances with chairs, and administered pills to his rag dolls. "He gets sticks and hobbles about," recorded his mother in her diary, "saying that he lost a leg at the Second battle of Manassas; tells wonderful stories of how he cut off Yankees' heads, bayoneted them, &c." He occasionally bid his mother goodbye, as his "furlough is out and he must go to his regiment again." Her three year old "also kills 'Lankees,' as he calls them, and can talk war lingo almost as well as George. . . . They can tell all about pickets, cavalry, cannon, ambulances, &c." On another occasion her children and their little friends interrupted a paper-doll dance when imaginary Yankees suddenly appeared and the paper soldiers had to dash off to fight them. Mrs. Preston no doubt spoke for many mothers when she complained that "the thought of war is never out of our minds. If it could be, our children would bring it back by their plays!"[36]

Some boys refused to settle for heckling raw recruits, maneuvering paper soldiers around bedroom floors, or shuffling through drills with broomstick rifles. Fascinated by the sudden militarization of their society and aching for adventure, they became obsessed with the idea of joining the army. Immediately after the president's call for troops, three Cambridge, Massachusetts, boys, all under age ten, marched into a Boston recruiting station. According to the younger brother of the leader, Charlie Skinner, the recruiting officers "received the lads with gravity, examined their eyes, noses, teeth, made them strip to the skin and thumped them," then passed them along to another recruiting office, where the examination was repeated. "Humiliation became abysmal" after Charlie reported their rejection to his father, who said the soldiers had simply been making fun of the boys.[37]

Indeed, most boys were denied their chances for martial glory, at least temporarily. When Union forces approached Vicksburg in the spring of 1862, seventeen-year-old Walter Stone and his brothers could hardly focus on school. Their older sister Kate reported that they could not "settle to any work and who can blame them." Walter's manly desire to fight the North conflicted with his boyish excitement, disappointment, and even embarrassment. Rebuffed in his earnest desire to do a man's duty, he shed a boy's tears. According to his big sister, he cried for a week when he failed to get his mother's permission to go to the army. Walter did, indeed, get his chance a few months later; he died of fever in a Confederate hospital in 1863. John Wesley Hardin was only nine but apparently serious enough about running away to join the army that his father could only "put an end to it all by giving me a sound thrashing." On at least two occasions boys' hard-headed patriotism collided with their parents' determination to keep them from harm. In the fall of 1862 a seventeen-year-old Ohio boy, angry that he was not allowed to join his two older brothers in the army, hanged himself in his father's barn. A year and a half later a thirteen-year-old Mississippian "had become a great annoyance to his mother about going to the army. After she whipped him for his continued begging, he shot his brains out" with a shotgun.[38]

Of course, thousands of underage boys ended up in the armies of both sides. In addition, especially in the manpower-strapped Confederacy, youngsters could live out their martial dreams short of enlisting. Very late in the war, for instance, boys as young as fourteen joined "Home Guard" companies assigned the task of clearing out nests of bandits. Others took advantage of their military school training. Dozens of cadets at the Georgia Military Institute fanned out to train recruits at county seats and training camps throughout the state. Like William Cain, a fourteen-year-old cadet at Hillsboro, North Carolina, Military Academy, they might at times command hundreds of men, many of whom were ignorant officers. Despite his age, "I gave them the devil," William reminisced years later.[59]

All Have Some Part to Perform

Children obviously made the war a part of their lives. Yet the war also created conditions that altered the material and emotional status quo of Civil War children. The absence and loss of fathers, the dangers brought by invading armies, the economic pressures, the stress placed on worried, busy mothers, and the fear for their own lives or the lives of loved ones all no doubt took a heavy psychological toll on children. Children also faced conflicting demands, such as keeping to daily routines even while preparing for violent disruptions in their lives and continuing to trust friends while learning to suspect potential enemies. Children normally are — and were — socialized to respect human life and believe in peace. During war, however, they are constantly pushed to dehumanize their enemies and rationalize their destruction. Studies of twentieth-century children in war zones have revealed that these conditions can break down discipline; increase antisocial and aggressive behavior and spark emotional outbursts; produce health problems such as sleep disorders, headaches, bedwetting, and decreased appetite; and create a whole range of what therapists now call post-traumatic stress disorders. Children over age eight or so often deny that danger actually exists or insist that it happens to other people, not to them. Very small children who lose a parent may "forget" how to use a toilet, fear sleep, and revert in other ways to less mature developmental stages. Older children may engage in self-destructive behavior by flouting community norms or taking unnecessary risks.[40]

Unfortunately for historians, few Civil War era children or parents recorded these kinds of reactions, although hints of "psychological casualties" appear in some contemporary sources. Anna Howard, nearly overwhelmed with the pressures of helping her mother sustain their family in the backwoods of Michigan, still remembered that life fifty years later as "a strenuous and tragic affair." A much younger girl revealed how war fears challenged even children living far behind the lines. Ruth Huntington Sessions, who was born only two years before the beginning of the war, heard the "almost daily horror" of the cannon fire on Boston Commons, which easily carried across the Charles River to her home in Cambridge, and how she dreaded hearing the tolling bells and the "dead march" of military funerals. Her nurses gossiped luridly about "wounds, and legs shot away and bullet-holes in foreheads." Even the happier sounds of victory marches and parades frightened her into a closet, where she would hide until they faded away.[41]

One aspect of the psychological effects of war on children noted by twentieth-century observers did emerge during the conflict: youth became more rebellious. The disruption of schools and of family discipline had, according to an Arkansas newspaper, "a most pernicious effect" on young Confederates, while the *Nashville Dispatch* lamented that with the closure of public schools, youth of both sexes had lapsed into "idleness and wickedness." Little Maggie Davis staged a brief rebellion early in the war when, according to a young visitor, she declared "that now her father was President she meant to have as much fire as she wanted," struck match after match, and threw them out the window. More seriously, a Richmond Sunday school teacher sadly noted that increasingly unruly boys spent far more time with one another than with adults, thus depriving themselves of the calm guidance of their elders. Gangs of city boys committed minor crimes, carelessly fired guns, bullied smaller children and African American refugees, and frequently injured innocent bystanders. An Oliver Twist-like gang of boy burglars prowled the streets of Chicago, while black and white boys in Philadelphia staged rock battles that became a "most serious . . . annoyance," according to a local newspaper. In some parts of the South, teenaged bandits terrorized country roads. Richmond authorities contended with gangs of "incipient blackguards," who vandalized houses and public buildings, as well as bands of "very mischievous urchins," who made a practice of robbing younger children. A number of preadolescents in Mobile were thrown into jail for gambling, while small "motherless boys, of both colors" had been caught carrying matches, kindling, and combustibles around town. Even Columbus, Georgia, suffered from boys spitting tobacco juice all over sidewalks, knocking out bridge and train lights, and stoning black carriage drivers. Gangs of young Atlantans disrupted baptisms, concerts, and other public gatherings. Early in the war, dismayed by the apparently negative effects on the behavior of boys throughout the South, the *Atlanta Intelligencer* complained of "these fast children that crowd up the side walks in the cities and towns of our country."[42]

Although it is impossible to know how much of this behavior can be attributed to conditions brought about by the crisis, some contemporaries did blame the war for the restlessness and willfulness of children. A northern expert on juvenile delinquency suggested that the absence of fathers and older brothers had "removed the restraints which had held in check many wayward boys," unleashing a "tide of disobedience and incipient crime," while another estimated that one-fourth of all wartime child offenders had fathers or brothers in the army. The managers of a Philadelphia refuge also blamed the departure of fathers for the army as the cause of "a very large number of children" to descend on the institution. Some reform schools made room for the wave of new offenders by releasing older inmates to military service, while officials at others, such as the Massachusetts State Industrial School for Girls, used alarming examples of wartime upheaval to justify their proactive policies. Interestingly, wartime annual reports mentioned the loyal service and steady habits of inmates of refuges and asylums who went into the Union army, no doubt to impress both current inmates and the politicians and philanthropists on whom they depended for funding.[43]

Less public but more annoying for mothers already hard pressed by wartime responsibilities, the apparent epidemic of delinquency sometimes carried over into children's behavior at home. Billy Neblett, showing the strain of the absence of his father, Will, and other family pressures, was a constant source of irritation to his mother, Lizzie, by refusing to do his chores and constantly bullying his younger brother Walter. "He grows worse all the time," Lizzie announced to Billy's father. He was "so hateful, such a mean, bad child, and you can't appeal to his feelings, he is too flinty to care for any thing." Lizzie threatened to "whip him every day" and predicted that Billy would "be a thorn in my heart as long as he lives." Although the other children missed their father, Billy "never speaks of you voluntarily." Later Lizzie remarked with obvious understatement, "children have lost their charm for me."[44]

These few anecdotes hardly show that the Civil War destroyed the psyches of northern and southern children. There were, of course, no social workers whose case files could reveal the underlying causes of the unsatisfactory behavior that so many observers noted. However, ample evidence shows what may be called stress-resistant behavior: developing a high tolerance for discomfort and becoming reliable, caring, and competent in the face of increased demands.[45] Many Civil War children met the challenges of war by taking on greater responsibilities and contributing to their families' survival. As Edward Pye reminded his son Ned, "fate has ordained that we should be *actors* in this dark chapter of the World's history— *You* and *I*—'*Ma*' and sister Edie—perhaps the little ones —all are actors—all have some *part* to perform." Both male and female children found themselves performing tasks usually reserved for older family members, ranging from caring for younger children to heavy farmwork to managing slaves to conducting business negotiations.[46]

The Fremaux children of Louisiana all took on more work when their father joined the Confederate army. Driven by an emotionally and physically abusive mother, fourteen-year-old Leon bargained for sugar and completed other tasks previously performed by his father, while for a time Celine spent long, freezing days stuffing ornery geese with corn and endured frustrating nights walking the floor with her crying baby brother. Later, after the family had relocated to Jackson, Louisiana, she went to school during the day, gave her younger brothers reading lessons, mended the family's clothes, and made dye from red oak and sweet gum bark. She also had to gather kindling and scrounge for dead animals from which to make soap. School provided her sole outlet from grinding physical labor.[47]

The Fremaux children's burdens were typical of the increased workload and heightened responsibility that southern youth had to accept. Seven- and eight-year-old Missourians fetched supplies in guerilla-infested territory and sold liquor to Union soldiers out of a rough grocery store. Teenaged boys made bare livings cutting wood for Confederate soldiers and rifling through abandoned supplies in old army camps. Louisa Sheppard once chased away a panther from her refugee party's campfire, rode for supplies, and taught a school of over twenty children, "some of them as old as I," after her own school term ended. Henry Huntington, fourteen, raced through the shells pouring down on Atlanta for milk for his baby brother and later cajoled a recalcitrant Mississippi provost marshal into granting his family a pass to leave Confederate lines. After Union troops evacuated Atlanta to begin their March to the Sea in November 1864, ten-year-old Carrie Berry joined other children in "plundering about . . . seeing what we could find." She spent three full days picking up nails among the ruins of the burned city. Later, after her mother gave birth, she did much of the cooking and cleaning for the family.[48]

The fortunes of war disrupted every aspect of southern children's lives, altering daily routines and forcing them to do everything for themselves, including work normally done by slaves. Sally Hawthorne was eight when Federal troops occupied Fayette, North Carolina. After their slaves vanished, each of the children in the formerly well-to-do family was assigned specific jobs: Sally swept the piazzas and halls and set the table, her brother fetched wood and tended fires, and her sister tidied the parlors and trimmed the candlesticks. "First of all," wrote Sally in a complaint indicating how unused to such responsibilities she actually was, "I had to learn to bathe and dress myself." More striking was her young cousins' chore of collecting stray kernels of corn from the farmyard for their mother to feed them. "We are so hungry," the starving girls told their grandfather, "and it is so good!"[49]

Of course, in the rural South most children had to pick up the slack on the plantations and farms that fed the soldiers and women and children of the Confederacy. Boys and probably many girls had helped their fathers with farmwork before, but the war thrust them into previously unknown positions of responsibility. Theodorick Montfort urged his thirteen-year-old son, in words echoed by independent-minded farmers through the ages, to "attend evry thing, see to it yourself, dont rely on any one else attending to it, but never go to sleep of a night untill you see that evry thing is attended to."[50]

Southern children did their best to fulfill these high expectations. When twelve-year-old Georgian Jacob Frederick took over his father's plantation, he supervised more than twenty slaves and ground sugarcane for the entire neighborhood. David Golightly Harris's young sons herded hogs, and his daughters pulled dried cotton stalks out of the fields. In addition to moral advice and affectionate stories, Confederate fathers carefully directed their sons on how to care for the livestock and crops. John William Fewell, seventeen, must have swelled with pride when his father's letters referred to "your wheat" and spoke to him as a man. "Let me hear from you and what you are doing and how the negroes are doing," he wrote. "You must make them mind you and each one attend to their respective duties." As the oldest child at home, Benny Fleet, fourteen, matter-of-factly wrote his brother in the army that he was "in charge," with the authority to "give orders without Pa's knowing anything about it." He performed all of the usual farm and marketing chores but also acted as man of the family in other ways. When his alcoholic father went on a binge, he had "the painful duty" of informing his absent, older brother that their father had "commenced drinking, & has been in quite a big frolic." With little help from his elders, Benny had to take an adult's role in every sense.[51]

Southern women and children moved outside the home to take work that supported themselves and contributed to the Confederate war effort. Government jobs allowed them to remain genteelly out of the public eye. A number of young girls were among the hundreds of women who applied to Secretary of the Treasury Christopher Memminger for jobs numbering and signing Confederate Treasury notes. Fifteen-year-old Hattie Hilby, an orphan, needed a job because the relative with whom she stayed was married to a low-paid private. Another fifteen-year-old orphan whose older brother was in the army needed work to provide for her younger sister and brother "and perhaps to continue them at school." Other girls desired to help their hard-pressed fathers and mothers support large families. Jane Tyler's father was only a clerk, and her oldest brother—of eight siblings—was only sixteen; so it was left to her to contribute to the family income. Sally Winfree declared that she was "a Virginian by birth and flatter myself as true to the Southern cause as any one who resides in this city," and that she wanted to help support her young nephew.[52]

Although tedious, Treasury jobs at least allowed women and girls to remain out of public view or even in their homes. Other young women and girls were forced to take on manual labor. Hundreds made uniforms and other war material at private and government plants in Augusta, Georgia. Southern girls also took jobs at the Confederate Laboratory on Brown's Island in Richmond, where late in the winter of 1863 an explosion killed three dozen workers and injured thirty more, many of whom were children. A newspaper account suggested that the workforce included over 300 females, mainly between the ages of twelve and twenty. Although the exact number of children is unknown, contemporary accounts stress the presence of very young, mostly female employees. A War Department official reported that "most of them were little indigent girls." After the explosion families streamed toward the wreckage in hopes of whisking their young daughters away to safety. "The most heartrending lamentations and cries issued from the ruins" as rescue workers pulled the killed and injured from the smoking rubble. "Mothers rushed wildly about, throwing themselves upon the corpses of the dead and persons of the wounded." Children "clamored" into ambulances, "crying bitterly in their search after sisters and brothers." [53]

Although the Union was better able than the Confederacy to keep men in the army and in the factory, northern children also had to fill in for absent fathers and brothers. Members of comfortable middle- and upper-class families may have settled into cozily patriotic, if rather detached, routines, revealing another major difference between northern and southern children's experiences. Yet thousands of farm children saw their responsibilities mount, and in manufacturing centers boys as young as fifteen or sixteen years frequently took the place of adults away in the army. Over 250 "boys" worked in the Washington Arsenal as early as June 1861, while enrollment in Baltimore high schools fell precipitously during the war when scores of boys chose employment over education.[54] Marion Drury, although only twelve years old, had "to assume the work and responsibilities" of a man because so many farmworkers had gone to the army. After his wounded father lost his mind—he later died in an asylum—seven-year-old Eddie Foy, the future comedian, helped his mother make ends meet by blacking boots all over lower Manhattan and by performing with a wandering fiddler in the bars and streets of New York, Brooklyn, and Jersey City.[55]

Of course, fathers did more for their families than collect paychecks or do farm chores, and some children literally took their fathers' places as heads of their families. Frank Rogers of Iowa interpreted the instructions to take care of the family left by his father, an army doctor, to include standing up for the Union against local Democrats. He even packed a gun when he accompanied his mother to the house of a local Copperhead leader. Frank's fondness for guns came in handy when the panic over the Minnesota Sioux uprising of 1862 drifted south into Iowa. Mrs. Rogers put her children on alert, giving her young sons her husband's sword and pistol and telling "them they were the men of the family and they must be soldiers and defend their mother if necessary." During the long night that followed, Frank and Fred refused to leave their mother's side. She recalled long afterward that "I felt quite safe with two such brave little soldiers." In addition to fetching the mail and caring for his younger nephews, when nine-year-old Levi Keeler's mother became seriously ill, he nursed her back to health. Jane Keeler wrote her husband that Levi "sat up with me all night and every little while he would ask Mother do you want anything, till one o'clock and then I could not stand it any longer so Levi went after the Doctor." Acknowledging the enormity of her son's contributions to her and the family's well-being, she declared, "Levi was my man." [56]

But whatever satisfaction children gained in doing extra work and fulfilling adult responsibilities, the fact remained that their lives could be hard, grinding, and more difficult than ever. One girl's memoir of pioneering in Michigan resembled the accounts of many southern boys and girls forced to work by the war. The father and two oldest brothers of Anna Howard joined the Union army soon after the war began, leaving Mrs. Howard and several children to fend for themselves in the Great Lakes wilderness. "I was the principal support of our family," Anna recalled as an adult. Little news trickled into this community forty miles from the nearest post office; work was "done by despairing women whose hearts were with their men." As the war dragged on, "the problem of living grew harder. . . . We eked out our little income in every way we could." She and her mother took in boarders from logging camps, sold quilts, sewed, and taught school. "It was an incessant struggle to keep our land, to pay our taxes, and to live." [57]

Slaves obviously knew what it was like to have to struggle for everything, even without a war draining vital resources. Although a few, including Booker T. Washington, claimed that the war had little effect on their lives, once the fighting started, the workloads of slave children almost invariably increased and their material lives worsened. A free father of three children still enslaved in Maryland complained to Secretary of War Edwin Stanton that his children's master only "half feed them and half Cloth them & beat them like dogs." As contrabands exposed to the filth and death of pestilential refugee camps, as victims of brutality and indifference from masters as well as Yankee soldiers, and as youngsters whose already vulnerable childhoods were taken away by economic pressures that forced them into the fields at very young ages, few slave children were able to act on the political beliefs they developed during the war.[58]

But most of those slave children who were allowed to act did not have to be politicized by the war; they already knew they hated slavery. Yet others, especially preadolescents, often identified closely with their white owners because these masters and mistresses were the locus of authority, the source of material well-being, and the bestowers of treats and gifts—the people who, in many ways, gave young blacks a value and sense of worth outside their families. So, not surprisingly, many young African Americans found themselves, at least at an emotional level, siding with the South. At times they sympathized with their Confederate families almost instinctively. Anna Johnson, a little girl when the war began, remembered her master's son's Rebel yell as he galloped past the slave quarters on his way to the fighting. "We answered back," Anna recalled. When word arrived of his death in battle, "We all cried." Like many white children, Ellen Claiborn of Georgia, who turned thirteen during the last year of the war, sewed clothes for Confederate soldiers and nursed sick and wounded Rebels. A number of teenaged slaves accompanied their masters to the army and served them faithfully throughout the war. Cicero Finch, only thirteen when the war began, cooked for and maintained the equipment of four of his master's sons, stole pigs and chickens for them, and nursed them when they were sick or hurt. During battles he and other servants acted as stretcher bearers; in one battle he was slightly wounded by a shell burst.[59]

One sad, lonely little African American loyally defended his white family against all comers. After capturing Jefferson Davis and his family in Georgia, Federal authorities sent Jim Limber, the free black boy rescued on a Richmond street by Varina Davis, to Union general Rufus Saxton, an old friend of the Davises posted at Beaufort, South Carolina. Jim stayed for several weeks and was cared for by teachers and missionaries to the freedmen. Elizabeth Botume sympathized with his confusion and with the "scorn and distrust" with which "he looked . . . upon all around him." Believing that he would soon be reunited with the Davises—he never was—he fought the black children when they sang about hanging Jeff Davis "to a sour apple tree." After one scuffle Jim vowed that if "he were a man he would kill every one of them."[60]

Southerners' belief that such determined loyalty proved their slaves' contentedness and love for their kindly masters misread the sophisticated dynamics of the master-slave relationship. Most bondspeople, of all ages, rejected the Confederacy and, when given the opportunity, rebelled against the institution of slavery. Mary Gladdy remembered attending secret religious meetings during the war, where the slaves would sing, pray, and testify throughout the night. The dream they returned to again and again during the meetings was, of course, freedom. On another Georgia plantation, as the war wound down to inevitable Confederate defeat, W. B. Allen's master desperately asked the fifteen year old, known to all as "a praying boy," "to pray to God to hold the Yankees back." W. B. refused, explaining bravely that he "wanted to be free and to see all the Negroes freed!" Furthermore, he declared, God "was using the Yankees to scourge the slave-holders" just as the Israelites had been chastised by "heathens and outcasts . . . centuries before." A teenaged slave in Texas refused to accompany his master to the Confederate army and suffered the consequences; the boy's sister saw him tied down and beaten "till . . . you couldn't tell what he look like." Others ran away as soon as they could. One twelve-year-old house servant in St. Louis took off, much to the astonishment of her master (who wrote to President Lincoln to complain), while a thirteen-year-old boy escaped to Knoxville, where he went to work for a Union captain and, later, in an army hospital. Similar stories were told by many other young slave boys.[61]

Some of the best-known African American leaders of the late nineteenth century got their starts as spirited Civil War children. Francis Grimké, the nephew of the famous abolitionist sisters, was born in 1850 and lived for much of his childhood in a semifree status in Charleston. His mother, Nancy, had shared a long relationship with Henry Grimké, her master; when he died, his will had vaguely suggested that his slave family be freed. However, his white son Montague ignored the provision and made Frank and his brother house servants. Frank resisted by taking two or three "holidays" and dressing carelessly on the job. After a severe whipping the twelve year old ran away and worked for Confederate officers at Castle Pinckney. Montague tracked him down, had him thrown into the Charleston workhouse, and sold him to a Confederate officer. Frank stayed behind when Charleston was evacuated in February 1865 and offered his services to Union soldiers, foraging for food among the poverty-stricken southerners along the route of Sherman's army. Finally, he fell ill and was sent back to Charleston to recover with his mother. Francis Grimké characterized the practical political responses of many slaves, even slave children, to the Civil War. Withholding their unqualified loyalty to either their masters or their liberators, they expressed their politicization by doing what they thought was best for them. Their only ideology was freedom — from slavery, from dependence, and from the narrow confines of their lives in bondage.[62]

Working Like Soldiers

Children not weighed down by extraordinary responsibilities and unable to talk their parents into allowing them to go into the army found more genteel forms of contributing to the war efforts of their sections. Perhaps the most often mentioned activity of children was producing lint to pack into wounds. Referred to as "scraping" or "picking," it was a nearly ubiquitous activity that children could do in their spare time; a New Orleans school devoted recess time to the chore. Sometimes it seemed a little anticlimactic to youngsters thrown into a frenzy by the war. When nine-year-old Maurice Egan and his Philadelphia friends failed to get into the army as drummers, he complained that they "were reduced to making lint for the army" with the girls. Others found the chore less degrading. In one small Wisconsin town, "even little children worked" with their mothers at Soldier's Aid Society meetings at the Baptist church. "Very important we children felt," Clara Lenroot remembered, "as we scraped away at the linen, making fluffy piles of the soft lint 'for the soldiers.'" Working with the older women helped the girls feel a part of the effort in other ways, too. Throughout the long afternoons of volunteer work, "they tried to comfort one another for the absence or the loss of dear ones. Long letters . . . were sometimes read aloud, describing camp scenes, or battle experiences, or hair-breadth escapes from Libby Prison." The tedious work, exciting stories, and sense of contributing to the larger community "thrilled us and left indelible memories."[63]

Children's most public contributions, however, usually consisted of raising money to buy flags and to support hospitals, soldiers' homes, and other war-related causes. As early as April 1861 a New Orleans resident reported little girls "trotting around" town with subscription lists to raise money for flags for local military companies. Schoolgirls in Grenada, Missouri, gathered at a classmate's house every Saturday to sew and knit clothing for Confederate soldiers and held tableaux, charades, and concerts to raise money for the soldiers. Outfitted in pink zouave jackets, students at the Atlanta Female Institute raised money for soldiers' families with a flower festival that included a "floral bombardment" of Fort Sumter. Individuals and groups of children sent money and mittens and socks and food to individual units and charitable organizations. They held tableaux, gave up long-planned class picnics and excursions, and hosted fairs at which they sold toys and "fancy" needlework. A Richmond girl remembered that women and children vowed not to eat meat on Fridays in order to leave more for the soldiers. Young ladies and other citizens sponsored a series of fairs and bazaars in Augusta, Georgia, to fund a wayside home for soldiers passing through town and to build a Confederate gunboat. Even as Sherman's army bore down on them, a "Ladies' Bazaar" was held in the State House at Columbia, South Carolina. Sixteen-year-old Emma Le Conte helped stage the event but found herself strangely detached from the festivities. With disaster looming so near, she wrote, "it seems like the dance of death."[64]

Early in the war, perhaps it was easier to feel pride than hopelessness. Like many school and church organizations, the Spartanburg, South Carolina, Methodist Sunday School Relief Society showed their enthusiasm by collecting supplies for the soldiers. Organized in July 1861, the society immediately began gathering as well as producing food and clothes. Led by the Sunday school teachers but largely comprised of students, the group held nearly weekly meetings, charged 25-cent dues, and established committees to purchase supplies, to "cut out" work and prepare projects for meetings, and to pack boxes for shipment.[65]

Although the secretary sometimes allowed her temper to surface—she twice seemed peeved when meetings began without a prayer "thanks to our punctual chaplain"—she devoted the bulk of her minutes to long lists of the contributions gathered and purchases made during the previous week or month. Sometimes she

Children frequently held their own fund-raisers—where they sold snacks, handicrafts, and even kisses—in conjunction with the great Sanitary Fairs in northern cities. (Frank B. Goodrich, *The Tribute Book: A Record of the Munificence, Self-Sacrifice, and Patriotism of the American People during the War for the Union* [New York: Derby and Miller, 1865], 98)

recorded that certain items were collected or sewn and sold; in their first six months they raised over $60 from the sale of "fancy work," and in August the children sold blackberries and blackberry wine. After three months of work the society completed its first shipment in September. It and succeeding boxes contained clothing, towels, bedding, cooking utensils, cakes, and dried fruit as well as a bottle of laudanum, a butter dish, a bundle of religious tracts, and a box of guava jelly. Attendance varied greatly over the two years for which records have survived. Two or three dozen members came to the first meetings. Later, sickness, bad weather, and, possibly, waning interest led to decreasing numbers.[66]

Northern soldiers also benefited from the efforts of youngsters back home. Prominent missionary Elizabeth W. Ross traced her "first missionary work" back to the moment when, at the behest of her beloved African American nanny, she made a "housewife"— a leather folder containing sewing supplies—for a Union soldier. Another young girl sent a cherished two-volume copy of *Grimm's Fairy Tales* to a soldiers' hospital; her older sister recalled it as "the dearest thing she could give to her country." In a period when army security was something of an oxymoron, children of all ages could easily wander around army encampments, especially in the early months of the war. Some sought to ease the hardships of army life by bringing gifts of food or blankets whenever they visited camp.[67]

Northern children directed most of their energy to raising money. Sometimes they mounted efforts on behalf of specific units or hospitals. Sunday school students in a Vermont town formed a "Juvenile Soldiers' Aid society" to buy religious tracts for soldiers. A flurry of "children's fairs" in Philadelphia early in the fall of 1862 took in cash and gathered supplies for a local zouave company and a U.S. Army hospital, while schools in Philadelphia's Eighteenth Ward gathered up two large wagons of food and linen in a single week. In the same city, black children from the Bethel African Methodist Episcopal Sabbath School sent money to the local Soldiers' Aid Society and to the hospital of a local black regiment.[68]

As they did for adult contributors and activists, the huge Sanitary Fairs sponsored by towns and cities all over the North tended to focus the fund-raising efforts of individual children as well as members of schools, orphanages, Sunday Schools, and other groups. At New York's 1864 fair a separate Children's Department, occupying the entire east wing of the Union Square Building, offered booths and displays by public and private schools, a toy store, and soldiers' orphans. According to the fair newspaper, the articles sold in the Children's Department "represent probably a greater devotion than in almost any other department." For instance, "the little children of the Home for the Friendless" gave hundreds of pennies and made "lamplighters" out of colored paper. The patriotism of these children stemmed from a very tangible source: more than sixty former inmates of the home had joined the army. Other institutions donating handmade items included the Deaf and Dumb Asylum, the Blind Asylum, the Wilson Industrial School, the Birch Church Mission School, the "girls of the House of Refuge," the Hebrew Orphan Asylum, children from the "Colored Home," unidentified "blind girls," and the "Children of the Sacred Heart" in Harlem.[69]

Chicago hosted two of the biggest Sanitary Fairs of the war, and young Chicagoans kicked into high gear to support the North-western Branch of the Sanitary Commission. At the opening cere-monies of the first fair, held in the late summer of 1863, 300 "young misses" sang "The Great Rebellion," a "patriotic musical allegory." Private entertainments were also held, and an Evans-ton doctor's children raised $10 with a "tableaux party." Other fairs aided the local Soldiers' Home and soldiers' families. Rock Island schoolchildren collected pickled tomatoes and vowed to contribute a nickel a month until the end of the war.[70]

Many children held their own "fairs" in backyards, front porches, or parlors. The *Chicago Tribune* described one of these "interesting and patriotic fairs of the little ones." Tables groaned with "choice" fruits, cream lemonade, and cake. Decorations in-cluded "flags, banners, emblems, and pictures," and the tables "were presided over by veritable fairy queens" charming "the quarters and dimes out of the purses of the visitors in an unac-countable manner." Back East, young Willie Kingsbury earned a penny for every pin he found, which he donated to soldiers' causes, and "soon he was selling everything he could to the neighborhood-children . . . by organizing little fairs entirely of his own." He enlisted his younger sister Alice to make a pin cushion and even sold kisses from a "pretty little fair-haired boy." His enthusiasm earned him a trip to the Sanitary Fair in New York. Ten-year-old Emma Andrews reported every Saturday morning to work with the Woman's Soldiers' Aid Society of Northern Ohio and by late in the war had made well over 200 small towels. Emptying their "tin boxes, savings' banks, and stockings," Chicago children con-tributed several hundred dollars to the Chicago fair, while young girls working in four-hour shifts at the Brooklyn fair and in other cities sold dolls dressed as "the old woman who lived in a shoe." The most famous was Nellie Grant, who delighted in her role at the St. Louis Sanitary Fair in 1864.[71]

Schools put together massive mobilization efforts in support of the Sanitary Fairs. Perhaps forty public and private schools in New York raised $24,000 by holding reading lessons and entertainments for their families and friends during the Metropolitan Fair. Phila-

Many Sanitary Fairs featured girls portraying "the old woman who lived in a shoe," who raised money by selling dolls. Nellie Grant, daughter of Gen. Ulysses S. Grant, is shown here, performing the role at the St. Louis Fair in 1864. (John Y. Simon, ed., *The Personal Memoirs of Julia Dent Grant* [Carbondale: Southern Illinois University Press, 1975]; copyright © 1975 by the Ulysses S. Grant Association, reprinted by permission of Southern Illinois University Press)

delphia's schoolchildren were even more active. Fourteen hundred teachers and 72,000 pupils worked for months sewing and soliciting; rehearsing concerts, readings, and tableaux; and holding tea parties and festivals to raise money for the Great Central Fair. Cincinnati schoolchildren put on "gymnastic exercises" and other entertainments at the Great Western Fair, while a chorus of children dressed in white and wearing wreaths of flowers opened Chicago's Great Northwestern Sanitary Fair. In St. Louis 1,700 students from the city's many German schools sang during the ceremonial procession and recession, while Nellie Grant read fairy tales to throngs of children. A single performance of *Cinderella*, featuring 200 child dancers and John C. and Jessie Benton Frémont's son as the prince, earned $2,500 in New York City.[72]

Other activities undertaken by children included picking blackberries and peaches for the soldiers on behalf of the Sanitary Commission. The "Alert Club" organized by the "little girls and young people" of Norwalk, Ohio, raised $560 from the town's 2,000 citizens for the local soldiers' aid society. In Kalamazoo, Michigan, Sunday school children met every Sunday in a cozy chapel called the Bird's Nest. When a visiting soldier donated a penny to the Sunday school, the children began the "Bird's Nest Bank." Every Saturday and Wednesday afternoon they sold shares in the bank for ten cents. Their efforts fired the imagination of northerners, and especially soldiers, around the country, and residents of virtually every northern state bought certificates. Eventually the children raised $200, most of which was devoted to freedmen's education.[73]

Another specific relief effort in which northern children participated was the East Tennessee Relief Fund, organized on behalf of the families of Union refugees from Tennessee. Centered in Massachusetts, it collected donations of all sizes from schools, Sunday schools, and individuals throughout the state. The students at Mr. Allen's school wrote a letter to accompany their donation. "The loyal boys of Massachusetts to the loyal boys of Tennessee send greeting," it began. It went on to sympathize with their plight and destitution "while your fathers and our fathers have been struggling side by side, for the support of the Union cause and in defence of liberty." Since "we have a united interest in the prosperity of our glorious country[,] . . . we wish to send you

Northern children raised thousands of dollars for the United States Sanitary Commission, rising through the ranks of the "Army of the American Eagle" by selling pictures of "Old Abe, the War Eagle." Emily Crouch of Wisconsin earned the second lieutenant's commission shown here by selling forty pictures. (State Historical Society of Wisconsin)

a trifle from our abundance" and to encourage "you to hold out, until better days shall come."[74]

The personal touch such a note gave to charitable giving ran counter to the increasing centralization, bureaucratization, and professionalization of philanthropy that characterized the massive efforts of the Sanitary Commission. The commission was not without its critics, despite the millions of dollars of aid it poured into soldiers' welfare. Yet its methods prevailed, providing a sense of unity to the war effort on the northern home front.[75] Very late in the war a Chicagoan named Alfred L. Sewell applied the principle of centrally organized giving to children's fund raising by devising the "Army of the American Eagle" as a way to raise money for the Northwestern Sanitary Fair. According to a short history of the movement that appeared in the first issue of *The Little Corporal*, a juvenile magazine Sewell also founded, he had been trying to think of a way to "marshal the children . . . and give them a chance to show how well they love their country and her brave defenders." His plan was to entice boys and girls to sell "beautiful Album pictures in oil colors" of "Old Abe," the "War Eagle" of the Eighth Wisconsin, which had led his regiment into numerous battles and emerged unscathed. The Chicago attorney made children "privates" in the Army of the American Eagle simply for buying pictures for a dime each. Recruits were then supposed to organize clubs and to sell copies of the pictures to other patriotic children and adults. As children sold more pictures, they advanced through the ranks of Sewell's army, starting with a corporal's rank for selling 10 copies and progressing up to major general for selling 4,000 copies. Other incentives included gold, silver, and bronze medals for the best salesmen and saleswomen, and a copy of the Old Abe booklet for every colonel and general. One picture at a time, over 12,000 children throughout the North raised well over $16,000.[76]

The War Was Continually Rising in Front of Me

Children experienced everything the war threw at northerners and southerners: danger and hardship, exhilaration and loss, and enhanced opportunities and crushing responsibilities. Although most committed youngsters refused to say so, by the end of the war many shared their parents' growing war-weariness. Robert Martin spoke for those southern children who "grew progressively tired of the continual night alarms," of "surly and threatening strangers" bursting into the house whenever they pleased, and of "the ever shorter rations of food that I could hardly eat." He began to feel that whenever he wanted something, "I was told that on account of the war I could not get it," and seemed to recall that before the war he could have anything he wanted. For him "the war was continually rising in front of me to bar me from something I wanted, whether food, clothes, or playthings." He wanted the South to win, of course, but if that was not possible, he wanted an end to "the war and . . . all these alarms and this killing and wounding and this long series of privations ever getting worse."[77]

Northern children, buoyed perhaps by the victories their armies won during the last few months of the war, may have felt differently. They certainly did not, as a general rule, witness the violence and deprivations that Martin, a Shenandoah Valley boy, experienced. But the war forced children in both sections to respond in some way to the events and issues and responsibilities thrust upon them. The conflict dominated their family relationships and schools, occupied energies and emotions, altered relationships and economic status, infected entertainment and play, and challenged assumptions and values. Moreover, the war politicized the children who fought it on the home front, inspiring ardent patriotism that could either lead to a life-long devotion to the Union or, in the case of Confederate children, make them permanently suspicious of the government of the United States and of the forces unleashed by the war. Gertrude Stein once wrote, "In time of peace what children feel concerns the lives of the children as children but in time of war there is not children's lives and grown up lives there is just lives." As the children of the Civil War grew up, they applied the political lessons of their childhoods to their adult lives, with important ramifications for the United States as it entered the twentieth century.[78]

6 Childhoods Lost and Found
Civil War Children as Adults

As the reunited United States lurched through an uneasy peace in the years following the war, a toy and a book suggested how the states of mind of northern and southern children may have differed. *The Myriopticon*, a child-sized panorama produced by Milton Bradley in 1866, presented a northern view of the Civil War. Less than one foot square, its crude but colorful drawings of military events from Fort Sumter through the evacuation of Richmond were turned from one reel to another inside a sturdy cardboard box gaudily decorated as a theater with red, white, and blue bunting and other patriotic flourishes. Included in the package were tickets to be distributed to patrons, a poster emulating claims that appeared in advertisements for adult panoramas ("This Splendid Work of Art is Painted on Nearly 1000 Square inches of Surface, And represents a great number of the most interesting and important events of the war—"), and a narration to be read aloud by the "proprietor." A certain jaunty cheeriness surfaced occasionally in the narrative, which suggested Union troops retreating from First Bull Run had not stopped as ordered at Centerville because the hotels were full. Other attempts at humor included a campfire with a sleeping sentinel (which in real life, of course, could have gotten him court-martialed and executed), a picture of Sherman's army "washing up" South Carolina, and the "pig-chew-resque" scene of a soldier chasing a southern pig. But most of the panorama's pictures featured stirring and ultimately victorious scenes of Union valor.[1]

Three years later *The Princess of the Moon*, published by a "Lady of Warrenton, Virginia," painted a much darker picture of the war and Reconstruction. Subtitled *A Confederate Fairy Story*, it was dedicated to "the children of the South, who suffered During the late War," but its fantastic plot must also have spoken to defeated southern adults. A returning Confederate veteran named Randolph finds his home destroyed and his parents dead. Whisked away on a flying horse given to him by a mysterious fairy, he explores the ravaged South and a North where Yankees in their prosperous houses decorate their mantles with belongings plundered from southern families. He soars to the moon, finds a tolerant kingdom of fairies, wins their friendship and sympathy with indignant stories about the plight of his defeated country, and falls in love with a princess. They eventually marry, and the former Confederate becomes the heir-apparent to the throne. Just then, huge balloons appear and disgorge crowds of nosy explorers with Yankee accents, as well as Randolph's former slave, who identifies his companions as the very men who had violated the hero's southern home. The fairy who had earlier befriended Randolph chases them away, clutching their carpetbags, and the generous and noble Confederate allows them to return safely home. The book's bittersweet ending shows that even the powerful fairies of the moon cannot redeem the South — or the greedy North, for that matter — and Randolph can find happiness only by leaving his beloved and ravaged homeland.[2]

The Princess of the Moon was privately printed and no doubt had a limited press run; few children, even in the North, could probably afford a toy as elaborate as *The Myriopticon*. But these two artifacts of children's postwar lives reveal much about the differences in children's experiences. Northern children, at least those not burdened with grief over dead fathers or brothers, could look forward with a sense of triumph and confidence and even good-natured humor; southern children, like their parents, faced disgrace, degradation, and a spiritual, if not physical, exile. This is partly explained by the intense trauma suffered by many southern children, but also important is the obvious fact that the political, economic, and social issues that had led to the crisis did not simply go away after the shooting stopped. The youngest Civil War children — at least those living in the South — became "Reconstruction children" and remembered the aftermath of war that stretched into the mid-1870s more clearly than the war itself; older children could make the connection between the war and the ragged attempts to resolve its issues. Children on both sides had warmed their hands by the fire that had, in the famous words of Oliver Wendell Holmes Jr., "touched" their fathers and brothers. Many southern children, however, were badly blistered, and the way they handled the war as adults once again distinguished them from their northern peers.

The greatest victors were also the worst victims of the war. Enduring grinding hardships and exhilarating release, former slaves embraced their new-found liberty but quickly discovered the limits of freedom. African American children had few public opportunities—as writers or politicians—to explore what they had learned in the war, but they did generally try to bring order to the jumble of conflicting emotions and experiences that the war and Reconstruction threw at them. As elderly, economically disadvantaged men and women in the 1930s, they sometimes regretted freedom itself; those former slave children who built careers for themselves as educators, ministers, or politicians had to carefully pick their battles. Even then, they had to face the fact that the promise of the war remained unfulfilled in the lives of the black children who survived it.

Most of the white children of war, like their African American counterparts, married, raised children, and finished their lives without setting down their thoughts on paper. Fortunately for historians, a few of them did explain their perceptions of the war and its place in their personal histories in memoirs or transformed their knowledge of the period into short stories or novels. This quest for relevance—the need to make sense out of the war—was particularly important to southerners. Northerners personally had less at stake and, of course, their side won; victory apparently demanded less soul-searching than defeat. For northern memoirists, for instance, the war ended with the assassination of Abraham Lincoln, which they often described in great detail, although virtually none of their published reminiscences mentioned Reconstruction. In fact, although a number of southerners published entire memoirs specifically detailing their childhood experiences during the war, most northerners relegated the conflict to a chapter or two in longer autobiographies. A similar distinction emerged from fictional accounts. Northern writers might set their stories in Civil War days, but southern writers were much more likely to make the war and its causes central components of their work.

Even — especially — in the political arena, northerners and southerners commemorated the war differently. A number of northern politicians traced certain of their attitudes to their experiences as Civil War children — Theodore Roosevelt and his friend Henry Cabot Lodge were especially affected — but southern politicians of the 1890s and later based their entire careers on reacting to the events of the 1860s and 1870s. As autobiographers, as writers, and as public servants, Civil War children proved that their war did not end when the armies laid down their weapons.

Reunion and Remembrance

At a very superficial level, children continued to be exposed to the war through toys, children's literature, and schoolbooks for decades after Appomattox. Tin monitors, card games, paper soldiers, and a walking "General Butler" doll were available into the 1870s. Few original juvenile novels related to the war appeared after the summer of 1865, although reprints of a number of popular dime novels came out in the mid-1870s, and editions of Oliver Optic's pair of trilogies appeared a few years later.[3]

Children's magazines in the North did, however, continue to offer war-related fare, getting a head start on the theme of sectional harmony that would characterize adult literature later in the century. Their version showed that southerners generally supported the Union during the war and fought for the Confederacy or paid Confederate taxes only because they could not resist the manipulations of the slaveocrat minority.[4] Oliver Optic presented a full-blown image of postwar reunification in a *Student and School-mate* "dialogue." After characters whose names obviously associate them with South, West, and North — Palmetto, Buckeye, and Jonathon — bicker over the advantages of the three leading sections of the country, their "Uncle Sam" calls on them to pull together and take pride in their nation's resources as well as their regional strengths. "We have come forth from our trial purified and strong, have agreed to let bygones be bygones," they declare, "and now we are ready to take the lead in the world's grand march to the highest civilization." Poems and stories published in the months following Appomattox also supported returning veterans, while *The Little Corporal* urged its readers to redirect their war work by aiding soldiers' orphans.[5]

Like northern adults, children welcomed the end of the war and celebrated by watching the assembled armies march in the Grand Review in May 1865, shown here in an engraving from *Harper's Weekly*, June 10, 1865. (Library of Congress)

Two new children's magazines touched from time to time on war themes and images without the partisanship that characterized wartime writings. Beginning in January 1867 Optic continued to explore war issues and subjects in *Oliver Optic's Magazine*. Although he ran articles on the human destruction wrought by the war and on the heroism displayed by Union soldiers, on individual battles and campaigns, and at least one humorous article about a "Dutch" regiment's encounter with a bull, most of the entries on the war were biographies of important Union generals, with at least seven separate items about General Grant. Even Optic, however, decided the well of war stories had run dry by 1870.[6]

The second magazine, and the lone southern children's publication from the immediate postwar period, was the *Southern Boys and Girls' Monthly*. Echoing prewar and wartime calls for a unique southern literature, the editors complained that "too much have we been disposed to rely on other sections of the land and other countries of the world to supply us with literature for the old and the young." Quickly denying any "unworthy sectional spirit," however, they promised to publish literature "commensurate with the wants of southern society." Most of the pieces published during the magazine's nearly two-year run consisted of highly moralistic stories about nature, travel, and history, as well as cheerful poems about death. A few recalled the war in generic or nonconfrontational ways. The first issue contained a long original poem, "The Colour-Bearer," which offered a battlefield hero without revealing the color of his uniform, while a later issue promoted Confederate Memorial Day. Puzzles and games occasionally utilized words or names associated with the war, while a humorous story about a dispute between neighbors ended with a little girl asking if her family would "secede" from the neighboring family.[7]

Many southern and northern children did not have to rely on store-bought toys or published stories to nurture their memories of the war. Letters written by brothers and fathers became treasured keepsakes tucked carefully away as bittersweet tributes to deceased loved ones. The daughter of Confederate Marion Fitzpatrick and his wife Amanda, conceived during her father's last furlough before he was killed at Petersburg, became the archivist of the letters written by a father she never knew. Lizzie Cary Daniel published her girlhood scrapbook of Confederate songs, speeches, poetry, and biographical articles in 1893 to raise money at Richmond's Memorial Bazaar for Confederate monuments. A more personal collection was kept by Lucretia Revere, widow of Col. Paul Revere, the grandson of the famous silversmith and patriot. Lucretia crowded obituaries, newspaper reports, and accounts of anniversaries, patriotic speeches, the construction of memorials, and other war-related material into the album for years afterward. It obviously became a family heirloom — Revere left two children under age four — that was eventually donated to the American Antiquarian Society.[8]

As Reconstruction ended, children who had actually lived through the war continued to be haunted by it. Not surprisingly, some grew up to hate war of any kind. As an old man George F.

Robertson wrote, "It is one thing to read about that terrible day" when Confederates fired on Fort Sumter, "but it is a very different thing to have passed through its awful hours of suspense." He hoped that "this will never be repeated," but admitted, "we hear of wars and rumors of wars every day . . . and that state of affairs will in all likelihood go on till the King of Peace shall come and sway His scepter of righteousness over his universal empire." Despite writing a memoir called *War Boy*, a Virginian urged the descendants for whom he wrote the book to resist calls to armed conflict. He pleaded with them to "not let the sound of fife and drum," which had led him during the war to found his own boy company, "stir your hot blood enough to break the peace." Even northerner Stephen Smith Burt, who had enthusiastically marched with Republican Wideawakes, attended a military academy during the war, and enjoyed Optic's wartime adventure stories, realized the cost of the war when he traveled through the South as a young man. Walking through southern cemeteries, he noted that "boys little older than I, when still at school and merely playing soldier, had gone to their death." An accident of birth, of geography, may have saved him from a similar battlefield tragedy. "War is the product of an age that has not entirely freed itself from barbarism," he concluded. "The entire question between the North and the South . . . could have been, in my belief, decided by arbitration . . . at what a saving of life, misery, suffering, and destruction."[9]

Southern children understood exactly what Burt meant. Wartime destitution extended into peacetime poverty, and despite the end of the fighting, emotionally challenging demands such as creating new relationships with freed slaves forced youngsters in the defeated South to reassess assumptions already shaken by the war. When Jane Friend's family returned to their ravaged home near Petersburg after the war ended, they found that the besieging Yankee army had stripped their 250 acres of trees as well as outhouses, slave quarters, barns, and fences. Fortifications and ramshackle huts scarred the landscape, roads were obliterated, and virtually no plants aside from weeds grew. Ten-year-old B. H. Wilkins's family had moved from Richmond to a Blue Ridge farm, where their first crop failed, then relocated to another farm on the James River, where B. H. helped make ends meet by scavenging bullets from nearby battlefields and bartering them at a country store for sugar and coffee. Not surprisingly, these difficult times led many children to lash out at the northern whites and southern blacks who represented their victorious enemies. A fifteen-year-old southern girl living with a grown sister in New Jersey just after the end of the war remained the consummate Rebel, complaining about the weather and the grating politeness of "these abominable" Yankee boys. Teenager Martha Moore came across a group of black children on their way to school in occupied New Orleans. Spotting Martha's geography text, one of them "called out, 'Sissy, is dat a jogafry?' Of course," Martha sniffed in her diary, "I took no notice of the impudent little monkey."[10]

Southern children reared in the crucible of war could trace their most violent impulses to wartime political and racial indoctrination. A case in point is the career of John Wesley Hardin, who was only eight when the war began. In his memoir he blamed his murderous career on the hatred of Yankees and African Americans he had learned as a boy. The outlaw recalled in his autobiography that "the principles of the Southern cause loomed up in my mind ever bigger, brighter, and stronger." Although he eventually killed over twenty men, spent sixteen years in prison, and was himself gunned down in El Paso at age forty-two, Hardin's exaggerated sense of southern grievance claimed his first victim: a black man who had threatened John after losing a wrestling match to the smaller white boy. The fifteen year old soon became a fugitive from the Federal soldiers occupying Texas. When a patrol of Yankees came after him, he killed three of them, including another black man. Hardin, still less than twenty years old, taught school for a time, but his anger mounted, he wrote, when he saw "impudent Negroes . . . insult or abuse old, wounded Confederates." In yet another fight with a squad of Federal soldiers, John and his companion each killed a Yankee. Hardin's Civil War childhood, at least as presented in his colorful autobiography, apparently turned him into a psychopath. He believed every rumor about the cruelties of northern troops and freedmen, took offense at any perceived slight, and generally believed that his actions were justified by conditions arising from the war and its aftermath.[11]

Up from Slavery

The children of those freedmen Hardin despised so much also had to deal with postslavery realities. Many had begun their Reconstruction experiences in the sad, wonderful contraband camps long before Lee's surrender. The end of the war forced all young slaves and their parents to change the ways they made decisions and related to the world around them. Their struggle to build lives out of the debris of plantation society, even as they were attacked politically and economically and physically by angry whites, scarred the memories of many black children about the Civil War.

Their immediate response to the destruction of slavery varied widely. Mary Ellen Johnson, seven when the war began, was a little surprised to hear that she did not "'long to anybody but Gawd and my pappy and mammy," because she "ain't never know I ain't free." Isom Norris recalled the equanimity of his master's son Joe, who had once predicted that Isom would be "free as I is wen de war is over." If that ever happened, Isom promised, the first thing he would do was to "give you a whipping." On the day freedom came, "the fus' thing I 'new I jumped right straddle of Little Massa Joe, and threw him down and give him a few licks wid my fist," reminding Joe of his prediction and Isom's vow. "He tuk it as a big joke, and . . . laughed at me gettin' so happy." [12]

Few blacks or whites laughed for long about the ramifications of freedom, and children no doubt absorbed the ambiguity that emancipation elicited in black adults. Booker T. Washington described the sober reflection that followed the celebrations. "There were the questions of a home, a living, the rearing of children, education, citizenship, and the establishment and support of churches," he wrote in his autobiography. "Was it any wonder that within a few hours the wild rejoicing ceased and a feeling of deep gloom seemed to pervade the slave quarters?" Unable, perhaps, to envision immediately a future outside the often unbearable but familiar confines of slavery, many freedmen and freedwomen soon began to ponder the futures they would have to make for themselves. "Gradually, one by one, stealthily at first, the older slaves" on Washington's farm "began to wander . . . to the 'big house' to have a whispered conversation with their former owners," to arrange at least temporary housing and employment. [13]

A whirlwind of new experiences and emotions greeted black children at the threshold of freedom. Young blacks' workloads may have declined after emancipation, as many black fathers tried to make a go of it without the full-time labor of children and women. Seeking help from Freedmen's Bureau agents and running ads in African American newspapers, men and women tracked down children and spouses across state lines, fighting illiteracy, the ravaged Confederacy's social chaos, and possessive white families. Poignant reunions were followed by equally touching weddings, as youngsters witnessed their parents' efforts to legalize long-term relationships and legitimate their offspring. Although it seemed to whites that all of "their negroes" were on the move, in actuality most slaves did not move far. Many only temporarily took to the road, seeking family members, returning to the farms or plantations of former masters where friends or fond memories drew them, or escaping brutal treatment from individual whites. Young children whose parents were dead or unable to recover them sometimes ended up in new orphanages, such as the home built with proceeds from an African American fair in Mobile, or the substantial four-building complex sponsored by black soldiers and their officers near Helena, Arkansas.[14]

The confusion and uncertainty that freedom produced in slaves were partly allayed by the unifying celebrations that inspired a sense of confidence and gave closure to lifetimes of slavery. Normal relationships with whites were shattered in both positive and negative ways. Freedpeople celebrated their new status by resisting discipline, ignoring plantation rules, or even pillaging their former owners' property. More organized expressions of jubilation occurred in southern towns and cities after their occupation by Union troops or after news arrived of the Confederate surrender. Four thousand Charleston blacks held a spontaneous parade as 10,000 spectators thronged the city's streets. The procession offered visions of the past as well as the future. It included a mock slave auction, a "slave gang," and a coffin draped in black and labeled, "Slavery Is Dead." But also joining the celebration were groups of black artisans carrying their tools, African American fire companies, the brass band of the Twenty-first U.S. Colored Troops, and black schoolchildren chanting, "We know no caste or color." Less than three years later, black Texans formed ranks in the black community of Webberville to ride as a group into Austin to vote. They entered the capital city with an American flag at the head of the column singing, "Rally 'round the Flag."[15]

Freed girls and boys discovered a sense of community existing beyond the borders of home plantations in the mass emancipation celebrations and, more substantively, in schoolhouses throughout the South. A majority of the young former slaves attended some sort of school. Freedmen's Bureau schools operated until 1870, reaching about 20,000 pupils in the State of Texas alone, while in 1867 at least 78,000 pupils attended hundreds of schools supported throughout the South by northern philanthropists. Many more attended Sunday schools as well as private and missionary schools. Those who had to work during the day attended night classes, while others shared desks with men and women the same age as their parents or even their grandparents. A substantial number of the schools were supported at least partly through tuition paid by the students or their parents. Although they applied to freedmen's education the standard and somewhat confining assumptions about Christian morality, free enterprise, and class consciousness found in most schools of the period, they nevertheless facilitated a dramatic rise in the literacy rate among former slaves of all ages. And despite the fairly obvious goal among educators of blacks to create a disciplined, responsible, and obedient labor force — another goal they shared with most white schools — education remained perhaps the most valuable postslavery experience for black Civil War children.[16]

Access to schooling may have been a highlight for African American children and their families during the war and Reconstruction, but the black community was soon besieged by discrimination and violence. Just after the war, southern legislatures imposed "Black Codes" to reassert white control over their former slaves; the so-called apprenticeship laws affected children most directly. Their official goal of caring for freedchildren without families — the laws generally required planters to educate and provide adequate room and board for their apprentices — thinly concealed their real purpose of retaining control of the labor of freedchildren. Often based on prewar customs of binding out black and white orphans and the children of indigent free blacks, the laws inevitably led to abuses. Planters often kept children in service against the wishes of their parents or took advantage of former slaves' often imprecise birth dates to keep grown "minors" at work. Eager to avoid having to support orphaned or impoverished blacks with government resources, Freedmen's Bureau agents frequently ignored the bureau's own regulations. Apprenticed youngsters rarely received the benefits mandated by law, which included a rudimentary education, a financial settlement upon completion of the indenture, and the skills necessary to practice a trade. Thousands of black children and teenagers throughout the South endured a de facto extension of their bondage through the manipulation of these laws.[17]

Former slave children also experienced with their elders the spasms of racial violence that racked the former Confederacy for years after the war. As victims and as witnesses, young blacks no doubt felt extremely vulnerable to the brutal and random attacks of groups such as the Ku Klux Klan and its clones, as well as individuals such as John Wesley Hardin and ad hoc mobs. Thousands of documented and at least as many undocumented cases of violence perpetrated by whites on blacks occurred during the Reconstruction years. Children witnessed racially inspired street fights, ambushes, lynchings, and outright executions. Throughout the South schools for freedchildren and the white and black teachers who taught them became special targets of terrorism. In St. Landry Parish, Louisiana, a white carpetbagger, Emerson Bentley, was severely beaten in front of a class of black children at a school he had founded; as many as 200 blacks were killed in methodical attacks on plantations in the same parish. During the Memphis riot of 1866, in addition to killing nearly four dozen African Americans, white rioters burned down twelve black schools. Twenty-six schools in Monroe County, Mississippi, closed due to violence, while night riders even burned white public schools in one corner of Alabama as symbols of the hated Radical Republicans. African Americans all over the South slept in the woods to avoid attacks from night riders, and hundreds fled from counties when violence reached epidemic proportions. In their nearly nightly attacks during one eleven-month period in York County, South Carolina, Klansmen murdered 11 people and assaulted 600 black men, women, and children. Some incidents were gothic in their horror. Twenty-five blacks were dragged out of a Houston church in 1875, slaughtered, and then drawn and quartered.[18]

The constant abuse took a toll on freedmen and freedwomen. Some no doubt internalized the low value placed on their lives.

One white Tennessean remarked plainly, "Nigger life's cheap now," and he was right. The value of blacks to the white community had, at least in the immediate aftermath of the war, vanished when they could no longer be bought or sold. Later in the century they endured another wave of violence as lynchings, already used by whites to punish or to warn recalcitrant blacks, soared to an average of 138 per year in the 1890s. As objects of sadistic abuse and as political threats to southern whites, blacks lived in constant fear for their lives and the lives of their families. As a former Texas slave reported, "In dem days when chillun wouldn't mind all dat I had to say was, 'All right de Ku Klux wil git yo!' " and "Dey'd come right into de yard and mind." More importantly, the violence and death had profound effects on the morale of black communities, which were disrupted, intimidated, and sometimes cast adrift without experienced leadership.[19]

Yet leaders did emerge from the last generation of slaves, the African American children of war. The brothers Archibald and Francis Grimké, sons of a slave mother and her white owner, had seized the chance to end their bondage during the war when they both escaped from their white half-brother and worked as servants to Confederate and Union officers. After the war they left Charleston for Lincoln University in Pennsylvania, later meeting their aunts, abolitionists Sarah and Angelina Grimké, who helped pay for their schooling. Francis became a well-known Presbyterian minister in Washington, D.C.—he married abolitionist Charlotte Forten in 1878—while Archibald became an editor, writer, and fiercely independent political activist. Both men drew strength from the independence they had asserted as young boys and from the confidence in their own abilities and self-worth that their wartime experiences had given them. Archibald directed his confrontational rhetoric at all forms of racism and discrimination, even challenging W. E. B. DuBois for his support of the First World War, and favored woman suffrage. Less radical but no less influential, Francis preached the importance of character in the development of his race; political power, education, and economic success would be a curse if not accompanied by a commitment to Christian morality.[20]

The first African American to graduate from West Point, Henry O. Flipper, had, like the Grimkés, lived as a boy in the path of William T. Sherman's army. Although born a slave, his father,

Festus, a skilled artisan, had bought his sons and wife and made a home with them in Atlanta, where, Henry remembered, they "lived happily" and "virtually free." After the war the elder Flipper hired the wife of a former Confederate officer to tutor Henry and his brother. They later attended Atlanta University. Flipper's seemingly charmed life—so unlike that of almost any other slave child's—ran headlong into the racism that plagued the U.S. Military Academy. He survived, however, and eventually served as the only black officer of the famed Tenth Cavalry in Texas. Yet personality conflicts, his own carelessness, and trumped-up charges eventually resulted in his dismissal from the service. He ultimately became a successful mining engineer, but his shattered military career bore witness to the fact that even relatively privileged slave children faced limits in postwar America.[21]

Few black leaders experienced the war and Reconstruction as intensely as newspaperman T. Thomas Fortune, born a slave in northwest Florida in 1856. Four of his relatives died fighting in the Union army, he became fast friends with the son of the Union soldier who taught school in his hometown of Marianna, and his father, Emanuel, served as a state legislator in the late 1860s. After Klan threats forced the family to move to Jacksonville, young Tim became acquainted with legislators as a bootblack and as a legislative page, worked as a printer's devil, and eventually entered Howard University in 1874.

Fortune never completed his college degree, but basing himself in New York, he made an often precarious living as reporter, editor, and sometimes publisher of African American newspapers. He published the *Globe* and the *New York Freeman* but sometimes had to scramble for jobs with papers as far afield as Cincinnati or Baltimore. His material rewards were few and the risks he took were high. He once called southern white men organized rape mobs and suggested that for every black man killed in the South a white man should be killed in retaliation. For fifty years he was a political independent unafraid to support Democrats (particularly Grover Cleveland) and to criticize Republicans (especially their exploitation of black voters and Theodore Roosevelt's handling of the infamous Brownsville Riot). In 1898 he formed the Afro-American Council, which promoted integration, education, and political rights for all African Americans, but particularly those in the South. This short-lived organization was a spiritual forerunner of the Niagara Movement, which led to the founding of the National Association for the Advancement of Colored People a decade later.[22]

Fortune's arch style often caused problems with other black leaders. He had a long but often tense relationship with Booker T. Washington, who by turns subsidized, exploited, and distanced himself from the sharp-penned journalist. Unlike Washington, Fortune and the Grimkés made their homes in the North, where they enjoyed political, economic, and emotional resources denied to all but a few freed slaves, the overwhelming majority of whom remained in the former Confederacy. Washington's cautious activism stemmed in part from his decision to live in the South but also from his life as a slave, much of which passed during the Civil War. Too young to escape bondage during the war, he did not feel the exhilaration of freedom until emancipation forced his family to fend for themselves. Unlike the Grimkés, who enjoyed the support of well-placed northern sponsors, life was a hand-to-mouth proposition for Booker, his siblings, his ailing mother, and his luckless stepfather. He wrote as an adult that he never remembered playing as a child and there was precious little time for leisure after freedom, either. After the war he worked for a time in a West Virginia salt mine and learned to read and write at night school. A much better situation emerged when he took a job as houseboy for a wealthy white family, where he learned notions of thrift, cleanliness, and hard work from his transplanted Yankee employer. Washington traveled a long way from his hard-knock life in Virginia and West Virginia to become the famed Wizard of Tuskegee, but his boyhood on a backwoods dirt farm and in the dreary salt mines taught him that emancipation had given his people nothing more than the freedom to work hard and that they could expect little more from whites than the opportunity to perform the hardest jobs available. No wonder his adult memories of the end of slavery were so ambiguous and his most consistent advice to other blacks was that only through diligent labor could they hope to conquer racism and forge better lives for themselves.[23]

Washington worked through his feelings about the war in speeches, articles, books, and his career as an educator. Other former slaves struggled in more personal ways to incorporate their own memories into some sort of coherent synthesis of what slavery and the war meant to them. Billy Slaughter, a Kentucky slave born in 1858, applied a scholarly zeal to his study of the causes and results of the Civil War. Interviewed in the 1930s by a Works Progress Administration worker, he revealed a quite up-to-date analysis of the war — secession and states' rights, not slavery, was its real cause, he argued — along with an admiration for John Brown and Abraham Lincoln. Slaughter was born near Lincoln's Kentucky birthplace, and he periodically made a "pilgrimage" to view the "Lincoln Farm." After asking his interviewer if she read much history, the old freedman gave her a brief lesson on the reasons for Lincoln's decision to emancipate the slaves, which he attributed to a desperate need for manpower rather than pure altruism.[24]

Few Civil War children could muster Slaughter's scholarly detachment, and most former slaves worked the war into their personal folklore in less comprehensive ways. Some could take comfort in merely surviving the war and living a long life. Clara Jones, born in 1848, remembered that Confederates "went off laffin' . . . and many did not come back." When the Yankees "come through, dey took what dey wanted; killed de stock; stole de horses; poured out de lasses and cut up a lot of meaness." But she had the last laugh, for unlike her, "most of 'em is dead and gone now." Others insisted that Abraham Lincoln had traveled through the South during the war to "just learn ever'thing 'bout de folks"; one woman had heard he was "'guised so nobody knowed who he wus." Another woman who witnessed Union soldiers plundering Spartanburg, South Carolina, remembered Lincoln, well armed and surrounded by soldiers, riding through town, assuring frightened blacks that they would not be harmed.[25]

These former slave children projected their obvious admiration for Lincoln into comforting tall tales that brought their emancipator closer to their childhoods. Even blacks who admired the memory of Lincoln as the source of their freedom, however, often tempered their memories with the cold reality of the difficult lives many had lived since emancipation. Jane Johnson could not remember much personally about Lincoln, since she "was too young to have much sense," but her "mammy and daddy say he was a good man and wanted everybody to be free, both white and black." That was all well and good, but what had the government done for her people since then? Jane reminded her interviewer that although "slavery was wrong . . . what 'bout hard times? . . . All dis hollerin' 'round 'bout freedom they has, shucks, all dat kind of talk ain't nothin'." William Pratt, only five when the war ended, went so far as to argue that "I think Abraham Lincoln didn't do just right, 'cause he threw all the negroes on the world without any way of getting along." Amy Penny, born in 1855 and battered by years of hardship capped by the Great Depression, bluntly declared, "I think slavery wus not such a bad thing 'pared wid de hard times now."[26]

Booker T. Washington's famous advice to his fellow southern blacks to remain in the rural South reflected, at least partly, his view of the war and of emancipation. Although obviously a turning point in the history of his people, it did not fundamentally change the daily challenges faced by African Americans. Yet southern and northern blacks did celebrate emancipation in ways that resembled the commemoration of the war by southern and northern whites. In fact, the national attention given to a group of black schoolchildren decorating the mass graves of Union soldiers outside Charleston on May 30, 1865, a day southerners had already dedicated to remembering the Confederate dead, helped inspire northerners to establish their own "decoration day." Starting even as the war still raged and extending into the present, black children in various parts of the country could participate in celebrations honoring a number of emancipation dates: January 1, the date the slave trade ended and the Emancipation Proclamation was issued; February 1, the passage of the Thirteenth Amendment ending slavery in the United States; July 4, the day slavery ended in New York; April 16, the day slaves in the District of Columbia were freed; and June 19, or "Juneteenth," the day Texas slaves received their freedom. Over the years, simple barbecues, picnics, worship services, and speech making evolved into ball games, beauty contests, historical pageants, and occasions for political protest. Even as younger generations were taught to mourn their ancestors' bondage, they also learned to honor the slaves' stubborn refusal to be dehumanized. By commemorating heroic resistance against slaveowners, preserving family folklore about slavery, and retelling old "trickster" tales, in which shrewd blacks turned the tables on dull whites, African Americans created a tradition of honoring their enslaved ancestors at the same time they celebrated their emancipation.[27]

Stern Realities

"Three years! I wonder if she'll know me!" began a poem in *The Student and Schoolmate* about a one-armed, sun-browned, "shaggy" veteran contemplating his return to wife and son. He imagines his wife watching for him from the corner near his house and the relief of finally putting down his burden and resting in familiar surroundings. Little Charlie, he knew, with "the laughing, three-years-old brown eyes / (His mother's eyes) will stare with pleased surprise!" Alas, those brown eyes had, while the soldier fought for his country, closed in death, and all the soldier found at home were two grass-carpeted graves.[28]

This excessively maudlin version of a soldier's homecoming hardly represented the typical experience of northern and southern children. Such reunions were rarely recorded in diaries or memoirs. When they were, the authors tended to focus on their relief and joy. Yet Civil War soldiers could not just shrug off all they had seen in camp and on the battlefield and resume interrupted lives. As a result, the happiness that shone over the reunions of soldiers and their families could be dimmed by the sometimes sudden arrival of these worn, somber men. Laura Ingalls Wilder recalled in her fictionalized reminiscences her Uncle George, who "was home from the army" but still wearing his blue army coat. Although he appeared to be a merry, gregarious soul, he apparently had been changed by his Civil War experience, which had begun when he ran away to be a drummer boy at age fourteen. According to Laura's father, George was "wild, since he came back from the war." Other children found that the cocky young men they had worshiped in photographs sent from the army came home ruined by their experiences. Mary Eliza Starbuck's cousin Seth had lost his strong physique and twinkling eye during a stint at Libby Prison. Mary recalled sitting on his knee, listening as he talked in that "quiet voice which had the curious hint of finality that I've always noticed in the returned soldier when telling his experiences." Never recovering from his ordeal, he died not long after returning home.[29]

The most complete description of a veteran's return to his family appeared in the first few pages of writer Hamlin Garland's autobiography; he had described the reunion nearly twenty years earlier in a short story. When Richard Garland arrived at his little

Wisconsin farm just after the war, Hamlin's mother Belle rushed into his arms, followed closely by their eldest child, Hattie. To five-year-old Hamlin, however, "he was only a strange man with big eyes and care-worn face." Yet he "submitted to his caresses" after his mother "urged me forward." Little Frank, however, who had been only nine months old when Richard marched off to war, "would not even permit a kiss. The gaunt and grizzled stranger terrified him," despite Richard's urgent, repeated plea to "come here, my little man." A shiny red apple eventually lured the scared toddler into his father's embrace. An idyllic day of lounging, eating, and talking followed, during which Richard's voice "sinks deeper into my remembrance," Garland recalled. At bedtime the children fell asleep listening to stories "of the battles he had seen, and the marches he had made." Their father was home, and all was well.

Yet all was not the same as before. Richard Garland had joined the army against his wife's wishes, serving through the latter months of the Vicksburg campaign and in Sherman's western army after that. Even as a boy, Hamlin retained a sense of the bitterness he must have instinctively learned from his mother. She had begged Richard not to enlist, but "he was of the stern stuff which makes patriots." "What sacrifice," Hamlin wrote as an adult, "what folly! Like thousands of others he deserted his wife and children for an abstraction, a mere sentiment." Garland admitted in his autobiography that his memory of the actual events of those war years was dim, but he held that "a large part of what I am is due to the impressions of these deeply passionate and poetic years." The children loved to hear their father tell stories — the war provided vivid additions to his repertoire of pioneer tales — and to recite Shakespearean scenes from memory. Yet a darker side of Richard Garland also emerged, "for my father brought back from his two years' campaigning . . . the temper and habit of a soldier." He became the dominant force in the family, a change of pace for Hamlin and Frank especially, who remembered nothing of their lives before Richard went away. "We soon learned . . . that the soldier's promise of punishment was swift and precise in its fulfillment." Although Hamlin entertained other, quite fond memories of his father, Richard was a strict man, and his oldest son believed his wartime experiences were the reason. "We knew he loved us," Garland wrote in words that could no doubt have been echoed by thousands of soldiers' children, "for he often took us to his knees of an evening and told us stories of marches and battles, or chanted war-songs for us." But "the moments of his tenderness were few," and the slightest misbehavior was corrected harshly and immediately.[50]

Garland's memories of how the war affected his father's relationships with his children stand virtually alone among the hundreds of books and articles written by the children of veterans. This should not be surprising, since even veterans were loath to write about the inevitable difficulties of their transition back to civilian lives. Indeed, although returning soldiers spent twenty years nursing old wounds and the disillusionment spawned by their combat experiences, both were supplanted in the 1880s by the patriotic, even nostalgic gloss put on the war by the Grand Army of the Republic (GAR), the United Confederate Veterans, and other organizations. By middle age and later, old soldiers spent a great deal of time and effort "veteranizing," as Sherwood Anderson called his father's postwar enthusiasm for martial displays and attributes.[31]

Yet veterans of Civil War combat were clearly exposed to traumas similar to those of twentieth-century soldiers, and although the memoir literature is virtually silent on the issue, psychological responses such as nightmares, delusions, and other manifestations of reliving the terrors of combat must have plagued many soldiers as well as their children. American veterans in the late 1940s or the 1970s felt awkward with their children, especially those born while they were away in the army. They tended to be critical of them, to focus on "childish" mannerisms such as thumb sucking, whining, and bed-wetting. Like Richard Garland, they maintained strict discipline. Guilty about their own survival when so many friends and comrades had died in battle, veterans may have demanded perfection of themselves and their children or, conversely, become anxious, overprotective parents. For their part, like Hamlin and his brother, children in this situation may have at least temporarily resented the sudden interruption of their cozy relationships with their mothers. The children of returning soldiers often had eating and sleeping problems and were difficult to toilet train. Of course, children whose fathers died on the battlefield or in the hospital were also affected permanently. Memoirists among children tended to focus on the nationalistic pride that assuaged their grief or the material hardships that followed their fathers' deaths. But researchers have shown that other physical and psychological symptoms often stem from the deaths of male parents in modern wars. Boys are often less likely to display masculine traits, while girls tend to exaggerate their femininity. Both genders tend to become more submissive and to delay gratification in their personal lives. Paternal bereavement often sparks emotional disturbances such as introversion, dependence on others, or even psychotic or suicidal behavior. Historians can only speculate that at least some of these symptoms surfaced in the postwar lives of veterans' children, for evidence of these manifestations of fathers' absences or deaths is virtually nonexistent.[32]

Although Victorian convention may have discouraged the sharing of such intimate, sad details, a number of children reflected on the war's immediate effect on their own lives. Southerners, especially girls, mourned the childhood that was a casualty of the war and resented missing the freedoms and pleasures normally reserved for youth. The girlhood of one woman "had slipped from me, never to return." Emma Le Conte confided the same sense of loss to her diary. Early in 1865 the sometime refugee and seventeen-year-old daughter of Confederate chemist Joseph Le Conte complained "how dreadfully sick I am" of the war that had monopolized her adolescence and robbed her of the joys and prerogatives girls of her class expected. "No pleasure, no enjoyment—nothing but rigid economy and hard work—nothing but the stern realities of life." Such tribulations would normally "come later" but due to the war "are made familiar to us at an age when gladness should surround us." Some revealed more than a little self-pity. Jane Friend was thirteen when the war ended with the destruction of her family's Petersburg home. She recalled long afterward her wartime belief that for a cousin who had lost a husband and a neighbor who had lost a son "the worst was over. They had no more sickening dread of news from the front"—her own father was in a Virginia regiment—"Their boy was past suffering, and his suffering, if at all, had been short. These were sad reasonings for a child of ten years," she wistfully stated in her reminiscences, "but war is transforming. At thirteen, when it closed, I was a full-fledged woman."[33]

Few northern children complained about a lost childhood, although the drudgery endured by Anna Shaw led her to greet the Confederate collapse with relief: "The end of the Civil War brought freedom to me, too," as well as to the slaves with whom she identified as an adolescent abolitionist. For most other northern children, it seems, the war enhanced rather than shortened their childhoods. Dan Beard cheerfully commented years later that "had a leader of boys arisen in '61, like that emotional shepherd lad who led the children's crusade of 1212, he could have gathered a vast army of small boys to fight for the Union."[34]

The hardening process may have affected northern children less than southern children, but many of the former did feel the pain and loss caused by the murder of Abraham Lincoln. Like children born in the 1950s who can remember exactly where they were when President John F. Kennedy was assassinated, the time and the place where they heard the news of the assassination were burned into the memories of children of the 1860s. Bliss Perry wrote over eighty years after the assassination that "I have never met a man old enough to recall Lincoln's death who did not remember precisely where he was and what he was doing."[35]

A Keokuk County, Iowa, boy and his family were riding home in a wagon when a neighbor gave them the news at a prairie crossroads. Long afterward he remembered "the feeling of depression and sorrow that came on us. His death seemed like a personal loss in the family." Anna Robertson was only five when her family drove into a nearby town and saw the black mourning bunting tacked to shops and houses. A storekeeper told her mother about the tragedy. Her cry, "Oh, what will become of us now?" burned the scene into her little daughter's memory. A sharply etched vignette of her mother "burying her face in her apron" and "running into her room sobbing as if her heart would break" made the moment memorable to eight-year-old Ida Tarbell. Images of boxes strewn around her new house, untouched because the demoralized family had just heard the news of Lincoln's death, occupied the memories of a Wisconsin girl. Others remembered small details about the days following Lincoln's death: the startling impression of men crying in public; wearing badges with the martyred president's picture framed in red, white, and blue; standing in line from supper time until nearly breakfast to see him lying in state; and a little girl remarking as she viewed his memorial procession, "That's the kind of coffin I'm going to get for my mother."[36]

Like their parents, northern children exhibited a wide variety of reactions to the death of the president. A future governor of Wyoming retreated daily to a mountain on his grandfather's Vermont farm and shouted, "Hurrah for Lincoln," then listened as his tribute echoed down the Otto Creek Valley. The conspirators obsessed Lizette Woodworth, a young Baltimore Rebel, who often dreamed of them after studying their pictures in the illustrated weeklies hanging in the window of a nearby stationery shop. On isolated Nantucket Island, nine-year-old Mary Starbuck and her friend Eliza, impressed by their parents' preparations for the local memorial service to which the girls were not invited, opened her mother's sewing bag and decorated every window on the first floor of their house. Black and white ribbons, garlands, ties, sashes, half-finished clothes, and rags illustrated the girls' attempts to join in the nation's mourning.[37]

The children of Craigie House, however, deflected their grief even more elaborately. Like children playing through their fears and hopes by "becoming" boy soldiers or reenacting personal dramas, they made it safe to think about the assassination by re-creating it. When the Longfellow children learned of the murder, according to neighbor and playmate Henrietta Dana, they "were stunned with amazement and vague terror . . . that such a thing could ever happen in our civilized age, in our own free country, to our own good and dear President." "Our love of the dramatic came to our rescue," wrote Henrietta, "and as descriptions of the scene of the assassination began to appear in the daily papers and illustrated weeklies, with one heart and mind we rushed to stage the scene in our outdoor theater." The east veranda of Longfellow's residence became the presidential box in Ford's Theater, and the croquet lawn became the stage on which scenes from "Our American Cousin" were enacted. Older girls directed and took the best roles, while Henrietta, the youngest, got only "the dummy roles which no one else wanted." The tallest girl played Lincoln as he entered the presidential box waving to the applauding audience, although Henrietta had to play Lincoln in the passive role of target and victim. The children reenacted the whole drama: the shooting, the stabbing of Major Rathbone, the leap onto the croquet lawn/stage, the escape and chase, and the capture of Booth—which, "as the lonely, crippled, hunted fugitive," was also a part suitable for the littlest and least powerful player. Even Long-fellow's "small fat Skye terrier" represented "a brace of manhunt-ing bloodhounds."[38]

Lincoln's death affected Civil War children far beyond their immediate grief and bewilderment. The president's martyrdom punctuated the end of the victorious war for the Union; to chil-dren, the coincidence amplified the significance of both events. Thrilling to the stories told again and again of battles and home-town heroes, Jane Addams especially admired President Lincoln, who was an acquaintance of her father, a member of the Illi-nois state senate. The Honorable Mr. Addams worshiped Lincoln, had at least two pictures of the Railsplitter hanging in the house, and when asked, would almost religiously take out the packet of "Mr. Lincoln's letters," a short stack of personal letters. When Addams died, friends eulogized him as a man who, during the days of fat contracts with the War Department, had not only not taken a bribe, but whose reputation for honesty had discouraged anyone from even offering him one. "For one or all of these reasons," Jane remembered fondly, "I always tend to associate Lincoln with the tenderest thoughts of my father." She was obviously shocked, then, when on an April morning when she was four and a half years old, she discovered mourning bands on her family's gate posts and her father tearfully announced that "the greatest man in the world had died."

Inspired by Lincoln's martyrdom and her father's devotion to his political ally, Jane came to see the former "as the standard bearer to the conscience of his countrymen" and as "an epitome of all that was great and good," and cultivated the values and strengths she believed both men possessed. Lincoln proved to be a powerful tool for helping the immigrants who crowded the Hull House complex cope with their shame and grief over repudiating their language and customs. Addams "held up Lincoln for their admiration as the greatest American" and emphasized his capacity for using his own awareness of how the past had shaped him as a potent method of adapting to new ideas and situations. For Jane Addams, who found herself a little wearied by the exces-sive scholarly apparatus surrounding the British settlement house movement that she otherwise admired, Lincoln was the only in-spiration required for going out into the world and making things better. "He made plain," she wrote, "once for all, that democratic government, associated as it is with all the mistakes and short-comings of the common people, still remains the most valuable contribution America has made to the moral life of the world."[39]

We Must Never Forget

Civil War children created their own meanings for the triumphs and tragedies of the war. At the same time, some children became a part of the meaning of the war constructed by adults. Soldiers' orphans were, to use a twentieth-century phrase, poster children for the cause, particularly in the North, as victims and as permanent symbols of the sacrifices endured by Americans. Although comprehensive statistics on children entering orphanages and asylums due to the deaths of soldier-fathers are unavailable, anecdotal evidence suggests there were thousands of war orphans. The number of boys seeking shelter in New York Newsboys' Lodging Homes nearly doubled during the war. The Northern Home for Friendless Children reported that half of its 160 residents were the children of soldiers, while of the 575 children admitted into Milwaukee asylums, 144 were related to soldiers. The war inspired philanthropists and religious denominations throughout the North and the South to establish institutions to care for the children of soldiers; as many orphanages opened in the 1860s as in the two previous decades. So great was the demand that Methodists in Boston, Baptists in Louisville, Jews in Cleveland, members of the Reformed Church in Philadelphia, and Roman Catholics in a number of cities opened new homes for orphans. African American women in Memphis organized informal orphanages to care for homeless child refugees, while the Brooklyn Colored Orphan Asylum, begun in 1866, served children uprooted by the collapse of slavery. Many institutions established before the war changed their policies to embrace children who were not technically orphans, including "half-orphans"—children with only one parent—and, as at the Protestant Orphan Asylum in St. Louis, children from refugee families.[40]

At the state level, the Soldiers' Orphans' Home movement begun in 1862 accelerated after the war. Even Congress got into the act in a modest way, chartering and exempting from federal and local taxes the National Soldiers' and Sailors' Orphans' Home in 1866, which by 1872 housed about seventy children.

Pennsylvania, Illinois, Kansas, Minnesota, Indiana, Iowa, Wisconsin, Rhode Island, Connecticut, and New Jersey all established state-supported institutions in the years immediately after the war. Some began as small, private schools or homes that state governments eventually took over. Others, as in Ohio, originated as projects supported by Republican politicians and the GAR. Orphans in Indiana originally lived in the state-sponsored soldiers' home, until their numbers overwhelmed those of the disabled veterans and a separate institution was established in 1870. An $8,000 grant from the Camden and Amboy Railroad—unpaid bounties for wartime volunteers who later deserted from the army—provided much of the seed money for the New Jersey home, while the Pennsylvania Railroad contributed the original $50,000 for soldiers' orphans' schools in the Keystone State. Eventually more than fifteen separate schools contracted with the state to provide homes and education for Pennsylvania's war orphans.[41]

Although some homes survived into the twentieth century by welcoming orphans of soldiers in later wars or all indigent children, many homes had relatively short lives. The Connecticut home, for example, had only 41 residents just a year or two before its demise in the mid-1870s, which its administrator attributed at least partly to a decline in contributions and interest on the part of the state's residents. Over 200 girls and boys lived in the New Jersey home in 1870, but the number had dwindled to 75 when the home closed six years later. Likewise, the Wisconsin home in Madison provided for between 250 and 300 children in any given year, but the legislature shut the doors on the crowded former soldiers' hospital in 1874. One of the few homes built expressly for African American orphans, the Shelter for Orphans of Colored Soldiers and Friendless Colored Children in Baltimore, had the resources to provide for only about a dozen children at a time.[42]

Despite the brief lives of some of these institutions, the soldiers' orphans' homes provided for the care, discipline, and education of thousands of poor orphans and half-orphans. Like the widows' and orphans' pensions established by Congress during the war, the homes represented the nation's commitment to the memory of the Union dead. Most homes were sponsored by state governments, however, and provided settings for political debates and patriotic displays in which politicians and veterans eagerly used the orphans' plight to make political points. Indeed, outraged when he discovered that 300 soldiers' orphans were living in county infirmaries and that as many as 2,000 others were homeless, Governor Rutherford B. Hayes of Ohio mobilized the GAR and other supporters to push a controversial orphans' bill through the Ohio legislature in 1870. Single-minded governors in Wisconsin and Pennsylvania, building on their reputations as the special friends of soldiers, helped win legislative funding for homes in their states. Governor Andrew Curtin of Pennsylvania traced his support for the idea to an encounter with two orphaned children who came begging at the governor's mansion on Thanksgiving Day 1863. The story may have been apocryphal, but it quickly became part of the folklore of the orphan schools that Curtin helped develop by the end of the war.[43]

Even after the homes and schools were safely established, controversies continued, inspired by Democratic Party attacks on their cost and on reports of abuse and mistreatment of their residents. After electing a governor and winning control of the Wisconsin legislature, for instance, Democrats quickly shut down the orphans' home in Madison, charging overcrowding and impractical educational goals. Accusations of misbehavior on the part of the children and of inadequate care prompted a special committee to investigate the New Jersey Soldiers' Children's Home in 1872. They concluded that most of the allegations were false, but the home closed four years later. As early as 1874 the superintendent of the Illinois home could say that after surviving "investigation after investigation," her staff could continue their "pure and holy . . . work." Yet her successors were also plagued with frequent accusations of harsh treatment and poor management during the long history of the home. The privately owned, profit-driven Pennsylvania system of orphans' schools was ripe for a wide array of abuses. The beginning of the end for them came with an 1886 exposé in the *Philadelphia Record* of corruption, profit mongering, and ill treatment. Income-producing work in shops and on farms was emphasized over education, critics charged. A newspaper campaign, a damning state investigation, and the withdrawal of support by the GAR led to the closing of most of the schools by 1892.[44]

Just as the care of orphans of Civil War soldiers became fodder for partisan politics, they and the institutions designed to accommodate them proved to be patriotic symbols of the war for the Union and potent reminders of the sacrifice of hundreds of thou-

Inspired by the true story of a dead soldier found clutching a photo of his children, the song "The Children of the Battle Field" helped popularize aid for soldiers' orphans. (Mary Ruth Collins)

sands of good northern men in that war. The most famous orphans' home grew from a nationwide campaign to locate the children of a soldier found dead on the battlefield at Gettysburg. Clutched in his hand was the picture of two boys and a girl who were quickly dubbed the "Children of the Battlefield." Sentimental northerners appreciated the symbolism of these youngsters, who came to represent all of the thousands of sons and daughters who lost their fathers in the cruel war. Newspapers and magazines around the country carried the story and the photo, and by November 1863 the widow and three children of Sgt. Amos Humiston had been located in Portville, New York.[45]

The poignant photo caught the imagination of the northern public, who bought thousands of copies of several different prints of the photograph and eagerly purchased sheets of the song "The Children of the Battlefield" by James G. Clark, winner of a poetry contest sponsored by the Philadelphia branch of the Sanitary Commission. Proceeds from the photographs went to Mrs. Humiston, but the composer of the song dedicated the money earned by his sentimental piece to "the support and education of the Orphan Children." Soon a campaign to establish a national orphanage for soldiers' orphans, promoted by Sabbath Schools around the country, was under way. By 1866 the former Gettysburg headquarters of Maj. Gen. O. O. Howard, Humiston's commanding general, had been purchased, and nearly two dozen children were living under the supervision of Philinda Humiston. She remained as matron for several years, and for nearly a decade the home flourished in reputation and in numbers until 1873, when seventy orphans resided there.[46]

The establishment and early years of the National Homestead at Gettysburg created a perfectly symmetrical progression of courage, sacrifice, loss, and reward. Yet the story of the orphans' refuge literally on the site of the bloodiest battle of the war ended with an ugly scandal. Revelations of abuse and embezzlement shocked Gettysburg residents. Rosa Carmichael, the matron, was convicted, fined, and thrown out of town, and others were also implicated in the widespread mistreatment of the children. Despite a waiting list of orphans needing homes, the facility closed in the fall of 1877.[47]

The descent of the National Homestead at Gettysburg into disgrace and oblivion ruptured the connection between Gettysburgians and their beloved symbol of the country's duty to the orphans of its departed heroes. Yet in other states and in other homes the relationship between patriotism and the care of orphans remained close. For one thing, the homes became nurseries of patriotism. In addition to the requirement in most homes that the children invest in their own maintenance by doing chores and working in home shops, boys at many of the schools and homes were formed into military companies and drilled at least once a week. The Home Cadets at the Ohio Soldiers' and Sailors' Orphan Home consisted of the oldest and most physically fit boys (and, after 1887, girls), who drilled, formed a drum corps, and received training in tactics and the use of rifles.[48]

In the decades following the end of the war, soldiers' orphans frequently appeared in public as reminders of the sacred duty of Americans to follow through on their collective responsibility. No less than veteran survivors, they became living monuments to the Federal cause. Year-end examinations offered the public a chance to see that their tax dollars were creating well-educated and orderly citizens, but more important were the ceremonies and events highlighting the special place the children filled in the patriotic soul of the North. In fact, one of the most effective displays of this child-sized "bloody shirt" came just after the war, when in a well-orchestrated effort to win support for public funding, a regiment of orphans invaded Harrisburg, Pennsylvania. After marching into the state capitol, they entertained and successfully moved politicians to action with patriotic and religious songs, speeches, and earnest pleas for help. Their message: patriotism would be rewarded and justice achieved by supporting these worthy offspring of devoted patriots.[49]

Of course, the nation expected something in return. In addition to the work that paid for part of their room and board, the orphans were also brought out on patriotic occasions. At the first Memorial Day ceremony at Arlington National Cemetery in 1868, orphans of Union soldiers spread flowers over 12,000 graves. Children at the Gettysburg National Homestead traditionally participated in local Decoration Day celebrations, strewing flowers on the graves at the national cemetery while chanting an ode beginning, "Lightly, lightly, lovingly tread / O'er the dust of the patriot dead." They also commemorated the battle of Gettysburg with a program on the anniversary of the last day of the battle, with the girls clad in white dresses with blue sashes and the boys in military-style uniforms, complete with miniature guns. Orphans also appeared when Pennsylvania's battle flags went on display in Philadelphia in 1866 and at Pennsylvania governor John F. Hartrauft's inauguration in 1873. Students at the New Jersey school "brought tears to eyes unused to weep," at least according to their administrator, when they sang patriotic songs at a flag raising on Independence Day. Drill teams and bands from other homes participated in GAR encampments and in dedication ceremonies for war monuments. In fact, the GAR incorporated children, orphans and non-orphans alike, into many of their rituals and projects. Women and children often visited GAR "campfires" and sometimes helped sing old war songs and stage patriotic and nostalgic tableaux. Union veterans sponsored Sons of Veterans chapters to perpetuate the memory of the veterans' sacrifices. In some states the GAR played active roles in reviewing schoolbooks (making sure the southerners' vain efforts were not presented too sympathetically) and encouraging the flying of American flags over public schools.[50]

Strapped for resources and more committed to local than federal or even state charities, the former Confederate states did not establish systems of schools or homes for children of their deceased soldiers. There had been attempts to do so during and just after the war, however. Committees were formed and contributions solicited in both North and South Carolina, for instance. A bill to establish an institution for orphans passed the Georgia state house of representatives, and late in the war Virginia Methodists proposed an "asylum" for soldiers' children. Scholarship funds were organized in several states, while local institutions were established for the care of orphans in Livingston, Alabama, Montgomery County, Tennessee, and Charleston, where orphans shared quarters with the widows and mothers of Confederate soldiers. Richmond finally established its own city orphanage, at least partly inspired by the plight of soldiers' orphans.[51]

Even though southerners failed to construct large-scale institutional supports for the orphans of soldiers, the fight for the souls of succeeding generations of children took on a special urgency in the South, where even the Ku Klux Klan swore to protect the orphans of dead Confederates. Organizations such as the United Confederate Veterans, the United Daughters of the Confederacy (UDC), the Sons of Confederate Veterans, the Children of the Confederacy, and other groups linked their status and self-images to the "Lost Cause." The UDC, which by 1912 had grown to 800 local chapters with 45,000 members, sponsored scholarships for the children of Confederate veterans, held essay contests on southern topics, campaigned to abolish the Lincoln's birthday holiday, encouraged "junior historians" in southern schools, and established children's auxiliaries as well as organizations such as the Junior Confederate Memorial Association in New Orleans and the Junior Hollywood Memorial Association in Richmond. These activities gave children important roles in preserving the memories and resting places of southern veterans. Children also regularly visited and entertained old Rebels living in the state-supported Confederate Soldiers' Homes that were founded beginning in the 1880s.[52]

Two young girls became the most potent symbols of children's participation in the southern war for independence. Winnie Davis, born to Jefferson and Varina Davis late in the war, was a regular guest at Confederate veterans' reunions late in the century. Although she was the spoiled daughter of fawning parents, educated in France and Germany, and a member of the South's cultural elite, Winnie never married and was the constant companion of her father. She was an essayist and published novelist, but as her father's reputation among southerners was gradually resurrected after Reconstruction, Winnie frequently accompanied him to his public appearances. From the 1880s until her death in 1898 she appeared before veterans' groups, who made her part of their ceremonies and followed former Confederate general John B. Gordon in calling her the "daughter of the Confederacy."[53]

Winnie Davis was a respected participant in the Lost Cause, but an aura of reverence surrounded the only surviving child of Gen. Stonewall Jackson; the difference in how southerners perceived them reflected the differences in the way the public had perceived their fathers. Born only a few months before Jackson's death at Chancellorsville and pushed by her mother, Mary Anna Jackson, into the Lost Cause limelight, Julia Jackson's short life was dominated by her status as the daughter of one of the Confederacy's greatest heroes. Although she never spoke in public, as a guest of honor she attended scores of monument dedications, receptions, and Confederate reunions, starting at age twelve with the unveiling of the Jackson statue in Richmond. She constantly received gifts honoring her father and was herself the object of a widely sold photograph labeled, "Julia, Daughter of Stonewall." After she died at age twenty-six, her young children took her place at numerous Confederate ceremonies.[54]

The presence of Winnie Davis and Julia Jackson — one historian has referred to the latter as a "professional orphan" — at Lost Cause events established a strong link between the Confederacy and its children. In typically southern fashion, larger-than-life individuals came to represent the children of the Confederacy, while in a corporate style familiar to most northerners, institutions and their sympathetic but largely nameless inmates usually illustrated the sacrifices of northern children.[55]

Yet southern patriots, including men and women who had been children during the war, did, in their own ways, look beyond nostalgia toward the future, attempting to shape the way succeeding generations of southerners viewed the war. For instance, they continued to expend a great deal of energy to influence the content of schoolbooks. Not every southern girl or boy could attend such safe and appropriately southern institutions as Charleston's Confederate Home School, where young teachers-to-be were inculcated with the appreciation and correct knowledge of the Confederacy; the Stonewall Jackson Institute; or Carr-Burdette College in Sherman, Texas, whose advertisements featured girls sporting Confederate uniforms and rifles. The struggle to assure the use of "safe" textbooks also complemented other publication projects, such as the UDC's 1912 *Catechism for Children*, a totally unreconstructed "history" of the war between the states. For many years and in virtually every former Confederate state, loyal southerners — especially members of the southern elite — guaranteed that the readers and histories put before the grandchildren and great-grandchildren of Rebels fully acknowledged the heroism of Confederate forebears and the correctness of the southern cause. Their campaign replicated the efforts of wartime educators and publishers to provide books appropriate for southern students and focused on the virtues, leadership, and sacrifices of the southern patriarchy. In addition to emphasizing the justice of the Confederate cause and the courage of its warriors, Lost Cause censors rejected Yankee authors' tendencies to immortalize Lincoln, to create the impression that slavery was the sole cause of the war, and to criticize the morality and leadership of southern slaveowners.[56]

A pair of southern high school teachers, W. N. McDonald

and J. S. Blackburn, produced the sort of history that southerners wanted in *A Southern School History of the United States
of America*, which labeled Puritans "extremists" who repeatedly
demonstrated "insolence and dictatorial arrogance"; justified slavery because, in Africa, "for many centuries that seems to have been
[the Africans'] natural condition"; blamed New Englanders for the
slave trade and applauded Virginia and other southern states for
outlawing it before 1808; called the Missouri Compromise "clearly
unconstitutional"; accused Republican "wide-awakes" of compris-
ing a "military organization"; and boasted of the victory of 20,000
Confederates over a well-equipped army of 60,000 Yankees at First
Manassas.[57]

Childhoods Found

There is no reason to believe that the girls who dressed in white
to decorate Confederate graves or the boys who executed military drills at GAR encampments did not, at least for the moment,
entertain patriotic thoughts. Yet the use of children as symbols of
the sacrifices endured and patriotism displayed by northerners and
southerners depended less on the children's own perceptions than
on the ambition of politicians and parents. But Civil War children
also sorted through their experiences and formed opinions about
what they witnessed during their nation's greatest crisis. The war
could become a foundation for personal beliefs and philosophies
as they applied the lessons of war to their careers. John Dewey's
winter in his quartermaster father's bleak Virginia camp helped
spawn his lifelong abhorrence of war. Henry Grady's father died
in battle, but his fortune remained intact, which no doubt helped
ease Henry's development into a moderate spokesman for the New
South. Anna Howard Shaw's obvious resentment at being left
with her sisters and mother to fend for themselves in the wilds of
Michigan by her father and brothers may have contributed to her
decision to fight for women's rights. Historian James Ford Rhodes
grew up in a Copperhead household in strongly Republican Cleveland, Ohio; the lessons of tolerance and intolerance he learned
there helped make the amateur historian a pioneer in the less partisan histories of the war that began to appear in the 1890s. As the
adult lives of these Civil War children reveal, if Civil War child-

hoods had been interrupted or lost, the search for meanings could salvage those battered years.[58]

Men and women who had experienced the war as southern children, who perceived it as a turning point in their lives and the lives of their fellow southerners, felt the greatest need to explain the war in memoirs and autobiographies. As such, they became their own historians, fitting their personal experiences into the larger sweep of events that had caught them up in their youths. In fact, the UDC strongly urged its members to write autobiographical accounts of their war experiences or at least brief histories of certain facets of the war — regiments, battles, and generals — from the southern point of view. Read aloud at chapter meetings, some were published as part of the UDC's commitment to preserving the Confederate version of history.[59]

A nearly ubiquitous topic in southerners' writing was the status of race relations during the ante- and postbellum periods. They saw the war as a watershed in southern race relations and often included nostalgic images of slavery that colored the grown-ups' memories of the institution and of the war. Some referred to fairly specific incidents or images of the institution or its aftermath: playing with slave children, eating "negro" food, and attending slaves' parties or worship services. Evelyn Ward, twelve when the war ended, remembered how strange it was to look at her father's former slaves and "know they were no longer our little maids and men." Some memories showed the lack of self-consciousness that many whites applied to what they believed to be idyllic images of preemancipation race relations. In his old age one Civil War child remembered with moist eyes the death of his favorite old slave who had once built him a wagon that the little white boy rode in behind a "team" of slave boys.[60]

The years before the war, for many southerners, "were the good old days and the good old ways," ruined by the war, and the more ambitious memoirists often included the standard justifications of African bondage in their happy, if one-sided, reminiscences. Before the war Thomas Ashby often "played and romped" with the slaves on his father's plantation. He argued fifty years later that slaves had been "free from care and responsibility . . . well fed, well clothed, well cared for in sickness and in old age." Hardships came to them due to their "vice and intemperance" and "bad temper and unruly disposition." The savagery of Africa, he asserted, had barely receded, even after centuries of civilizing contact with whites. Elizabeth Randolph Preston assured readers that the slaves were well treated and responded with absolute faithfulness to their masters. Emancipation had disrupted the relationship and thrown them onto their own meager mental resources. Cynical Rhode Island slave traders were responsible for the establishment and growth of the institution, believed a nephew of Confederate general Leonidas Polk, and northern Radicals made a bad situation—emancipation—worse, requiring southerners to "calmly, but firmly, put . . . down [the] lawlessness to which the negroes were incited" and restore them to "their places." Even a passage in another autobiography of a Confederate child that began by blaming slavery for the "death and misfortune" of "so many" ended with the reminder that it was also "an agency which brought many members of the Negro race out of the dark jungles of Africa."[61]

Similar reflections on the benefits of slavery also surfaced as a theme in the fiction published by Civil War children. Southern writers of the last few decades of the nineteenth century and the first decades of the twentieth often used the war and Reconstruction as backdrops to their stories in which slaves and freedmen are a constant presence. But just as southern and northern memoirs differed in their emphasis on the war, so did fictional accounts. Acknowledging their section's near-obsession with the war, many southern writers built careers explaining the war's impact on southern institutions and racial relationships. Northern writers, on the other hand, visited the conflict only occasionally; no single theme emerged from their fictional war. Caught up, perhaps, in the dramatic Gilded Age growth of industry and of cities, Yankee authors saw the war as unworthy of their complete attention, as merely a step in the larger economic and social transformations they so avidly explored in their writing.

A trio of northeastern writers displayed this intermittent interest in the war. Sarah Orne Jewett experienced the war as a girl on the threshold of adolescence at Berwick Academy in Maine. Her father served as a government surgeon, and Sarah participated in patriotic schoolgirl oratory, watched neighbors march from Berwick to fight for the Union, and attended funerals of boys not much older than she. A recent biographer explained her decision not to marry and her long-term relationship with another woman in terms of the postwar shortage of marriageable New England men. Yet Sarah rarely wrote about the war, as such. However, after attending in the mid-1890s a veterans' parade in Berwick and the dedication ceremonies for the Fifty-fourth Massachusetts monument on Boston Commons, she did write a story of a town's efforts to commemorate the war. Her touching "Decoration Day" told of three old veterans' successful attempts to reawaken their sleepy Maine town's gratitude to the boys in blue. On the other hand, Jewett also wrote novels dealing sympathetically with the southern aristocracy and their loyal slaves.[62]

Edward Bellamy, about a year younger than Jewett, also embraced the patriotism that dominated his little hometown of Chicopee Falls, Massachusetts, and, caught up in the spirit of the war, considered a military career. He failed the West Point physical examination, but his generally positive ideas about war as a unifying force and as a means of demonstrating the efficiency of centralization became crucial to his version of utopia. *Looking Backward* shows these positive effects of war in a general way. A less well known short story, "An Echo of Antietam," offers realistic, sensitive, and emotionally wrenching scenes of a local company departing for the front. When the hero inevitably falls in battle, his heartbroken lover is able to see his death and her own sacrifice as part of a noble and ultimately victorious cause.[63]

A third well-known northern writer, Harold Frederic, who turned five in the war's first year, viewed the war in a decidedly unromantic way. He seemed to have enjoyed the ceremony most little boys relished but also remembered the mounting losses and the political confusion in his home town of Utica, New York, where Democrats and Republicans fought over war aims. Best known for *The Damnation of Theron Ware*, Frederic also wrote extensively about the war in two novellas and a pair of short stories collected in an 1897 book he called *In the Sixties*. With a cynicism rivaling his older contemporary Ambrose Bierce, Frederic showed hypocritical and intolerant patriots persecuting a gruff but sympathetic Copperhead, a manipulative belle enticing men to enlist in the army, and a kind of class conflict emerging from the relationship between two sisters-in-law, one married to an officer, the other to a private.[64]

Of course southern writers, unlike northern authors such as

Jewett or Bellamy, could not frame their war memories in the context of victory. In addition, although northern children who went on to memorialize their war in literature could and did ignore Reconstruction, southern children—especially those who grew to adulthood during the decade following the war—could not separate its social, political, economic, and racial confusion from the war itself. This is not to say that southern authors publishing from the 1880s to the 1910s presented bitter critiques of northern motives and harsh descriptions of southern destruction and defeat. A few authors naturally did, including Mary Noailles Murfree who, writing as Charles Egbert Craddock, published *Where the Battle was Fought* two decades after the war ended. Murfree's family plantation had been destroyed by the war, and her dark novel shows shattered survivors hopelessly struggling in a tiny Tennessee town near a haunted battlefield. To Murfree's sad characters, the New South is a pipe dream and the Old South is only an empty memory.[65]

But Murfree was a mournful exception. Depending almost entirely on northern publishers and nearly as much on northern readers, southern children, as adult writers, focused on two themes: the romance of the Old South—the centerpiece of the Lost Cause myth—and sectional reconciliation. Obsessed with their region's romantic antebellum past, southern writers nevertheless rarely touched on the bitterness of the war. Reconstruction remained an unhappy and unfortunate and even tragic element of the relationship between the sections, but it came to represent less a serious rupture than an aberration in the generally noble, tolerant, and intertwined histories of the North and the South.[66]

Ironically, their narrow focus meant that southern writers actually had few useful things to say about the war. Limited by their northern markets, the conventions of victorian romances, and the constrictions of the local-color school, the books and stories of grown-up southern children, with a few exceptions, became rather predictable and nearly interchangeable. Joel Chandler Harris was best known for his versions of old slave tales, but he also fictionalized his wartime experiences as an apprentice newspaperman in *On the Plantation.* His war included casualty lists, corrupt Confederate officials, civilian hardships and poverty, Confederate defeats, and other inevitabilities of war, but those hard times are undercut by the good-natured tone of the book and a plot frequently interrupted by slave tales and hunting adventures. At one point he even writes that "it was agreed on all sides that times were very hard," but "they seemed very pleasant and comfortable" to the young protagonist. A more serious approach was taken by the less well known but more versatile Will N. Harben, who wrote in the local-color mode about his native northern Georgia but also tackled in meaningful and sympathetic ways postwar issues such as race, class, and wartime dissension.[67]

Like Harris, Thomas Nelson Page, born in 1853, clearly adapted his own experiences during the war to his best-selling fiction late in the century. According to his brother, in fact, numerous real-life incidents and individuals, including former slaves, appear in his novels and stories. The deeply conservative Page was only the most prolific of the writers of sectional reconciliation and the most noted of southern apologists. He believed that the war had robbed him of an idyllic life, and he spent his entire adulthood idealizing that world. The ugly side of this romantic Old South image was his insistence that African Americans were best suited for slavery. In his fiction, his essays, and his public addresses Page hammered away at the notion that blacks could function competitively with whites. They lacked courage, culture, and intellect, and Page insisted that white and black southerners should be left to work out their relationships without northern interference. Despite his strong preference that the North stay out of southern race relations, Page became an enthusiastic proponent of sectional reconciliation, offering praiseworthy northern and southern characters. His novel for youngsters, *Two Little Confederates*, is full of adventures and hardships but also features friendly Yankees who admire the little boys' spunk and a wounded sergeant who dies despite the young hero's ministrations. After the war, the soldier's wife and son arrive to take the body home, and the families become friends, winning a small victory for the process of national reunion.[68]

A coterie of female authors also attempted to explain the South to the rest of America. Drawing on their experiences as adolescent Rebels in the wartime South and as young wives and mothers in New Orleans during Reconstruction, Grace King, Ruth McEnery Stuart, and Kate Chopin won critical and popular acclaim for their stories and novels. The settings for their work rarely include the war itself, although King's "Bayou l'Ombre" is a humorous look at the dynamics of Confederate spies, marauding Yankees, and jubilant slaves on a backwater Louisiana plantation in the last days of the war, and Chopin's "The Locket" briefly visits a battlefield. Yet all three women detailed the challenges facing southern women due to the social, economic, and racial upheaval following the war. Ignoring the antebellum political and economic issues that had driven the sections apart, they focused instead on the destruction of a way of life that had previously shielded women from hardship and responsibility. Their politics emerges from their rose-colored view of the Old South and their portrayal of African American characters as hopelessly dependent and ever loyal to their former masters. King's *Balcony Stories*, for example, emphasize female orphans or widows overcoming deprivation and loss, while her *The Pleasant Ways of St. Medard* counterposes a doomed black family with a white family who recoup their prewar status and wealth. Stuart made her black characters even more pathetic in their slow wittedness and childlike nostalgia for the good old days on the plantation. Even Chopin, who explored uncharted feminist waters in her controversial *The Awakening*, presented blacks as subordinate and sentimentally attached to their white employers.[69]

These women did not generally use the actual events of their wartime and Reconstruction lives as sources of plots, but their writings did reflect a deep loyalty to the South and an anguish over the effects that the war had had on southern assumptions and institutions. Chopin's loss at age eleven of a half-brother in the Confederate army and her shame at having to endure life in Union-controlled St. Louis were followed by her marriage to Oscar Chopin, a member of Louisiana's White League. King's and Stuart's own families lost their social standing due to wartime dislocations; in fact, Stuart became a writer, editor, and well-paid lecturer because she knew of no other way to earn a living. Of course, the destruction of a family's fortunes by the war did not necessarily make a southerner an apologist for the Old South. Few southern families fell as far or as fast as William Sidney Porter's, who wrote under the pen name O. Henry. His birth in Greensboro, North Carolina, in 1862 was soon followed by his mother's death and his physician father's descent into alcoholism, apparently due to the stress of being an overworked Confederate surgeon, his despair over the South's defeat, and the loss of his young wife. Although Henry wrote primarily about the West and about life in the big city, his few stories on Civil War topics tend to gently lampoon Old South types—honor-bound patriarchs, the seedy gentility, and professional Confederates—and to promote a refreshing New South point of view.[70]

The North Carolina-raised Charles Waddell Chesnutt provided a nearly symmetrical counterpoint to the complacent racism of southern white writers. Born to free black parents in Ohio in 1858, he frequently wrote about the hardening of racial attitudes in the postwar South. Yet he also addressed the institution of slavery in terms understandably ignored by Page and his Lost Cause colleagues. Although he often wrote in the "Negro dialect," he used it to expose the humanity rather than exploit the comic inferiority of blacks, who in his stories experience the tragedy of separation, cleverly manipulate obtuse whites, and endure the trials and tribulations of courtship and marriage. The pieces in *The Wife of His Youth and Other Stories of the Color Line* present the richness of black culture during slavery and after emancipation, including the sometimes bitter struggles between "pure" Africans and mulattos and the conflicts between middle-class and working-class blacks. His novels examine the problems of a light-skinned woman trying to "pass" as white and the difficulties faced by educated blacks in a small southern town. In later works he also looked at the wide variety of racial and political attitudes of southern whites. Chesnutt's postwar South, including its black community, presents a far more complex and nuanced set of options and behaviors than readers devoted to the writings of Harris or Page or King or even Chopin would ever dream of.[71]

Searching for Order

Literary-minded Civil War children sought to exorcise demons, pay tribute to heroes, or cast nostalgic glances through the lens of the war. Other public figures drew on their wartime childhoods in forming their political ideologies and in developing government policies as state and federal officials. By the late nineteenth century, men were coming to political power who had been children during the Civil War. Although their childhood experiences did not necessarily translate into predictable political ideas, rhetoric, and behavior, a few noted northern and southern politicians displayed a spectrum of reactions. In many cases their attitudes about the war and the lessons they took from it were deeply affected by their relationships with important individuals or with certain institutions. These contacts could balance or mediate or amplify their gut-level reactions to the war and help guide their political careers.

No line led Civil War children straight from particular wartime experiences to particular adult beliefs. The war could become an important and in some cases vital contributing factor in the development of ideas and attitudes, but other components also added to the psychological and political mix. At one end of the spectrum of southern reactions were those boys who refused to become Lost Cause proponents as adults. Walter Hines Page, who would serve as ambassador to England before and during the First World War, spent most of his adult life as an editor and publisher. His wartime childhood was fairly detached from the fighting, and even when the Yankees finally appeared at his father's home near Raleigh, North Carolina, their three-week sojourn was interesting and pleasant rather than threatening. Page enjoyed fishing and hunting with friendly Confederate veterans, but a more important influence on the formation of Page's attitudes were the years he spent at Randolph-Macon College before going on to Johns Hopkins University. A remarkable spirit of tolerance and national rather than sectional interests prevailed at Randolph-Macon. Page was especially influenced by a speech given on campus by editor and former Confederate John Hampden Chamberlayne, who urged the students to forget the old northern-southern issues, especially race, and to forge ahead in an accepting, national point of view. Although a conservative on the "negro question"—he published Thomas Dixon's sensationally racist novels—Page did develop a hatred of the southern obsession with race and, as editor of a Raleigh newspaper and a nationally known columnist and magazine editor, promoted economic and educational development in the South. He adopted the model of self-help and economic growth put forward by Booker T. Washington—ironically, another one of his authors at Doubleday, Page—as the key to humane and peaceful race relations. His autobiographical novel, *The Southerner*, states his views through the fictional and not altogether successful career of its hero, Nicholas Worth, a reform-minded politician fighting to pull his native North Carolina out of the shadows of ignorance, worship of the Confederacy, and race baiting of the late nineteenth century.[72]

Woodrow Wilson, an acquaintance of Page's at Johns Hopkins, also took a moderate line on the war that had disrupted his Augusta, Georgia, childhood. Four when the war began, "Tommy" Wilson's Presbyterian minister father enthusiastically raised money to buy Bibles for Rebel soldiers, traveled for the Georgia Relief and Hospital Association, and served as a Confederate chaplain. Although Wilson's hometown was not actually invaded, his father's church became a hospital, his mother worked long hours as a nurse, and food shortages and a general lawlessness characterized the last month of the war in Augusta.[73]

Wilson's lack of bitterness about the war stemmed, no doubt, from his relatively mild experiences but also, perhaps, from his close relationship with his maternal grandfather, a Presbyterian minister in Ohio. Even as a young law student in Virginia, Wilson published an essay in which he declared that "*because* I love the South, I rejoice in the failure of the Confederacy." The war, he argued, had actually benefited the South by destroying slavery and by preserving the United States. Years later, long after giving up the study of law and just before entering politics, the professor and university president published *Division and Reunion*, a survey of American history from 1829 through 1909. His scholarly version of these troubled years hardly displayed a nostalgia for the Old South or an attraction to the Lost Cause. Although he treated slavery much more as a constitutional and a political issue than as a social or moral problem, and although his brief analysis of congressional Reconstruction was a standard southern critique of the Radical Republicans, Wilson's sympathies clearly did not lie exclusively with the South or with the Confederates. He expressed admiration for tough-minded presidents who upheld the law and the Constitution — including Andrew Jackson, Zachary Taylor, and Abraham Lincoln — and, in the historiographical fashion of the day, criticized both fanatical abolitionists and aggressive and unrealistic southerners. Wilson could admire the Confederacy's spirit, devotion, and quixotic willingness to sacrifice everything for its cause but insisted that it fought for "a belated principle of government, an outgrown economy, an impossible purpose."[74]

Wilson became president of the United States three years after publishing *Division and Reunion*. As chief executive he largely ignored sectional in favor of economic issues and appeared largely indifferent to racial concerns. Although he seemed inclined to accept the two-decades-old legal doctrine of "separate but equal" in allowing subordinates to segregate some areas of federal office buildings and to dismiss some black federal employees, he committed himself neither to the hard policies advocated by his fellow southern Democrats nor to the pleadings of African American activists. Even his famous comment about the aggressively racist film *Birth of a Nation*—that it was "history written with lightning"—was probably more enigmatic than his former classmate at Hopkins, Thomas Dixon, would have liked to believe.[75]

Other southern moderates who stood out in the immoderation of the late nineteenth-century South included James Stephen Hogg, the Texas progressive whose father died in the Confederate army, who lost his mother when he was twelve, and who, after the war, worked as a sharecropper, a farmhand, and a printer's devil. Yet his career as Democratic attorney general and governor in the 1880s and 1890s belied his own hard times during the war. In addition to his progressive battles against the railroad and oil interests, he improved public education, eschewed the virulently racist language spat out by many of his gubernatorial colleagues in the 1890s, disapproved of the poll tax, and assured his constituents that African Americans rightly sought only economic and political justice, not social equality. An important influence in his temperate stance on these touchy issues was the famous Texas Unionist, Confederate postmaster general, and congressional moderate John Reagan, whom Hogg had befriended as a teenager. Reagan's middle-of-the-road approach throughout his long career earned him the criticism of both northerners and southerners at various times, but it was his model of intelligent pragmatism that Hogg eagerly emulated.[76]

On the other hand, harsh wartime experiences could obviously push individuals in an entirely different direction. Some men became professional Confederates, even though they had been in knee breeches when the war was fought. Longtime congressman and senator John Sharp Williams of Mississippi, who lost his father at Shiloh, made defending the interests and reputations of Rebel veterans one of his special causes. Jeff Davis, born in 1863 and named by his Rebel father, rose to represent Arkansas as governor and senator on the basis of demagogic attacks on businessmen and "high-collared" Yankee aristocrats and on a shrewd pandering to Confederate veterans. Davis went so far as to guarantee another

Civil War if southern interests failed to receive more consideration from the federal government. Yet it is too simple to say that the loss of a father or of economic security or some other tragedy led directly to the southern mindset of the 1890s. For instance, the "White Chief," James K. Vardaman of Mississippi, lost everything as a boy in Texas during the war. Yet equally influential in his development was his friendship with Dr. B. F. Ward, a curmudgeonly Confederate veteran contemptuous of the so-called New South and committed to an extreme form of white superiority. Borrowing the words and attitudes of his mentor, Vardaman, as a state legislator, newspaper editor, and governor, frequently and publicly used the term "nigger," advocated lynching "Negro rapists," attacked public schools for blacks, and lectured throughout the country on the "dangers" posed by "Negro equality."[77]

African Americans and Yankees found an even more dangerous enemy in Georgian Tom Watson, who turned five early in the war's first autumn. Raised on his grandfather's plantation, he loved the large, plain house, the satisfying seasonal routines of the fields, and the status and security that his strong-willed grandfather— owner of more than forty slaves, including a nearly stereotypical "Mammy" beloved by Tom—was poised to pass along to his grandson. But the war intervened, and the young boy's father and uncles left for the army and came back wounded or even crippled. Added to the tragedy was the debilitating stroke Grandfather Watson suffered in 1863, which eventually killed him just after the war. These difficult moments were accompanied by the normal memories of patriotic songs and plays, hardships and excitement, and hopelessness and defeat.[78]

Although Watson's professions as a writer and a politician took two seemingly dissimilar turns, his careers as a populist and a race demagogue both grew out of his treasured boyhood on his grandfather's small plantation. Never admitting that a better life could be imagined, he constantly attacked northeastern capitalists for condemning farmers to poverty and despair. He traced the decline of the power of southern farmers and planters to their defeat in the Civil War, which also gave rise to the very forces that had since then conspired to keep them down. Indeed, as the only southern Populist in Congress in the late 1880s and early 1890s, Watson forcefully advocated cooperation between hard-pressed black and white farmers, whose enemies were using race to divide and conquer. Frustrated in his attempt to reassert agrarian power, he deserted the Democratic Party that he believed had hypocritically forsaken its earnest southern supporters and donned the mantle of the Lost Cause, arguing that the political and economic thralldom of the South could be traced directly to its defeat on the battlefields of the 1860s. His later turn against African Americans was at first aimed at eliminating race as a political issue. If the Democratic establishment could no longer threaten poor farmers with the specter of black political power, the masses would be free to vote their own interests, he believed. Eventually, however, an extreme version of white supremacy radicalized his successful push for disfranchisement. In addition to his unequivocal support of lynching — he once wrote that "in the South, we have to lynch [the Negro] occasionally, and flog him, now and then, to keep him from blaspheming the Almighty, by his conduct, on account of his smell and his color" — he also poured out abuse at both Jews and Catholics.[79]

Joining Watson on this bitter, racist end of the spectrum was "Pitchfork" Ben Tillman, from neighboring South Carolina, who grew up after his 1847 birth in the chronically violent Edgefield District. Ben's family was nearly a parody of the southern obsession with violence as a way to settle matters of honor. His father and many male siblings regularly participated in duels and brawls, and the Mexican and Civil Wars each claimed the life of a brother. Despite his upbringing in a wealthy upcountry family and his extensive landholdings as an adult, Tillman, like Watson, came to represent the "wool-hat boys," the renters and small farmers who resented the power and privilege and cozy relationships with industrialists and bankers of such Confederate "Bourbons" as South Carolina's Gen. Wade Hampton. Tillman's prestige during two terms as governor in the early 1890s and three terms as a U.S. senator was hardly a memorial to the Lost Cause represented by Hampton. In fact, at one level Tillman seemed to be rejecting his Civil War childhood with his violent attacks on southern aristocrats. Although a life-threatening infection cost him the sight of one eye and kept the teenager out of the army, his wartime experiences did apparently affect him in his racial views. In addition to accompanying his widowed mother in her search through Confederate hospitals for a wounded brother, Ben also found himself as the only white male on a plantation worked by nearly ninety slaves, one-third of whom were native Africans. Part of one of the last cargoes of smuggled slaves to reach the American South, these wretched, confused, and exotic men and women gave the impressionable young South Carolinian a glimpse of what he would later interpret as the alarming potential for "retrogression" among African Americans released from the stabilizing influence of slavery. Virtually no leader among post-Reconstruction southerners displayed more enthusiastic bitterness toward blacks than Tillman, who by the 1890s espoused lynching, accused black schools of creating rapacious monsters, and successfully insisted on driving them completely out of the political system. "Whoever doubts that civilization depends on white supremacy is a fool and a knave," he declared unambiguously. It may be too simple to trace the origins of hateful statements such as these back to experiences that took place decades before. But it seems clear that at least part of the urge to explain their present by recalling the past was animated by the disruption of these men's childhoods by the Civil War. Watson's only attempt to write a novel, for instance, featured a young boy who shares many of Watson's youthful experiences.[80]

Northern politicians also drew on their wartime childhoods for political lessons, although their reactions seem to have been more idiosyncratic than those of their southern colleagues, presenting a less coherent picture of the way northern children applied their wartime educations to later political careers. Thomas R. Marshall, a Democratic governor of Indiana and Woodrow Wilson's vice-president during World War I, traced his first memories to the start of the war, when he believed as a five year old just learning his Presbyterian catechism that, like disputants in the Old Testament, the two sides would each choose a champion to settle the issue man to man. However, what he really learned from the war was political tolerance. As a member of a steadfastly Democratic family—his grandfather, angered at the overt Republicanism of a local minister, said that "he was willing to take his chance on Hell but never on the Republican party"—he knew what it was like to be criticized for holding unpopular political opinions. "Perhaps it was the experience of those youthful days," he wrote in retirement, "that has led me to be rather charitable in my judgment of the political opinions of the other men."[81]

On the other hand, one of those Republicans whom Marshall's grandfather distrusted, Theodore Roosevelt, took an entirely different approach to the war he had witnessed between his second and seventh birthdays. His father was, as Roosevelt wrote, "a strong Lincoln Republican," while his mother was an "entirely 'unreconstructed'" southerner. Their political disagreement caused only mild and, to the adult Theodore, amusing conflicts in their New York household. Young Teddy enjoyed the war immensely, playing "Running the Blockade" with his sister in Central Park (his southern uncles were blockade-runners) and wearing a custom-made Zouave uniform. These childhood activities were amplified by his acquaintance through his father with Generals Grant, Sherman, and McClellan, and wars and warriors dominated his reading. Roosevelt's fascination with war has, in turn, fascinated historians. His analysis of the Civil War as peculiarly noble, virtuous, and necessary helps explain his own enthusiasm for the Spanish-American and First World Wars; his belief that waging war could be a form of individual as well as national cleansing fit into his obsession with the strenuous life. His own rather exaggerated machismo took on martial qualities, especially when he castigated pacifists and slandered opponents like Wilson, whom he called an "astute, unprincipled, and physically cowardly demagogue." His own father's failure to serve in the army during the war, according to a recent biographer, fueled much of Theodore's later enthusiasm for military glory and his excessive admiration for the veterans who had risked their lives for the Union.[82]

Roosevelt's combative nature, his rush to volunteer for both of the wars the United States fought during his adult life, and his rhetoric reflected his obsession and admiration for the great war that filled his earliest memories. He wanted the nation and the Republican Party to renew the wartime spirit of disinterested nationalism in order to design and carry out wisely progressive reforms. He frequently applauded aging Union veterans and in 1904 raised their pensions, sparking a partisan controversy just before the presidential campaign. He regretted that, as president, he had not been called on to lead his country through war and projected his jealousy over Wilson's chance to be a war president into immoderate attacks on the Virginian. He characterized his last run for political office, the "Bull Moose" campaign of 1912, as a military operation, even giving a speech to a Milwaukee crowd a few minutes after he was shot in the chest.[83]

The attitudes that Roosevelt took from the war resembled in

their fury the belligerence of Tom Watson more than they suggested the lessons learned by most northern children. Like the
noncelebrity northern memoirists who devoted only a few pages
or a chapter to the war, most northern politicians did not focus on
the war as a major influence on their later political ideals. An exception was Roosevelt's friend and colleague Henry Cabot Lodge,
who penned the most thoughtful self-analysis by a former Civil
War child. In an early chapter of his 1913 memoir, Lodge, who
aged from a youngster of ten to a teenager during the war, described his view of the conflict from the lofty height of the Boston
elite. Still, he clearly drank deeply from the cup of war.

Ever aware of his family's Federalist and Whig background,
Lodge remembered that, at his father's urging, he "hollered for
Frémont" in 1856 and wore a Lincoln badge in 1860. Charles
Sumner frequently dined at the Lodge table, and Henry's father
had talked a great deal about John Brown's raid; but the great
military events of the war overshadowed the boy's interest in politics. Too young to fight, Lodge nevertheless remembered himself
as a great patriot who took pride that the officer who stopped the
Boston draft riot with a blast of grapeshot was a relative, and who
lashed out at "our Democratic Irish groom" when he suggested
that Sherman would never reach the sea. His daily life was dominated by the war. "You saw it in the streets," he wrote, "in the dis-
appearance of silver and gold, in the early makeshifts for money,
in the paper currency, in the passing soldiers, in the neighboring
camps." He watched Governor John Andrew send regiments off to
war, saw Robert Gould Shaw's Fifty-fourth Massachusetts march
out of town, and drilled with his school's military company. At
theaters "every sentence which could be twisted into a patriotic
allusion was loudly cheered." He and his friends attended Sanitary
Fairs and affected military caps. And like boys and girls everywhere, he worried over absent relatives and friends. "This reading
the death-roll and scanning bulletins to see how many men whom
you have known and cared for, whose people are your people and
whose fate is dear to you, have been killed is not an experience
that one ever forgets."

But these were superficial impressions and fleeting images.
Lodge also believed that the war had had a profound effect on
him. "The feeling about the country of those to whom the Civil
War is not mere history, but a living memory, is, I am certain,

a little different from that of any others." Having witnessed their "country . . . at death grips with a destroying antagonist, reeling on the edge of the abyss," they came to appreciate its value and to know the cost of sustaining it. Those men "who lived through the war times have a more tender sentiment about their country[,] . . . are more easily moved by all that appeals to their sense of patriotism, and . . . are less dispassionate no doubt in judging America and the American people than others."

The war left Lodge with several "profound convictions which nothing can ever shake." First, it made him an optimist about the future of the United States. Despite all the problems caused by the growth of industry, the centralization of wealth, and immigration in the decades since the Civil War, having seen "the nation come through the most terrible ordeal which any nation can undergo" made him believe that the American people could and would rise to meet any crisis. Second, he naturally admired deeply the heroes of the northern war effort and acknowledged southerners' right to glorify their own great warriors and to memorialize their lost cause. Yet he decried the fashion among northerners, fifty years after the war, to also accept uncritically the southern side of the war and to implicitly or explicitly reject the values and ideas that had fuelled the patriotism of the North. "We should think ill of the Southern people if they did not" cherish their own institutions and patriots, but "that which is most praiseworthy in Southerners is discreditable in a Northerner." What Lodge had learned from the war was the importance of committed patriotism. "I can understand and I profoundly admire the man who was loyal to the nation against his State. I can understand the man who was loyal to his State against the nation. But I cannot understand the men who were loyal neither to their State nor to their nation." Men who were "loyal to nothing . . . risked nothing" and were, in fact, worse than the most determined Rebels. Another "lesson" Lodge took from the war was "the hostility which I imbibed against England," due particularly to the "stupidity" displayed by its government in dealing with the United States during the war. His hatred was later replaced by a contempt that influenced his opposition to the proposed League of Nations after the First World War; Lodge admitted that he had never "felt the slightest deference to English opinion."

Finally, Lodge declared in his memoir that these "truisms" had been "pushed aside" recently "as if they were something to be ashamed of, as if they might be true but were certainly disagreeable and might possibly hurt somebody's feelings." He wanted Americans to remember that "there was a right and a wrong in the Civil War." Slavery was wrong. Southerners were certainly courageous, worthy, and principled opponents, but they were clearly mistaken in trying to break up the United States on behalf of "a crime against humanity." Those in the North who "try to pretend that both sides were right" ignored history and the truth. "Events have shown inexorably that it was the right which triumphed at Appomattox." The old Brahmin pointedly closed his section on the war by insisting that "forgiveness is admirable and cannot be too complete, but in the affairs and the history of nations it is not wise wholly to forget."[84]

Lodge believed that he spoke for an important, if shrinking, minority of northern men. In fact, as always, he and his fellow politicians and novelists and memoirists must represent the ideas and attitudes of the vast majority of Americans unable or unwilling to articulate what they thought about the war. Yet it is also clear that, as adults, their generation did apparently respond to national issues in a fairly coherent spectrum of ways. As they came of age and into political power in the 1880s, 1890s, and early decades of the twentieth century, they applied the political lessons of the war that marred their childhoods to later issues and crises in ways that marked them as a generation separate from the men who fought the war. New economic challenges and threats from third parties such as the Populists forced the newcomers to national politics in the 1890s to ignore the old sectional issues and to forge into tariff, currency, civil service, and regulatory issues. The symbolic transition from the Civil War veteran William McKinley to the Civil War child Theodore Roosevelt completed this shift from old issues to new concerns.[85]

Yet the work of their fathers and grandfathers was not entirely forgotten. Descendants of the tiny band of northern abolitionists continued to work for racial justice. Themselves the children of war, they transformed the fight against slavery into campaigns to help African Americans achieve equality, especially through education and legal challenges to discrimination. Arthur A. Birney, grandson of James G. Birney, was a civil rights lawyer; Francis J. Garrison, William Lloyd Garrison's grandson, raised money for

Tuskegee Institute and promoted publications setting the record straight on the character of American blacks. Others took on high-profile and difficult positions as presidents of the new black colleges founded after the war. Wilbur P. Thirkield headed a Methodist seminary in Atlanta as well as Howard University, while William Goodell Frosts was president of Berea College, an integrated school in Kentucky, and stirred controversy among reformers when he established the blacks-only Lincoln Institute in the 1910s after Kentucky passed a law segregating its colleges. A number of Civil War children descended from abolitionists helped found the National Association for the Advancement of Colored People in the early twentieth century.[86]

Young southern men also shrugged off Civil War issues — even as they may have conceded the attractiveness of mythic Lost Cause rhetoric — feeling that the war haunted their own careers. By 1888 three-fourths of southern voters were too young to have voted for Jefferson Davis, and the Young Turks of the state and local Democratic parties eagerly moved forward with their own agendas, which included less cooperation with local Republicans and a much harsher attitude toward African Americans. They made their political marks by disfranchising black voters, strengthening state party organizations (to eliminate perennial threats from third parties), and in some places boosting their towns and cities as commercial and industrial centers. In North Carolina, New South advocates from among those men who had been too young to serve in the Confederate army revamped public education, making it more centralized, more professionalized, and strictly segregated.[87]

Joel Williamson has isolated a more sinister strain of shared response among the generation of southern children of war. In his chilling analysis of southern racial attitudes after the Civil War, he wrote that "many of these men and women" active in constructing racial barriers and encouraging racial violence "had been children during the Civil War when great numbers of fathers left home for the war and many never returned, when starvation became a real possibility, and powerlessness in the face of a despicable enemy" was a reality. Reconstruction only encouraged them to dwell on their wartime powerlessness and hardships and to attempt to establish absolute control over their own lives and region. Since the North was no longer a threat, they turned on the African Americans in their midst as living symbols of their lost civilization

and defeat. Frightening economic shifts and a long-term southern depression amplified their fears and lent greater urgency to
their efforts to locate and crush scapegoats. The words and actions
of the Watsons and Vardamans and Tillmans reflected perfectly
their constituents' frustrations and attitudes. Their experiences as
Civil War children, shared by untold thousands of silent witnesses,
shaped southern politics and race relations for decades.[88]

The attempts by both northerners and southerners to fashion
political or racial paradigms from childhood experiences reflect
the sociological premise that children need to be shown that their
own activities are worthwhile and that the goals society sets for
them make sense. Of course, too often the way a teenager wants
the world to be crashes head-on into the way it is, creating disillusionment about society and cynicism about making long-range
plans. Southern children obviously found themselves not only cut
loose from the United States they had at least, as very young
children, nominally been taught to honor, but also thrust into
the heady excitement of a Confederate nationalism that collapsed
around them after a frightening and confusing war. Although they
continued to honor the memory of fallen Confederates, they felt
free — indeed, felt compelled — to leave behind at least some of the
old political ways and assumptions. Times of crisis tend to inter-
rupt the already imperfect transmission of the political heritage
from one generation to the next; yet if children have internalized
facets of a strong worldview or ideology, they can often make some
sort of sense out of even the most senseless wars. It should come as
no surprise, then, that the Civil War sparked major changes in the
ways that its children, at least in the South, carried on the business of politics, even as they continued to believe in, even to exaggerate, certain traditional assumptions. Civil War children shared
several "frames of remembrance," as a recent book on collective
memory calls the meanings applied to shared events that become
more important than the objective facts of those memories.[89]

Those memories helped Civil War children face an unsettling
conjunction of economic, social, ethnic, and political disruptions
during the forty years after Reconstruction. The startling increase
and centralization of wealth, the alarming influx of immigrants,
the rise of political machines in the cities, disillusionment with
government after the debacle of Reconstruction, looming race
problems, and periodic economic crises set American politicians

and policy makers scrambling for solutions. Robert Wiebe calls their quest a "search for order," and that search is what unifies the northern and southern child-veterans of the Civil War. Former Yankee and Rebel children went about creating order in their worlds in somewhat different ways, but their response to the chaos they witnessed or feared during the war of their childhoods was a fervent desire to establish order in their lives and in their society as adults.[90]

Northern children adapted and refined the businesslike ideas about centralization and efficiency their parents had applied to the massive mobilization of manpower and resources that won the war. Their new attitudes shifted reform and benevolence from an evangelical, individualistic footing to one of scale and pragmatism that eventually included a willingness to allow at least a modicum of government-controlled reform. They targeted outlaw trusts, the most egregious social ills, and some of the problems caused by rapid urbanization and unregulated immigration in attempting to bring order to their section.[91] Southern children — who, despite rejecting parts of their political heritage, hung onto their section's tradition of states' rights — focused almost entirely on reestablishing the sedate, tightly controlled, and elite-centered political systems of the antebellum South. At the same time they dismissed traditional southern efforts to cooperate with the North and chose to give up entirely on "finding" a workable relationship with former slaves and their descendants. Disfranchisement of both blacks and the poorest whites enabled them to create order out of the chaos of their fathers' generation.[92]

These reformers in both sections frequently shared the title "progressive," which indicated less an agreement on the issues than a willingness to use at least a little of the state's power to rationalize the political and economic systems. Many boys of the Civil War generation shared another characteristic: a need to live up to the reputations of their fathers and uncles, to demonstrate "manly" virtues in acceptable ways. In his recent analysis of the evolution of the forms and assumptions of manhood in the United States, Michael Kimmel labels the Civil War a "gendered war" fought at the symbolic level over competing visions of manhood related to wealth, manners, and freedom. Although the war may have briefly settled the issue, by the turn of the century it had become increasingly difficult to define what it meant to be a man, as industrialization; the entry of women, blacks, and immigrants into the public sphere; and the closing of the frontier eliminated niches typically reserved for men. As a result, white American males felt they had lost their bearings and sought ways to regain their roles as men in American society. Some grew beards, frequented billiard parlors and saloons, went to gyms, and took up outdoor sports. Others found more profound ways of regaining their self-images. Southerners demonstrated their courage and character and resurrected their role as masculine protectors through racial vigilantism—lynching, disfranchisement, and other forms of racial control. Many northerners, and a number of southerners, became avid supporters of expansion in general and specifically of intervention in Cuba. Military expansion and the acquisition of colonies would create new frontiers, project American-style manliness onto other cultures, and provide exciting venues for heroic action. Perhaps, men like Theodore Roosevelt might have hoped, war would restore turn-of-the-century manhood to its Civil War era glory.[93]

This attempt to recapture a model of manhood—of Caucasian manhood—that had somehow vanished since the glorious 1860s, to establish feelings of place and a sense of order, and to utilize political lessons learned as children of war should not obscure the fact that women and African American men also processed their war experiences. Gender and race shaped the forms rather than the impulses to explain and interpret the war. White men could not only publish memoirs and attend celebrations and compose novels, they could also win elections, set policies, and project their memories of the war onto a panorama-sized public canvas. Women and blacks had fewer options. A few women, such as Jane Addams, could apply their Lincolnian passion for justice to the public sphere, while others found outlets as professional writers. Most blacks had to settle for private responses and applications of their war lessons, although leaders such as Booker T. Washington could publicly—if carefully—express what the war meant to them.

Even though their venues differed, the crucial thing to remember is that Civil War children felt compelled to explain the war. Informed by personal experiences, by knowledge imparted by caring fathers, or by magazines, novels, and schoolbooks, children of war were politicized and, in turn, mobilized, not just to seek more information about the war or to raise money for soldiers or to pick lint for bandages or to pray for absent loved ones, but to see their lives as products of the war. It may be only a modest exaggeration to argue that the Civil War was an event as central in their lives as it was for the soldiers who fought it. Although they did not march down dusty streets on haunted Decoration Days or hold quaint and poignant reunions commemorating their roles in the conflict, they never forgot the war they had witnessed as children. Like twentieth-century Americans whose childhoods were permanently shaped by the Great Depression, by the Second World War, or by the youthful rebellion of the 1960s, Civil War children insisted on testing the events of their adult lives against what the war had taught them. For some this meant replaying old themes in tedious novels and idealized celebrations; for others it meant inventing hideous racial codes or progressive government policies; for still others it meant quietly reflecting on the meanings of the great events they had experienced in their youths. Being a child of war was an honor for some, a burden for others. Although no monuments were forged and no medals were cast for Civil War children, they left as their legacy the history of a generation whose unique experiences led them to insist that the circumstances of their collective childhood meant something to them and to the nation.

Notes

INTRODUCTION

1. "Picture of the Week," *Life*, October 4, 1937, 102; "The Cost of a Bombing Error in Vietnam," *Life*, June 23, 1972, 4–5; Esther Forbes, *Johnny Tremain: A Novel for Old and Young* (Boston: Houghton Mifflin, 1960); Johanna Hurwitz, *Anne Frank: A Life in Hiding* (Philadelphia: Jewish Publications Society, 1988); "Forbidden Games," *Life*, January 12, 1953, 42–44; Richard Corliss, "Hard Rites of Passage," *Time*, February 22, 1988, 92; Tim O'Brien, "Obsession and Memory," *Commonweal*, December 4, 1987, 94–95, and "Yesterday's Children," *Commonweal*, March 25, 1988, 181; "Massacre of the Innocents," *Nation*, February 4, 1991, 114; Zlata Filipovic, *Zlata's Diary: A Child's Life in Sarajevo* (New York: Viking, 1994).

2. For examples of books that have attempted to provide relatively comprehensive accounts of Civil War soldiers' experiences and ideologies, see Bell I. Wiley, *The Life of Johnny Reb: The Common Soldier of the Confederacy* (Indianapolis: Bobbs-Merrill, 1943; reprint, Baton Rouge: Louisiana State University Press, 1970) and *The Life of Billy Yank: The Common Soldier of the Union* (Indianapolis: Bobbs-Merrill, 1952; reprint, Baton Rouge: Louisiana State University Press, 1971); Gerald F. Linderman, *Embattled Courage: The Experience of Combat in the American Civil War* (New York: Free Press, 1987); Reid Mitchell, *Civil War Soldiers: Their Expectations and Their Experiences* (New York: Viking, 1988); James I. Robertson, *Soldiers Blue and Gray* (Columbia: University of South Carolina Press, 1988); Earl J. Hess, *Liberty, Virtue, and Progress: Northerners and Their War for the Union* (New York: New York University Press, 1988); and James M. McPherson, *For Cause and Comrades: Why Men Fought in the Civil War* (New York: Oxford University Press, 1997).

3. See, for example, Mary Elizabeth Massey, *Bonnet Brigades* (New York: Knopf, 1966); Bell I. Wiley, *Confederate Women* (Westport, Conn.: Greenwood, 1975); George Rable, *Civil Wars: Women and the Crisis of Southern Nationalism* (Urbana: University of Illinois Press, 1989); Catherine Clinton, *Tara Revisited: Women, War, and the Plantation Legend* (New York: Abbeville, 1995); and Drew Gilpin Faust, *Mothers of Invention: Women of the Slaveholding South in the American Civil War* (Chapel Hill: University of North Carolina Press, 1996). Northern women have been far less studied, although Elizabeth D. Leonard has recently offered *Yankee Women: Gender Battles in the Civil War* (New

York: Norton, 1994), and Stephen B. Oates has published *A Woman of Valor: Clara Barton and the Civil War* (New York: Free Press, 1994).

4. See, for example, Bell I. Wiley, *Southern Negroes, 1861–1865* (New York: Rinehart, 1938); Robert Francis Engs, *Freedom's First Generation: Black Hampton, Virginia, 1861–1890* (Philadelphia: University of Pennsylvania Press, 1979); John Cimprich, *Slavery's End in Tennessee, 1861–1865* (University: University of Alabama Press, 1985); Clarence L. Mohr, *On the Threshold of Freedom: Masters and Slaves in Civil War Georgia* (Athens: University of Georgia Press, 1986); and Joseph T. Glatthaar, *Forged in Battle: The Civil War Alliance of Black Soldiers and White Officers* (New York: Free Press, 1990).

5. For the record, I have defined children not only as people who had not yet reached their majority, but also as girls and boys who *acted* like children. They lived with at least one parent, attended school more or less regularly—at least in normal times—and worked part time, if at all (such rules of thumb were obviously harder to enforce for black children). These self-imposed guidelines disqualified drummer boys and underage soldiers, of course, but also young women finished with their schooling but still living at home, self-supporting seventeen-year-old boys, and teenaged girls on the brink of marriage and motherhood. In effect, I allowed my subjects to define themselves as children.

6. For underage soldiers and drummer boys, see Francis A. Lord and Arthur Wise, *Bands and Drummer Boys of the Civil War* (New York: Yoseloff, 1966; reprint, Da Capo, 1979), 100–21, and Jim Murphy, *The Boys' War: Confederate and Union Soldiers Talk about the Civil War* (New York: Clarion, 1990). The latter, intended for adolescent readers, is a brief and heavily illustrated volume consisting mostly of personal narratives of boys under age sixteen who served in the Union and Confederate armies. Books about the Union's most famous drummer boy, John Clem, include a novel, James A. Rhodes's *Johnny Shiloh* (Indianapolis: Bobbs-Merrill, 1959), and a brief book for children, George C. Grant's *Lincoln's Littlest Soldier* (Minneapolis: Denison, 1969). It is difficult to get anything approaching a confident estimate of how many underage boys ended up in the army. Murphy suggests without citing a source that between 10 and 20 percent of all soldiers were underage, while Bell Wiley cited a U.S. Sanitary Commission actuary's no doubt low estimate that only 1 percent of Union soldiers were under age eighteen. His own sampling of Confederate soldiers came up with about 5 percent under eighteen. See Murphy, *Boys' War*, 2; Wiley, *Life of Billy Yank*, 299; Wiley, *Life of Johnny Reb*, 331.

7. Ruth Huntington Sessions, *Sixty-Odd: A Personal History* (Brattleboro, Vt.: Stephen Daye, 1936), 31.

8. Francis T. Miller, ed., *The Photographic History of the Civil War*, 10 vols. (New York: Review of Reviews, 1911; reprint, Yoseloff, 1957), 2:148, 4:13, 5:249, 6:267, 7:276–77, 283, 322–23; William C. Davis,

ed., *Image of War*, vol. 1, *Shadows of the Storm* (New York: Doubleday, 1981), 399, and vol. 6, *End of an Era* (New York: Doubleday, 1984), 145.

CHAPTER ONE

1. Hermon W. DeLong Sr., *Boyhood Reminiscences (Life in Dansville, 1855–1872), with Other Sketches* (Dansville, N.Y.: Dansville Press, 1913, 1982), 70–73.
2. Sue M. Chancellor, "Personal Recollections of the Battle of Chancellorsville," *Register of the Kentucky Historical Society* 66 (April 1968): 137–46. A nearly identical version appeared as "Recollections of Chancellorsville," in *Confederate Veteran* 29 (1921): 213–15.
3. George P. Rawick, ed. *The American Slave: A Composite Autobiography*, 19 vols. (Westport, Conn.: Greenwood, 1972–74), 8(2):138–41.
4. Bureau of the Census, *Historical Statistics of the United States: Colonial Times to 1970, Pt. 1* (Washington, D.C.: Government Printing Office, 1975), 23, and *Statistical Abstract of the United States, 1990* (Washington, D.C.: Government Printing Office, 1990), 18. Children under fifteen made up 47 percent of the population in 1790.
5. *Frank Leslie's Illustrated Newspaper*, May 25, 1861, 27; July 6, 1861, 125; September 7, 1861, 260–61; October 18, 1862, 25–26; September 24, 1864, 1; February 11, 1865, 328; *Harper's Weekly*, September 27, 1862, 616–17; January 31, 1863, 68; April 23, 1864, 265; December 17, 1864, 812; December 24, 1865, 824–825; *Harper's New Monthly Magazine*, April 1862, 717; July 1864, 145; Currier and Ives, *Off for the War*, *The Soldier's Dream of Home*, and *The American Patriot's Dream: The Night before the Battle*; G. White, *Departure for the War*; *The Veteran on Furlough*, Prints and Photographs Division, Library of Congress, Washington, D.C.; Carter Smith, ed., *Behind the Lines: A Source Book on the Civil War* (Brookfield, Conn.: Millbrook Press, 1993), 43.
6. David English Henderson, *Departure from Fredericksburg before the Bombardment*, and William D. Washington, *The Burial of Latane*, in *Mine Eyes Have Seen the Glory: The Civil War in Art*, by Mark E. Neely Jr. and Harold Holzer (New York: Orion, 1993), 209, 219; Lilly Martin Spencer, *The War Spirit at Home: Celebrating the Victory at Vicksburg*, in *The Civil War: The Artists' Record*, by Hermann Warner Williams Jr. (Boston: Beacon, 1961), 227; Joseph W. John, *Harvest Home: When the War Was Over*; Currier and Ives, *The Domestic Blockade*; William Morris Hunt, *Playing Field Hospital*, and Eastman Johnson, *Writing to Father* and *Knitting for the Soldiers*, in Neely and Holzer, *Mine Eyes Have Seen the Glory*, 207–8, 221, 212, 213.
7. John Davidson to Julia Davidson, February 14, 1863, "A Wartime Story: The Davidson Letters, 1862–1865," ed. Jane Bonner Peacock, *Atlanta Historical Bulletin* 19, no. 1 (1975): 45; J. W. Cotton to Mariah Cotton, May 5, 1862, April 27, 1863, *Yours till Death: Civil War Letters of John W. Cotton*, ed. Lucille Griffith (University: University of Ala-

bama Press, 1951), 4, 65; Marcus Spiegel to his wife, May 25, 1863, *Your True Marcus: The Civil War Letters of a Jewish Colonel*, ed. Frank L. Byrne and Jean P. Soman (Kent, Ohio: Kent State University Press, 1985), 285; Marion Fitzpatrick to Amanda Fitzpatrick, June 9, 1862, *Letters to Amanda from Sergeant Major Marion Hill Fitzpatrick, Company K, 45th Georgia Regiment, Thomas's Brigade, Wilcox Division, Hill's Corps, CSA, to his wife Amanda Olive Elizabeth White Fitzpatrick, 1862–1865*, ed. Henry Hammock (Culloden, Ga.: Mansel Hammock, 1976), 7; J. A. McMurtrey to Lucinda McMurtrey, September 28, 1862, *Letters to Lucinda, 1862–1864*, comp. Mary Frances Hosea Johnston (Huntsville, Ala.: Mrs. J. H. Johnston, 1985), 5.

8. Annie L. Burton, *Memories of Childhood's Slavery Days* (Boston: Ross, 1909), 11–12; Amelia E. Barr, *All the Days of My Life: An Autobiography* (New York: Appleton, 1913), 251.

9. Calvin Henderson Wiley et al., *Address to the People of North Carolina* (Raleigh: n.p., [1861]), 1–2, 4, 11, 13.

10. O. L. Davis Jr., "The Educational Association of the C.S.A.," *Civil War History* 10 (March 1964): 67–79; *Proceedings of the Convention of Teachers of the Confederate States, Assembled at Columbia, S.C., April 28, 1863* (Macon, Ga.: Burke, Boykin, 1863), 8, 11–14.

11. Roy P. Basler, ed., *The Collected Works of Abraham Lincoln*, 9 vols. (New Brunswick, N.J.: Rutgers University Press, 1953), 8:333; *Report of the Directors of the Soldiers' Children's Home, to the Senate and General Assembly* (Trenton, N.J., 1866), 1245.

12. *Harper's Weekly*, August 23, 1862, December 10, 1864; *Chicago Tribune*, August 23, 1861; Institute of Reward for Orphans of Patriots, *Fifth Annual Report* (New York, 1866), 1–8; *Washington Daily Morning Chronicle*, January 1, 1864; Board of Managers, Patriot Orphan Home, *Annual Report, 1866* (New York: Holt Brothers, 1866), 9; Kenneth L. Lyftogt, *From Blue Mills to Columbia: Cedar Falls and the Civil War* (Ames: Iowa State University Press, 1993), 165; Alexander Downing Diary, March 14, 1865, *Downing's Civil War Diary*, ed. Olynthus B. Clark (Des Moines: Historical Department of Iowa, 1916), 261.

13. C. K. Marshall, *Orphans of Our Soldiers and How to Educate Them* (Columbus, Ga.: n.p., 1864), Mississippi Department of Archives and History, Jackson, 1–8, quote on p. 1.

14. David Wallace Adams and Victor Edmunds, "Making Your Move: The Educational Significance of the American Board Game, 1832 to 1904," *History of Education Quarterly* 17 (Winter 1977): 359–84.

15. *Visit to Camp* (New York: McLoughlin, [1865]); *The Commanders of Our Forces: A Game for Old and Young* (Concord, N.H.: Eastman, [1865]); *The Game of the Union* (Boston: Williams, [1862]), all in Games and Puzzles Collection, American Antiquarian Society, Worcester, Mass.; *Running the Blockade* (New York: Magnus, [1863–65]), Lithograph Collection, American Antiquarian Society; Blair Whitton, *American Clockwork Toys, 1862–1900* (Exton, Pa.: Schiffer, 1981), 26;

Anne D. Williams, *Jigsaw Puzzles: An Illustrated History and Price Guide* (Radnor, Pa.: Wallace-Homestead, 1990), 92; Bernard Barenholtz and Inez McClintock, *American Antique Toys, 1830–1900* (New York: Abrams, 1980), 91.

16. *Catalogue of Photographic Incidents of the War, from the Gallery of Alexander Gardner, Photographer to the Army of the Potomac* (Washington, D.C.: H. Polkinhorn, 1863); Edward W. Earle, ed. *Points of View: The Stereograph in America, a Cultural History* (Rochester, N.Y.: Visual Studies Workshop, 1979); W. Fletcher Thompson Jr., *The Image of War: The Pictorial Reporting of the American Civil War* (New York: Yoseloff, 1961); William C. Darrah, *The World of Stereographs* (Gettysburg, Pa.: Times and News Publishing, 1977), 21–26, 153–54; Harold F. Jenkins, *Two Points of View: A History of the Parlor Stereoscope* (Elmira, N.Y.: World in Color Productions, 1957); O. G. Brockett and Lenyth Brockett, "Civil War Theater: Contemporary Treatments," *Civil War History* 1 (September 1955): 239–40; Maxwell Bloomfield, "Wartime Drama: The Theater in Washington, 1861–1865," *Maryland Historical Magazine* 64 (Winter 1969): 404–6; Terry Theodore, "The Confederate Theatre: Theatre Personalities and Practices during the Confederacy," *Lincoln Herald* 76 (Winter 1974): 190, and "The Confederate Theatre: The Confederate Drama," *Lincoln Herald* 77 (Spring 1975): 34–35. For a richly illustrated description of the illusions and technology of this precursor to motion pictures, see Richard Balzer, *Optical Amusements: Magic Lanterns and Other Transforming Images* (Watertown, Mass.: Richard Balzer, 1987); Norborne T. N. Robinson III, "Blind Tom, Musical Prodigy," *Georgia Historical Quarterly* 51 (September 1967): 336–58; *A Union of Hearts and Hands: Chicagoans during the Civil War* (Chicago: Chicago Historical Society, 1996) (exhibit pamphlet); Civil War Pictorial Envelopes Collection, Southern Historical Collection, University of North Carolina, Chapel Hill (this collection contains 350 Union and 215 Confederate envelopes bound in a volume labeled Envelopes of the Great Rebellion); Valentine Collection, American Antiquarian Society; E. L. Rudolph, *Confederate Broadside Verse: A Bibliography and Finding List of Confederate Broadsides Ballads and Songs* (New Braunfels, Tex.: Book Farm, 1950).

17. John L. Marsh, "Drama and Spectacle by the Yard: The Panorama in America," *Journal of Popular Culture* 10 (Winter 1976): 581–92; Charlotte Willard, "Panoramas, the First 'Movies,'" *Art in America* 47 (1959): 65–69.

18. *Philadelphia Public Ledger and Transcript*, June 10, August 21, 1861, July 24, October 21, December 20, 1862; Brockett and Brockett, "Civil War Theater," 239–40; *Atlanta Daily Intelligencer*, April 30, 1862; *Savannah Daily Morning News*, May 7, 1862; *Charleston Mercury*, May 19, October 13, 1862, May 1, October 6, 1863, December 31, 1866.

19. *Savannah Daily Morning News*, April 3, 1862; "Gen. Fremont and Staff! Are invited and expected to be present at the Tremont Temple!

To witness the Exhibition of the Great War Painting," Theatrical Programs Collection, American Antiquarian Society; Bloomfield, "Wartime Drama," 404–6.

20. *Chicago Tribune*, April 4, 1865; Brockett and Brockett, "Civil War Theater," 240; broadside for *Cutting's National Polyrama*, Iowa State Historical Society, Iowa City; *Philadelphia Public Ledger and Transcript*, December 20, 1862; *Milwaukee Sentinel*, March 27, 1863; *Charleston Mercury*, May 19, 1862. For a description of the techniques used to create panoramas and their competitors, see Richard Carl Wickman, "An Evaluation of the Employment of Panoramic Scenery in the Nineteenth-Century Theatre" (Ph.D. diss., Ohio State University, 1961).

21. *Philadelphia Ledger and Transcript*, June 18, 1861; Lyftogt, *From Blue Mills to Columbia*, 20; *Chicago Tribune*, April 23, 1861; *Savannah Daily Morning News*, September 14, 1861.

22. *Magnus' Universal Picture Books, Series N. 1–12* (New York: Charles Magnus, 1863), Lithograph Collection, American Antiquarian Society.

23. William Y. Thompson, "Sanitary Fairs of the Civil War," *Civil War History* 4 (March 1958): 51–67; Beverly Gordon, "A Furor of Benevolence," *Chicago History* 15 (Winter 1986–87): 48–65.

24. *Chicago Tribune*, October 25, 1863, May 30, 1865; *Philadelphia Public Ledger and Transcript*, June 15, 1864; *Frank Leslie's Illustrated Newspaper*, April 23, June 25, 1864; *The Canteen* (Albany), February 20, 27, 29, March 4, 1864; *The Drumbeat* (Brooklyn and Long Island), March 1, 1864.

25. Anne C. Rose, *Victorian America and the Civil War* (Cambridge: Cambridge University Press, 1992), 147, 184.–89; Steven Mintz, *A Prison of Expectations: The Family in Victorian Culture* (New York: New York University Press, 1983), 20, 28, 37, 67; Michael Grossberg, *Governing the Hearth: Law and the Family in Nineteenth-Century America* (Chapel Hill: University of North Carolina Press, 1985), 9–11; Robert Elno McGlone, "Suffer the Children: The Emergence of Modern Middle Class Family Life in America, 1820–1870" (Ph.D. diss., University of California, Los Angeles, 1971), viii; Sylvia D. Hoffert, *Private Matters: American Attitudes toward Childbearing and Infant Nurture in the Urban North, 1800–1860* (Urbana: University of Illinois Press, 1989), 2; Viviana A. Zelizer, *Pricing the Priceless Child: The Changing Social Value of Children* (New York: BasicBooks, 1985), 11–15; Jerome Kagan, "The Child in the Family," in *The Family*, ed. Alice S. Rossi, Jerome Kagan, and Tamara K. Hareven (New York: Norton, 1977), 42–43; Mary P. Ryan, *The Empire of the Mother: American Writing about Domesticity, 1830–1860* (New York: Haworth, 1982), 48–55.

26. Daniel Blake Smith, *Inside the Great House: Planter Life in Eighteenth-Century Chesapeake Society* (Ithaca: Cornell University Press, 1980), 41–53; Jan Lewis, *The Pursuit of Happiness: Family and Values in Jefferson's Virginia* (Cambridge: Cambridge University Press, 1983),

179–86; Jane Turner Censer, *North Carolina Planters and Their Children, 1800–1860* (Baton Rouge: Louisiana State University Press, 1984), esp. 18–21; Sally G. McMillen, "Antebellum Southern Fathers and the Health Care of Children," *Journal of Southern History* 60 (August 1994): 513–32; Mary Frances Berry, *The Politics of Parenthood: Child Care, Women's Rights, and the Myth of the Good Mother* (New York: Viking, 1993), 42–52; Geraldine Youcha, *Minding the Children: Child Care in America from Colonial Times to the Present* (New York: Scribner, 1995), 40–42; Mary P. Ryan, *Cradle of the Middle Class: The Family in Oneida County, New York, 1790–1865* (New York: Cambridge University Press, 1981), 99–102; Robert L. Griswold, *Fatherhood in America: A History* (New York: BasicBooks, 1993), 13–17; E. Anthony Rotundo, "Manhood in America: The Northern Middle Class, 1770–1920" (Ph.D. diss., Brandeis University, 1981), 179–237; John Demos, *Past, Present, and Personal: The Family and the Life Course in American History* (New York: Oxford University Press, 1986), 41–67.

27. James Marten, ed., "The Diary of Thomas H. DuVal: The Civil War in Austin, Texas, February 26 to October 9, 1863," *Southwestern Historical Quarterly* 94 (January 1991): 435–58; Ross D. Parke and Peter N. Stearns, "Fathers and Child Rearing," in *Children in Time and Place: Developmental and Historical Insights*, ed. Glen H. Elder Jr., John Modell, and Ross D. Parke (Cambridge: Cambridge University Press, 1993), 147–48; Berry, *Politics of Parenthood*, 52–53; Youcha, *Minding the Children*, 40–41.

28. One way the census measured family size was by counting the number of children under age five per 1,000 mothers. In 1800 that number was 1,342 among whites; although 1860 represented a small spike above 1850, the number on the eve of the Civil War had shrunk to only 905, with New England registering only 622 and the Southeast 918. See Bureau of the Census, *Historical Statistics*, 54.

29. Carl Degler, *At Odds: Women and the Family in America from the Revolution to the Present* (New York: Oxford University Press, 1980), 66–75, 88–94; Mary Lynn Stevens Heininger, "Children, Childhood, and Change in America, 1820–1920," in *A Century of Childhood, 1820–1920*, by Mary Lynn Stevens Heininger et al. (Rochester, N.Y.: Margaret Woodbury Strong Museum, 1984), 1–32; Anne M. Boylan, "Growing Up Female in America, 1800–1860," in *American Childhood: A Research Guide and Historical Handbook*, ed. Joseph M. Hawes and N. Ray Hiner (Westport, Conn.: Greenwood, 1985), 159; Barbara Finkelstein, "The Reconstruction of Childhood in the United States, 1790–1870," in Hawes and Hiner, *American Childhood*, esp. 123–35.

30. Boylan, "Growing Up Female," 161–62; Maris A. Vinovskis, "Schooling and Poor Children in Nineteenth-Century America," *American Behavioral Scientist* 35 (January/February 1992): 313–31; Carl F. Kaestle, *Pillars of the Republic: Common Schools and American Society, 1780–1860* (New York: Hill and Wang, 1983); Robert K. Weis, "To Please

and Instruct the Children," *Essex Institute Historical Collections* 123 (1987): 117–49; Dickson D. Bruce Jr., "Play, Work, and Ethics in the Old South," *Southern Folklore Quarterly* 40 (1977): 33–38, 41; Bernard Mergen, *Play and Playthings: A Reference Guide* (Westport, Conn.: Greenwood, 1982), 21–37, 43–44; David K. Wiggins, "The Play of Slave Children in the Plantation Communities of the Old South, 1820–1860," *Journal of Sport History* 7 (Summer 1980): 25–26.

31. J. Merton England, "The Democratic Faith in American Schoolbooks, 1783–1860," *American Quarterly* 15 (Summer 1963): 191–99; Carol Billman, "McGuffey's Readers and Alger's Fiction: The Gospel of Virtue According to Popular Children's Literature," *Journal of Popular Culture* 11 (Winter 1977): 614–19; Carolyn L. Karcher, "Lydia Maria Child and the Juvenile Miscellany: The Creation of an American Children's Literature," in *Periodical Literature in Nineteenth-Century America*, ed. Kenneth M. Price and Susan Belasco Smith (Charlottesville: University Press of Virginia, 1995), 90–114; John H. Westerhoff III, *McGuffey and His Readers: Piety, Morality, and Education in Nineteenth-Century America* (Nashville: Abingdon, 1978); John G. Cawelti, *Apostles of the Self-Made Man* (Chicago: University of Chicago Press, 1965), 104–8. See also Robert Franklin Berman, "The Naive Child and the Competent Child: American Literature for Children and the American Culture, 1830–1930" (Ph.D. diss., Harvard University, 1978), esp. chaps. 2 and 3. John Morton Blum appropriately refers to mid-century writing for juvenile readers as "the incidental work of leading British and American authors, and the major work of some incidental writers of Victorian prose and poetry" (John Morton Blum, ed., *Yesterday's Children: An Anthology Compiled from the Pages of Our Young Folks, 1865–1873* [Boston: Houghton Mifflin, 1959], xiii).

32. Ann Scott MacLeod, *A Moral Tale: Children's Fiction and American Culture, 1820–1860* (Hamden, Conn.: Archon, 1975), 104–16; Anne M. Boylan, *Sunday School: The Formation of an American Institution, 1790–1880* (New Haven: Yale University Press, 1988), 80–85; Mary E. Quinlaven, "Race Relations in the Antebellum Children's Literature of Jacob Abbott," *Journal of Popular Culture* 16 (Summer 1982): 27–36; John C. Crandell, "Patriotism and Humanitarian Reform in Children's Literature, 1825–1860," *American Quarterly* 21 (Spring 1969): 3–22; John B. Crume, "Children's Magazines, 1826–1857," *Journal of Popular Culture* 6 (Spring 1973): 698–707. Some antebellum children's publications foreshadowed the more aggressively political wartime literature. In 1847, for instance, *The Anti-Slavery Alphabet* (Philadelphia: Merrihew and Thompson, 1847) was published and sold to make money for the Anti-Slavery Fair in Philadelphia, while Harriet Beecher Stowe considered her *Uncle Tom's Cabin* to be appropriate reading for children as well as adults. See Susan Belasco Smith, "Serialization and the Nature of Uncle Tom's Cabin," in Price and Smith, *Periodical Literature in Nineteenth-Century America*, 70–71.

33. David Easton and Jack Dennis, *Children in the Political System: Origins of Political Legitimacy* (New York: McGraw-Hill, 1969), 78–83; Fred I. Greenstein, *Children and Politics* (New Haven: Yale University Press, 1965), 71–72; R. W. Connell, *The Child's Construction of Politics* (Melbourne: Melbourne University Press, 1970), 43–44, 48–49, 59; Richard M. Merelman, "The Role of Conflict in Children's Political Learning," in *Political Socialization, Citizenship Education, and Democracy*, ed. Orit Ichilov (New York: Teachers College Press, 1990), 47–65. For studies of children growing up in the context of long-term wars and political conflicts, see M. Fraser, *Children in Conflict* (New York: BasicBooks, 1973); J. J. M. Harbison and J. I. Harbison, eds., *A Society under Stress: Children and Young People in Northern Ireland* (Somerset: Open Books, 1980); and J. J. Harbison, ed., *Children of the Troubles: Children in Northern Ireland* (Belfast: Straumillis College Learning Resources Unit, 1983).

34. Ed Cairns, "Social Identity and Intergroup Conflict in Northern Ireland: A Developmental Perspective," in *Growing Up in Northern Ireland*, ed. Joan Harbison (Belfast: Straumillis College, 1989), 115–30; Norman Adler and Charles Harrington, eds., *The Learning of Political Behavior* (Glenview, Ill.: Scott, Foresman, 1970), 46; Connell, *Child's Construction of Politics*, 81–82; Greenstein, *Children and Politics*, 5; Howard Tolley, *Children and War: Political Socialization to International Conflict* (New York: Teachers College Press, 1973), 9–10, 124–25; Robert Coles, *The Political Life of Children* (Boston: Atlantic Monthly Press, 1986), 35, 87–88, 101–2. Some child psychologists concluded that the Second World War had little permanent effect on the American children who lived through it; Sioux City, Iowa, schoolkids, at least, were not preoccupied with the war or war-related activities. See A. L. Rautman and Edna Brower, "War Themes in Children's Stories," *Journal of Psychology* 19 (1945): 191–202, and "War Themes in Children's Stories: II. Six Years Later," *Journal of Psychology* 31 (1951): 263–70.

35. Thomas Davey, *A Generation Divided: German Children and the Berlin Wall* (Durham, N.C.: Duke University Press, 1987), 10.

36. Joanna L. Stratton, *Pioneer Women: Voices from the Kansas Frontier* (New York: Simon and Schuster, 1981), 25–26; John Burnett, ed., *Destiny Obscure: Autobiographies of Childhood, Education, and Family from the 1820s to the 1920s* (London: Penguin, 1982), 10, 24–27; Elizabeth Hampsten, *Read This Only to Yourself: The Private Writings of Midwestern Women, 1880–1915* (Bloomington: Indiana University Press, 1982), 25.

37. David Lowenthal, *The Past Is a Foreign Country* (Cambridge: Cambridge University Press, 1985), 7, 194–97, 200–201; John Kotre, *White Gloves: How We Create Ourselves through Memory* (New York: Free Press, 1995), 143–50, quotes on 148; Liahna Babener, "Bitter Nostalgia: Recollections of Childhood on the Midwestern Frontier," in *Small*

Worlds: Children and Adolescents in America, 1850–1950, ed. Elliott West and Paula Petrik (Lawrence: University Press of Kansas, 1992), 303. See also Paul Connerton, *How Societies Remember* (Cambridge: Cambridge University Press, 1989), for the origins and uses of memory from a social science perspective.

38. Rawick, *American Slave*; supplement, ser. 1, 12 vols. (1978); supplement, ser. 2, 10 vols. (1979).

39. Paul D. Escott, "The Art and Science of Reading WPA Slave Narratives," and John W. Blassingame, "Using the Testimony of Ex-Slaves: Approaches and Problems," in *The Slave's Narrative*, ed. Charles T. Davis and Henry Louis Gates Jr. (New York: Oxford University Press, 1985), 40–48, 79–98, esp. 83–92. James Olney's remark about published narratives seems appropriate for the WPA narratives, too: "Memory creates the significance of events in discovering the pattern into which those events fall" (" 'I Was Born': Slave Narratives, their Status as Autobiography and as Literature," in Davis and Gates, *Slave's Narrative*, 149).

40. Lowenthal, *Past Is a Foreign Country*, 217–19.

41. Arnold Gesell and Frances L. Ilg, *The Child from Five to Ten* (New York: Harper and Brothers, 1946), 447–49.

42. William M. Tuttle Jr., *"Daddy's Gone to War": The Second World War in the Lives of America's Children* (New York: Oxford University Press, 1993); W. D. Halls, *The Youth of Vichy France* (Oxford: Clarendon, 1981); Ruth Inglis, *The Children's War: Evacuation, 1939–1945* (London: William Collins Sons, 1989). A recent dissertation covers much of the same ground as Tuttle's work, with more emphasis on children's participation in the war effort. See Robert William Kirk, "Hey Kids! The Mobilization of American Children in the Second World War" (Ph.D. diss., University of California, Davis, 1991).

CHAPTER TWO

1. Gerald Norcross Diaries, May 28, 1863, November 11, December 24, 1864, February 24, March 12, 1865, American Antiquarian Society, Worcester, Mass. Gerald also managed to fit in a few potboiler westerns with titles such as *Speaking Rifle, the Indian Slayer, Snaky Snodgrass*, and *The Dacotah Queen*. See Norcross Diaries, February 4, 9, March 19, 1865.

2. John B. Boles, "Jacob Abbott and the Rollo Books: New England Culture for Children," *Journal of Popular Culture* 6 (Spring 1972): 507–28. Other entries in the series included *Rollo Learning to Read, Rollo Learning to Work, Rollo's Philosophy*, and *Rollo's Correspondence*.

3. Jane Clement Stone, "The Evolution of Civil War Novels for Children" (Ph.D. diss., Ohio State University, 1990), 155–67. These thematic threads also match a recent interpretation of mid-century children's literature as focusing on boys overcoming fear as a demonstration of virtue. See Peter N. Stearns and Timothy Haggerty, "The Role of Fear:

Transitions in American Emotional Standards for Children, 1850–1950," *American Historical Review* 96 (February 1991): 66–72.

4. Sarah Law Kennerly, "Confederate Juvenile Imprints: Children's Books and Periodicals Published in the Confederate States of America, 1861–1865" (Ph.D. diss., University of Michigan, 1956), 1–2, 55–180; George C. Rable, *The Confederate Republic: A Revolution against Politics* (Chapel Hill: University of North Carolina Press, 1994), 178–85.

5. *Our Young Folks*, April 1865, 285; *Little Corporal*, May 1867, 80; Mrs. M. B. C. Slade, "A Song of Hope," *Student and Schoolmate*, January 1864, 32; L. Adams, "On to Richmond!," *Student and Schoolmate*, August 1864, 64; *Little Pilgrim*, December 1861, 163, and July 1863, 97.

6. "Teacher's Desk," *Student and Schoolmate*, June 1863, 189; "Major Gen. George B. McClellan," *Merry's Museum*, November 1861, 115–16; Wilforley, "A Summer Trip Eastward," *Merry's Museum*, December 1861, 138–41; "Aunt Sue's Scrap-Bag," *Merry's Museum*, October 1861, 117, and September 1862, 88–89; Charles C. Coffin, "Letters from the Army," *Student and Schoolmate*, January 1862, 16–19; February 1862, 55–58; March 1862, 90–93; "Campaigning," *Student and Schoolmate*, July 1864, 21–22; August 1864, 47–48; October 1864, 108–10; December 1864, 175–78; February 1865, 39–42; April 1865, 117–18; William H. Armstrong, ed., *Gerty's Papa's Civil War* (New York: Pilgrim Press, 1984); Charles C. Nott, *Sketches of the War: A Series of Letters to the North Moore Street School of New York*, 4th ed. (New York: Anson D. F. Randolph, 1865), viii, 29–41, 75–87, 88–108, 135–53. Proceeds from the sale of Nott's book benefited disabled soldiers.

7. J. T. Trowbridge, *Frank Manly, the Drummer Boy: A Story of the War* (Boston: William F. Gill, 1876); Lavinia S. Goodwin, *The Little Helper* (Boston: Lee and Shepard, [1867]), 68–69; Charles Fosdick, *Frank on a Gun-Boat* (Philadelphia: Porter and Coates, 1864), 129.

8. "The Little Prisoner," *Our Young Folks*, January 1865, 33–37; April 1865, 240–44; May 1865, 327–29; July 1865, 462–65. In a similar story the twelve-year-old protagonist survives the battle of Chancellorsville and a stay in Libby Prison and encounters a villainous Robert E. Lee. See "The Boy of Chancellorsville," ibid., September 1865, 600–608.

9. Christie Pearl, "The Fort and How It Was Taken," *Student and Schoolmate*, August 1862, 273–74; "Union Boys in Kentucky," *Student and Schoolmate*, May 1863, 151–56; Louisa May Alcott, "Nelly's Hospital," *Our Young Folks*, April 1865, 267–77; Mrs. Phebe H. Phelps, "A Box for the Soldier," *Student and Schoolmate*, March 1864, 71–74. For a real-life instance in which each child added to a soldier's box "some little thing that father would like," see Mrs. M. A. Rogers, "An Iowa Woman in Wartime," *Annals of Iowa* 35 (Winter 1961): 541.

10. Lydia Maria Child, "The Two Christmas Evenings," *Our Young Folks*, January 1866, 2–13; "The Cloud with the Silver Lining," *Our Young Folks*, December 1865, 557–61; "The Discontented Girl," *Little Pilgrim*, November 1862, 150–51.

11. Holly Clyde, "The Soldier's Little Boy," *Little Pilgrim*, August 1863, 110.

12. Emily Huntington Miller, "The House That Johnny Rented," *Little Corporal*, July 1865, 7–9; August 1865, 19–21; September 1865, 42–45.

13. Louisa May Alcott, *Little Women* (Boston: Roberts Bros., 1868–69; reprint, London: Puffin Books, 1953); Horatio Alger Jr., *Frank's Campaign; or, What Boys Can Do on the Farm for the Camp* (Boston: Loring, 1864). See also Sarah Stuart Robbins, *Ned's Motto; or, Little by Little* (St. Paul: Merrill, 1864).

14. Amanda M. Douglas, *Kathie's Soldiers* (Boston: Lee and Shepard, 1870); Mary G. Darling, *Battles at Home* (Boston: Horace B. Fuller, 1870), 246–47.

15. Two examples of this metaphorical war appearing in children's periodicals are Gail Hamilton, "Small Fighting," *Student and Schoolmate*, January 1862, 7–11, and "About Being a Soldier," *Little Corporal*, September 1865, 33–34. The only mention of the war in the church magazine *Little American* came when a character named Captain Drummond tells the troubled main character, a little girl who wants to become a Christian soldier, about his experiences as a soldier in the war. See "Melbourne House," *Little American*, November 1, 1862, 18–19.

16. Sophie May, *Captain Horace* (Boston: Lee and Shepard, 1864); *Kate Morgan and Her Soldiers* (Philadelphia: American Sunday School Union, 1862), 121–22; Caroline E. Kelly, *Andy Hall: The Mission Scholar in the Army* (Boston: Henry Hoyt, 1863); Sarah S. Baker, *Charlie the Drummer Boy* (New York; American Tract Society, n.d.); Sarah Towne Smith, "The Drummer-Boy of the Twenty-Sixth," in *Our Village in War-Time* (New York: American Tract Society, 1864), 50–79.

17. J. T. Trowbridge, "Turning of the Leaf," *Our Young Folks*, June 1865, 399; "The Home Society," *Merry's Museum*, June 1863, 164–65, quoted in Patricia Ann Pflieger, "A Visit to Merry's Museum; or, Social Values in a Nineteenth-Century American Periodical for Children" (Ph.D. diss., University of Minnesota, 1987), 190; Charles Carleton Coffin, *My Days and Nights on the Battlefield* (Boston: Ticknor and Fields, 1864), 14, 19, and *Following the Flag* (Boston: Ticknor and Fields, 1865), 5–6.

18. "The Comedy of Secession," *Student and Schoolmate*, August 1862, 279–83; September 1862, 314–19.

19. Steven V. Ash, *When the Yankees Came: Conflict and Chaos in the Occupied South, 1861–1865* (Chapel Hill: University of North Carolina Press, 1995), 13–37; James M. McPherson, *Ordeal by Fire: The Civil War and Reconstruction*, 2nd ed. (New York: McGraw-Hill, 1992), 142–43; Kenneth M. Stampp, *And the War Came: The North and the Secession Crisis, 1860–1861* (Baton Rouge: Louisiana State University Press, 1950, 1970), 16–21; Trowbridge, "Turning of the Leaf," 400.

20. George Levy, *To Die in Chicago: Confederate Prisoners at Camp Douglas, 1862–1865* (Evanston, Ill.: Evanston Pub. Co., 1994), 56–65, 271–73; J. T. Trowbridge, "A Visit to Camp Douglas," *Our Young Folks*, April

1865, 252–60; May 1865, 291–300; June 1865, 357–60; "Battle-Field of Fredericksburg," *Our Young Folks*, March 1866, 163–70; "Richmond Prisons," *Our Young Folks*, April 1866, 298–304; "A Tennessee Farm-House," *Our Young Folks*, June 1866, 370–76. Trowbridge also published a book for adults describing his travels in the South, *The South: A Tour of Its Battle-fields and Ruined Cities* (Hartford: Stebbuis, 1866). Trowbridge makes this political point a crucial element of the plot of his novel *The Three Scouts*, especially in the character of a young Confederate conscript who joins the heroes of the story after his parents are killed by guerillas. He later sacrifices his own life to hold off the attacking guerilla band, allowing the fugitives to escape. See J. T. Trowbridge, *The Three Scouts* (Boston: Tilton, 1865).

21. G. N. Coan, "Correspondence," *Little Pilgrim*, June 1864, 81–82; Clara C. Clark, "An Appeal," ibid., July 1862, 93.

22. Christie Pearl, "The Contraband," *Student and Schoolmate*, February 1862, 45–48.

23. "Jim Dick; or, the Best Revenge," *Forrester's Playmate*, May 1864, 45–46. For Jacob Abbott's treatment of sympathetic black characters — in which young African Americans persevere in the face of discrimination and name-calling — see Mary E. Quinlaven, "Race Relations in the Antebellum Children's Literature of Jacob Abbott," *Journal of Popular Culture* 16 (Summer 1982): 27–36.

24. J. Thomas Warren, *Old Peggy Boggs; or, The Old Dominion Inside Out: A Tale of the Great Rebellion* (New York: Beadle and Adams, 1865); Donnarae C. MacCann, "The White Supremacy Myth in Juvenile Books about Blacks, 1830–1900" (Ph.D. diss., University of Iowa, 1988), 48–89; Jane Goodwin Austin, *Dora Darling: The Daughter of the Regiment* (Boston: Tilton, 1865); Mrs. Sarah Kip Brandegee, *The Bugle Call: A Summons to Work in Christ's Army* (New York: American Tract Society, [1870]), 20.

25. Trowbridge, *Three Scouts*; "Anecdotes and Sayings of Children," *Little Pilgrim*, September 1862, 125.

26. Albert Johannsen, *The House of Beadle and Adams and Its Dime and Nickel Novels: The Story of a Vanished Literature* (Norman: University of Oklahoma Press, 1950), 1:128–30. Representative titles (all published by Beadle and Company in New York), included Edward Willett, *True Blue; or, The Writing in Cipher* (1865); Willett, *The Loyal Specter; or, The True Hearts of Atlanta* (1865); Willett, *The Vicksburg Spy; or, Found and Lost: A Story of the Siege and Fall of the Great Rebel Stronghold* (1864); Lt. Col. Hazeltine, *The Prisoner of the Mill; or, Captain Hayward's Bodyguard* (1864); and Stephen Holmes Jr., *The Guerillas of the Osage; or, The Price of Loyalty on the Border* (1864).

27. Oliver Optic, *The Soldier Boy; or, Tom Somers in the Army: A Story of the Great Rebellion* (Boston: Lee and Shepard, 1863), 5–6. The sequels are *The Young Lieutenant; or, The Adventures of an Army Officer* (Boston: Lee and Shepard, 1865) and *Fighting Joe; or, the Fortunes of a Staff*

Officer (Boston: Lee and Shepard, 1866). Sam Pickering calls the Optic series juvenile versions of the *Iliad* (following Tom through his army career) and the *Odyssey* (Jack's adventures at sea). See Pickering, "A Boy's Own War," *New England Quarterly* 48 (September 1975): 371.

28. Oliver Optic, *The Yankee Middy; or, The Adventures of a Naval Officer: A Story of the Great Rebellion* (Boston: Lee and Shepard, 1866). The other books in the series are *The Sailor Boy; or, Jack Somers in the Navy: A Story of the Great Rebellion* (Boston: Lee and Shepard, 1863) and *Brave Old Salt; or, Life on the Quarterdeck* (Boston: Lee and Shepard, 1867). Another popular trilogy came from the pen of Charles Fosdick, who wrote the Gunboat Series about a young boy named Frank who served on the Mississippi through the entire war. Although the action in the first book, *Frank on a Gun-Boat* (Philadelphia: Porter and Coates, 1864), is restricted primarily to waterborne fights against Confederate forts or with guerillas firing from shore, Frank actually spends most of the Vicksburg campaign fighting in the trenches, smuggling supplies, and scouting. See Fosdick, *Frank on a Gun-Boat*, 99–111, 123. Fosdick's other books are *Frank before Vicksburg* (Philadelphia: Porter and Coates, 1864) and *Frank on the Lower Mississippi* (Philadelphia: R. W. Carroll, 1867). All three books feature the common pattern of capture and escape. For a postwar series following the exploits of a single soldier, see Dennis Moran's *The Banner Series*, which appeared in 1874. Written for very young readers, the books nevertheless featured the espionage efforts of young Ned Harris, whose exploits in Tennessee — complete with several captures and escapes — raised him from the rank of corporal to lieutenant. See Dennis Moran, *The Banner Series*, vol. 1, *The Little Corporal*; vol. 2, *The Young Sergeant*; vol. 3, *Lieutenant Edward Harris* (Pittsburgh: W. B. Quartz Jr., 1874).

29. Austin, *Dora Darling*, 168.

30. Paula Petrik, "The Youngest Fourth Estate: The Novelty Toy Printing Press and Adolescence, 1870–1886," in *Small Worlds: Children and Adolescents in America, 1850–1950*, ed. Elliott West and Paula Petrik (Lawrence: University Press of Kansas, 1992), 125–42. See also Elizabeth Harris's catalog for a recent National Museum of American History exhibition on novelty presses, *The Boy and His Press* (Washington, D.C.: Smithsonian Institution Press, 1992).

31. *Sunbeam*, October 1, 2, 28, 1863, January 22, June 24, 1864. All of the quotes are from newspapers in the Amateur Newspaper Collection, American Antiquarian Society.

32. *Once a Fortnight*, September 12, 26, 1864; *Union*, May, June, October 1861; *Monthly Chronicle*, August 1865.

33. Newark High School *Athenaeum*, October 1863, April, May, June 1864, New Jersey Historical Society, Newark. The dates provided are estimates drawn from internal evidence; the paper itself was undated.

34. Worcester *Monthly Chronicle*, June 1865.

35. Thomas Wentworth Higginson, "Children's Books of the Year," *North American Review* 102 (January 1866): 241–43.

36. Kennerly, "Confederate Juvenile Imprints," 256–302, 422–26; *Raleigh Daily Confederate*, December 22, 1864. At least one adult magazine, *The Southern Magnolia*, published in Richmond, featured a children's department with games whose clues often dealt with the war. See Carlton P. Brooks, *"The Magnolia*: A Literary Magazine for the Confederacy," *Virginia Cavalcade* 32 (Spring 1983): 151.

37. "What Children Should Do," *Child's Index*, September 1863, 19, and August 1863, 29; "The Two Revolutions," *Child's Index*, September 1863, 33; "Is Slavery Right?," *Child's Index*, December 1863, 47; "Angel Rose," *Child's Index*, March 1864, 12; "A War Picture," *Child's Index*, November 1863, 44; Kennerly, "Confederate Juvenile Imprints," 269–71.

38. Some publishers brought out their own versions of well-known fairy tales and stories. See, for instance, *Aladdin; or, The Wonderful Lamp* (Richmond: George L. Bidgood, 1865); Sophie May, *Christmas Fairies* (Memphis, Tenn.: Geo. Pattison, 1861), originally published before the war in *Little Pilgrim*; and *Mother Goose's Melodies* (Richmond: George L. Bidgood, 1865). Very small children could enjoy a short, apparently original tale about a woodman, his dog, and a bear in *Grandpapa and One of His Stories* (Richmond: Enquirer Book and Job Office, 1863). A Confederate edition of a favorite prewar adventure story for boys, *Robert and Harold; or, the Young Marooners on the Florida Coast*, came out in 1863 (Macon, Ga.: Burke, Boykin; "First Confederate [Edition]: from the Eighth United States Edition"), while the Presbyterian Church published *Wee Davie* (Richmond: Presbyterian Committee of Publication, 1864), a very popular, extremely morbid English parable of the religious and moral influence brought to a poor blacksmith's family by the interminable but pious death of their young son.

39. *For the Little Ones* (Savannah: John M. Cooper, n.d.), 6–7, 32–33. *The Illustrated Alphabet* (Columbia, S.C.: B. Duncan, [1862–65]), on the other hand, contained no material related to the war. An anonymously written and apparently unpublished "New Alphabet for Rebel Children," written even before First Manassas, criticized northern motivations and political figures. "A" was for Governor Andrew of Massachusetts, "so gallant & brave / He's shed oceans of blood to unshackle the slave," while "B" was for Butler, "D" was for Doubleday, and "G" was for "Greeley, the mighty Tribune / Just as safe in this war as the man in the moon." The alphabet ended with "Zouaves, pet-lambs of New York / I'm afraid they won't fatten on crackers & pork" ("A New Alphabet for Rebel Children," June 8, 1861, Maryland Historical Society, Baltimore).

40. *Uncle Buddy's Gift Book for the Holidays, Containing a Variety of Tales, Translations, Poetry, Chronology, Games, Anecdotes, Conundrums, &c,*

&c (Augusta: Blome and Tehan, 1863), 14–16, 51–52; Uncle William, *The Boys and Girls Stories of the War* (Richmond: West and Johnston, n.d.), 2–3, 7, 30–31. Although it may have been read by children, the anonymous thirty-two-page "epic" poem *Adventures of the Marion Hornets, Co. H, 7th Regt Fla. Vols.* (Knoxville: by the author, 1863), was apparently meant for adults. Its often breezy style included a number of references to drinking, running out of whisky, or getting "tight" — hardly appropriate reading material for southern children by the standards of the day.

41. A. McDowell to Calvin H. Wiley, July 4, 1861, Calvin Henderson Wiley Papers, Southern Historical Collection, University of North Carolina, Chapel Hill. Unfortunately, historians have paid little attention to the schoolbooks published in the Confederacy, although they frequently refer to the most colorful titles and most dramatic examples of southern pride, such as the well-known arithmetic problem that asked students, "If one Confederate soldier can whip 7 Yankees, how many soldiers can whip 49 Yankees?" See, for instance, Clement Eaton, *The Waning of the Old South Civilization, 1860–1880* (New York: Pegasus, 1969), 106, and *A History of the Southern Confederacy* (New York: Free Press, 1954), 209; Frank E. Vandiver, *Their Tattered Flags: The Epic of the Confederacy* (New York: Harper's Magazine Press, 1970), 211; Charles P. Roland, *The Confederacy* (Chicago: University of Chicago Press, 1960), 162–63, and *An American Iliad: The Story of the Civil War* (New York: McGraw-Hill, 1991), 228–29; Bell Irvin Wiley, *The Plain People of the Confederacy* (Baton Rouge: Louisiana State University Press, 1944), 56–57; E. Merton Coulter, *The Confederate States of America, 1861–1865* (Baton Rouge: Louisiana State University Press, 1950), 518.

42. Ruth Miller Elson, *Guardians of Tradition: American Schoolbooks of the Nineteenth Century* (Lincoln: University of Nebraska Press, 1964), 7–8, 91–93, 294–95, 321–23; John A. Nietz, *Old Textbooks* (Pittsburgh: University of Pittsburgh Press, 1961), 263; Louise L. Stevenson, *The Victorian Homefront: American Thought and Culture, 1860–1880* (New York: Twayne, 1991), 92–93; C. A. Apple to Calvin H. Wiley, May 1863, Wiley Papers.

43. Roland, *American Iliad*, 228; Eaton, *History of the Southern Confederacy*, 208–9; Eaton, *Waning of the Old South Civilization*, 103–6; Christie Farnham Pope, "Preparation for Pedestals: North Carolina Antebellum Female Seminaries" (Ph.D. diss., University of Chicago, 1977), 269–74. Similar strains seriously impeded the educational mission of schools in Maryland. See Richard R. Duncan, "The Impact of the Civil War on Education in Maryland," *Maryland Historical Magazine* 61 (March 1966): 37–52.

44. *Atlanta Daily Intelligencer*, October 10, 1861; Edward S. Joynes, *The Education of Teachers in the South* (Lynchburg: Virginia Power-Press Book and Job Office, 1864), 5–6.

45. T. Michael Parrish and Robert W. Willingham Jr., *Confederate Imprints: A Bibliography of Southern Publications from Secession to Surrender* (Austin: Jenkins, 1984), 630–54; Rev. Robert Fleming, *The Elementary Spelling Book, Revised and Adapted to the Youth of the Southern Confederacy, Interspersed with Bible readings on Domestic Slavery* (Atlanta: J. J. Toon, 1863), 4–5; *The New Texas Primary Reader, for the Use of Primary Schools* (Houston: E. H. Cushing, 1863), 2; Adelaide De Vendel Chaudron, *Chaudron's Spelling Book, Carefully Prepared for Family and School Use* (Mobile: S. H. Goetzel, 1864), 5.

46. John H. Rice, *A System of Modern Geography, Compiled from Various Sources and Adapted to the Present Condition of the World; Expressly for the Use of Schools and Academies in the Confederate States of America* (Atlanta: Franklin, 1862), 3; Allen M. Scott, *A New Southern Grammar of the English Language, Designed for the Use of Schools and Private Learners* (Memphis, Tenn.: Hutton and Freleigh, 1861), iv. For southerners' antebellum criticism of northern textbooks, see John McCardell, *The Idea of a Southern Nation: Southern Nationalists and Southern Nationalism, 1830–1860* (New York: Norton, 1979), 177–83, 203–8; Elson, *Guardians of Tradition*, 1–2.

47. *Columbia Daily Southern Guardian*, July 15, 1861; *Charleston Mercury*, February 16, 1864; *Mobile Daily Advertiser and Register*, December 12, 1863.

48. Richard Sterling, *Our Own Second Reader: For the Use of Schools and Families* (Greensboro, N.C.: Sterling, Campbell and Albright; Richmond: W. Hargrave White, 1862), iv; William A. Campbell, *The Child's First Book* (Richmond: Ayres and Wade, 1864), 3. Charles Smythe's *Primary Grammar for the Use of Beginners* (Greensborough, N.C.: Sterling and Campbell; Richmond: W. Hargrave White; Charleston: M'Carter and Dawson, 1861) was unusual in that, in addition to ignoring the war, it also lacked biblical injunctions, focusing almost solely on behavioral expectations for children. "The Confederate primers," writes Charles Carpenter, "aside from regional touches, were in a general way similar in text outline to those of the North" but were "nearly always" of inferior physical quality (*History of American Schoolbooks* [Philadelphia: University of Pennsylvania Press, 1963], 56).

49. See, for example, J. C. R. Taylor, *The Southern Primer, or the Child's First Book* (Charleston: A. E. Miller, 1864); Mrs. M. B. Moore, *The Dixie Primer, for the Little Folks*, 2nd ed. (Raleigh: Branson Farrar, 1863); *The Virginia Primer* (Richmond: J. R. Keiningham, 1864); *Confederate Rhyming Primer; or, First Lessons Made Easy* (Richmond: George L. Bidgood, 1863); Thomas Rambaut, *The Child's Primer* (Atlanta: J. J. Toon, 1863); *The Tract Primer* (Petersburg: Evangelical Tract Society, 1864); Rev. Peter Bullions, *An Analytical and Practical Grammar of the English Language* (Raleigh: North Carolina Christian Advocate, 1864); *The New Texas Spelling Book, Revised and Enlarged* (Houston: E. H. Cushing, 1865); *The First Confederate Speller: On a*

Strictly Philosophical and Progressive Plan (Nashville: Association of Southern Teachers, 1861); *The Second Confederate Speller* (Nashville: Southern Methodist Publishing, 1861); [Richard McAllister Smith], *The Confederate Primer*, 3rd ed. (Richmond: George L. Bidgood, 1863; [Richard McAllister Smith], *The Confederate First Reader: Containing Selections in Prose and Poetry; as Reading Exercises for the Young Children in the Schools and Families of the Confederate States* (Richmond: George L. Bidgood, 1864); [Roswell Chamberlain Smith], *Louisiana English Grammar* (Shreveport: Southwestern, 1865); *The Confederate Spelling Book, Compiled Principally from the National Speller* (Austin: D. Richardson, 1864).

50. *The Confederate Speller, Embracing Easy Lessons in Reading*, 3rd ed. (Mt. Lebanon, La.: W. F. Wells, 1864), 80–81; *The Old Dominion Speller* (Richmond: J. R. Keiningham, 1862), 27; *The Pictorial Primer: Designed for the Use of Schools and Families, Embellished with Fine Engravings* (Richmond: West and Johnson, 1863), 19, 24; Charles W. Smythe, *Our Own Elementary Grammar, Intermediate between the Primary and High School Grammars, and Especially Adapted to the Wants of the Common Schools* (Greensboro, N.C.: Sterling, Campbell and Albright; Richmond: W. Hargrave White; Columbia: Townsend and North, 1863), 14; Allen M. Scott, *New Southern Grammar*, 29, 74.

51. Adelaide De Vendel Chaudron, *The Second Reader, Designed for the Use of Primary Schools* (Mobile: Daily Advertiser and Register, 1863), 57–58 (*Chaudron's Spelling Book* and *Chaudron's First Reader, Designed for the Use of Primary Schools*, 2nd ed. [Mobile: W. G. Clark, 1864] contained virtually no war imagery or examples); Richard M. Smith, *The Confederate Spelling Book with Reading Lessons for the Young, Adapted to the Use of Schools or for Private Instruction* (Richmond: George L. Bidgood, 1863), 58, 85–87, 123; *The First Reader, for Southern Schools* (Raleigh: North Carolina Christian Advocate, 1864), 12; Levi Branson, *First Book in Composition, Applying the Principles of Grammar in the Art of Composing . . .* (Raleigh: Branson, Farrar, 1863), 14, 22.

52. Adelaide De Vendel Chaudron, *The Third Reader: Designed for the Use of Primary Schools* (Mobile: W. G. Clark, 1864), 13, 16, 27, 138.

53. Rev. Charles E. Leverett, *The Southern Confederacy Arithmetic, for Common Schools and Academies, with a Practical System of Book-Keeping* (Augusta: J. T. Paterson, 1864), 1, 20, 122; Rev. George Y. Browne, *Browne's Arithmetical Tables, Combined with Easy Lessons in Mental Arithmetic for Beginners* (Atlanta: Franklin, 1865), 27; Warren Colburn, *Intellectual Arithmetic, upon the Inductive Method of Instruction* (Nashville: Southern Methodist Publishing, 1862), 113; Samuel Lander, *Our Own School Arithmetic* (Greensboro, N.C.: Sterling, Campbell and Albright, 1863), 136, 157, 158, 222.

54. L. Johnson, *An Elementary Arithmetic, Designed for Beginners* (Ra-

leigh: Branson and Farrar, 1864), 15, 16, 18–19, 22, 34, 42, 43, 44, 45, 121–22.

55. Mrs. M. B. Moore, *The Dixie Speller, to Follow the First Dixie Reader* (Raleigh: Branson and Farrar, 1864), 23, 33.

56. John Neely, *The Confederate States Speller and Reader: Containing the Principles and Practice of English Orthography and Orthoepry, Systematically Developed* (Augusta: A. Bleakley, 1865), 53, 62, 80, 100; Fleming, *Elementary Spelling Book*, 90, 97, 106. The biblical supports for slavery appear on pp. 45–46, 57–58, 64, 71–72, 94–95, 127, and 154–55.

57. Rice, *System of Modern Geography*, 21, 51, 85; Mrs. M. B. Moore, *The Geographical Reader, for the Dixie Children* (Raleigh: Branson, Farrar, 1863), 13–14, 19–20.

58. *The New Texas Reader, Designed for the Use of Schools in Texas* (Houston: E. H. Cushing, 1864).

59. N. P. Henderson, *Henderson's Test Words in English Orthography* (New York: Clark and Maynard, 1865), 6, 16, 19, 20, 22, 35, 37, 40, 51; Marcus Willson, *Willson's Primary Speller: A Simple and Progressive Course of Lessons in Spelling with Reading and Dictation Exercises, and the Elements of Oral and Written Compositions* (New York: Harper and Brothers, 1863), 60; Edward Brooks, *The Normal Written Arithmetic, by Analysis and Synthesis: Designed for Common Schools, Normal Schools, High Schools, Academies, Etc.* (Philadelphia: Sower, Barnes, and Potts, 1863), 188, 190, 196, 198, 273, 322, 327; Charles Davis, *Practical Arithmetic: Embracing the Science and Applications of Numbers* (New York: Barnes and Burr, 1863), 37, 39, 51, 52, 113, 211, 288; James S. Eaton, *The Common School Arithmetic: Combining Analysis and Synthesis* (Boston: Taggard and Thompson; San Francisco: H. H. Brancroft, 1864), 252–53, 262, 263, 266; G. A. Walton, *A Written Arithmetic, for Common and Higher Schools* (Boston: Brewer and Tileston, 1865), 23–24.

60. G. S. Hillard, *The Intermediate Reader: For the Use of Schools* (Boston: Brewer and Tileston, 1863), 94–95, 190–91; G. S. Hillard, *The Sixth Reader: Consisting of Extracts in Prose and Verse, with Biographical and Critical Notices of the Authors* (Boston: Brewer and Tileston; New York: J. W. Schermerhorn; Portland: Bailey and Noyes, 1865), 125–26, 425–26, 428, 430–33; G. S. Hillard and L. J. Campbell, *The Third Reader for Primary Schools* (Philadelphia: Eldredge and Brother; Boston: Brewer and Tileston, 1864), 186–91.

61. *The Union ABC* (Boston: Degen, Estes, 1864), unpaginated.

62. Robert R. Raymond, *The Patriotic Speaker: Consisting of Specimens of Modern Eloquence, together with Poetical Extracts Adapted for Recitation, and Dramatic Pieces for Exhibitions* (New York: Barnes and Burr; Chicago: Geo. and C. W. Sherwood, 1864), v.

63. New England Branch of the American Tract Society, *Fifth Annual Re-*

port (Boston: The Branch, 1864), 19–20. These educational publications joined other ATS books for freedmen, such as *Friendly Counsels for Freedmen*, *A Warning to Freedmen against Intoxicating Drinks*, *Southern Planters and the Freedmen*, *John Freeman and His Family*, and *Out of the House of Bondage*. The total number of pages distributed by the society in 1863 was more than 1,643,500; total number of pages sent to freedmen comprised about 43,500 of that total. See *Fifth Annual Report*, 6.

64. Robert C. Morris, *Reading, 'Riting, and Reconstruction: The Education of Freedmen in the South, 1861–1870* (Chicago: University of Chicago Press, 1981), 198–201; Ronald E. Butchart, *Northern Schools, Southern Blacks, and Reconstruction: Freedmen's Education, 1862–1875* (Westport, Conn.: Greenwood, 1980), 135–39, 155–59; *The Freedman's Spelling Book* (Boston: American Tract Society, 1866), 4–5, 42–71.

65. American Tract Society, *Fifty-Second Annual Report, Presented at Boston* (Boston: American Tract Society, 1866), 8, 15, 48, 53, 55; "The Camp," *Freedman*, September 1864, 33; "Introduction for the Freedmen," *Freedman*, January 1864, 1; April 1865, 15.

66. *Freedman*, April 1865, 13; June 1864, 21.

67. Ibid., January 1864, 4; March 1864, 12; April 1864, 16; May 1864, 20; August 1864, 29, 30; March 1865, 12.

68. *Freedman's Spelling Book*, 22; *Freedman*, November 1864, 41; January 1865, 4; April 1865, 14; May 1865, 17–18. Northern missionaries to foreign lands — including, at least by the figures in the accompanying illustration, Africa — also deserved the admiration of freedmen. Yet another article stressed the hardships and sacrifices the first immigrants to New England endured. "They did not know when they first came here . . . what a great nation God was going to make of them" (*Freedman*, March 1865, 9; December 1864, 45).

69. Lydia Maria Child, *The Freedman's Book* (Boston: Ticknor and Fields, 1865), 14–23, 33–83, 86–92, 156–75, 265–76.

70. Butchart, *Northern Schools, Southern Blacks, and Reconstruction*, 135–59. For the American Tract Society's own views of the remedial needs of freedmen, reared in slavery and supposedly ignorant of religious, family, and political knowledge, see *Fifty-Second Annual Report*, 17–18.

71. *Freedman*, June 1865, 22.

72. For instance, the public schools of Mobile adopted Chaudron's school readers, according to an ad in the December 23, 1863, *Charleston Mercury*.

73. John Morton Blum, ed., *Yesterday's Children: An Anthology Compiled from the Pages of Our Young Folks, 1865–1873* (Boston: Houghton Mifflin, 1959), xv.

CHAPTER THREE

1. Title quote, Rufus Andrews to Agnes Andrews, September 20, 1862, *"Kiss Each Other For Me": The Civil War Letters of Rufus Andrews, 1861–1863,* by Rufus Andrews (Iron Mountain, Mich.: Mid-Peninsula Library Cooperative, 1979), 31; Edward Pye to his family, December 16, 1863, "Letters from the Confederate Medical Service in Texas, 1863–1865," ed. Frank E. Vandiver, *Southwestern Historical Quarterly* 55 (January 1952): 382; Fred Fleet to Bessie Fleet, October 12, 1862, *Green Mount: A Virginia Plantation Family during the Civil War: Being the Journal of Benjamin Robert Fleet and Letters of His Family,* ed. Betsy Fleet and John D. P. Fuller (Lexington: University Press of Kentucky, 1962), 172–73; Norman Riley to "Dear Wife," August 12, 1865, *Freedom: A Documentary History of Emancipation, 1861–1867,* ed. Ira Berlin, Joseph P. Reidy, and Leslie S. Rowland, ser. 2, *The Black Military Experience* (Cambridge: Cambridge University Press, 1982), 703.

2. Joshua Jones to Celia Jones, November 7, 1861, " 'Absent So Long from Those I Love': The Civil War Letters of Joshua Jones," ed. Eugene H. Berwanger, *Indiana Magazine of History* 88 (September 1992): 217; Winston Stephens to Octavia Stephens, November 10, 1861, "Children of Honor: Letters of Winston and Octavia Stephens, 1861–1862," ed. Ellen E. Hodges and Stephen Kerber, *Florida Historical Quarterly* 56 (July 1977): 55; Edward Pye to Molly Pye, December 16, 1864, Vandiver, "Letters from the Confederate Medical Service in Texas" (April 1952), 467; William Stoker to Elizabeth Stoker, July 27, 1862, "The War Letters of a Texas Conscript in Arkansas," ed. Robert W. Glover, *Arkansas Historical Quarterly* 20 (Winter 1961): 358.

3. Drew Gilpin Faust, *Mothers of Invention: Women of the Slaveholding South in the American Civil War* (Chapel Hill: University of North Carolina Press, 1996), 116–18; George C. Rable, *Civil Wars: Women and the Crisis of Southern Nationalism* (Urbana: University of Illinois Press, 1989), 55; Bell I. Wiley, *The Life of Johnny Reb: The Common Soldier of the Confederacy* (Indianapolis: Bobbs-Merrill, 1943; reprint, Baton Rouge: Louisiana State University Press, 1970), 192–216. For Victorian courtship correspondence, see Ellen K. Rothman, *Hands and Hearts: A History of Courtship in America* (New York: BasicBooks, 1984), 11–13. Letters from distraught wives have often been held up as a major cause of desertion from the Confederate army. See, for example, Ella Lonn, *Desertion during the Civil War* (Gloucester, Mass.: Peter Smith, 1966), 12–14; Bessie Martin, *Desertion of Alabama Troops from the Confederate Army: A Study in Sectionalism* (New York: AMS Press, 1966), 127–55; Reid Mitchell, "The Perseverance of the Soldiers," in *Why the Confederacy Lost,* ed. Gabor S. Boritt (New York: Oxford University Press, 1992), 126–29.

4. Louisa May Alcott, *Little Women* (Boston: Roberts Bros., 1869–69; reprint, London: Puffin Books, 1953), 20.

5. Donna Rebecca Donde Krug, "The Folks Back Home: The Confederate Homefront during the Civil War" (Ph.D. diss., University of California, Irvine, 1990), 229–300; Wiley, *Life of Johnny Reb*, 192–216, esp. 208. Wiley's volume on northern soldiers neglects to mention children as correspondents; see *The Life of Billy Yank: The Common Soldier of the Union* (Indianapolis: Bobbs-Merrill, 1952. Reprint, Baton Rouge: Louisiana State University Press, 1971.), 183–91. For the "Psychic Control" model of child rearing, which some of these soldier-fathers no doubt followed in giving advice, see Glenn Davis, *Childhood and History in America* (New York: Psychohistory Press, 1976), 37–89.

6. "Anecdotes and Sayings of Children," *Little Pilgrim*, March 1863, 41; Helen Sharp to John Sharp, July 29, October 10, 1862, "The Sharp Family Civil War Letters," ed. George Mills, *Annals of Iowa*, 3rd ser., 34 (January 1959): 515; Mitchell Thompson to Eliza Thompson, July 18, 1864, *Dear Eliza . . . : The Letters of Mitchell Andrew Thompson, May 1862–August 1864*, ed. Michael Andrew Thompson (Ames, Iowa: Carter Press, 1976), 96–97; William Nugent to Eleanor Nugent, November 18, 1862, *My Dear Nellie: The Civil War Letters of William L. Nugent to Eleanor Smith Nugent*, ed. William M. Cash and Lucy Somerville Howorth (Jackson: University Press of Mississippi, 1977), 146.

7. Joseph Willis Young to Anna Young, April 20, 1863, *The Personal Letters of Captain Joseph Willis Young: 97th Regiment, Indiana Volunteers, 4th Division, 15th A.C., Army of the United States, Civil War*, by Joseph Willis Young (Bloomington, Ind.: Monroe County Historical Society, 1974), 23–24; Jedediah Hotchkiss to Sara Hotchkiss, March 25, 26, 27, April 4, 1862, Jedediah Hotchkiss Papers, Family Correspondence, Library of Congress, Washington, D.C.

8. James Williams to Eliza Williams, May 8, August 10, 1863, *From That Terrible Field: Civil War Letters of James W. Williams, Twenty-first Alabama Infantry Volunteers*, ed. John Kent Folmar (University: University of Alabama Press, 1981), 111, 118; Alexander Fewell to Martha Fewell, November 6, 1864, *"Dear Martha . . .": The Confederate War Letters of a South Carolina Soldier, Alexander Faulkner Fewell*, ed. Robert Harley Mackintosh Jr. (Columbia, S.C.: R. L. Bryan, 1976), 158.

9. Nancy Schrom Dye and Daniel Blake Smith, "Mother Love and Infant Death, 1750–1920," *Journal of American History* 73 (September 1986): 329–53; Sylvia D. Hoffert, *Private Matters: American Attitudes toward Childbearing and Infant Nurture in the Urban North, 1800–1860* (Urbana: University of Illinois Press, 1989), 169–87; Sally G. McMillen, *Motherhood in the Old South: Pregnancy, Childbirth, and Infant Rearing* (Baton Rouge: Louisiana State University Press, 1990), 165–79.

10. Edwin Fay to his wife, August 2, 1862, *"This Infernal War": The Confederate Letters of Sgt. Edwin H. Fay*, ed. Bell I. Wiley (Austin: University of Texas Press, 1958), 130–31; Henry Ankeny to Fostina Ankeny,

September 22, 1862, *Kiss Josey For Me!*, ed. Florence Marie Ankeny Cox (Santa Anna, Calif.: Friis-Pioneer Press, 1974), 31; John Cotton to Mariah Cotton, November 8, 1862, *Yours till Death: Civil War Letters of John W. Cotton*, ed. Lucille Griffith (University: University of Alabama Press, 1951), 32.

11. Mary Minor to W. B. Minor, December 27, 1863, Mary J. Minor Papers, transcript, Center for American History, University of Texas, Austin; Charles Blacknall to Oscar Blacknall, August 2, 1861, Oscar W. Blacknall Papers, typescript, North Carolina Division of Archives and History, Raleigh; Jacob Heffelfinger to Jennie Heffelfinger, April 15, 1862, "'Dear Sister Jennie—Dear Brother Jacob': The Correspondence between a Northern Soldier and His Sister in Mechanicsburg, Pennsylvania, 1861–1864," ed. Florence C. McLaughlin, *Western Pennsylvania Historical Magazine* 60 (April 1977): 132; Elijah Cavins to Ann Cavins, February 27, 1863, *The Civil War Letters of Col. Elijah H. C. Cavins, 14th Indiana*, comp. Barbara A. Smith (Owensboro, Ky.: Cook-McDowell, 1981), 144, 179; Henry Kyd Douglas, *I Rode with Stonewall* (St. Simons Island, Ga.: Mockingbird Books, 1974), 209.

12. Thomas Wentworth Higginson, *Army Life in a Black Regiment* (Boston: Fields, Osgood, 1870; reprint, New York: Norton, 1984), 177–86. Higginson published another version of this story as "The Baby of the Regiment" in *Our Young Folks*, February 1865, 102–9. Not everyone approved of the presence of children in camp. Although Mitchell Thompson apparently enjoyed watching several little girls who "play and cut around just like" his daughter Corry, he protested that only "parents that don't care how children are brought up and are willing to let them run at large in every kind of company" would bring their youngsters to an army camp (Mitchell Thompson to Eliza Thompson, June 8, March 13, 1864, Michael Andrew Thompson, *Dear Eliza*, 90, 75).

13. Alfred Lacey Hough to Mary Jane Hough, May 26, June 18, 1861, *Soldier in the West: The Civil War Letters of Alfred Lacey Hough*, ed. Robert G. Athearn (Philadelphia: University of Pennsylvania Press, 1957), 43; William Wallace to Sarah Wallace, September 1, 1864, "William Wallace's Civil War Letters: The Atlanta Campaign," ed. John O. Holzhueter, *Wisconsin Magazine of History* 57 (Winter 1973–74): 108; David Coon to Isabel Coon, July 14, 1864, David Coon Letters, Library of Congress; John West to Mary West, November 15, 1863, *A Texan in Search of a Fight*, by John West (Waco, Tex.: J. S. Hill, 1901), 129.

14. G. W. Peddy to Kate Peddy, January 10, 1862, *Saddle Bag and Spinning Wheel: Being the Civil War Letters of George W. Peddy, M.D., and His Wife Kate Featherston Peddy*, ed. George Peddy Cuttino (Macon, Ga.: Mercer University Press, 1981), 29; William Stoker to Elizabeth Stoker, January 22, 1863, Glover, "War Letters of a Texas Conscript," 379; David B. Danbom, "'Dear Companion': Civil War Letters of a Story County Farmer," *Annals of Iowa*, 3rd ser., 47 (Fall 1984):

543; Mitchell Thompson to Eliza Thompson, August 7, 1863, Michael Andrew Thompson, *Dear Eliza*, 50; Joseph Adams to Elizabeth Adams, June 13, 1863, *Dear Wife: Captain Joseph Adams' Letters to His Wife Eliza Ann, 1861–1864*, ed. Jeanne Anne Hudder (n.p., 1985), 81.

15. James A. Garfield to Lucretia Garfield, August 22, 1861, *The Wild Life of the Army: Civil War Letters of James A. Garfield*, ed. Frederick D. Williams (East Lansing: Michigan State University Press, 1964), 28; William Dorsey Pender to Fanny Pender, September 22, 1861, *The General to His Lady: The Civil War Letters of William Dorsey Pender to Fanny Pender*, ed. William W. Hassler (Chapel Hill: University of North Carolina Press, 1965), 66; Shephard to Penelope Pryor, August 17, 1861, *"Dear Mother: Don't grieve about me. If I get killed, I'll only be dead." Letters from Georgia Soldiers in the Civil War*, ed. Mills Lane (Savannah: Library of Georgia, 1990), 51; Alfred Lacey Hough to Mary Jane Hough, August 26, 1863, Athearn, *Soldier in the West*, 131–32; Chamberlain quoted in Michael Golay, *To Gettysburg and Beyond: The Parallel Lives of Joshua Lawrence Chamberlain and Edward Porter Alexander* (New York: Crown, 1994), 106.

16. Theophilus Perry to Harriet Perry, April 28, 1863, Theophilus Perry Letters, Presley Carter Person Papers, Manuscript Division, Perkins Library, Duke University, Durham, N.C.; Krilla Gordon to George Gordon, June 28, 1863, George A. Gordon Papers, Center for American History; Julia Davidson to John Davidson, February 14, 1863, "A Wartime Story: The Davidson Letters, 1862–1865," ed. Jane Bonner Peacock, *Atlanta Historical Bulletin* 19, no. 1 (1975): 43–44; C. R. Burckmyer to C. L. Burckmyer, August 20, 1863, *The Burckmyer Letters, March, 1863–June, 1865*, ed. Charlotte R. Holmes (Columbia, S.C.: State Co., 1926), 117; Helen Sturtevant to Josiah Sturtevant, September 1, 1862, March 29, April 7, 1863, *Josiah Volunteered: A Collection of Diaries, Letters, and Photographs of Josiah H. Sturtevant, His Wife, Helen, and His Four Children*, ed. Arnold H. Sturtevant (Farmington, Maine: Knowlton and McLeary, 1977), 34–35, 40, 42, 44.

17. Margaret King to Philander King, February 9, April 29, 1864, Margaret A. King Correspondence, Illinois Historical Survey, University of Illinois, Urbana-Champaign; Laura DuVal to Thomas H. DuVal, January 31, 1864, Thomas H. DuVal Papers, Center for American History; Kate Peddy to G. W. Peddy, November 10, December 22, 1861, Cuttino, *Saddle Bag and Spinning Wheel*, 13; Susan Caldwell to Lycurgus Caldwell, letter fragment, ca. 1862, *"My Heart Is So Rebellious": The Caldwell Letters, 1861–1865*, ed. J. Michael Welton (Warrenton, Va.: Fauquier National Bank, 1991), 104, 112; Laura Bryan to Guy Bryan, October 23, 1864, Guy M. Bryan Papers, Center for American History.

18. Harriet Perry to Theophilus Perry, August 3 (the letter still bears a yellow stain), September 3, 24, 1862, Perry Letters. Lila Chunn also circled kisses from her daughter Helen; see Lila Chunn to William

Chunn, September 12, 1862, William A. Chunn Papers, Duke University.

19. Lizzie Simons Diary, typescript, September 4, 21, October 10, 24, 1862, Center for American History; Elizabeth Blair Lee to Samuel P. Lee, January 29, 1862, *Wartime Washington: The Civil War Letters of Elizabeth Blair Lee*, ed. Virginia Jeans Laas (Urbana: University of Illinois Press, 1991), 97.

20. Mary Anna Jackson, *Memoirs of Stonewall Jackson* (Louisville: Prentice Press, 1895), 361–53; Agnes Gordon to George Gordon, March 15, 1863, Gordon Papers; Leander Stem to Amanda Stem, December 20, 1862, "Stand by the Colors: The Civil War Letters of Leander Stem," *Register of the Kentucky Historical Society* 73 (October 1975): 410; Mary Lewis to Andrew Lewis, August 13, 1861, "The Civil War Letters of Captain Andrew Lewis and His Daughter," ed. Michael Barton, *Western Pennsylvania Historical Magazine* 60 (October 1977): 374, quoted in Marilyn Mayer Culpepper, *Trials and Triumphs: Women of the American Civil War* (East Lansing: Michigan State University Press, 1991), 286; Mary Neblett to Will Neblett, October 24, 1863, February 12, 1864, Lizzie Neblett Papers, Center for American History.

21. Nannie Whatley to William Whatley, June 11, 1862, William J. Whatley Letters, Center for American History; Ann Valentine to Andrew Valentine, January 19, 1864, Berlin et al., *Black Military Experience*, 686–87.

22. William Dorsey Pender to Fanny Pender, June 28, 1863, Hassler, *General to His Lady*, 255; John Davidson to Julia Davidson, December 24, 1862, Peacock, "Wartime Story," 32; Rufus Andrews to Agnes Andrews, March 21, September 25, 1862, Rufus Andrews, *"Kiss Each Other for Me,"* 9, 32; William Wallace to Sarah Wallace, February 16, 1862, "William Wallace's Civil War Letters: The Virginia Campaign," ed. John O. Holzhueter, *Wisconsin Magazine of History* 57 (Autumn 1973): 36; Henry Matrau to "Dear Mother," March 3, 1863, June 26, 1864, *Letters Home: Henry Matrau of the Iron Brigade*, ed. Marcia Reid-Green (Lincoln: University of Nebraska Press, 1993), 45, 81; Henry Livermore Abbott to Carrie Abbott, December 21, 1862, and to "Dear Papa," November 12, 1861, January 17, 1862, *Fallen Leaves: The Civil War Letters of Major Henry Livermore Abbott*, ed. Robert Garth Scott (Kent, Ohio: Kent State University Press, 1991), 75, 97–99, 155; Cordello Collins to John and Dolly Collins, November 1, 1861, "A Bucktail Voice: Civil War Correspondence of Pvt. Cordello Collins," ed. Mark Reinsberg, *Western Pennsylvania Historical Magazine* 48 (July 1965): 237; Joseph Young to Anna Young, July 2, 1863, Young, *Personal Letters*, 35; G. W. Peddy to Kate Peddy, August 2, 1864, Cuttino, *Saddle Bag and Spinning Wheel*, 271.

23. Lizzie Neblett to Will Neblett, February 6, 1864, Neblett Papers; James Marten, "The Making of a Carpetbagger: George S. Denison and the South, 1854–1866," *Louisiana History* 34 (Spring 1993): 151–52.

24. Golay, *To Gettysburg and Beyond*, 194; Elijah Cavins to Ann Cavins, October 10, December 21, 1862, May 17, 1863, Barbara A. Smith, *Civil War Letters of Col. Elijah H. C. Cavins*, 97, 122, 161; John McKitrick to Sophia McKitrick, May 21, 1863, *The Civil War Letters of John McKitrick to his wife Sophia*, comp. Doris C. Griffin (Lincoln: University of Nebraska Press, 1982), 14; Henry Matrau to "Dear Mother," June 26, 1864, Reid-Green, *Letters Home*, 81; William A. Crawford to Sarah Crawford, May 31, 1861, "A Saline Guard: The Civil War Letters of Col. William Ayers Crawford, C.S.A., 1861–1865," ed. Charles G. Williams, *Arkansas Historical Quarterly* 31 (Winter 1972): 335; Joshua Jones to Celia Jones, January 8, 1862, Berwanger, "Absent So Long from Those I Love," 222; Franklin Gaillard to Maria Porcher, December 31, 1861, July 17, 1863, Franklin Gaillard Letters, typescript, Southern Historical Collection, University of North Carolina, Chapel Hill; Luther Cowan to Molly Cowan and to Josephine Cowan, May 3, 27, 1862, Luther H. Cowan Letters, State Historical Society of Wisconsin, Madison; Matilda Lamb Morton Memoirs, Southern Historical Collection; Joseph Adams to Elizabeth Adams, February 6, 1862, Hudder, *Dear Wife*, 31; Marcus Spiegel to his wife, September 7, 1862, *Your True Marcus: The Civil War Letters of a Jewish Colonel*, ed. Frank L. Byrne and Jean P. Soman (Kent, Ohio: Kent State University Press, 1985), 258; Hans C. Heg to Hilda Heg, June 1, 1863, *The Civil War Letters of Colonel H. C. Heg*, ed. Theodore C. Blegen (Northfield, Minn.: Norwegian-American Historical Association, 1936), 214; Silas Browning to Minnie Browning, March 27, February 26, 1863, Silas Browning Papers, Library of Congress. It is unclear how serious Browning was in offering a young African American to his daughter, but at least one Union soldier, a chaplain from Iowa, did bring home an adult contraband. See Mrs. M. A. Rogers, "An Iowa Woman in Wartime," *Annals of Iowa* 36 (Summer 1961): 17–18.

25. E. Grey Dimond and Herman Hattaway, eds., *Letters from Forest Place: A Plantation Family's Correspondence, 1846–1881* (Jackson: University Press of Mississippi, 1993), 257; Bertram Wyatt-Brown, *Southern Honor: Ethics and Behavior in the Old South* (New York: Oxford University Press, 1982), 120–25; James I. Robertson, *Soldiers Blue and Gray* (Columbia: University of South Carolina Press, 1988), 7, 9; James M. McPherson, *What They Fought For, 1861–1865* (Baton Rouge: Louisiana State University Press, 1994), 18–21, 29–30; Reid Mitchell, *The Vacant Chair: The Northern Soldier Leaves Home* (New York: Oxford University Press, 1993), 14.

26. James M. McPherson, *For Cause and Comrades: Why Men Fought in the Civil War* (New York: Oxford University Press, 1997), 22–29, 134–39; Henry Hitchcock to Mary Hitchcock, November 4, 1864, Henry Hitchcock Papers, Library of Congress.

27. Joshua Chamberlain to Daisy Chamberlain, May 1863, quoted in Alice Rains Trulock, *In the Hands of Providence: Joshua L. Chamberlain*

and the American Civil War (Chapel Hill: University of North Carolina Press, 1992), 113; Joseph Young to Anna Young, November 4, 1862, Young, *Personal Letters*, 4–5.

28. Josiah Patterson to his Sons, December 13, 1861, Lane, *"Dear Mother: Don't grieve about me,"* 88–89; Isaac Austin Brooks to ——, October 13, 1861, *Yankee Correspondence: Civil War Letters between New England Soldiers and the Home Front*, ed. Nina Silber and Mary Beth Sievans (Charlottesville: University of Virginia Press, 1996), 60.

29. James Hall to Jesse and Mary Hall, June 11, 1861, July 8, 1864, James Iredell Hall Papers, Southern Historical Collection.

30. Henry Hitchcock to Mary Hitchcock, November 11, 1864, Hitchcock Papers; Luther Cowan to Mollie, Josephine, and George Cowan, January 18, 25, May 3, 27, 1862, typescript, Cowan Letters; William Watson to Marie Watson, September 4, 1864, *Letters of a Civil War Surgeon*, ed. Paul Fatout (West Lafayette, Ind.: Purdue University Press, 1961), 84–85; Marcus A. Turner to Liz Turner, July 6, 1861, Marcus A. Turner Papers, Southern Historical Collection; Franklin Gaillard to David Gaillard, June 28, 1863, Gaillard Letters. On northern soldiers' perceptions of the southern populace and countryside, see Reid Mitchell, *Civil War Soldiers: Their Expectations and Their Experiences* (New York: Viking, 1988), 90–147.

31. "Emery" to Laura Stebbins, November 13, December 25, 1862; Reuben Currier to Laura Stebbins, November 23, 1862; and C. J. Lakin to "Dear Teacher and friends," November 15, 1862, all in Laura W. Stebbins Papers, Duke University.

32. Jacob Heffelfinger to Jennie Heffelfinger, April 15, 1862, McLaughlin, " 'Dear Sister Jennie—Dear Brother Jacob,' " 133; Hugh N. Jones to "My Little Dear Niece," June 23, 1861, Hugh N. Jones Papers, Center for American History; Marcus Spiegel to his wife, March 30, 1862, Byrne and Soman, *Your True Marcus*, 90–91.

33. William H. Armstrong, ed., *Gerty's Papa's Civil War* (New York: Pilgrim Press, 1984), 19–20.

34. John West to Stark West, July 8, 1863, John West, *Texan in Search of a Fight*, 84–86.

35. William R. Stimson to "Dear Wife and little Children," April 10, 1862, William R. Stimson Letters, Library of Congress; J. G. Meacham to "My Dear wife and Children," April 18, 1862, "Civil War Letters," *Register of the Kentucky Historical Society* 72 (July 1974): 270.

36. Edward Pye to Matilda Pye, December 27, 1863, Vandiver, "Letters from the Confederate Medical Service in Texas" (January 1952), 381–82.

37. David Coon to "Dear Wife and Children," March 11, 1864, and to Emma Coon, June 5, 1864, transcript, Coon Letters; Theodore Montfort to David, Molly, and Tebo Montfort, November 3, 1861, Lane, *"Dear Mother: Don't grieve about me,"* 80.

38. Franklin Gaillard to David Gaillard, October 27, 1861, Gaillard Letters.

39. Marilyn Dell Brady, "The New Model Middle-Class Family," in *American Families: A Research Guide and Historical Handbook*, ed. Joseph M. Hawes and Elizabeth I. Nybakken (New York: Greenwood, 1991), 98–103; Daniel Blake Smith, *Inside the Great House: Planter Life in Eighteenth-Century Chesapeake Society* (Ithaca: Cornell University Press, 1980), 55, 82–125; Wyatt-Brown, *Southern Honor*, 126–27, 131–40; E. Anthony Rotundo, "Manhood in America: The Northern Middle-Class, 1770–1920" (Ph.D. diss., Brandeis University, 1981), 210–22; William H. Pease and Jane H. Pease, "Paternal Dilemmas: Education, Property, and Patrician Persistence in Jacksonian Boston," *New England Quarterly* 53 (June 1980): 147–67, esp. 150–59.

40. Joseph Young to Anna Young, November 16, 1862, Young, *Personal Letters*, 6; Willis Jones to Martha Buford Jones, December 1, 1863, *Peach Leather and Rebel Gray: Bluegrass Life and the War, 1860–1865*, ed. Mary E. Wharton and Ellen F. Williams (Lexington, Ky.: Helicon, 1986), 133–34.

41. James Goodnow to Nancy Goodnow, November 20, 1862, James Harrison Goodnow Papers, Library of Congress.

42. James Goodnow to Sam Goodnow, November 20, 1862, February 20, 1863, Goodnow Papers.

43. Ibid., January 11, February 20, April 6, 1863.

44. James Goodnow to Dan Goodnow, January 11, February 20, 1863; to Johnny Goodnow, February 20, 1863; to Dan and Johnny, October 25, 1863, Goodnow Papers.

45. James Goodnow to Sam Goodnow, October 25, 1863, and to Dan Goodnow, January 11, February 20, 1863, Goodnow Papers.

46. Spotswood Rice to "My Children," September 3, 1864, Berlin et al., *Black Military Experience*, 689; Thomas Charles Brady to Jane Brady, April 8, 1865, Charles Thomas Brady Family Papers, Center for American History; James Hall to Jesse and Mary Hall, June 13, 1864, Hall Papers; Luther Cowan to Josephine Cowan, April 27, 1862, typescript, Cowan Letters; J. A. McMurtrey to Lucinda McMurtrey, April 20, 24, 1864, *Letters to Lucinda, 1862–1864*, comp. Mary Frances Hosea Johnston (Huntsville, Ala.: Mrs. J. H. Johnston, 1985), 40, 41.

47. John L. Bridgers Sr. to John L. Bridgers Jr., August 27, September 22, October 12, 1864, John L. Bridgers Jr. Papers, Southern Historical Collection.

48. Edgeworth Bird to Sallie Bird, January 12, March 15, 1862, August 28, 1863, April 19, August 10, 1864, *The Granite Farm Letters: The Civil War Correspondence of Edgeworth and Sallie Bird*, ed. John Rozier (Athens: University of Georgia Press, 1988), 57–58, 76, 143, 163, 185.

49. Harriet Perry to Theophilus Perry, September 15, 1862, Perry Letters; William Whatley to Nannie Whatley, December 4, 1862, Whatley Letters; Jestin Hampton to Thomas B. Hampton, April 10, 1864, Thomas B. Hampton Papers, Center for American History.

50. William Dorsey Pender to Fanny Pender, September 28, 1861, Hassler,

General to His Lady, 69; William Nugent to Eleanor Smith Nugent, June 9, 1864, Cash and Howorth, *My Dear Nellie*, 181; Winston Stephens to Octavia Stephens, November 10, 1861, Hodges and Kerber, "Children of Honor," 54; Octavia Stephens to Winston Stephens, February 14, 1863, " 'Rogues and Black Hearted Scamps': Civil War Letters of Winston and Octavia Stephens, 1862–1863," ed. Ellen E. Hodges and Stephen Kerber, *Florida Historical Quarterly* 57 (July 1978): 79; James A. Garfield to Lucretia Garfield, March 10, 1862, Frederick D. Williams, *Wild Life of the Army*, 76. A number of these tidbits of advice also appeared in antebellum child-rearing manuals, which suggests that some fathers may have done a little research on child care. See Nancy F. Cott, "Notes toward an Interpretation of Antebellum Childrearing," *Psychohistory Review* 6 (1978): 7.

51. William Dorsey Pender to Fanny Pender, October 4, 1861, Hassler, *General to His Lady*, 75; Joel Blake to Laura Blake, April 11, 1863, "Letters of Joel C. Blake," ed. J. Russell Reaver, *Apalachee* 5 (1957–62): 16; John Duncan to Alma Duncan, May 5, 1864, "Letters of John W. Duncan, Captain, Confederate States of America," ed. Herbert L. Ferguson, *Arkansas Historical Quarterly* 9 (Winter 1956): 298–312; James Goodnow to Nancy Goodnow, November 20, 1863, Goodnow Papers.

52. Henry Livermore Abbott to "Dear Mama," October 19, 1861; to Grafton Abbott, May 8, 1862; to Arthur Abbott, May 8, 1862; and to Samuel Abbott, September 28, 1863, all in Robert Garth Scott, *Fallen Leaves*, 58, 117, 220–21.

53. Willie Sivley to Jane Sivley, October 21, 1863, Jane Sivley Papers, Southern Historical Collection; Leo M. Kaiser, ed., "Letters from the Front," *Journal of the Illinois State Historical Association* 61 (Summer 1963): 158, 160, 162.

54. Jasper Barrett to Marion Barrett, December 26, 1863, September 14, 1864, and to Matilda Barrett, March 15, 1865, Jasper N. Barrett Papers, Library of Congress.

55. Holiday Ames to his wife, April 23, 1865, "Waiting for the War's End: The Letter of an Ohio Soldier in Alabama after Learning of Lincoln's Death," ed. Louis Filler, *Ohio History* 74 (Winter 1965): 61; John Davidson to Julia Davidson, May 10, 1863, Peacock, "Wartime Story," 55; William Nugent to Eleanor Smith Nugent, August 2, 1864, Cash and Howorth, *My Dear Nellie*, 195; Marion Fitzpatrick to Amanda Fitzpatrick, May 26, 1864, *Letters to Amanda from Sergeant Major Marion Hill Fitzpatrick, Company K, 45th Georgia Regiment, Thomas's Brigade, Wilcox Division, Hill's Corps, CSA, to his wife Amanda Olive Elizabeth White Fitzpatrick, 1862–1865*, ed. Henry Hammock (Culloden, Ga.: Mansel Hammock, 1976), 132; Ernst Damkoehler to Mathilde Damkoehler, June 22, 1863, *From Wisconsin to Andersonville*, by Ernst Damkoehler (n.p., 1961); Volney Ellis to Mary Ellis, December 8, 1862, " 'An Experience in Soldier's Life': The Civil War Letters of Volney Ellis, Adjutant, Twelfth Texas Infantry, Walker's

Texas Division, C.S.A.," ed. Thomas W. Cutrer, *Military History of the Southwest* 22 (Fall 1992): 121.

56. William Nugent to Eleanor Smith Nugent, July 6, 1864, Cash and Howorth, *My Dear Nellie*, 187; C. L. Burckmyer to C. R. Burckmyer, December 30, 1864, Holmes, *Burckmyer Letters*, 460–61.

57. L. Gaylord Clark, "Childhood: A Letter to the Editor," *Knickerbocker* 50 (October 1857): 302–98.

58. Charles Blacknall to Oscar Blacknall, August 30, 1864, Blacknall Papers; Leander Huckaby to "Dear Father, Mother and sisters," June 7, 1863, "A Mississippian in Lee's Army: The Letters of Leander Huckaby," ed. Donald E. Reynolds, *Journal of Mississippi History* 36 (August 1974): 281.

CHAPTER FOUR

1. John H. Krenkel, ed., *Serving the Republic: Richard Yates, Illinois Governor and Congressman, Son of Richard Yates, Civil War Governor, an Autobiography* (Danville, Ill.: Interstate Publishers, 1968), 3–4.

2. George W. Donaghey, *Autobiography of George W. Donaghey, Governor of Arkansas, 1909–1913* (Benton, Ark.: L. B. White, 1939), 15–16; Annie P. Marmion, *Under Fire: An Experience in the Civil War*, ed. William Vincent Marmion Jr. (n.p., 1959), 7, 16. For a mostly military account of wartime in this beleaguered Virginia town, see Chester G. Hearn, *Six Years of Hell: Harpers Ferry during the Civil War* (Baton Rouge: Louisiana State University Press, 1996).

3. For a brief but effective overview, see Peter W. Bardaglio, "The Children of Jubilee: African American Childhood in Wartime," in *Divided Houses: Gender and the Civil War*, ed. Catherine Clinton and Nina Silber (New York: Oxford University Press, 1992), 213–29.

4. E. Anthony Rotundo, "Boy Culture: Middle-Class Boyhood in Nineteenth-Century America," in *Meaning for Manhood: Constructions of Masculinity in Victorian America*, ed. Mark Carnes and Clyde Griffin (Chicago: University of Chicago Press, 1990), 15–36.

5. Jesse R. Grant, *In the Days of My Father General Grant* (New York: Harper and Brothers, 1925), 15, 23–25.

6. Opie Read, *I Remember* (New York: R. R. Smith, 1930), 11–13.

7. Cornelia Peake McDonald Diary, March 1862, June 4, 1863, *A Woman's Civil War: A Diary, with Reminiscences of the War, from March 1862*, ed. Minrose C. Gwin (Madison: University of Wisconsin Press, 1992), 35–36, 156.

8. James W. Sullivan, *Boyhood Memories of the Civil War, 1861–1865: Invasion of Carlisle* (Carlisle, Pa.: Hamilton Library Association, 1933), 17, 18, 20–21; Robert L. Bloom, "'We Never Expected a Battle': The Civilians at Gettysburg, 1863," *Pennsylvania History* 55 (October 1988): 166, 167, 170. Some children no doubt cursed their luck for missing the battle. Enoch and Charlotte Lewis of Altoona, for example, sent their children to their grandparents' home in Philadelphia when

the Confederates entered Pennsylvania. See Michael R. Gannett, ed., "Twelve Letters from Altoona, June–July, 1863," *Pennsylvania History* 46 (January 1980): 39–56.

9. McCurdy quoted in Elizabeth Daniels, "The Children of Gettysburg," *American Heritage* 40 (May–June 1989): 99; William Hamilton Bayly, *Stories of the Battle* (Gettysburg, Pa.: Gettysburg National Military Park Library, 1939) (*Gettysburg Compiler* Scrapbook), 4; Daniel Alexander Skelly, *A Boy's Experiences during the Battle of Gettysburg* (Gettysburg, Pa.: n.p., 1932), 18–20.

10. Bloom, " 'We Never Expected a Battle,' " 182; Albertus McCreary, "Gettysburg: A Boy's Experience of the Battle," *McClure's Magazine*, July 1909, 243–53. A former slave remembered black children collecting spent ammunition near Fort Donelson for years after the war. See George P. Rawick, ed. *The American Slave: A Composite Autobiography*, 19 vols. (Westport, Conn.: Greenwood, 1972–74), 6:95.

11. Read, *I Remember*, 11–13.

12. Patrick J. Geary, ed., *Celine: Remembering Louisiana, 1850–1871* (Athens: University of Georgia Press, 1987), 106, 129.

13. Iver Bernstein, *The New York City Draft Riots: Their Significance for American Society and Politics in the Age of the Civil War* (New York: Oxford University Press, 1990), 29; Eric F. Goldman, ed., "Young John Bach McMaster: A Boyhood in New York City," *New York History* 20 (October 1939): 324; Eddie Foy, *Clowning through Life* (New York: Dutton, 1928), 14.

14. Jacob Michaux, "Youth's Impressions of War between States," photocopy, Manuscript Collection, Fredericksburg and Spotsylvania National Military Park, Va.

15. William Wallace to Sarah Wallace, May 27, 1862, July 24, 1864, "William Wallace's Civil War Letters: The Atlanta Campaign," ed. John O. Holzhueter, *Wisconsin Magazine of History* 57 (Winter 1973–74): 49, 103, 108; May 30, 31, 1862, *A Confederate Girl's Diary*, ed. James I. Robertson Jr. (Bloomington: Indiana University Press, 1960), 51; Rawick, *American Slave*, 4(1):81.

16. Eliza Ann Lanier Recollections, Alcinda Timberlake Papers, Mississippi Department of Archives and History, Jackson; Annie Laurie Broidrick, "A Recollection of Thirty Years Ago," typescript, Southern Historical Collection, University of North Carolina, Chapel Hill; Mrs. W. W. Lord Journal, typescript, Library of Congress, Washington, D.C., 3–4.

17. A. A. Hoehling, *Vicksburg: Forty-seven Days of Siege* (Englewood Cliffs, N.J.: Prentice-Hall, 1969), 126; "War Diary of a Union Woman in the South," ed. G. W. Cable, May 1, June 25, 1863, *Famous Adventures and Prison Escapes of the Civil War* (New York: Century, 1904), 59–60, 73; Mrs. Mary A. Loughborough, *My Cave Life in Vicksburg* (New York: Appleton, 1864), 79, 91–92, 129; Anne Shannon to Emmie Crutcher, April 23, 1863, and Lavinia Shannon to Emmie Crutcher, July 13, 1863,

Crutcher-Shannon Family Papers, Center for American History, University of Texas, Austin. (For confirmation of this particularly gruesome incident, see Emma Balfour Diary, May 24, 1863, Balfour Collection, Mississippi Department of Archives and History.)

18. Julia Davidson to John Davidson, July 26, August 4, 1864, "A Wartime Story: The Davidson Letters, 1862–1865," ed. Jane Bonner Peacock, *Atlanta Historical Bulletin* 19, no. 1 (1975): 96, 99; Lee Kennett, *Marching through Georgia: The Story of Soldiers and Civilians during Sherman's Campaign* (New York: HarperCollins, 1995), 89. Perhaps twenty Atlantans were killed or hurt during the bombardment; there were so few civilian casualties because of the dwindling number of residents remaining in the city and the unreliable Union shells. See Stephen Davis, "'A Very Barbarous Mode of Carrying on War': Sherman's Artillery Bombardment of Atlanta, July 20–August 24, 1864," *Georgia Historical Quarterly* 79 (Spring 1995): 57–90.

19. Ann Banister, "Incidents in the Life of a Civil War Child," Harrison Henry Cocke Papers, Southern Historical Collection.

20. M. Viatora Schuller, "A History of Catholic Orphan Homes in the United States from 1727 to 1884." (Ph.D. diss., Loyola University of Chicago, 1954), 231; *Richmond Examiner*, October 17, 1863, March 3, 1864; *Mobile Advertiser and Register*, October 21, 1863; *Raleigh Daily Confederate*, February 17, 1865; McCreary, "Gettysburg," 253; *Chicago Tribune*, January 30, November 11, 1863; J. Matthew Gallman, *Mastering Wartime: A Social History of Philadelphia during the Civil War* (Cambridge: Cambridge University Press, 1990), 208, 212; *Baltimore Daily Gazette*, November 30, 1863, November 17, 1864, February 4, 1865; *Atlanta Daily Intelligencer*, February 28, 1864.

21. Drew Gilpin Faust, *Mothers of Invention: Women of the Slaveholding South in the American Civil War* (Chapel Hill: University of North Carolina Press, 1996), 35–37, 236–38; Joan E. Cashin, *Our Common Affairs: Texts from Women in the Old South* (Baltimore: Johns Hopkins University Press, 1996), 22.

22. Anna Freud and Dorothy Burlingham, *War and Children* (New York: Ernst Willard, 1943), 33–35; George C. Rable, *Civil Wars: Women and the Crisis of Southern Nationalism* (Urbana: University of Illinois Press, 1989), 57–58, 65–72, 96–99, 155–58, 202–20; Victoria E. Bynum, *Unruly Women: The Politics of Social and Sexual Control in the Old South* (Chapel Hill: University of North Carolina Press, 1992), 111–50; Elizabeth Fuller to Solon Fuller, March 29, 1863, Solon L. Fuller Papers, Manuscript Division, Perkins Library, Duke University, Durham, N.C.; Cornelia M. Noble Diary, typescript, June 30, November 1, 8, 1863, Center for American History.

23. Lizzie Neblett to Will Neblett, April 13, May 6, June 9, 1863, February 12, 1864, and Will Neblett to Lizzie Neblett, August 23, 1863, Lizzie Neblett Papers, Center for American History.

24. "Grandmother to Granddaughter," December 15, 1864, Maryland His-

torical Society, Baltimore; Anna Burwell to Edmund Burwell, August 8, 1863, and letter fragment, 1865, Edmund S. Burwell Papers, Southern Historical Collection.

25. Lucy Hull Baldwin, "My Autobiography," typescript, Lucy Hull Baldwin Papers, Southern Historical Collection; Earl Schenck Miers, ed., *When the World Ended: The Diary of Emma Le Conte* (New York: Oxford University Press, 1957), 91; Carrie M. Berry Diary, September 10, 1864, Atlanta History Center, Atlanta, Ga.; F. C. Jones to "My Dear Major," January 3, 1863, Civil War Papers, American Antiquarian Society, Worcester, Mass.

26. Jeannette Leonard Gilder, *Autobiography of a Tomboy* (New York: Doubleday, Page, 1904), 213; Phoebe Jane Morrison Hutchison Reminiscences, Illinois Historical Survey, University of Illinois, Urbana-Champaign, 18–20; George W. Norris, *Fighting Liberal: The Autobiography of George W. Norris* (New York: Macmillan, 1946), 9–11.

27. Quoted in Marilyn Mayer Culpepper, *Trials and Triumphs: Women of the American Civil War* (East Lansing: Michigan State University Press, 1991), 286; Emma Balfour Diary, May 20, 30, 1863, Balfour Collection; William A. MacCorkle, *Recollections of Fifty Years of West Virginia* (New York: Putnam's, 1928), 11–12, 14.

28. Hans Heg to Hilda Heg, December 19, 1862, January 12, 1863, *The Civil War Letters of Colonel H. C. Heg*, ed. Theodore C. Blegen (Northfield, Minn.: Norwegian-American Historical Association, 1936), 157, 175; Marcus Spiegel to Hamlin, Lizzie, and Moses Spiegel, March 22, 1862, *Your True Marcus: The Civil War Letters of a Jewish Colonel*, ed. Frank L. Byrne and Jean P. Soman (Kent, Ohio: Kent State University Press, 1985), 80–81; Henry Livermore Abbott to Grafton Abbott, May 8, 1862, *Fallen Leaves: The Civil War Letters of Major Henry Livermore Abbott*, ed. Robert Garth Scott (Kent, Ohio: Kent State University Press, 1991), 117.

29. Henrietta Dana Skinner, *An Echo from Parnassus: Being Childhood Memories of Longfellow and His Friends* (New York: Sears, 1928), 174; Andrew Hilen, "Charley Longfellow Goes to War," *Harvard Library Bulletin* 14 (Spring 1960): 295–303.

30. Rolla Wells, *Episodes of My Life* (St. Louis: Rolla Wells, 1933), 14–15; John Philip Sousa, *Marching Along: Recollections of Men, Women, and Music* (Boston: Hale, Cushman and Flint, 1928), 6–7; Elizabeth Kipp Vincent, *In the Days of Lincoln: Girlhood Recollections and Personal Reminiscences of Life in Washington during the Civil War* (Gardena, Calif.: Spanish American Institute Press, 1924), 12–15; Addie Hibbard Gregory, *A Great-Grandmother Remembers* (Chicago: Kroch, 1940), 23–25.

31. A. B. Morong Diary, April 3, 10, 11, 15, 19, 27, 1865, J. D. Phillips Library, Peabody Essex Museum, Salem, Mass.; Mary E. Cunningham, ed., "The Background of an American (Being the True Chronicle of a Boy of Twelve)," *New York History* 27 (January, July 1946): 76–

87, 213–23; Marion F. Overton, "Wintertime in Old Brooklyn," *Long Island Forum* 11 (February 1948): 23–24; Sarah Cook Williamson Diary, George H. Cook Papers, Special Collections and Archives, Rutgers University Library, New Brunswick, N.J.

32. Lizzie H. Corning Diary, February 23, March 18, May 21, August 19, October 4, 5, 26, 29, November 12, 27, December 2, 17, 1862, January 1, 1863, New Hampshire Historical Society, Concord; "The Civil War Home Front: Diary of a Young Girl, 1862–1863," February 7, June 24, July 21, August 12, 1862, January 1, 1863, ed. Virginia Mayberry and Dawn E. Bakken, *Indiana Magazine of History* 87 (March 1991): 35, 47, 52, 54, 61.

33. Marion Richardson Drury, *Reminiscences of Early Days in Iowa* (Toledo, Iowa: Toledo Chronicle Press, 1931), 44–45; Mary Eliza Starbuck, *My House and I: A Chronicle of Nantucket* (Boston: Houghton Mifflin, 1929), 193–94, 197.

34. "Diary of John Magill Steele and Sarah Eliza Steele," April 3, June 11, 1863, *Diaries, Letters, and Recollections of the War between the States* (Winchester, Va.: Winchester–Frederick County Historical Society, 1955), 69, 75.

35. Kevin Rawlings, *We Were Marching on Christmas Day: A History and Chronicle of Christmas during the Civil War* (Baltimore: Toomey, 1995), 91, 90, 118, 119; Stephen V. Ash, *When the Yankees Came: Conflict and Chaos in the Occupied South, 1861–1865* (Chapel Hill: University of North Carolina Press, 1995), 106; Mary Elizabeth Massey, *Refugee Life in the Confederacy* (Baton Rouge: Louisiana State University Press, 1964), 196–200; Rable, *Civil Wars*, 99–100.

36. *Richmond Examiner*, December 25, 1862; Mary Ann Cobb to John A. Cobb, December 29, 1861, *Athens, 1861–1865: As Seen through Letters in the University of Georgia Libraries*, ed. Kenneth Coleman (Athens: University of Georgia Press, 1969), 35–36; Susan Caldwell to Lycurgus Caldwell, December 28, 1862, *"My Heart Is So Rebellious": The Caldwell Letters, 1861–1865*, ed. J. Michael Welton (Warrenton, Va.: Fauquier National Bank, 1991), 166; George Gordon to Krilla Gordon, December 25, 1862, Gordon Papers.

37. Virginia Ingraham Burr, ed., *The Secret Eye: The Journal of Ella Gertrude Clanton Thomas, 1848–1889* (Chapel Hill: University of North Carolina Press, 1990), 213, 220, 250; Lucy Wood Butler Diary, typescript, December 24, 1862, University of Virginia Library, Charlottesville; Susan Bradford Eppes, *Through Some Eventful Years* (Macon, Ga.: J. W. Burke, 1926), 253; Alice West Allen, "Recollections of the War in Virginia," *Confederate Veteran* 23 (June 1915): 268–69; John B. Jones Diary, December 25, 26, 1865, *A Rebel War Clerk's Diary*, ed. Earl Schenck Miers (New York: Sagamore Press, 1958; reprint, Baton Rouge: Louisiana State University Press, 1993), 466–67.

38. Margaret Lawrence Lindsley Journal, December 25, 1864, Margaret Lawrence Ramsey Collection, Library of Congress; Florence Ashmore

Cowles Hamlett Martin, ed., *Courageous Journey: The Civil War Journal of Laetitia Lafon Ashmore Nutt* (Miami: E. A. Seemann, 1975), 45; Dolly Sumner Lunt, *A Woman's Wartime Journal* (New York: Century, 1918), 44–45; Robert Hugh Martin, *A Boy of Old Shenandoah* (Parsons, W.Va.: McClain, 1977), 47.

39. Lee Ann Whites, *The Civil War as a Crisis in Gender: Augusta, Georgia, 1860–1890* (Athens: University of Georgia Press, 1995), 98–99; *Richmond Examiner*, December 15, 1862, October 3, 1864 (copying Macon *Confederate*); *Raleigh Daily State Journal*, January 10, 1863; Louisa Gilmer to Jeremy Gilmer, September 26, 1863, Jeremy F. Gilmer Papers, Southern Historical Collection; William C. Harris, "East Tennessee's Civil War Refugees and the Impact of the War on Civilians," *Journal of East Tennessee History* (January 1993): 13–14; Newton B. Jones, "The Charleston Orphan House, 1860–1876," *South Carolina Historical Magazine* 62 (October 1961): 210; Schuller, "History of Catholic Orphan Homes," 229–31; Hartwell T. Bynum, "Sherman's Expulsion of the Roswell Women," *Georgia Historical Quarterly* 54 (Summer 1970): 178–80; *Baltimore Daily Gazette*, August 11, 1864; Michael D. Hitt, *Charged with Treason: Ordeal of 400 Mill Workers during Military Operations in Roswell, Georgia, 1864–1865* (Monroe, N.Y.: Library Research Associates, 1992).

40. James M. Merrill, ed., " 'Nothing to Eat but Raw Bacon': Letters from a War Correspondent, 1862," *Tennessee Historical Quarterly* 17 (June 1958): 152–53. For a still useful description of the experiences of refugees in the South; their motivations; their options; their economic, social, and moral priorities and disappointments; their relationships with other southerners and with Federal authorities; and myriad other aspects of their wartimes lives, see Massey, *Refugee Life in the Confederacy*. Although Massey rarely separates the experiences of children from those of their parents, she does comment briefly on their education, their relationships with nonrefugee children, and Christmas celebrations.

41. August 16, October 29, 30, 1863, *Brokenburn: The Journal of Kate Stone, 1861–1868*, ed. John Q. Anderson (Baton Rouge: Louisiana State University Press, 1955), 238, 249–50.

42. Mary Jane Lucas to Anne Lucas Ashely, June 11, 1862, Lucas-Ashley Family Papers, Duke University.

43. Faust, *Mothers of Invention*, 39, 143–44; Mary Jane Warde, "Now the Wolfe Has Come: The Civilian Civil War in the Indian Territory," *Chronicles of Oklahoma* 71 (Spring 1993): 68; Lucie Blackwell Malone Thompson Autobiographical Sketch, Thompson Family Papers, Southern Historical Collection; Sister Aloysius Mackin, ed., "Wartime Scenes from Convent Windows: St. Cecilia, 1860 through 1865," *Tennessee Historical Quarterly* 39 (Winter 1980): 409.

44. Baldwin, "My Autobiography"; Charles Nagel, *A Boy's Civil War Story* (St. Louis: Eden, 1934), 261, 265–71.

45. *Philadelphia Public Ledger and Transcript*, July 4, 1863; Sullivan, *Boy-hood Memories of the Civil War*, 14; Jennie Love, "War as a Girl Saw It: Chambersburg, Pennsylvania, During the Invasion of Lee and Ewell into Pennsylvania," *National Tribune*, May 12, 1910.

46. Peggy Robbins, "Jim Limber and the Davises," *Civil War Times Illustrated* 17 (November 1978): 22–27.

47. Bardaglio, "Children of Jubilee," 218–19; Booker T. Washington, *Up from Slavery: An Autobiography* (New York: Doubleday, Page, 1901; reprint, Garden City, N.Y.: Doubleday, 1963), 6–7, 13–14.

48. Clarence L. Mohr, *On the Threshold of Freedom: Masters and Slaves in Civil War Georgia* (Athens: University of Georgia Press, 1986), 210–14; Rawick, *American Slave*, 3(1):162; 3(2):171–72; 4(3):1141; 7:167.

49. Bell Irvin Wiley, *Southern Negroes, 1861–1865* (New York: Rinehart, 1938), 32–36; Washington, *Up from Slavery*, 5; Rawick, *American Slave*, supplement, ser. 2, 2(1):64; 9(3):63.

50. Joseph T. Glatthaar, *Forged in Battle: The Civil War Alliance of Black Soldiers and White Officers* (New York: Free Press, 1990), 70–71, 93–95; Lt. William Argo to Brig. Gen. William A. Pyle, March 21, 1864, *Freedom: A Documentary History of Emancipation, 1861–1867*, ed. Ira Berlin, Joseph P. Reidy, and Leslie S. Rowland, ser. 1, vol. 1, *The Destruction of Slavery* (New York: Cambridge University Press, 1985), 481–82; testimony of Col. George H. Hanks, February 6, 1864, *Freedom: A Documentary History of Emancipation, 1861–1867*, ed. Ira Berlin, Joseph P. Reidy, and Leslie S. Rowland, ser. 1, vol. 3, *The Wartime Genesis of Free Labor: The Lower South* (New York: Cambridge University Press, 1990), 519; T. E. Hall to Gen. O. O. Howard, June 22, 1865, *Freedom: A Documentary History of Emancipation, 1861–1867*, ed. Ira Berlin, Joseph P. Reidy, and Leslie S. Rowland, ser. 2, *The Black Military Experience* (Cambridge: Cambridge University Press, 1982), 718.

51. Mohr, *On the Threshold of Freedom*, 173–74; Deborah Gray White, *Ar'n't I a Woman? Female Slaves in the Plantation South* (New York: Norton, 1985), 137–38; Randolph B. Campbell, *An Empire for Slavery: The Peculiar Institution in Texas, 1821–1865* (Baton Rouge: Louisiana State University Press, 1989), 243–45; Rawick, *American Slave*, 4(2):94; 7:221–22.

52. *Douglass' Monthly*, March 1862, 617; Olynthus B. Clark, ed., *Downing's Civil War Diary* (Des Moines: Historical Department of Iowa, 1916), 85, 131; Joseph T. Glatthaar, *The March to the Sea and Beyond: Sherman's Troops in the Savannah and Carolinas Campaigns* (New York: New York University Press, 1985), 54, 60–62.

53. Robert Francis Engs, *Freedom's First Generation: Black Hampton, Virginia, 1861–1890* (Philadelphia: University of Pennsylvania Press, 1979), 38; Willie Lee Rose, *Rehearsal for Reconstruction: The Port Royal Experiment* (New York: Vintage, 1967), 243–44, 322; *Statistics of the Operations of the Executive Board of Friends' Association of Philadel-*

phia, and Its Vicinity, for the Relief of Colored Freedmen (Philadelphia: Inquirer Printing Office, 1864), 11, 12, 19; Frank R. Levstik, ed., "A Journey among the Contrabands: The Diary of Walter Totten Carpenter," *Indiana Magazine of History* 73 (September 1977): 210–11. Lee Kennett estimates that 30,000 to 32,000 former slaves joined Sherman's men as they marched through Georgia. See Kennett, *Marching through Georgia*, 289.

54. Cam Walker, "Corinth: The Story of a Contraband Camp," *Civil War History* 20 (March 1974): 5–22; Felix James, "The Establishment of Freedman's Village in Arlington, Virginia," *Negro History Bulletin* 33 (1970): 90–93; Rawick, *American Slave*, 7:358; Engs, *Freedom's First Generation*, 31–32; John Cimprich, *Slavery's End in Tennessee, 1861–1865* (University: University of Alabama Press, 1985), 53, 50, 58; Gaines M. Foster, "The Limitations of Federal Health Care for Freedmen," *Journal of Southern History* 48 (August 1982): 349–72; Cornelia Hancock to unknown, November 15, 1863, and to "My Dear Mother," December 23, 1863, *South after Gettysburg: Letters of Cornelia Hancock, 1863–1868*, ed. Henrietta Stratton Jaquette (New York: Thomas Y. Crowell, 1937), 33–34, 37.

55. Cimprich, *Slavery's End in Tennessee*, 47, 50, 53; Engs, *Freedom's First Generation*, 34, 38, 41; *Statistics of the Operations of the Executive Board*, 12, 14; New England Freedmen's Aid Society (Education Commission), *Second Annual Report* (Boston: The Society, 1864), 38, quoted in Martha Mitchell Bigelow, "Vicksburg: Experiment in Freedom," *Journal of Mississippi History* 26 (February–November 1964): 39; Lt. W. T. Truxton to Flag Officer S. F. DuPont, June 13, 1862, and Adj. Gen. Lorenzo Thomas to Edwin M. Stanton, August 23, 1863, both in Berlin et al., *Destruction of Slavery*, 125–27, 308–9; James Bryan to Edwin M. Stanton, July 27, 1863, Berlin et al., *Wartime Genesis of Free Labor*, 716; Maria R. Mann to "Elisa," February 10, 1863, Mary Tyler Peabody Papers, Library of Congress.

56. *Statistics of the Operations of the Executive Board*, 30; *Philadelphia Christian Recorder*, March 4, 1864, quoted in Henry Rowntree, "Freedmen at Davis Bend, April 1864," ed. James T. Currie, *Journal of Mississippi History* 46 (May 1984): 122; *New Orleans Times*, April 8, 1864.

57. E. S. Philbrick to "Dear Ned," April 12, 1862, and Edward L. Pierce to Salmon P. Chase, June 2, 1862, Berlin et al., *Wartime Genesis of Free Labor*, 185, 192; Louis S. Gerteis, *From Contraband to Freedman: Federal Policy toward Southern Blacks, 1861–1865* (Westport, Conn.: Greenwood, 1973), 124, 149, 157–58; Elizabeth Hyde Botume, *First Days amongst the Contrabands* (Boston: Lee and Shepard, 1893; reprint, New York: Arno Press, 1968), 94. For the gradual incorporation of slave children into the plantation work routine, see Wilma King, *Stolen Childhood: Slave Youth in Nineteenth-Century America* (Bloomington: Indiana University Press, 1995), 21–41; John W. Blassingame, *The Slave Community: Plantation Life in the Antebellum South*, 2nd ed.

(New York: Oxford University Press, 1979), 185–91; and White, *Ar'n't I a Woman?*, 91–97.

58. Ronald E. Butchart, *Northern Schools, Southern Blacks, and Reconstruction: Freedmen's Education, 1862–1875* (Westport, Conn.: Greenwood, 1980), 9, 4; "The Freedmen at Port Royal," *Atlantic Monthly*, September 1863, 303; Engs, *Freedom's First Generation*, 26, 53; Cimprich, *Slavery's End in Tennessee*, 76; Beula May Price, ed., "'Yank' Girl Visits Occupied Corinth," *Daily Corinthian, Civil War Centennial Souvenir Edition* (1961), 2, 15; Robert D. Parmet, "Schools for the Freedmen," *Negro History Bulletin* 34 (1971): 128; Sing-Nan Fen, "Notes on the Education of Negroes at Norfolk and Portsmouth, Virginia, during the Civil War," *Phylon* 28 (Summer 1967): 204; William F. Messner, "Black Education in Louisiana, 1863–1865," *Civil War History* 22 (March 1976): 46, 48; Elisabeth Joan Doyle, "Nurseries of Treason: Schools in Occupied New Orleans," *Journal of Southern History* 26 (May 1960): 175–79; Lucy Chase to Miss Lowell, April 20, 1865, *Dear Ones at Home: Letters from Contraband Camps*, ed. Henry L. Swint (Nashville: Vanderbilt University Press, 1966), 157.

59. May 16, 17, 1865, *From a New England Woman's Diary in Dixie in 1865*, by Mary Ames (New York: Negro Universities Press, 1969), 26, 29; Botume, *First Days amongst the Contrabands*, 64–65, 68, 69; "Freedmen at Port Royal," 303–7; *New Orleans Times*, June 22, 1865; B. Rush Plumly, *Report of the Board of Education for Freedmen, Department of the Gulf, for the Year 1864* (New Orleans: True Delta, 1865), 6, 7. For a hypothetical, but useful, description of a typical day of instruction in a freedchildren's school, see Robert C. Morris, *Reading, 'Riting, and Reconstruction: The Education of Freedmen in the South, 1861–1870* (Chicago: University of Chicago Press, 1981), 174–77.

60. Messner, "Black Education in Louisiana," 51; Fen, "Notes on the Education of Negroes at Norfolk and Portsmouth," 204; May 17, 19, 24, 1865, Ames, *From a New England Woman's Diary*, 29, 34, 39; Botume, *First Days amongst the Contrabands*, 89.

61. Laura M. Towne Diary, June 11, August 26, 1862, *Letters and Diary of Laura M. Towne: Written from the Sea Islands of South Carolina, 1862–1864*, ed. Rupert Sargent Holland (Cambridge, Mass.: Riverside Press, 1912; reprint, New York: Negro Universities Press, 1969), 67, 87; Botume, *First Days amongst the Contrabands*, 41–43.

62. Sandra E. Small, "The Yankee Schoolmarm in Freedmen's Schools: An Analysis of Attitudes," *Journal of Southern History* 45 (August 1979): 390–91; introduction to Holland, *Letters and Diary of Laura M. Towne*, 6; Patricia Brady, "Trials and Tribulations: American Missionary Association Teachers and Black Education in Occupied New Orleans, 1863–1864," *Louisiana History* 31 (Winter 1990): 11; Towne Diary, May 23, 1862, May 3, 1863, Holland, *Letters and Diary of Laura M. Towne*, 6, 59, 104–5; Rawick, *American Slave*, 2(4):184.

63. Lucy Chase to "Dear ones at home," April 1, June 13, 1863, Swint,

Dear Ones at Home, 61–62, 81–82; July 3, 10, 15, 1865, Ames, *From a New England Woman's Diary*, 74, 83, 88–89; Laura M. Towne Letter, December 25, 1864, Holland, *Letters and Diary of Laura M. Towne*, 145; Nellie F. Stearns to "Lizzie," November 5, 1865, Nellie F. Stearns Letter, Duke University. For examples of the material and social difficulties faced by northern teachers among the contrabands, including the danger of attack by angry southern whites, see Patricia Brady, "Trials and Tribulations," 10–13; Joe M. Richardson, "The American Missionary Association and Black Education in Civil War Missouri," *Missouri Historical Review* 69 (July 1975): 444–46; Joe M. Richardson, *Christian Reconstruction: The American Missionary Association and Southern Blacks, 1861–1890* (Athens: University of Georgia Press, 1986), 28–29, 178; *New Orleans Times*, November 15, 1863; Plumly, *Report of the Board of Education for Freedmen*, 7–11.

64. Richardson, *Christian Reconstruction*, 191, 198; Clara Merritt De Boer, *His Truth Is Marching On: African Americans Who Taught the Freedmen for the American Missionary Association, 1861–1877* (New York: Garland, 1995), 27–28, 50–53, 56, 60–64, 84, 90–91.

65. New England Freedmen's Aid Society (Educational Commission) *Extracts from Letters of Teachers and Superintendents*, 5th ser. (Boston: John Wilson and Son, 1864), 13; Elizabeth Ware Pearson, ed., *Letters from Port Royal, 1862–1868* (Boston: W. B. Clarke, 1906; reprint, New York: Arno Press, 1969), 65–67. The graveside scene was memorialized in the poem "The Negro Burying Ground," by William C. Gannett, one of the teachers present.

66. Thomas L. Webber, *Deep Like the Rivers: Education in the Slave Quarter Community, 1831–1865* (New York: Norton, 1978), 31–32; *Charleston Mercury*, April 8, 1864; *Richmond Examiner*, June 10, 1864; Rawick, *American Slave*, 9(4):60; 13(3):116; 15(2):383; 16:29.

67. Rawick, *American Slave*, 5(3):130–31, 270–71; 6:125; 7:95–96; 12(1):21; 12(2):54–55; 14(1):35, 343; 15(2):201; 17:231.

68. Glatthaar, *March to the Sea*, 54–59; Bell I. Wiley, *The Life of Billy Yank: The Common Soldier of the Union* (Indianapolis: Bobbs-Merrill, 1952; reprint, Baton Rouge: Louisiana State University Press, 1971), 109–19; Glatthaar, *Forged in Battle*, 81–92; Rawick, *American Slave*, 2(1):177.

69. *Philadelphia Christian Recorder*, March 25, 1865.

70. Reid Mitchell, *Civil War Soldiers: Their Expectations and Their Experiences* (New York: Viking, 1988), 122; Rawick, *American Slave*, 2(2): 329–30; 6:225, 251–52; 7:361; 9(3):85; 10(5):1, 367; 10(6):40, 45; 15(2): 353.

71. Willie Lee Rose, *Rehearsal for Reconstruction*, 322–23; Glatthaar, *March to the Sea*, 64; Mohr, *On the Threshold of Freedom*, 92–93; Rawick, *American Slave*, 6:219; 10(5):233.

72. Sallie Hunt, "Boys and Girls in the War," in *Our Women in the War: The Lives They Lived, the Deaths They Died* (Charleston: News and

Courier Book Presses, 1885), 41, 45; Grace Elizabeth King, *Memories of a Southern Woman of Letters* (New York: Macmillan, 1932), 5; Eliza Freleigh Shippery, "Some War Experiences," in *Reminiscences of the Women of Missouri during the Sixties*, by Missouri Division, United Daughters of the Confederacy (Jefferson City, Mo.: Hugh Stephens, n.d.), 136–37.

73. For the dynamics of civilian/military relations in the occupied South, see Ash, *When the Yankees Came*, 38–75. For an analysis of the Federal policies stemming from those relationships, see Mark Grimsley, *The Hard Hand of War: Union Military Policy toward Southern Civilians, 1861–1865* (Cambridge: Cambridge University Press, 1995).

74. Emmie Sublett to Emily Anderson, April 29, 1865, Manuscript Division, Eleanor S. Brockenbrough Library, Museum of the Confederacy, Richmond, Va.; Read, *I Remember*, 10; Delia White Woodward, Civil War Memorandum, Augustus White Long Papers, Southern Historical Collection.

75. Mrs. W. D. Chadwick Diary, August 21, 1863, "Civil War Days in Huntsville: A Diary by Mrs. W. D. Chadwick," by Mrs. W. D. Chadwick, *Alabama Historical Quarterly* 9 (Summer 1947): 231; Juliette Low, "When I Was a Girl," in *Juliette Low and the Girl Scouts: The Story of an American Woman, 1860–1927*, ed. Anne Hyde Choate and Helen Ferris (Garden City, N.Y.: Doubleday, Doran, 1928), 4.

76. May 15, 16, 1862, January 12, 1863, *Sad Earth, Sweet Heaven: The Diary of Lucy Rebecca Buck during the War between the States*, ed. William P. Buck (Birmingham, Ala.: Cornerstone, 1973), 68, 72; Carol Wells, ed., *War, Reconstruction, and Redemption on Red River: The Memoirs of Dosia Williams Moore*. Ruston, La.: McGinty, 1990), 21–22.

77. Eppes, *Through Some Eventful Years*, 272–73.

78. Harriet E. Keatinge, "Narrative of the Burning of Columbia, S.C., February 17, 1865, and Journey to Fayetteville, N.C., with Sherman's Army, February–March 1865," typescript, Library of Congress.

79. *Columbia Daily Southern Guardian*, April 6, 1864; Winston Stephens to Octavia Stephens, March 13, 1862, "'Rogues and Black Hearted Scamps': Civil War Letters of Winston and Octavia Stephens, 1862–1863," ed. Ellen E. Hodges and Stephen Kerber, *Florida Historical Quarterly* 57 (July 1978): 58; Geary, *Celine*, 112; Maria Wacker Fleet and Dr. Benjamin Fleet to Fred Fleet, June 12, 1864, *Green Mount: A Virginia Plantation Family during the Civil War: Being the Journal of Benjamin Robert Fleet and Letters of His Family*, ed. Betsy Fleet and John D. P. Fuller (Lexington: University Press of Kentucky, 1962), 329; Charles W. Turner, ed., "General David Hunter's Sack of Lexington, Virginia, June 10–14, 1864: An Account by Rose Page Pendleton," *Virginia Magazine of History and Biography* 83 (April 1975): 182. On the impact of the war on families and on children as participants in

the deadly struggle in Missouri, see Michael Fellman, *Inside War: The Guerilla Conflict in Missouri during the American Civil War* (New York: Oxford University Press, 1989), 193–230. For brief accounts of the more than thirty rapes by Union soldiers—none clearly involving a child—that made it to trial, see Thomas P. Lowry, *The Story the Soldiers Wouldn't Tell: Sex in the Civil War* (Mechanicsburg, Pa.: Stackpole, 1994), 123–31.

80. Robert Jay Lifton, *Home from the War: Vietnam Veterans, Neither Victims nor Executioners* (New York: BasicBooks, 1973, 1983), 206–7.

81. Hoehling, *Vicksburg*, 106; Berry Diary, August 3, 25, 28, September 16, October 1, 15, 25, 1864.

82. Cora Warren Beck Memoirs, pp. 9–10, East Carolina Manuscript Collection, J. Y. Joyner Library, East Carolina University, Greenville, N.C.

83. Ambrose Bierce, "Chickamauga," in *The Civil War Short Stories of Ambrose Bierce* (Lincoln: University of Nebraska Press/Bison Books, 1988), 53–58, quotes on 54, 55, 56, 58.

84. Grace King, "Bayou l'Ombre: An Incident in the War," in *Civil War Women: The Civil War Seen through Women's Eyes*, ed. Frank McSherry Jr., Charles G. Waugh, and Martin Greenberg (New York: Simon and Schuster, 1990), 100–132, quotes on 101, 103.

CHAPTER FIVE

1. Margaret Wade Campbell Deland, *If This Be I, As I Suppose It Be* (New York: Appleton-Century, 1936), 17–19; Elizabeth Randolph Preston Allan, *A March Past: Reminiscences of Elizabeth Randolph Preston Allan* (Richmond: Dietz, 1938), 111; Betty Herndon Maury Diary, May 22, 1862, *The Confederate Diary of Betty Herndon Maury, 1861–1863*, ed. Alice Maury Parmelee (Washington, D.C.: privately printed, 1938), 77; Journal of Baby Maud, October 25, 1863, April 10, 1865, New Hampshire Historical Society, Concord; Howard Pyle, "When I Was a Little Boy," *Woman's Home Companion*, April 1912, 5.

2. Susan Bradford Eppes, *Through Some Eventful Years* (Macon: J. W. Burke, 1926), 141–46; Samuel A. Steele, *The Sunny Road: Home Life in Dixie during the War* (Memphis, Tenn.: n.p., [1924]), 59, 68, 69.

3. Lizette Woodworth Reese, *A Victorian Village: Reminiscences of Other Days* (New York: Farrar and Rinehart, 1929), 69–72.

4. Maurice F. Egan, *Recollections of a Happy Life* (New York: George H. Doran, 1924), 42–48.

5. See, for instance, Norman Adler and Charles Harrington, eds., *The Learning of Political Behavior* (Glenview, Ill.: Scott, Foresman, 1970), 10; R. W. Connell, *The Child's Construction of Politics* (Melbourne: Melbourne University Press, 1970), 81–82.

6. Eric F. Goldman, ed., "Young John Bach McMaster: A Boyhood in New York City," *New York History* 20 (October 1939): 323; *Milwaukee Sentinel*, June 11, 28, 1861; *Philadelphia Public Ledger*, April 22, 23, 24,

25, 27, May 6, 1861; Norman B. Wilkinson, "The Brandywine Home Front during the Civil War," pt. 2, "1862," *Delaware History* 10 (April 1963): 206.

7. Gerald Norcross Diaries, October 24, November 10, 1864, January 26, February 13, 1865, American Antiquarian Society, Worcester, Mass.; *Philadelphia Public Ledger and Transcript*, July 4, 1863; *Extracts from the College Album, Spring Hill College* (Mobile: Register and Advertiser, 1861), 13, 21–22, 30–31, 35–36. For an example of a teacher who used class time — contrary to school policy — to infuse his students with good Republican ideas in the years just before the war, see Elizabeth McL. Gould Rowland, *Story of the Girls' High School of Portland, Maine, 1850–1863* (Lee, Maine: Press of the Valley Gleaner, 1897), 30–31.

8. [Charles Stratton], "Extracts from the Diary of a Member of the Graduating Class of the Boston Public Latin School," pp. 14–15, Department of Rare Books and Manuscripts, Boston Public Library, Boston, Mass.

9. *New York Weekly Anglo African*, March 8, 29, 1862; Sandra E. Small, "The Yankee Schoolmarm in Freedmen's Schools: An Analysis of Attitudes," *Journal of Southern History* 45 (August 1979): 394; Laura Towne Diary, July 3, 4, 1863, *Letters and Diary of Laura M. Towne: Written from the Sea Islands of South Carolina, 1862–1884*, ed. Rupert Sargent Holland (Cambridge, Mass.: Riverside Press, 1912; New York: reprint, Negro Universities Press, 1969), 113–14; *New Orleans Union*, July 12, 1864; "Life on the Sea Islands," *Atlantic Monthly*, May 1864, 591; "The Freedmen at Port Royal," *Atlantic Monthly*, September 1863, 303–6; *Philadelphia Christian Recorder*, July 23, 16, 1864.

10. Elisabeth Joan Doyle, "Nurseries of Treason: Schools in Occupied New Orleans," *Journal of Southern History* 26 (May 1960): 161–79; *New Orleans Times*, March 5, 13, 1864; Gerald H. Capers, *Occupied City: New Orleans under the Federals, 1862–1865* (Lexington: University Press of Kentucky, 1965), 67, 185–89.

11. Martha Josephine Moore Diary, May 7, 1863, Frank Liddell Richardson Papers, Southern Historical Collection.

12. Carl M. Becker, "'Disloyalty' and the Dayton Public Schools," *Civil War History* 11 (March 1956): 58–68; *Chicago Tribune*, May 12, 1863.

13. M. Viatora Schuller, "A History of Catholic Orphan Homes in the United States from 1727 to 1884." (Ph.D. diss., Loyola University of Chicago, 1954), 154–55; Margaret Lawrence Lindsley Journal, November 9, 1864, Margaret Lawrence Ramsey Collection, Library of Congress, Washington, D.C.; Opie Read, *I Remember* (New York: R. R. Smith, 1930), 7; Jesse R. Grant, *In the Days of My Father General Grant* (New York: Harper and Brothers, 1925), 21.

14. Mary Robinson Kemper, "Civil War Reminiscences at Danville Female Academy," ed. Mary Lee Kemper, *Missouri Historical Review* 62 (April 1968): 314–20.

15. James W. Sullivan, *Boyhood Memories of the Civil War, 1861–1865: In-*

vasion of Carlisle (Carlisle, Pa.: Hamilton Library Association, 1933), 2–4. Adolescent Israelis who lost an older sibling in war tend to become more conservative and nationalistic and are more interested in politics. Their bereavement forces them to reevaluate their religion, their residence in Israel, and their sense of purpose. See Anita Morawetz, "The Impact on Adolescents of the Death in War of an Older Sibling," in *Stress and Anxiety*, ed. Norman A. Milgram, vol. 8 (Washington, D.C.: Hemisphere, 1982), 267–74.

16. Alice Williamson Diary, February 19, March 11, 12, April 7, 26, 1864, Manuscript Division, Perkins Library, Duke University, Durham, N.C.; Emmie Sublett to Emily Anderson, April 29, 1865, Manuscript Division, Eleanor S. Brockenbrough Library, Museum of the Confederacy, Richmond, Va.; Susan Caldwell to Lycurgus Caldwell, May 14, 1862, *"My Heart Is So Rebellious": The Caldwell Letters, 1861–1865*, ed. J. Michael Welton (Warrenton, Va.: Fauquier National Bank, 1991), 117.

17. Andrew James Miller, *Old School Days: A Memoir of Boyhood* (New York: Abbey Press, 1900), 38–39; Marion Ramsey Furness, "Childhood Recollections of Old St. Paul," *Minnesota History* 29 (June 1948): 116.

18. Archer Woodson Vaughan Diary, April 28, 29, May 5, June 7, 1861, April 19, 1862, Archer Woodson Vaughan Papers, East Carolina Manuscript Collection, J. Y. Joyner Library, East Carolina University, Greenville, N.C.

19. Cora Owens Hume Diary, April 30, 1863, Filson Club Historical Society, Louisville, Ky.; Emma Cassandra Riley Macon, *Reminiscences of the Civil War* (Cedar Rapids, Iowa: Torch Press, 1911), 116; Madge Preston to May Preston, February 22, 1863, *A Private War: Letters and Diaries of Madge Preston, 1862–1867*, ed. Virginia Walcott Beauchamp (New Brunswick, N.J.: Rutgers University Press, 1987), 48 (letter), 75; James McLachlan, ed., "The Civil War Diary of Joseph H. Coit," *Maryland Historical Magazine* 60 (September 1965): 249–51; Moore Diary, April 6, 7, 9, 1863; John B. Jones Diary, March 14, 1863, *A Rebel War Clerk's Diary*, ed. Earl Schenck Miers (New York: Sagamore Press, 1958; reprint, Baton Rouge: Louisiana State University Press, 1993), 176.

20. Eliza McLeague to "Aunt Mary," August 9, 1861, Scarborough Family Papers, Duke University; Lucy A. Cannon Diary, April 6, 1864, Lucy A. Cannon Papers, Maryland Historical Society, Baltimore; Hume Diary, January 23, 30, 1863; Betsy Swint Underwood, "War Seen through a Teen-ager's Eyes," *Tennessee Historical Quarterly* 20 (June 1961), 177–87, quotes on p. 181.

21. *Concord Observor*, August 17, 31, 1862, September 28, 1864; *Worcester Once a Fortnight*, October 10, 1864. All amateur newspapers, unless otherwise noted, are located in the Amateur Newspaper Collection, American Antiquarian Society.

22. Newark High School *Athenaeum*, November, June, January, May, September 1864, New Jersey State Historical Society, Newark.

23. Kathryn Grover, *Hard at Play: Leisure in American, 1840–1940* (Amherst: University of Massachusetts Press; Rochester: Strong Museum, 1992), 163; Mary Ellen Goodman, *The Culture of Childhood: Child's-Eye Views of Society and Culture* (New York: Teachers College Press, 1970), 132–33; Jean Piaget, *Play, Dreams, and Imitation in Childhood* (New York: Norton, 1962), 73, 78, 87, 107, 140; Anna Freud and Dorothy Burlingham, *War and Children* (New York: Ernst Willard, 1943), 3–32, 21–24; Joseph Levy, *Play Behavior* (New York: John Wiley and Sons, 1978), 169–77; James M. Ellis, *Why People Play* (Englewood Cliffs, N.J.: Prentice-Hall, 1973), 59, 62; Frank Caplan and Theresa Caplan, *The Power of Play* (New York: Anchor, 1974), 37–49; Lili E. Peller, "Models of Children's Play," in *Child's Play*, ed. R. E. Herron and Brian Sutton-Smith (New York: John Wiley and Sons, 1971), 110–25.

24. R. L. Punamaki, "Childhood in the Shadow of War: A Psychological Study on Attitudes and Emotional Life of Israeli and Palestinian Children," *Current Research on Peace and Violence* 5 (1982): 26–41; Norah Rosenan, "The Sources of Children's Political Concepts: An Application of Piaget's Theory," in *New Directions in Political Socialization*, ed. David C. Schwartz and Sandra Kenyon Schwartz (New York: Free Press, 1975), 177–79; Daniel Glaser, "Violence in the Society," in *Violence in the Home: Interdisciplinary Perspectives*, ed. Mary Lystad (New York: Brunner/Mazel, 1986), 18–21; Thomas Davey, *A Generation Divided: German Children and the Berlin Wall* (Durham, N.C.: Duke University Press, 1987), 53; Roger Rosenblatt, *Children of War* (Garden City, N.Y.: Anchor/Doubleday, 1983), 40, 44; M. Fraser, *Children in Conflict* (New York: BasicBooks, 1973), 105; George Eisen, *Children and Play in the Holocaust: Games among the Shadows* (Amherst: University of Massachusetts Press, 1988), 49–50, 78, 80–81, 104–5, 122. Over 80 percent of the boys and nearly half of the girls responding to a 1943 U.S. survey reported taking part in "war play." See Ralph C. Preston, "What Children Think of War Play," *Parents' Magazine*, March 1943, 21, 79.

25. Robert Elno McGlone, "Suffer the Children: The Emergence of Modern Middle Class Family Life in America, 1820–1870" (Ph.D. diss., University of California, Los Angeles, 1971), 274; Karin Calvert, *Children in the House: The Material Culture of Early Childhood, 1600–1900* (Boston: Northeastern University Press, 1992), 112. See, for example, the Christmas illustrations in *Frank Leslie's Illustrated Newspaper*, December 31, 1864, December 30, 1865.

26. *Richmond Examiner*, May 6, 1863; Daniel E. Sutherland, *Seasons of War: The Ordeal of a Confederate Community, 1861–1865* (New York: Free Press, 1995), 38; Drew Gilpin Faust, *Mothers of Invention: Women of the Slaveholding South in the American Civil War* (Chapel Hill: University of North Carolina Press, 1996), 203; Evelyn D. Ward, *The Children of Bladensfield* (New York: Viking, 1978), 32; Patrick J. Geary, ed.,

Celine: Remembering Louisiana, 1850–1871 (Athens: University of Georgia Press, 1987), 99.

27. George P. Rawick, ed., *The American Slave: A Composite Autobiography*, 19 vols. (Westport, Conn.: Greenwood, 1972–74), 2(2):6; 4(1):171; 4(2):227; 15(2):326; *Charleston Mercury*, September 16, 1861; Ward, *Children of Bladensfield*, 77; Peter Bardaglio, "The Children of Jubilee: African American Childhood in Wartime," in *Divided Houses: Gender and the Civil War*, ed. Catherine Clinton and Nina Silber (New York: Oxford University Press, 1992), 220.

28. T. M. Eddy, *The Patriotism of Illinois: A Record of the Civil and Military History of the State in the War for the Union* (Chicago: Clark, 1865), 1:75; John Y. Simon, ed., *The Personal Memoirs of Julia Dent Grant* (New York: Putnam's, 1975), 89; quoted in George S. May, "Ann Arbor and the Coming of the Civil War," *Michigan History* 36 (September 1952): 253; Ruth Painter Randall, *Lincoln's Sons* (Boston: Little, Brown, 1955), 108, 110–11, 112–14. Ironically, northern children, particularly in urban areas, would have witnessed fairly extensive public ridicule of militia units before the war. In Philadelphia, for instance, mock militia companies paraded in mismatched uniforms and armed themselves with wooden swords and broomsticks. See Susan G. Davis, *Parades and Power: Street Theatre in Nineteenth-Century Philadelphia* (Philadelphia: Temple University Press, 1986), 71–72, 78–96, 105–6.

29. Jeannette Leonard Gilder, *Autobiography of a Tomboy* (New York: Doubleday, Page, 1904), 202–10.

30. Daniel Carter Beard, *Hardly a Man Is Now Alive: The Autobiography of Dan Beard* (New York: Doubleday, Doran, 1939), 102, 151; George F. Robertson, *A Small Boy's Recollections of the Civil War* (Clover, S.C.: G. F. Robertson, 1932), 19–20, 57–59; Thomas A. Ashby, *The Valley Campaigns: Being the Reminiscences of a Non-Combatant While between the Lines in the Shenandoah Valley during the War of the States* (New York: Neale, 1914), 208–9.

31. Peter W. Bardaglio, "On the Border: Children and the Politics of War in Maryland, 1861–1865" (paper presented at the annual meeting of the Organization of American Historians, Chicago, March 1996); Charles Mount to Charley Mount, March 13, 1862, Charles Greene McChesney Mount Papers, Ohio Historical Society, Columbus.

32. George F. Robertson, *Small Boy's Recollections*, 72–74; B. H. Wilkins, *"War Boy": A True Story of the Civil War and Re-Construction Days* (Tullahoma, Tenn.: Wilson Brothers, 1990), 23, 41–42.

33. D. F. Morrow, *Then and Now: Reminiscences and Historical Romance, 1856–1865* (Macon, Ga.: J. W. Burke, 1926), 67–73.

34. Frank Towers, ed., "Military Waif: A Sidelight on the Baltimore Riot of 19 April 1861," *Maryland Historical Magazine* 89 (Winter 1994): 427–46; Norcross Diaries, April 26, May 24, 26, 1862, January 11, February 8, 25, 1863, July 29, 1864.

35. Mrs. M. A. Rogers, "An Iowa Woman in Wartime," *Annals of Iowa*

35 (Winter 1961): 529; Alice Eliza Kingsbury, *In Old Waterbury: The Memoirs of Alice E. Kingsbury* (Waterbury, Conn.: Mattatuck Historical Society, 1942), [2]; Otis Skinner, *Footlights and Spotlights: Recollections of My Life on the Stage* (Indianapolis: Bobbs-Merrill, 1924), 16–17; Maury Diary, August 4, 1862; Parmelee, *Confederate Diary of Betty Herndon Maury*, 89.

36. Elizabeth Preston Allan, ed., *The Life and Letters of Margaret Junkin Preston* (Boston: Houghton Mifflin, 1903), 158–59, 179.

37. Otis Skinner, *Footlights and Spotlights*, 17–18.

38. May 22, 1862, *Brokenburn: The Journal of Kate Stone, 1861–1868*, ed. John Q. Anderson (Baton Rouge: Louisiana State University Press, 1955), 108–9; John Wesley Hardin, *The Life of John Wesley Hardin, as Written by Himself* (Norman: University of Oklahoma Press, 1961), 5–6; *Chicago Tribune*, September 5, 1862; *Raleigh Daily Confederate*, February 2, 1864.

39. Stephen V. Ash, *When the Yankees Came: Conflict and Chaos in the Occupied South, 1861–1865* (Chapel Hill: University of North Carolina Press, 1995), 210; Keith Bohannon, "Cadets, Drillmasters, Draft Dodgers, and Soldiers: The Georgia Military Institute during the Civil War," *Georgia Historical Quarterly* 79 (Spring 1995): 8–10; William Cain Reminiscences, Southern Historical Collection.

40. Mooli Lahad and Ofra Ayalon, "Preserving Children's Mental Health under Threat of War," in *Children and Death*, ed. Danai Papadatou and Costas Papadatou (New York: Hemisphere, 1991), 65–76; J. Langmeier and Z. Matejcek, *Psychological Deprivation in Childhood* (New York: Halsted Press, 1975), 122, 127, 155; Norman Garmezy, "Stressors of Childhood," in *Stress, Coping, and Development in Children*, ed. Norman Garmezy and Michael Rutter (New York: McGraw-Hill, 1983), 62–68; Frances E. Merrill, *Social Problems on the Home Front: A Study of War-time Influences* (New York: Harper and Brothers, 1948), 55–59, 81–82; M. Fraser, *Children in Conflict* (New York: BasicBooks, 1973), 61, 124–25; J. D. Curran, E. F. Jardine, and J. J. M. Harbison, "Factors Associated with the Development of Deviant Attitudes in Northern Ireland Schoolboys," in *A Society under Stress: Children and Young People in Northern Ireland*, ed. J. J. M. Harbison and J. I. Harbison (Somerset: Open Books, 1980), 141–52; Cole P. Dodge and Magne Raundalen, *Reaching Children in War: Sudan, Uganda, and Mozambique* (Bergen, Norway: Sigma Forlag; Uppsala, Sweden: Scandinavian Institute of African Studies, 1991), 28–35; Ed Cairns, *Caught in Crossfire: Children and the Northern Ireland Conflict* (Belfast: Appletree; Syracuse: Syracuse University Press, 1987), 50–69; Erna Furman, "Children's Patterns in Mourning the Death of a Loved One," in *Childhood and Death*, ed. Hannelore Wass and Charles A. Corr (Washington, D.C.: Hemisphere, 1984), 185–203; James Garbarino, Nancy Dubrow, Kathleen Koztelny, and Carole Pardo, *Children in Danger: Coping with*

the *Consequences of Community Violence* (San Francisco: Jossey-Bass, 1992), 50–55.

41. Anna Howard Shaw, *The Story of a Pioneer* (New York: Harper and Brothers, 1915), 52–53; Ruth Huntington Sessions, *Sixty-Odd: A Personal History* (Brattleboro, Vt.: Stephen Daye, 1936), 32–34.

42. *Fort Smith New Era*, July 15, 1865, and *Nashville Dispatch*, July 23, 1863, quoted in Ash, *When the Yankees Came*, 200; Mrs. H. K. Cantley, "Little Folks in War Times," *Philadelphia Weekly Times*, October 4, 1884; Mary Elizabeth Glade, "The Boy Gangs of Richmond: A Juvenile Search for Manhood after the Civil War" (paper presented at the annual meeting of the Organization of American Historians, Chicago, March 1996); *Chicago Tribune*, November 27, 1861; *Philadelphia Public Ledger and Transcript*, May 1, 1863; Ash, *When the Yankees Came*, 207–8; *Baltimore Daily Gazette*, December 27, 1862; *Washington Daily Morning Chronicle*, December 5, 1862; *Richmond Examiner*, January 21, November 6, 1862, April 21, 1863, January 20, 22, 1864; *Mobile Daily Advertiser and Register*, March 5, 8, 1864; Leon Bosik, " 'Soiled Dresses are Better than Soiled Modesty': Decency and Delinquency in Columbus, Georgia, 1861–1865," *Lincoln Herald* 83 (Spring 1981): 577; Paul D. Lack, "Law and Disorder in Confederate Atlanta," *Georgia Historical Quarterly* 66 (Summer 1982): 177; *Atlanta Daily Intelligencer*, October 11, 1861.

43. Children's Aid Society, *Thirteenth Annual Report* (New York: Wynkoop and Hollenbeck, 1866), 23; M. L. Elbridge, "History of the Massachusetts Nautical Reform School," in *Children and Youth in America: A Documentary History*, ed. Robert H. Bremner, vol. 1, *1600–1865* (Cambridge, Mass.: Harvard University Press, 1970), 713; Edith Abbott, "The Civil War and the Crime Wave of 1865–1870," *Social Service Review* 1 (June 1927): 222; Robert M. Mennel, *Thorns and Thistles: Juvenile Delinquents in the United States, 1825–1940* (Hanover, N.H.: University Press of New England, 1973), 57–58; Barbara M. Brenzel, *Daughters of the State: A Social Portrait of the First Reform School for Girls in North America, 1856–1905* (Cambridge, Mass.: MIT Press, 1983), 96–97; Managers of the Society for the Reformation of Juvenile Delinquents, *Thirty-Ninth Annual Report* (Albany: Comstock and Cassidy, 1864), 62–68, and *Fortieth Annual Report* (Albany: C. Wendell, 1865), 52–57, 61–63. A number of historians of juvenile delinquency have not noted any major effect of the war on the problem. See, for example, Joseph M. Hawes, *Children in Urban Society: Juvenile Delinquency in Nineteenth-Century America* (New York: Oxford University Press, 1971); Anthony Platt, *The Child Savers: The Invention of Delinquency*, 2nd ed. (Chicago: University of Chicago Press, 1977); and John R. Sutton, *Stubborn Children: Controlling Delinquency in the United States, 1640–1981* (Berkeley: University of California Press, 1988).

44. Faust, *Mothers of Invention*, 129–33; Lizzie Neblett to Will Neblett,

October 25, 1863, Lizzie Neblett Papers, Center for American History, University of Texas, Austin.

45. Norman Garmezy, "Stress-Resistant Children: The Search for Protective Factors," in *Recent Research in Developmental Psychopathology*, ed. J. E. Stevenson (Oxford: Pergamon, 1985), 225–26.

46. Edward Pye to Neddie Pye, November 7, 1864, "Letters from the Confederate Medical Service in Texas, 1863–1865," ed. Frank E. Vandiver, *Southwestern Historical Quarterly* 55 (April 1952): 465–66. For examinations of the ways that environment and economic considerations created similar patterns of responsibility and freedom in the lives of nineteenth- and early twentieth-century children, see Elliott West, *Growing Up with the Country: Childhood on the Far-Western Frontier* (Albuquerque: University of New Mexico Press, 1989), and David Nasaw, *Children of the City: At Work and at Play* (New York: Oxford University Press, 1985).

47. Geary, *Celine*, 71, 102, 115–16.

48. Henry Smith Pritchett Reminiscences, Library of Congress; William A. MacCorkle, *Recollections of Fifty Years of West Virginia* (New York: Putnam's, 1928), 14; Cornelia Peake McDonald Diary, December 1864, March 1865, *A Woman's Civil War: A Diary, with Reminiscences of the War, from March 1862*, ed. Minrose C. Gwin (Madison: University of Wisconsin Press, 1992), 222, 227; Ben Kremenak, ed., "Escape from Atlanta: The Huntington Memoir," *Civil War History* 11 (June 1965): 166–67, 172; Carrie M. Berry Diary, November 18, 26, 28, 29, December 7, 8, 9, 1864, Atlanta History Center, Atlanta, Ga.

49. Sally Hawthorne Reminiscence, North Carolina Division of Archives and History, Raleigh.

50. Theodorick Montfort to David Montfort, November 14, 1861, *Rebel Lawyer: Letters of Theodorick W. Montfort, 1861–1862*, ed. Spencer B. King Jr. (Athens: University of Georgia Press, 1965), 34–35.

51. Gerald J. Smith, ed., "Reminiscences of the Civil War by J. W. Frederick," *Georgia Historical Quarterly* 59, supplement (1975): 157–58; David Golightly Harris Farm Journals, February 16, 1864, Southern Historical Collection; Alexander Fewell to Martha Fewell, October 27, 1864, *"Dear Martha . . .": The Confederate War Letters of a South Carolina Soldier, Alexander Faulkner Fewell*, ed. Robert Harley Mackintosh Jr. (Columbia, S.C.: R. L. Bryan, 1976), 154; Benny Fleet to Fred Fleet, September 21, December 12, 1861, and Benny Fleet Journal, December 31, 1861, *Green Mount: A Virginia Plantation Family during the Civil War: Being the Journal of Benjamin Robert Fleet and Letters of His Family*, ed. Betsy Fleet and John D. P. Fuller (Lexington: University Press of Kentucky, 1962), 77, 90, 191.

52. Hattie Hilby to Memminger, September 17, 1863; Mary Rankin to Memminger, n.d.; Jane Tyler to Memminger, October 11, 1862; Sally Winfree to Memminger, November 26, 1862, all in Letters to Con-

federate Secretary of the Treasury Christopher Memminger, Civil War Papers, American Antiquarian Society.

53. Lee Ann Whites, *The Civil War as a Crisis in Gender: Augusta, Georgia, 1860–1890* (Athens: University of Georgia Press, 1995), 86–87, 89; *Richmond Examiner*, March 14, May 22, 1863; Jones Diary, March 13, 1863, Miers, *Rebel War Clerk's Diary*, 175.

54. Joseph F. Kett, *Rites of Passage: Adolescence in America, 1790 to the Present* (New York: BasicBooks, 1977), 130; *Chicago Tribune*, June 20, 1861; Richard R. Duncan, "The Impact of the Civil War on Education in Maryland," *Maryland Historical Magazine* 61 (March 1966): 46–47. Similar statistics came out of the Second World War, when more teenagers took full-time employment and fewer attended school. See Frances E. Merrill, *Social Problems on the Home Front*, 79. Few statistics are available for child labor in industry during the Civil War. In northern Vermont, where immigrants from Quebec provided the labor in the expanding textile mills of Burlington and Colchester, the number of teenagers working in the mills seems to have actually declined during the 1860s. See Betsy Beattie, "Migrants and Millworkers: The French Canadian Population of Burlington and Colchester, 1860–1870," *Vermont History* 60 (Spring 1992): 95–117.

55. Marion Richardson Drury, *Reminiscences of Early Days in Iowa* (Toledo, Iowa: Toledo Chronicle Press, 1931), 45; Eddie Foy, *Clowning through Life* (New York: Dutton, 1928), 9–10, 15, 16–17.

56. Rogers, "Iowa Woman in Wartime," 606–7, 626–27; Jane Keeler to Elnathan Keeler, March 24, 27, 1864, *Portrait of Elnathan Keeler, a Union Soldier*, ed. Helen Klaas (Wappingers Falls, N.Y.: Goldlief Reproductions, 1977), 19, 20–21.

57. Shaw, *Story of a Pioneer*, 52–53.

58. Booker T. Washington, *Up from Slavery: An Autobiography* (New York: Doubleday, Page, 1901; reprint, Garden City, N.Y.: Doubleday, 1963), 7–8; John Q. A. Dennis to Edwin Stanton, July 26, 1864, *Freedom: A Documentary History of Emancipation, 1861–1867*, ed. Ira Berlin et al., ser. 1, *The Destruction of Slavery* (New York: Cambridge University Press, 1985), 1:386; Bardaglio, "Children of Jubilee," 221, 223–24.

59. Lester Alston, "Children as Chattel," in *Small Worlds: Children and Adolescents in America, 1850–1950*, ed. Elliott West and Paula Petrik (Lawrence: University Press of Kansas, 1992), 208–31, esp. 211–14; Rawick, *American Slave*, 3(3):40; 12(1):187; John W. Blassingame, ed., *Slave Testimony: Two Centuries of Letters, Speeches, Interviews, and Autobiographies* (Baton Rouge: Louisiana State University Press, 1977), 583.

60. Elizabeth Hyde Botume, *First Days amongst the Contrabands* (Boston: Lee and Shepard, 1893; reprint, New York: Arno Press, 1968), 182–90.

61. Rawick, *American Slave*, 12(1):12–13; 12(2):26–27; 5(3):256; Charles Jones to Abraham Lincoln, March 24, 1863, and Statement of Jim

Hiskell, March 30, 1864, both in Berlin et al., *Freedom*, ser. 1, 1:451, 320–22. See also Blassingame, *Slave Testimony*, 619–20, 623–24.

62. Henry Justin Ferry, "Francis James Grimké: Portrait of a Black Puritan" (Ph.D. diss., Yale University, 1970), 27–40.

63. Minnie Hauk, *Memories of a Singer* (London: A. M. Philpot, 1925), 26; Maurice Francis Egan, *Recollections of a Happy Life*, 45; Clara C. Lenroot, *Long, Long Ago* (Appleton, Wis.: Badger Printing, 1929), 14.

64. "War Diary of a Union Woman in the South," ed. G. W. Cable, April 20, 1861, *Famous Adventures and Prison Escapes of the Civil War* (New York: Century, 1904), 9; "A Glimpse of Both Sides," in *Reminiscences of the Women of Missouri during the Sixties*, by Missouri Division, United Daughters of the Confederacy (Jefferson City, Mo.: Hugh Stephens, n.d.), 223–27; *Atlanta Daily Intelligencer*, May 3, 1861; *Charleston Mercury*, January 29, September 10, 1862, January 23, June 30, 1863; *Raleigh Daily Confederate*, February 8, 1864; *Richmond Examiner*, June 16, 1864; *Our Women in the War: The Lives They Lived, the Deaths They Died* (Charleston: News and Courier Book Presses, 1885), 43; Whites, *Civil War as a Crisis in Gender*, 56–57, 60; Earl Schenck Miers, ed., *When the World Ended: The Diary of Emma Le Conte* (New York: Oxford University Press, 1957), 12–13; Sue to Isabella Ann Roberts, August 17, 1861, Isabella Ann Roberts Woodruff Letters, Duke University.

65. Based on the presence or absence of titles such as Mrs., Miss, Mr., and Master, it seems apparent that at least 28 girls and 8 boys were preadolescents, while only 6 appear to have been adults (4 women and 2 men). All told, there were 53 female and 13 male members.

66. Spartanburg, S.C., Methodist Sunday School Relief Society, minutes, Thomas Dillard Johnston Papers, Southern Historical Collection.

67. Elizabeth W. Ross, *A Road of Remembrance* (Cincinnati: Powell and White, 1923), 13; Caroline M. Hewins, *A Mid-Century Child and Her Books* (New York: Macmillan, 1926), 65; Lizzie H. Corning Diary, December 2, 1862, New Hampshire Historical Society.

68. New England Branch of the American Tract Society, *Sixth Annual Report* (Boston: The Branch, 1865), 38; *Philadelphia Public Ledger and Transcript*, June 11, August 23, September 12, October 1, 1862; *Philadelphia Christian Recorder*, October 15, 1864, April 1, 1865.

69. *Spirit of the Fair*, April 4, 6, 7, 15, 16, 18, 22, 1864.

70. *Chicago Tribune*, August 20, 25, 1863, July 28, August 17, September 11, 20, 1864.

71. Ibid., October 1864; Kingsbury, *In Old Waterbury*; Frank B. Goodrich, *The Tribute Book: A Record of the Munificence, Self-Sacrifice, and Patriotism of the American People during the War for the Union* (New York: Derby and Miller, 1865), 116, 166, 190, 193–94; Simon, *Personal Memoirs of Julia Dent Grant*, 131.

72. Goodrich, *Tribute Book*, 219–22, 258; *Ladies Knapsack*, December 29, 1863; Thomas Jean Walters, "Music of the Great Sanitary Fairs: Cul-

ture and Charity in the American Civil War" (Ph.D. diss., University of Pittsburgh, 1989), 119, 237, 249, 278–79.

73. Goodrich, *Tribute Book*, 87–88, 102, 373–75.

74. Ibid., 400–406. See also William C. Harris, "The East Tennessee Relief Movement of 1864–1865," *Tennessee Historical Quarterly* 48 (Summer 1989): 86–96.

75. Phillip Shaw Paludan, *"A People's Contest": The Union and Civil War, 1861–1865* (New York: Harper and Row, 1988), 354–55; Jeanie Attie, "Warwork and the Crisis of Domesticity in the North," in Clinton and Silber, *Divided Houses*, 247–59.

76. "Officer's Commission," Army of the American Eagle, Emily J. Crouch File, State Historical Society of Wisconsin, Madison; *Chicago Tribune*, May 31, 1865; "How I Came to Print the Little Corporal," and "The Army of the American Eagle," *Little Corporal*, July 1865, 1–2, 3; "The Veteran Eagle, and What the Children Did," *Little Corporal*, December 1866, 88–90. Abe became one of the most popular attractions at the fair; the crowds gathering in the Alcove of the Eagle inspired P. T. Barnum to vainly offer $20,000 for the eagle. See Richard H. Zeitlin, *Old Abe the War Eagle: A True Story of the Civil War and Reconstruction* (Madison: State Historical Society of Wisconsin, 1986), 76. The "army" recruited by Sewell provided a ready-made subscription base for *The Little Corporal*; he reported 35,000 subscribers in December 1866.

77. Robert Hugh Martin, *A Boy of Old Shenandoah* (Parsons, W.Va.: McClain, 1977), 45–46.

78. Gertrude Stein, *Wars I Have Seen* (New York: Random House, 1945), 7, quoted in William M. Tuttle Jr., *"Daddy's Gone to War": The Second World War in the Lives of America's Children* (New York: Oxford University Press, 1993), 241.

CHAPTER SIX

1. *The Myriopticon: A Historical Panorama of the Rebellion* (Springfield, Mass.: Milton Bradley, [1866]). The Prints and Photographs Division of the Library of Congress, Washington, D.C., and the Games and Puzzles Collection of the American Antiquarian Society, Worcester, Mass., each own a copy of *The Myriopticon*; the former is complete except for the poster, while the latter has a poster but is in more fragile condition. Other contemporary miniature panoramas include *Uncle Sam's Panorama of Rip Van Winkle and Yankee Doodle* (New York: McLoughlin Brothers, [1870]) and [*Panorama of the Visit of Santa Claus to the Happy Children*] (Springfield, Mass.: Milton Bradley, n.d.), both at the American Antiquarian Society.

2. A Lady of Warrenton, Virginia, *The Princess of the Moon: A Confederate Fairy Story* (Warrenton, Va: n.p., 1869).

3. Bernard Barenholtz and Inez McClintock, *American Antique Toys, 1830–1900* (New York: Abrams, 1980), 92; Katharine Morrison McClinton, *Antiques of American Childhood* (New York: Clarkson N. Potter,

1970), 227; Lee Dennis, *Warman's Antique American Games, 1840–1940* (Elkins Park, Pa.: Warman, 1986), 130; Blair Whitton, *Paper Toys of the World* (Cumberland, Md.: Hobby House Press, 1986), 85; Blair Whitton, *American Clockwork Toys* (Exton, Pa.: Schiffer, 1981), 92; Albert Johannsen, *The House of Beadle and Adams and Its Dime and Nickel Novels: The Story of a Vanished Literature* (Norman: University of Oklahoma Press, 1950), 1:164–65.

4. See, for instance, Trowbridge's articles in *Our Young Folks* about his travels to southern battlefields, published between the spring of 1865 and the spring of 1866.

5. "Uncle Sam's Boys after the War," *Student and Schoolmate*, December 1865, 152; Emily J. Bugbee, "The Last Review," *Little Corporal*, August 1865, 28, and "Give Them Work," *Little Corporal*, November 1865, 139–40; Glance Gaylord, "Soldiers' Orphans," *Little Corporal*, January 1866, 3.

6. "Little Things" and "The Fallen Heroes," January 19, 1867, 32, 34; "Eminent Living Men," January 25, 1867, 57, and January 18, 1868, 42; "Our Fallen Heroes," August 3, 1867, 2; "Grant," August 5, 1868, 524; "Incidents in the Life of General Grant," August 29, 1868, 554; "Our Picture Gallery," October 3, 1868, 632; "Anecdote of General Grant," October 31, 1868, 698; "The Bull and the Dutch Regiment," June 26, 1869, 407; "Battle of Nashville," July 24, 1869, 470; "Capture of Morris Island," November 20, 1869, 742; "Bombardment of Sumter," January 8, 1870, 25, all in *Oliver Optic's Magazine*.

7. "Salutary" and "The Colour-Bearer," January 1867, 1–2, 11–13; "What Will We Do When We Secede," October 1867, 341; Fanny Downing, "Memorial Flowers," April 1867, 127; June 1867, 223; July 1867, 255; June 1868, 208; July 1868, 279, all in *Southern Boys and Girls' Monthly*.

8. Introduction to Henry Hammock, *Letters to Amanda from Sergeant Major Marion Hill Fitzpatrick, Company K, 45th Georgia Regiment, Thomas's Brigade, Wilcox Division, Hill's Corps, CSA, to His Wife Amanda Olive Elizabeth White Fitzpatrick, 1862–1865* (Culloden, Ga.: Mansel Hammock, 1976); preface to Lizzie Cary Daniel, *Confederate Scrap-Book* (Richmond: J. L. Hill, 1893); Lucretia Revere Scrapbook, American Antiquarian Society.

9. George F. Robertson, *A Small Boy's Recollections of the Civil War* (Clover, S.C.: G. F. Robertson, 1932), 17; B. H. Wilkins, *"War Boy": A True Story of the Civil War and Re-Construction Days* (Tullahoma, Tenn.: Wilson Brothers, 1990), 23, 83; Stephen Smith Burt, *Recollections and Reflections Chiefly of My Boyhood* (New York: S. S. Smith, 1912), 10–11, 17–18.

10. Jane Minge Friend Dangerfield Recollections, pp. 60–61, White Hill Plantation Books, Southern Historical Collection, University of North Carolina, Chapel Hill; Wilkins, *"War Boy,"* 57–58; Anne Rose Diary, typescript, September 24, 1865, Hermione Ross Walker Collection, Southern Historical Collection; Martha Josephine Moore Diary, April

14, 1863, Frank Liddell Richardson Papers, Southern Historical Collection.

11. John Wesley Hardin, *The Life of John Wesley Hardin, as Written by Himself* (Norman: University of Oklahoma Press, 1961), 5–6, 11–15, 16–17.

12. George P. Rawick, ed., *The American Slave: A Composite Autobiography*, 19 vols. (Westport, Conn.: Greenwood Press, 1972–74), 4(2):224; supplement, ser. 2, 10 vols. (1979), 8(7):2934.

13. Booker T. Washington, *Up from Slavery: An Autobiography* (New York: Doubleday, Page, 1901; reprint, Garden City, N.Y.: Doubleday, 1963), 15–16.

14. William Cohen, *At Freedom's Edge: Black Mobility and the Southern White Quest for Racial Control, 1861–1915* (Baton Rouge: Louisiana State University Press, 1991), 14–15; Leon F. Litwack, *Been in the Storm So Long: The Aftermath of Slavery* (New York: Vintage, 1980), 229–42, 305–10; Wilma King, *Stolen Childhood: Slave Youth in Nineteenth-Century America* (Bloomington: Indiana University Press, 1995), 144–49.

15. Litwack, *Been in the Storm So Long*, 135–49, 177–78; Vennie Deas-Moore, "I've Got Something to Celebrate," in *Jubilation! African-American Celebrations in the Southeast*, ed. William H. Wiggins Jr. and Douglas De Natale (Columbia: McKissick Museum, University of South Carolina, 1993), 29–30; James Marten, *Texas Divided: Loyalty and Dissent in the Lone Star State, 1856–1874* (Lexington: University Press of Kentucky, 1990), 163.

16. Alton Hornsby Jr., "The Freedmen's Bureau Schools in Texas, 1865–1870," *Southwestern Historical Quarterly* 76 (April 1973): 397–417; Ronald E. Butchart, *Northern Schools, Southern Blacks, and Reconstruction: Freedmen's Education, 1862–1875* (Westport, Conn.: Greenwood, 1980), 13–31, 172–73, 201–2.

17. Rebecca Scott, "The Battle over the Child: Child Apprenticeship and the Freedmen's Bureau in North Carolina," *Prologue* 10 (Summer 1978): 100–113; Wilma King, *Stolen Childhood*, 151–54.

18. George C. Rable, *But There Was No Peace: The Role of Violence in the Politics of Reconstruction* (Athens: University of Georgia Press, 1984), 39, 76, 86, 96, 128; Eric Foner, *Reconstruction: America's Unfinished Revolution, 1863–1877* (New York: Harper and Row, 1988), 120, 392, 428; Marten, *Texas Divided*, 176–77; Litwack, *Been in the Storm So Long*, 275; Allen W. Trelease, *White Terror: The Ku Klux Klan Conspiracy and Southern Reconstruction* (New York: Harper and Row, 1971), 122, 124, 206, 294.

19. Trelease, *White Terror*, 365; Joel Williamson, *The Crucible of Race: Black-White Relations in the American South since Emancipation* (New York: Oxford University Press, 1984), 185; Marten, *Texas Divided*, 168; Foner, *Reconstruction*, 442–43.

20. Henry Justin Ferry, "Francis James Grimké: Portrait of a Black Puri-

tan" (Ph.D. diss., Yale University, 1970); Dickson D. Bruce Jr., *Archibald Grimké: Portrait of a Black Independent* (Baton Rouge: Louisiana State University Press, 1993).

21. Charles M. Robinson III, *The Court-Martial of Lieutenant Henry Flipper* (El Paso: University of Texas, 1994), 1–3, 6–7, 111–14.

22. Emma Lou Thornbough, *T. Thomas Fortune, Militant Journalist* (Chicago: University of Chicago Press, 1972), 3–24, 65–65, 86–88, 89, 184–86, 281–85. For his relationship with Washington, see 177–286.

23. Washington, *Up from Slavery*, 5, 18–19; Louis R. Harlan, *Booker T. Washington: The Making of a Black Leader, 1856–1901* (New York: Oxford University Press, 1972), 28–52.

24. Rawick, *American Slave*, 6:176–77.

25. Ibid., 6:316–17; 3(2):203–4, 207.

26. Ibid., 3(1):51, 279; 15(2):160–61.

27. Paul H. Buck, *The Road to Reunion, 1865–1900* (New York; Vintage, 1937), 120–21; William H. Wiggins Jr., *O Freedom! Afro-American Emancipation Celebrations* (Knoxville: University of Tennessee Press, 1987), esp. xix–xx; Lawrence W. Levine, *Black Culture, Black Consciousness: Afro-American Folk Thought from Slavery to Freedom* (New York: Oxford University Press, 1977). For differences among African Americans about how to commemorate their emancipation (which often reflected class distinctions), see Willard B. Gatewood, *Aristocrats of Color: The Black Elite, 1880–1920* (Bloomington: Indiana University Press, 1990), 51–52, and David W. Blight, " 'What Will Peace among the Whites Bring?': Reunion and Race in the Struggle over the Memory of the Civil War in American Culture," *Massachusetts Review* 34 (Autumn 1993): 397–400.

28. "The Return," *Student and Schoolmate*, September 1865, 86.

29. Laura Ingalls Wilder, *Little House in the Big Woods* (New York: Harper and Brothers, 1932; reprint, New York: HarperCollins, 1971), 136–37, 146; Mary Eliza Starbuck, *My House and I: A Chronicle of Nantucket* (Boston: Houghton Mifflin, 1929), 202–4.

30. Hamlin Garland, *A Son of the Middle Border* (New York: Macmillan, 1917; reprint, Lincoln: University of Nebraska Press, 1979), 1–8; Hamlin Garland, "The Return of a Private," in *Main-Travelled Roads* (New York: Harper and Brothers, 1899).

31. Gerald F. Linderman, *Embattled Courage: The Experience of Combat in the American Civil War* (New York: Free Press, 1987), 266–97, quote on 280.

32. Eric T. Dean Jr., " 'We Will All Be Lost and Destroyed': Post-Traumatic Stress Disorder and the Civil War," *Civil War History* 37 (June 1991): 138–53; Lois Meek Stolz et al., *Father Relations of War-Born Children: The Effect of Postwar Adjustment of Fathers on the Behavior and Personality of First Children Born While the Fathers Were at War* (New York: Greenwood, 1968); Robert Jay Lifton, *Home from the War: Vietnam Veterans, Neither Victims nor Executioners* (New York: BasicBooks,

1973, 1983), 400; Ellen B. Berlinsky and Henry B. Biller, *Parental Death and Psychological Development* (Lexington, Mass.: Lexington Books, 1982), 65–67, 78–80, 119, 123. Two famous Civil War veterans — Lewis Paine, the Lincoln conspirator, and Ambrose Bierce, the cynical writer — both exhibited the sorts of symptoms of post-traumatic stress that other veterans may well have demonstrated, such as an obsession with death, a violent temper, and an inability to get along with their families. See Herbert Hendin and Ann Pollinger Haas, *Wounds of War: The Psychological Aftermath of Combat in Vietnam* (New York: Basic-Books, 1984), 16–21.

33. Patrick J. Geary, ed., *Celine: Remembering Louisiana, 1850–1871* (Athens: University of Georgia Press, 1987), 102; Earl Schenck Miers, ed., *When the World Ended: The Diary of Emma Le Conte* (New York: Oxford University Press, 1957), 21–22; Dangerfield Recollections, p. 37.

34. Anna Howard Shaw, *The Story of a Pioneer* (New York: Harper and Brothers, 1915), 54; Daniel Carter Beard, *Hardly a Man Is Now Alive: The Autobiography of Dan Beard* (New York: Doubleday, Doran, 1939), 151.

35. Merrill D. Peterson, *Lincoln in American Memory* (New York: Oxford University Press, 1994), 5–6; Bliss Perry, "The Butterfly Boy," in *When I Was a Child*, ed. Edward Wagenknecht (New York: Dutton, 1946), 60.

36. D. C. Mott, *Fifty Years in Iowa* (Marengo, Iowa: Marengo Republican, n.d.), 3–4; Otto Kallir, ed., *Grandma Moses: My Life's History* (New York: Harper and Brothers, 1946), 18–19; Ida M. Tarbell, *All in the Day's Work: An Autobiography* (New York: Macmillan, 1939), 11; Clara C. Lenroot, *Long, Long Ago* (Appleton, Wis.: Badger Printing, 1929), 24–25; Mary J. Newson, "Memories of Fort Snelling in Civil War Days," *Minnesota History* 15 (December 1934): 403; Anne Eliza Sterling Neely, *Just Me: An Autobiography* (Philadelphia: Dorrance, 1949), 14; Edward James Cattell, *Fighting Through* (Philadelphia: Dunlap, 1936), 8; Lizette Woodworth Reese, *A Victorian Village: Reminiscences of Other Days* (New York: Farrar and Rinehart, 1929), 75.

37. Fenimore Chatterton, *Yesterday's Wyoming: The Intimate Memoirs of Fenimore Chatterton, Territorial Citizen, Governor, and Statesman* (Aurora, Colo.: Powder River Publishers, 1957), 15; Reese, *Victorian Village*, 76; Starbuck, *My House and I*, 189–93. Not surprisingly, southern children reacted differently. Future governor of Arkansas George W. Donaghey, only five when the war began, remembered Abraham Lincoln as the villain of the war, "a person to be feared and hated" and "the direct cause" of poverty, the death of neighbors in the army, and Donaghey's own father's suffering in a Union prison camp. When Lincoln was assassinated, George and other local schoolboys rejoiced "with boyish savagery" (George W. Donaghey, *Autobiography of George W. Donaghey, Governor of Arkansas, 1909–1913* [Benton, Ark.: L. B. White, 1939], 17–18). Samuel Steele, who grew up on the Mississippi Delta during the war, devoted a portion of his memoir to debunking the

Lincoln of northern mythology. He declared that "Lincoln was responsible for the so-called 'Civil War'" and accused the North of making "a
demi-god of Lincoln" (Samuel A. Steele, *The Sunny Road: Home Life
in Dixie during the War* [Memphis, Tenn., (1924)], 85).

38. Henrietta Dana Skinner, *An Echo from Parnassus: Being Childhood
Memories of Longfellow and His Friends* (New York: Sears, 1928), 175–
79.

39. Jane Addams, *Twenty Years at Hull-House, with Autobiographical Notes*
(New York: Macmillan, 1929), 23–42.

40. Charles Loring Brace, *The Dangerous Classes of New York and Twenty
Years' Work among Them*, 3rd ed. (New York: Wynkoop and Hollenbeck, 1880; reprint, Montclair, N.J.: Patterson-Smith, 1967), 109; *Philadelphia Public Ledger and Transcript*, May 3, 1864; Peter Leo Johnson,
Daughters of Charity in Milwaukee, 1846–1946 (Milwaukee: Daughters
of Charity, 1946), 158; Robert H. Bremner, *The Public Good: Philanthropy and Welfare in the Civil War Era* (New York: Knopf, 1980), 86;
Peter C. Holoran, *Boston's Wayward Children: Social Services for Homeless Children, 1830–1930* (Rutherford, N.J.: Fairleigh Dickinson University Press, 1989), 56, 122; M. Viatora Schuller, "A History of Catholic
Orphan Homes in the United States from 1727 to 1884." (Ph.D. diss.,
Loyola University of Chicago, 1954), 140–42, 149–52, 160–61, 172, 173–
74, 213, 223, 262–63; Keith Harper, "The Louisville Baptist Orphan's
Home: The Early Years," *Register of the Kentucky Historical Society*
90 (Summer 1992): 237; Marian J. Morton, "Homes for Poverty's Chil-
dren: Cleveland's Orphanages, 1851–1933," *Ohio History* 98 (Winter-
Spring 1989): 6; Thomas M. Yundt, *A History of the Bethany Orphans
Home of the Reformed Church in the United States* (Reading, Pa.:
Daniel Miller, 1888), 23–24, 37; John Cimprich, *Slavery's End in Ten-
nessee, 1861–1865* (University: University of Alabama Press, 1985), 75;
Carleton Mabee, "Charity in Travail: Two Orphan Asylums for Blacks,"
New York History 55 (January 1974): 55–77; Clare L. McCausland,
*Children of Circumstances: A History of the First 125 Years (1849–
1974) of the Chicago Child Care Society* (Chicago: Chicago Child Care
Society, 1976), 39; Priscilla Ferguson Clement, "Children and Charity:
Orphanages in New Orleans, 1817–1914," *Louisiana History* 27 (Fall
1986): 344–45; Susan Whitelaw Downs and Michael W. Sherraden,
"The Orphan Asylum in the Nineteenth Century," *Social Science Re-
view* 57 (June 1987): 279–80.

41. Officers of the Home, *Report of the Lady Managers of the National
Soldiers' and Sailors' Orphans' Home* ([Washington, D.C.], 1872), 7–8,
2; Bremner, *Public Good*, 86; Paul C. Graham, comp., *History of the
Indiana Soldiers' and Sailors' Orphans' Home, 1865–1904* (Knightstown,
Ind.: Home Journal, 1905), 5–9; *Report of the Directors of the Soldiers'
Children's Home of the State of New Jersey* ([Trenton, N.J.], 1865), 9;
O. David Gold, "The Soldiers' Orphans' Schools of Pennsylvania, 1864–
1889" (Ph.D. diss., University of Maryland, 1971), 25, 41.

42. Edward W. Hughes and William C. McCracken, *History of the Ohio Soldiers' and Sailors' Orphan Home* (Xenia, Ohio: Association of Ex-Pupils, 1963), 8; Board of Trustees of the Illinois Soldiers' Orphans' Home, *Fourth Biennial Report* (Springfield, Ill.: D. W. Lusk, 1877), 10, and *Sixteenth Biennial Report* (Springfield, Ill.: Phillips Brothers, 1900), 19; W. Pierce, "The Iowa Home for Soldiers' Orphans," *Proceedings of the Sixth National Conference of Charities and Corrections* (New York, 1879), 153; *Report of the Connecticut Soldiers' Orphans' Home* (Hartford: Case, Lockwood and Brainard, 1873), 5–6, 8; *Sixth Annual Report of the Soldiers' Children's Home of the State of New Jersey* (Trenton, N.J.: n.p., 1870), [3]; *Report of [the] Joint Committee on Soldiers' Children's Home* ([Trenton, N.J.], 1876), 3; Patricia G. Harrsch, " 'This Noble Monument': The Story of the Soldiers' Orphans' Home," *Wisconsin Magazine of History* 76 (Winter 1992–93): 83–120; Shelter for Orphans of Colored Soldiers and Friendless Colored Children, *Fourth Annual Report* (Baltimore: J. Jones, 1871), 4. For a history-memoir of the Iowa Soldiers' Orphans' Home by a former resident, see George Gallarno, "How Iowa Cared for Orphans of Her Soldiers of the Civil War," *Annals of Iowa*, 3rd ser., 15 (January 1926): 163–93.

43. Megan J. McClintock, "Civil War Pensions and the Reconstruction of Union Families," *Journal of American History* 83 (September 1996): 456–80; Gold, "Soldiers' Orphans' Schools," 9–25, 36; Hughes and McCracken, *History of the Ohio Soldiers' and Sailors' Orphan Home*, 20, 60–71; Harrsch, " 'This Noble Monument,' " 86–87; George L. Heiges, "The Mount Joy Soldier's Orphan School," *Papers of the Lancaster County Historical Society* 48 (1944): 110.

44. Harrsch, " 'This Noble Monument,' " 107–18; *Report of the Committee Appointed by His Excellency Gov. Parker, to Inquire into the Condition and Management of the Soldiers' Children's Home of New Jersey* (Trenton, N.J., 1872), 14–21; Board of Trustees of the Illinois Soldiers' Orphans' Home, *Third Biennial Report* (Springfield, Ill.: State Journal, 1875), 15; Joan Gittens, *Poor Relations: The Children of the State in Illinois, 1818–1990* (Urbana: University of Illinois Press, 1994), 24–26, 49–50; Gold, "Soldiers' Orphans' Schools," 64–69; Stuart McConnell, *Glorious Contentment: The Grand Army of the Republic, 1865–1900* (Chapel Hill: University of North Carolina Press, 1992), 130–31. The GAR did not support the homes in every state; just a few years before the decline of the Pennsylvania system of schools, the trustees of the Illinois home wistfully mentioned the lack of interest in the home among members of the GAR in Illinois, especially compared with the active interest displayed by Pennsylvania veterans. See Board of Trustees of the Illinois Soldiers' Orphans' Home, *Eighth Biennial Report* (Springfield, Ill.: H. W. Rokker, 1885), 10.

45. Mary Ruth Collins and Cindy A. Stouffer, *One Soldier's Legacy: The National Homestead at Gettysburg* (Gettysburg, Pa.: Thomas Publications, 1993), 9–13.

46. Ibid., 14–23, 57.
47. Ibid., 60–81.
48. James Laughery Paul, *Pennsylvania's Soldiers' Orphan Schools* (Philadelphia: Claxton and Remson, 1876), 99–101; Hughes and McCracken, *History of the Ohio Soldiers' and Sailors' Orphan Home*, 135–37. Critics of the Wisconsin home complained that inmates were "well versed in the knowledge required from the study of books" but failed to receive an education that would prepare them for jobs in the trades. See Harrsch, "'This Noble Monument,'" 109–10.
49. G. Kurt Piehler, *Remembering War the American Way* (Washington, D.C.: Smithsonian Institution Press, 1995), 58; Heiges, "Mount Joy Soldier's Orphan School," 113; *Ceremonies at the Reception of the Orphan Children of Pennsylvania Soldiers, who Perished Defending the Government, by the Governor and the Legislature, in the State Capitol* (Harrisburg, Pa.: George Bergner, 1866).
50. Collins and Stouffer, *One Soldier's Legacy*, 29–32; Paul, *Pennsylvania's Soldiers' Orphan Schools*, 147–48, 197; *Report of the Soldiers' Children's Home of the State of New Jersey for the Year 1867* ([Trenton, N.J., 1868]), 856–57; Hughes and McCracken, *History of the Ohio Soldiers' and Sailors' Orphan Home*, 135; Graham, *History of the Indiana Soldiers' and Sailors' Orphans' Home*, 63, 132; McConnell, *Glorious Contentment*, 180, 202–5; Charles F. Speierl, "Civil War Veterans and Patriotism in New Jersey Schools," *New Jersey History* 110 (Fall/Winter 1992): 41–55.
51. *Raleigh Daily Confederate*, May 28, June 30, October 20, 26, December 30, 1864; *Charleston Mercury*, March 12, 1864, December 1, 6, 1866; *Atlanta Daily Intelligencer*, December 20, 1863; *Richmond Examiner*, August 6, 1864; C. K. Marshall, *Orphans of Our Soldiers and How to Educate Them* (Columbus, Ga.: n.p., 1864), Mississippi Department of Archives and History, Jackson, 1–8; E. Merton Coulter, *The Confederate States of America, 1861–1865* (Baton Rouge: Louisiana State University Press, 1950), 518–19; Ursula Smith Beach, *Along the Wariota; or, A History of Montgomery County, Tennessee* (Clarksville, Tenn.: n.p., 1964), 230–31; *City of Charleston Yearbook, Appendix* (Charleston, 1885), 361–70; Barbara Lawrence Bellows, "Tempering the Wind: The Southern Response to Urban Poverty, 1850–1865" (Ph.D. diss., University of South Carolina, 1983), 95.
52. Piehler, *Remembering War the American Way*, 62; Mary B. Poppenheim et al., *The History of the United Daughters of the Confederacy* (Richmond: Garrett and Massie, 1938), 84–85; *History of the Confederated Memorial Associations of the South* (New Orleans: Graham Press, 1904), 191–93, 302–4; Catherine Clinton, *Tara Revisited: Women, War, and the Plantation Legend* (New York: Abbeville, 1995), 183–84; Gaines M. Foster, *Ghosts of the Confederacy: Defeat, the Lost Cause, and the Emergence of the New South* (New York: Oxford University Press, 1987), 172–73; R. B. Rosenburg, *Living Monuments: Confeder-*

ate *Soldiers' Homes in the New South* (Chapel Hill: University of North
Carolina Press, 1993), 145–47.

53. Foster, *Ghosts of the Confederacy*, 96–97; Charles Clifton Ferrell, " 'The
Daughter of the Confederacy': Her Life, Character, and Writings,"
Publications of the Mississippi Historical Society 2 (1899): 69–84.

54. Robin Veder, " 'Julia, Daughter of Stonewall': Julia Thomas Jackson,"
Virginia Cavalcade 46 (Summer 1996): 4–19.

55. Ibid., 14.

56. Foster, *Ghosts of the Confederacy*, 48; Charles Reagan Wilson, *Baptized
in Blood: The Religion of the Lost Cause, 1865–1920* (Athens: University
of Georgia Press, 1980), 147, 140; Fred Arthur Bailey, "Free Speech and
the 'Lost Cause' in Texas: A Study of Social Control in the New South,"
Southwestern Historical Quarterly 97 (January 1994): 453–78; Fred
Arthur Bailey, "The Textbooks of the 'Lost Cause': Censorship and the
Creation of Southern State Histories," *Georgia Historical Quarterly* 75
(Fall 1991): 507–33; Louise L. Stevenson, *The Victorian Homefront:
American Thought and Culture, 1860–1880* (New York: Twayne, 1991),
94–96.

57. W. N. McDonald and J. S. Blackburn, *A Southern School History of the
United States of America, from the Earliest Discoveries to the Present
Time* (Baltimore: George Lycett, 1869), 45, 48–49, 273, 386, 398, 409.
Interestingly, McDonald and Blackburn grudgingly admired northern
patriotism in defending the flag and the capital of the United States
and admitted that on Gettysburg's third day, "Never did Americans
evince greater valor, than both Federals and Confederates exhibited
that day" (ibid., 403, 450).

For examples of the sort of pro-Union, pro-Lincoln, and anti-
slavery histories that southerners loved to hate, see William Makepeace
Thayer, *A Youth's History of the Rebellion*, 4 vols. (Boston: Walker,
Fuller, 1864–65); John Bonner, *A Child's History of the United States*,
vol. 3 (New York: Harper and Brothers, 1866); Mary S. Robinson, *A
Household Story of the American Conflict*, 4 vols. (New York: N. Tibbals,
1866, 1871); Thomas Wentworth Higginson, *Young Folks' History of the
United States* (Boston: Lee and Shepard, 1875); and J. D. Champlin Jr.,
Young Folks History of the War for the Union (New York: Holt, 1881).

More neutral northern texts, at least to the extent that race issues
are downplayed and Confederates are not painted as villains, included
Samuel G. Goodrich, *The American Child's Pictorial History of the
United States* (Philadelphia: E. H. Butler, 1865); M. J. Kerney, *The First
Class Book of History, Designed for Pupils Commencing the Study of
History* (Baltimore: John Murphy, 1868); and G. P. Quackenbos, *Illus-
trated School History of the United States and the Adjacent Parts of
America, from the Earliest Discoveries to the Present Times* (New York:
Appleton, 1884).

58. Steven C. Rockefeller, *John Dewey: Religious Faith and Democratic
Humanism* (New York: Columbia University Press, 1991), 34–35, 290–

311; Raymond B. Nixon, *Henry W. Grady, Spokesman of the New South* (New York: Knopf, 1943), 36, 39–41, 70, 80–84, 98–99, 160–62, 314–15; Shaw, *Story of a Pioneer*; Thomas J. Pressly, *Americans Interpret Their Civil War* (Princeton: Princeton University Press, 1954; reprint, New York: Free Press, 1965), 169–79.

59. Sarah Elizabeth Gardner, "'Blood and Irony': Southern Women's Narratives of the Civil War, 1861–1915" (Ph.D. diss., Emory University, 1996), 173–78.
60. Carol Wells, ed., *War, Reconstruction, and Redemption on Red River: The Memoirs of Dosia Williams Moore* (Ruston, La.: McGinty, 1990), 8–11; Evelyn Douglas Ward, *The Children of Bladensfield* (New York: Viking/Sand Dune Press, 1978), 111–12; John George Clinkscales, *On the Old Plantation: Reminiscences of His Childhood* (Spartanburg, S.C.: Band and White, 1916), 35–36, 55.
61. Mrs. D. Giraud Wright, *A Southern Girl in '61: The Wartime Memories of a Confederate Senator's Daughter* (New York: Doubleday, Page, 1905), 17–18; Thomas A. Ashby, *The Valley Campaigns: Being the Reminiscences of a Non-Combatant While between the Lines in the Shenandoah Valley during the War of the States* (New York: Neale, 1914), 12–15; Elizabeth Randolph Preston Allan, *A March Past: Reminiscences of Elizabeth Randolph Preston Allan.* (Richmond: Dietz, 1938), 80–82; George Washington Polk, "Some Reflections and Reminiscences," typescript, pp. 21–22, George Washington Polk Papers, Southern Historical Collection; George Wilcox McIver Autobiography, typescript, p. 11, Southern Historical Collection.
62. Elizabeth Silverthorne, *Sarah Orne Jewett: A Writer's Life* (Woodstock, N.Y.: Overlook Press, 1993), 42–44, 108–9; Paula Blanchard, *Sarah Orne Jewett: Her World and Her Work* (Reading, Mass.: Maddison-Wesley, 1994), 306–7; Sarah Orne Jewett, "Decoration Day," in *A Native of Winby and Other Tales* (Boston: Houghton Mifflin, 1893), 39–64.
63. Sylvia E. Bowman, *The Year 2000: A Critical Biography of Edward Bellamy* (New York; Bookman Associates, 1958), 18–19, 48; George Frederickson, *The Inner Civil War: Northern Intellectuals and the Crisis of the Union* (New York: Harper and Row, 1965), 225–27; Edward Bellamy, "An Echo of Antietam," in *The Blindman's World and Other Stories* (Boston: Houghton Mifflin, 1898), 30–58.
64. Robert M. Myers, *Reluctant Expatriate: The Life of Harold Frederic* (Westport, Conn.: Greenwood, 1995), 6–7; Harold Frederic, "The Copperhead," "Marsena," and "The War Widow," in *In the Sixties* (New York: Charles Scribner's Sons, 1897; reprint, New York: AMS Press, 1971), 1–149, 151–228, 229–70.
65. Gardner, "'Blood and Irony,'" 150–54.
66. Edmund Wilson wrote that "the chloroform of magazine prose" would help blur the issues that had once separated the sections; southern writers were "doing . . . nothing more than applying soft poultices of

words not merely to the suppurating wounds of the South but also to the feelings of guilt of the North" (*Patriotic Gore: Studies in the Literature of the American Civil War* [New York: Oxford University Press, 1962], 605, 615).

67. John C. Inscoe, "The Confederate Home Front Sanitized: Joel Chandler Harris' *On the Plantation* and Sectional Reconciliation," *Georgia Historical Quarterly* 76 (Fall 1992): 652–74; Joel Chandler Harris, *On the Plantation: A Story of a Georgia Boy's Adventures during the War* (New York: Appleton, 1892), 124; Robert Bush, ed., "Will N. Harben's Northern Georgia Fiction," *Mississippi Quarterly* 20 (1967): 103–17.

68. Roswell Page, *Thomas Nelson Page: A Memoir of a Virginian Gentleman* (New York: Charles Scribner's Sons, 1923), 31–42; Theodore L. Gross, *Thomas Nelson Page* (New York: Twayne, 1967), 9–33, 49–53, 105–12; Thomas Nelson Page, *Two Little Confederates* (New York: Charles Scribner's Sons, 1888), 125–41, 146–50, 155–56. A writer in the Page tradition whose work has not survived in the nation's literary memory is James Lane Allen, who did not write about the war often but promoted the gentility of the prewar South and lavished praise on the southerners' heroism and bravery. See Grant C. Knight, *James Lane Allen and the Genteel Tradition* (Chapel Hill: University of North Carolina Press, 1935).

69. Robert Bush, ed., *Grace King: A Southern Destiny* (Baton Rouge: Louisiana State University Press, 1983), 106–8; Per Seyerstad, *Kate Chopin: A Critical Biography* (Baton Rouge: Louisiana State University Press, 1969), 77; Helen Taylor, *Gender, Race, and Region in the Writings of Grace King, Ruth McEnery Stuart, and Kate Chopin* (Baton Rouge: Louisiana State University Press, 1989), 18, 24–25, 62–63, 67–68, 106–7, 116–18, 155–57.

70. Seyerstad, *Kate Chopin*, 20–21, 42; Robert Bush, ed., introduction to *Grace King of New Orleans: A Selection of Her Writings* (Baton Rouge: Louisiana State University Press, 1973), 4; Helen Taylor, *Gender, Race, and Region*, 84–97; Eugene Current-Garcia, *O. Henry* (New York: Twayne, 1965), 18–19, 46, 56–59. For another southern woman who applied the lessons of the war and Reconstruction that she witnessed to her art, see Hubert Horton McAlexander, *The Prodigal Daughter: A Biography of Sherwood Bonner* (Baton Rouge: Louisiana State University Press, 1981).

71. Francis Richardson Keller, *An American Crusade: The Life of Charles Waddell Chesnutt* (Provo, Utah: Brigham Young University Press, 1978); Hugh M. Gloster, "Charles W. Chesnutt: Pioneer in the Fiction of Negro Life," *Phylon* 2 (Spring 1941): 57–65; Kenneth M. Price, "Charles Chesnutt, the *Atlantic Monthly*, and the Intersection of African-American Fiction and Elite Culture," in *Periodical Literature in Nineteenth-Century America*, ed. Kenneth M. Price and Susan Belasco Smith (Charlottesville: University Press of Virginia, 1995), 257–76.

72. John Milton Cooper Jr., *Walter Hines Page: The Southerner as American, 1855–1918* (Chapel Hill: University of North Carolina Press, 1977), xxv, 77–79, 145–49; Burton J. Hendrick, *The Training of an American: The Earlier Life and Letters of Walter H. Page, 1855–1913* (Boston: Houghton Mifflin, 1928), 17–23, 57–59, 165–71.
73. George C. Osborn, *Woodrow Wilson: The Early Years* (Baton Rouge: Louisiana State University Press, 1968), 12–17.
74. Ibid., 17–18; John Milton Cooper Jr., *The Warrior and the Priest: Woodrow Wilson and Theodore Roosevelt* (Cambridge, Mass.: Harvard University Press, 1983), 45; Woodrow Wilson, *Division and Reunion, 1829–1909* (New York: Longmans, Green, 1909), 30–35, 116–32, 166–67, 172, 211–12, 216–17, 239, 266–72.
75. Williamson, *Crucible of Race*, 385–95.
76. Robert C. Cotner, *James Stephen Hogg: A Biography* (Austin: University of Texas Press, 1959), 23–33, 39–41, 312–13, 353–54, 562–63, 571–72.
77. George Coleman Osborn, *John Sharp Williams: Planter-Statesman of the Deep South* (Gloucester, Mass.: Peter Smith, 1964), 5–6, 185–87, 420–21; Raymond Arsenault, *The Wild Ass of the Ozarks: Jeff Davis and the Social Bases of Southern Politics* (Philadelphia: Temple University Press, 1984), 3, 26–27, 237; William F. Holmes, *The White Chief: James Kimble Vardaman* (Baton Rouge: Louisiana State University Press, 1970), 4–5, 7–8, 36, 43, 59, 121–22, 198, 383–86.
78. C. Vann Woodward, *Tom Watson: Agrarian Rebel* (New York: Rinehart, 1938), 1–5.
79. Ibid., 220–23, 348–51, 370–73, 380, 432, 435–39.
80. Francis Butler Simkins, *Pitchfork Ben Tillman: South Carolinian* (Baton Rouge: Louisiana State University Press, 1944), 33–34, 39, 44–45, 224–25, 295–303, 399–400, 552; Williamson, *Crucible of Race*, 137–38; Thomas E. Watson, *Bethany: A Story of the Old South* (New York: Appleton, 1910).
81. Thomas R. Marshall, *Recollections of Thomas R. Marshall, Vice President and Hoosier Philosopher: A Hoosier Salad* (Indianapolis: Bobbs-Merrill, 1925), 70–72.
82. Wayne Andrews, ed., *The Autobiography of Theodore Roosevelt* (New York: Charles Scribner's Sons, 1958), 10; Kathleen Dalton, "Theodore Roosevelt and the Idea of War," *Theodore Roosevelt Association Journal* 7 (Fall 1981): 6, 7, 9; Cooper, *Warrior and the Priest*, 12–13.
83. Cooper, *Warrior and the Priest*, 84–85, 111, 201, 283–85.
84. Henry Cabot Lodge, *Early Memories* (London: Constable, 1913), 112–34.
85. R. Hal Williams, *Years of Decision: American Politics in the 1890s* (New York: John Wiley and Sons, 1978), 4–7, 32–36, 59, 96; Lewis L. Gould, "Party Conflict: Republicans versus Democrats, 1877–1901," in *The Gilded Age: Essays on the Origins of Modern America*, ed. Charles W.

Calhoun (Wilmington, Del.: Scholarly Resources, 1996), 215–34. For two very different analyses of Civil War children's political values and attitudes, see Earl J. Hess, *Liberty, Virtue, and Progress: Northerners and Their War for the Union* (New York: New York University Press, 1988), 123–27, and Robert M. Crunden, *Ministers of Reform: The Progressives' Achievement in American Civilization, 1889–1920* (New York: BasicBooks, 1982), ix, 1–6, 275–77.

86. James M. McPherson, *The Abolitionist Legacy: From Reconstruction to the NAACP* (Princeton: Princeton University Press, 1975), 155–56, 159, 253–60, 350, 364, 368–93.

87. Edward L. Ayers, *The Promise of the New South: Life after Reconstruction* (New York: Oxford University Press, 1992), 28, 48–50, 53, 64–65; James L. Leloudis, *Schooling the New South: Pedagogy, Self, and Society in North Carolina, 1880–1929* (Chapel Hill: University of North Carolina Press, 1996), esp. 73–106.

88. Williamson, *Crucible of Race*, 180–81, 301–2.

89. Mihaly Csikszentmihaly and Reed Larson, *Being Adolescent: Conflict and Growth in the Teenage Years* (New York: BasicBooks, 1984), 4, 85, 233; Robert D. Hess and Judith V. Torney, *The Development of Political Attitudes in Children* (Chicago: Aldine, 1967), 213–14; Roberts S. Sigel and Marilyn B. Hoskin, *The Political Involvement of Adolescents* (New Brunswick, N.J.: Rutgers University Press, 1981), 5; James Garbarino, Kathleen Koztelny, and Nancy Dubrow, *No Place to Be a Child: Growing Up in a War Zone* (Lexington, Mass.: Lexington Books, 1991), 22–23; Iwona Irwin-Zarecka, *Frames of Remembrance: The Dynamics of Collective Memory* (New Brunswick, N.J.: Tranaction Publishers, 1994), 9, 49, 54.

90. Robert H. Wiebe, *The Search for Order, 1877–1920* (New York: Hill and Wang, 1967), 11–75.

91. Frederickson, *Inner Civil War*, esp. 111–12; Lori D. Ginzberg, *Women and the Work of Benevolence: Morality, Politics, and Class in Nineteenth-Century United States* (New Haven: Yale University Press, 1990), 133–35, 158; Lawrence Cremin, *American Education: The National Experience, 1783–1876* (New York: Harper, 1980), 511–17. For an account of the far-flung philanthropic efforts undertaken in the North and the South between the 1850s and the 1870s, see Bremner, *Public Good*.

92. See, for instance, Raymond H. Pulley, *Old Virginia Restored: An Interpretation of the Progressive Impulse, 1870–1930* (Charlottesville: University Press of Virginia, 1968), 4–23, 57–63, 81–91, 186–88; J. Morgan Kousser, *The Shaping of Southern Politics: Suffrage Restriction and the Establishment of the One-Party South, 1880–1910* (New Haven: Yale University Press, 1974), 250–61.

93. Michael Kimmel, *Manhood in America: A Cultural History* (New York: Free Press, 1996), 72–78, 89–96, 111–12, 117–41; Gerald F. Linderman, *The Mirror of War: American Society and the Spanish-American*

War (Ann Arbor: University of Michigan Press, 1974), 92–93; John J. Leffler, "From the Shadows into the Sun: Americans in the Spanish-American War" (Ph.D. diss., University of Texas, Austin, 1991), 21–22, 123, 176–77. Leffler suggests that the Civil War also offered quite negative images that, for southerners especially, inhibited enthusiasm for intervening in Cuba.

Bibliography

MANUSCRIPT COLLECTIONS

American Antiquarian Society, Worcester, Mass.
  Amateur Newspaper Collection
  Civil War Papers
  Games and Puzzles Collection
  Etta R. Harlow Diary
  Gerald Norcross Diaries
  Nathaniel Paine Scrapbook
  Lucretia Revere Scrapbook
  Theatrical Handbills Collection
  Valentines Collection
  Caroline Barrett White Diaries
  Worcester Children's Friend Society Records
Atlanta History Center, Atlanta, Ga.
  Carrie M. Berry Diary, typescript
Boston Public Library, Boston, Mass.
  Extracts from the Diary of a Member of the Graduating Class of the
    Boston Public Latin School, April–July 1862
Center for American History, University of Texas, Austin
  George F. Atkinson Reminiscences
  William Pitt Ballinger Diary
  Charles Thomas Brady Family Papers
  Guy M. Bryan Papers
  Crutcher-Shannon Family Papers
  Thomas H. DuVal Papers
  Sam W. Farrow Papers
  W. B. Foster Reminiscences
  George A. Gordon Papers
  Mrs. L. D. Ledbetter Collection
  Lizzie Neblett Papers
  Cornelia M. Noble Diary
  Mary Rabb Papers
  Lizzie Simons Diary
  William J. Whatley Letters
Duke University, Perkins Library, Manuscript Division, Durham, N.C.
  Tilman F. Baggarly Papers
  William A. Chunn Papers
  Solon F. Fuller Papers

Lucas-Ashley Family Papers
Theophilus Perry Letters, Presley Carter Person Papers
Hugh N. Ponton Letters
Scarborough Family Papers
Nellie F. Stearns Letter
Laura W. Stebbins Papers
Alice Williamson Diary
Isabella Ann Roberts Woodruff Letters
Filson Club Historical Society, Louisville, Ky.
Cora Owens Hume Diary
Lizzie Schrieber Diary, Smith-Moreman Families Papers
Sally Yandell Diary
Historical Society of Pennsylvania, Philadelphia
R. Laird McCormic Diary
Lizzie Marchand Diary
Illinois Historical Survey, University of Illinois, Urbana-Champaign
Phoebe Jane Morrison Hutchison Reminiscences
Margaret A. King Correspondence
J. Y. Joyner Library, East Carolina University, Greenville, N.C.
Cora Warren Beck Memoirs
Archer Woodson Vaughan Papers
Library of Congress, Washington, D.C.
Jasper N. Barrett Papers
Chauncey E. Barton Letter
Elizabeth Johnston Burt Papers
David Coon Letters, transcripts
John H. Craven Papers
Family Correspondence, Jedediah Hotchkiss Papers
James Harrison Goodnow Papers
Henry Hitchcock Papers
George A. Hudson Letters
Margaret Lawrence Lindsley Journal, Margaret Lawrence Ramsey
    Collection
Mrs. W. W. Lord Journal, typescript
Mary Tyler Peabody Mann Papers
Charles D. Mitchell Memoir
Henry Smith Pritchett Reminiscences, typescript
William H. Shriver Papers
William E. Stimson Letters
Thomas Thweatt Tredway Collection
United States Sanitary Commission Papers
Maryland Historical Society, Baltimore
Autobiography of Mrs. Enoch Louis Lowe, Bond-McCulloch Family
    Papers
Lucy A. Cannon Diary
Rebecca D. Davis Diary

"Grandmother to Granddaughter," letter
Mrs. Benjamin G. Harris Diaries
Margaret Mehring Diary
"A New Alphabet for Rebel Children"
Milwaukee County Historical Society, Milwaukee, Wis.
    Cornelius Wheeler Collection
Mississippi Department of Archives and History, Jackson
    Emma Balfour Diary, typescript
    Eliza Ann Lanier Recollections, typescript, Alcinda Timberlake Papers
    C. K. Marshall, *Orphans of Our Soldiers and How to Educate Them*
      (Columbus, Ga.: n.p., 1864)
Museum of the Confederacy, Eleanor S. Brockenbrough Library,
    Richmond, Va.
    Emmie Sublett Letter
New Hampshire Historical Society, Concord
    Lizzie M. Corning Diary
    Journal of Baby Maud
    George E. Upton Papers
New Jersey Historical Society, Newark
    Newark High School *Athenaeum*
New York Public Library, New York
    Louis Pope Gratacard Diary
North Carolina Division of Archives and History, Raleigh
    Oscar W. Blacknall Papers
    Sally Hawthorne Reminiscence
    Isaac Lefevers Correspondence
    Lowry Shuford Collection
Ohio Historical Society, Columbus
    Charles Green McChesney Mount Papers
J. D. Phillips Library, Peabody Essex Museum, Salem, Mass.
    Annie B. Brown Correspondence, Brown Family Papers
    A. B. Morong Diary
Rutgers University Library, Special Collections and Archives, New
    Brunswick, N.J.
    Sarah Cook Williamson Diary, George H. Cook Papers
Southern Historical Collection, University of North Carolina, Chapel Hill
    Lucy Hull Baldwin Papers
    Anne Banister, "Incidents in the Life of a Civil War Child," Harrison
      Henry Cocke Papers
    John L. Bridgers Jr. Papers
    Annie Laurie Broidrick, "A Recollection of Thirty Years Ago"
    Edmund S. Burwell Papers
    William Cain Reminiscences
    Civil War Pictorial Envelopes
    Elizabeth Collier Diary
    Creecy Family Papers

Jane Minge Friend Dangerfield Recollections, White Hill Plantation
Books
Ellen H. Easton, "Thoughts on My History"
Julia Johnson Fisher Diary
Franklin Gaillard Letters
Jeremy F. Gilmer Papers
James Iredell Hall Papers
David Golightly Harris Farm Journals
Hermon Hawkins, "Christmas in Jackson in 1865"
Hubbard Family Papers
Myra Inman Diary
Augustus White Long Papers
George Wilcox McIver Autobiography
Letitia Miller Recollections
Martha Josephine Moore Diary, Frank Liddell Richardson Papers
Matilda Lamb Morton Memoirs
George Washington Polk Papers
Alice Ready Diary
Anne Rose Diary, Hermione Ross Walker Collection
Louisa A. Sheppard Recollections
Jane Sivley Papers
Spartanburg, S.C., Methodist Sunday School Relief Society, minutes,
Thomas Dillard Johnston Papers
Thompson Family Papers
Marcus A. Turner Papers
Sarah Lois Wadley Diary
Lucita Hardie Wait, "Memories of a Childhood Spent in Brasil"
Mary D. Waring Journal
Calvin Henderson Wiley Papers
State Historical Society of Wisconsin, Madison
Alva Cleveland Diary, typescript
Luther H. Cowan Letters, typescript
Emily J. Crouch File
Warden Wood Papers
University of Virginia Library, Manuscript Department, Charlottesville
Lucy R. Buck Diary, typescript
Lucy Wood Butler Diary, typescript

NEWSPAPERS

Canteen (Albany)
Christian Recorder (Philadelphia)
Daily Morning Chronicle (Washington, D.C.)
Daily Morning News (Savannah)
Daily State Journal/Daily Confederate (Raleigh)

Drumbeat (Brooklyn)
Examiner (Richmond)
Freedman (Boston)
Public Ledger and Transcript (Philadelphia)
Sanitary Commission Bulletin (Philadelphia)
Spirit of the Fair (New York)
Volunteer, or North-Western Fair Gazette (Chicago)

CHILDREN'S PERIODICALS

Child's Banner (Salisbury, N.C.)
Child's Index (Macon)
Children's Friend (Dayton)
Children's Friend (Richmond)
Children's Guide (Macon)
Forrester's Playmate (Boston)
Frank Leslie's Chimney Corner (New York)
Little American (New York)
Little Corporal (Chicago)
Little Pilgrim: An Illustrated Journal for Boys and Girls (Philadelphia)
New Church Magazine for Children (Boston)
Oliver Optic's Magazine
Our Young Folks (Boston)
Southern Boys' and Girls' Monthly (Richmond)
Student and Schoolmate (Boston)

OFFICIAL DOCUMENTS

Auxiliary Association in Aid of the Home for the Mothers, Widows, and Orphans of Confederate Soldiers. Charleston: Courier Job Presses, 1870.
Board of Managers, Patriot Orphan Home. *Annual Report, 1866*. New York: Holt Brothers, 1866.
Board of Trustees of the Illinois Soldiers' Orphans' Home. *Biennial Reports, 1875–1900* (3rd through 16th). Springfield, Ill.: State Printer, 1875–1900.
———. *Special Report to the Governor of Illinois*. Springfield, Ill.: State Journal Printing Office, 1874.
Ceremonies at the Reception of the Orphan Children of Pennsylvania Soldiers, Who Perished Defending the Government, by the Governor and the Legislature, in the State Capitol. Harrisburg, Pa.: George Bergner, 1866.
Children's Aid Society. *Annual Reports, 1863–1868* (10th through 15th). New York: Wynkoop, Hallenbeck, and Thomas, 1863–64; Wynkoop and Hallenbeck, 1865–68.

Institute of Reward for Orphans of Patriots. *Fifth Annual Report.* New York, 1866.

Managers of the Society for the Reformation of Juvenile Delinquents. *Annual Reports, 1863–1865* (39th through 41st). Albany, N.Y.: Comstock and Cassidy, 1864; C. Wendell, 1865–66.

New England Branch of the American Tract Society. *Sixth Annual Report.* Boston: The Branch, 1865.

New England Freedmen's Aid Society (Educational Commission). *Extracts from Letters of Teachers and Superintendents.* 5th ser. Boston: John Wilson and Son, 1864.

———. *Second Annual Report.* Boston: The Society, 1864.

Officers of the Home. *Report of the Lady Managers of the National Soldiers' and Sailors' Orphans' Home.* [Washington, D.C.], 1872.

Plumly, B. Rush. *Report of the Board of Education for Freedmen, Department of the Gulf, for the Year 1864.* New Orleans: True Delta, 1865.

Report of the Connecticut Soldiers' Orphans' Home. Hartford: Case, Lockwood and Brainard, 1873.

Shelter for Orphans of Colored Soldiers and Friendless Colored Children. *Fourth Annual Report.* Baltimore: J. Jones, 1871.

State of Iowa. *Report of the Joint Committee of the Eighteenth General Assembly Appointed to Visit the Soldiers' Orphans' Home Located at Davenport.* Des Moines: F. M. Mills, 1880.

———. *Report of the Joint Committee of the Twenty First General Assembly Appointed to Visit the Soldiers' Orphans' Home Located at Davenport.* Des Moines: Geo. E. Roberts, 1886.

———. *Report of the Joint Committee of the Twenty Second General Assembly Appointed to Visit the Soldiers' Orphans' Home Located at Davenport.* Des Moines: Geo. E. Roberts, 1888.

———. *Report of the Joint Committee of the Twenty Third General Assembly Appointed to Visit the Soldiers' Orphans' Home Located at Davenport.* Des Moines: G. H. Ragsdale, 1890.

CHILDREN'S BOOKS AND TEXTBOOKS

Adley, Markinfield. *"Little Mac," and How He Became a Great General: A Life of George Brinton McClellan, for Young Americans.* New York: James G. Gregory, 1864.

Adventures of the Marion Hornets, Co. H, 7th Regt Fla. Vols. Knoxville: by the author, 1863.

Alcott, Louisa May. *Little Women.* Boston: Roberts Bros., 1868–69. Reprint, London: Puffin Books, 1953.

Alger, Horatio, Jr. *Frank's Campaign; or, What Boys Can Do on the Farm for the Camp.* Boston: Loring, 1864.

The Anti-Slavery Alphabet. Philadelphia: Merrihew and Thompson, 1847.

Austin, Jane Goodwin. *Dora Darling: The Daughter of the Regiment.* Boston: Tilton, 1865.

Baker, Sarah S. (Sarah Schoonmaker). *Charlie the Drummer-Boy.* New York: American Tract Society, n.d.

[Barrow, Frances]. *Red, White, and Blue Socks.* New York: Leavitt and Allen, 1863.

Bonner, John. *A Child's History of the United States.* 3 vols. New York: Harper and Brothers, 1866.

Brandegee, Mrs. Sarah Kip. *The Bugle Call: A Summons to Work in Christ's Army.* New York: American Tract Society, [1870].

Branson, Levi. *First Book in Composition, Applying the Principles of Grammar in the Art of Composing . . . .* Raleigh: Branson, Farrar, 1863.

Brooks, Edward. *The Normal Written Arithmetic, by Analysis and Synthesis: Designed for Common Schools, Normal Schools, High Schools, Academies, Etc.* Philadelphia: Sower, Barnes, and Potts, 1863.

Browne, Rev. George Y. *Browne's Arithmetical Tables, Combined with Easy Lessons in Mental Arithmetic for Beginners.* Atlanta: Franklin, 1865.

Bullions, Rev. Peter. *An Analytical and Practical Grammar of the English Language.* Raleigh: North Carolina Christian Advocate, 1864.

Burnham, Catharine Lydia. *"I Can't"; or, Nelly and Lucy.* New York: Leavitt and Allen, 1870.

Campbell, William A. *The Child's First Book.* Richmond: Ayres and Wade, 1864.

Champlin, J. D., Jr. *Young Folks History of the War for the Union.* New York: Holt, 1881.

Chaudron, Adelaide De Vendel. *Chaudron's First Reader, Designed for the Use of Primary Schools.* 2nd ed. Mobile: W. G. Clark, 1864.

———. *Chaudron's Spelling Book, Carefully Prepared for Family and School Use.* Mobile: S. H. Goetzel, 1864.

———. *The Second Reader, Designed for the Use of Primary Schools.* Mobile: Daily Advertiser and Register, 1863.

———. *The Third Reader: Designed for the Use of Primary Schools.* Mobile: W. G. Clark, 1864.

Child's Scripture Question Book: Southern Edition. Macon, Ga.: J. W. Burke, 1862.

Civil War Stories, Retold from St. Nicholas. New York: Century, 1905.

Coffin, Charles Carleton. *Following the Flag.* Boston: Ticknor and Fields, 1865.

———. *My Days and Nights on the Battlefield.* Boston: Ticknor and Fields, 1864.

Colburn, Warren. *Intellectual Arithmetic, upon the Inductive Method of Instruction.* Nashville: Southern Methodist Publishing, 1862.

Confederate Rhyming Primer; or, First Lessons Made Easy. Richmond: George L. Bidgood, 1863.

The Confederate Speller, Embracing Easy Lessons in Reading. 3rd ed. Mt. Lebanon, La.: W. F. Wells, 1864.

The Confederate Spelling Book, Compiled Principally from the National Speller. Austin: D. Richardson, 1864.

Darling, Mary G. *Battles at Home.* Boston: Horace B. Fuller, 1870.

Davis, Charles. *Practical Arithmetic: Embracing the Science and Applications of Numbers.* New York: Barnes and Burr, 1863.

Dodge, M. E. *The Irvington Stories.* New York: James O'Kane, 1865.

Douglas, Amanda M. *Kathie's Soldiers.* Boston: Lee and Shepard, 1870, 1877.

Eaton, James S. *The Common School Arithmetic: Combining Analysis and Synthesis.* Boston: Taggard and Thompson; San Francisco: H. H. Brancroft, 1864.

The First Confederate Speller: On a Strictly Philosophical and Progressive Plan. Nashville: Association of Southern Teachers, 1861.

The First Reader, for Southern Schools. Raleigh: North Carolina Christian Advocate, 1864.

Fleming, Rev. Robert. *The Elementary Spelling Book, Revised and Adapted to the Youth of the Southern Confederacy, Interspersed with Bible Readings on Domestic Slavery.* Atlanta: J. J. Toon, 1863.

For the Little Ones. Savannah: John M. Cooper, n.d.

Fosdick, Charles. *Frank before Vicksburg.* Philadelphia: Porter and Coates, 1864.

———. *Frank on a Gun-Boat.* Philadelphia: Porter and Coates, 1864.

———. *Frank on the Lower Mississippi.* Philadelphia: R. W. Carroll, 1867.

The Freedman's Spelling Book. Boston: American Tract Society, 1866.

Goodwin, Lavinia S. *The Little Helper.* Boston: Lee and Shepard, [1867].

Goulding, Rev. F. R. *Robert and Harold; or, the Young Marooners on the Florida Coast.* Macon, Ga.: Burke, Boykin, 1863.

Harris, Joel Chandler. *On the Plantation: A Story of a Georgia Boy's Adventures during the War.* New York: Appleton, 1892.

Hazeltine, Lt. Col. *The Prisoner of the Mill; or, Captain Hayward's Bodyguard.* New York: Beadle and Adams, 1864.

Headley, P. C. *Fight It Out on This Line, the Illustrated Story Life of General Grant, Boy-Soldier-President.* New York: George A. Leavitt, 1870.

Henderson, N. P. *Henderson's Test Words in English Orthography.* New York: Clark and Maynard, 1865.

Higginson, Thomas Wentworth. *Young Folks' History of the United States.* Boston: Lee and Shepard, 1875.

Hillard, G. S. *The Intermediate Reader: For the Use of Schools.* Boston: Brewer and Tileston, 1863.

———. *The Sixth Reader; Consisting of Extracts in Prose and Verse, with Biographical and Critical Notices of the Authors.* Boston: Brewer and Tileston; New York: J. W. Schermerhorn; Portland: Bailey and Noyes, 1865.

Hillard, G. S., and L. J. Campbell. *The Third Reader for Primary Schools.* Philadelphia: Eldredge and Brother; Boston: Brewer and Tileston, 1864.

John, Cousin. *The Drummer Boy: A Story of the War*. Boston: Crosby and Nichols, 1862.

Johnson, L. *An Elementary Arithmetic, Designed for Beginners*. Raleigh: Branson, Farrar, 1864.

Kate Morgan and Her Soldiers. Philadelphia: American Sunday School Union, 1862.

Kelly, Caroline E. *Andy Hall: The Mission Scholar in the Army*. Boston: Henry Hoyt, 1863.

A Lady of Warrenton, Virginia. *The Princess of the Moon: A Confederate Fairy Story*. Warrenton, Va.: n.p., 1869.

Lander, Samuel. *Our Own School Arithmetic*. Greensboro, N.C.: Sterling, Campbell and Albright, 1863.

Leverett, Rev. Charles E. *The Southern Confederacy Arithmetic, for Common Schools and Academies, with a Practical System of Book-Keeping*. Augusta: J. T. Paterson, 1864.

Little Clare's Voyage. New York: Henry Hoyt, [1865].

McDonald, W. N., and J. S. Blackburn. *A Southern School History of the United States of America, from the Earliest Discoveries to the Present Time*. Baltimore: George Lycett, 1869.

Magnus' Universal Picture Books. New York: Charles Magnus, [1863–64].

May, Sophie. *Captain Horace*. Little Prudy Series. Boston: Lee and Shepard, 1864.

Moore, Mrs. M. B. *The Dixie Primer, for the Little Folks*. Raleigh: Branson, Farrar, 1863.

————. *The Dixie Speller, to Follow the First Dixie Reader*. Raleigh: Branson, Farrar, 1864.

————. *The First Dixie Reader*. Raleigh: Branson, Farrar, 1863.

————. *The Geographical Reader, for the Dixie Children*. Raleigh: Branson, Farrar, 1863.

Moran, Dennis. *The Banner Series*. Vol. 1, *The Little Corporal*. Vol. 2, *The Young Sergeant*. Vol. 3, *Lieutenant Edward Harris*. Pittsburgh: W. B. Quartz Jr., 1874.

Neely, John. *The Confederate States Speller and Reader: Containing the Principles and Practice of English Orthography and Orthoepry, Systematically Developed*. Augusta: A. Bleakley, 1865.

The New Texas Primary Reader, for the Use of Primary Schools. Houston: E. H. Cushing, 1863.

The New Texas Reader, Designed for the Use of Schools in Texas. Houston: E. H. Cushing, 1864.

The New Texas Spelling Book, Revised and Enlarged. Houston: E. H. Cushing, 1865.

The Old Dominion Speller. Richmond: J. R. Keiningham, 1862.

The Old Flag. Philadelphia: American Sunday-School Union, 1864.

Optic, Oliver. *Brave Old Salt; or, Life on the Quarterdeck*. Boston: Lee and Shepard, 1867.

———. *Fighting Joe; or, The Fortunes of a Staff Officer*. Boston: Lee and Shepard, 1866.

———. *The Sailor Boy; or, Jack Somers in the Navy: A Story of the Great Rebellion*. Boston: Lee and Shepard, 1863.

———. *The Soldier Boy; or, Tom Somers in the Army: A Story of the Great Rebellion*. Boston: Lee and Shepard, 1863.

———. *The Yankee Middy; or, The Adventures of a Naval Officer: A Story of the Great Rebellion*. Boston: Lee and Shepard, 1866.

———. *The Young Lieutenant; or, The Adventures of an Army Officer*. Boston: Lee and Shepard, 1865.

Page, Thomas Nelson. *Two Little Confederates*. New York: Charles Scribner's Sons, 1888.

The Pictorial Primer: Designed for the Use of Schools and Families, Embellished with Fine Engravings. Richmond: West and Johnson, 1863.

Quackenbos, G. P. *First Lessons in Composition*. 1851. New York: Appleton, 1862.

A Rainy Day in Camp. Philadelphia: Protestant Episcopal Book Society, ca. 1865.

Rambaut, Thomas. *The Child's Primer*. Atlanta: J. J. Toon, 1863.

Raymond, Robert R. *The Patriotic Speaker: Consisting of Specimens of Modern Eloquence, together with Poetical Extracts Adapted for Recitation, and Dramatic Pieces for Exhibitions*. New York: Barnes and Burr; Chicago: Geo. and C. W. Sherwood, 1864.

Rice, John H. *A System of Modern Geography, Compiled from Various Sources and Adapted to the Present Condition of the World; Expressly for the Use of Schools and Academies in the Confederate States of America*. Atlanta: Franklin, 1862.

Robbins, Sarah Stuart. *Ned's Motto; or, Little by Little*. St. Paul: Merrill, 1864.

Robinson, Mary S. *A Household Story of the American Conflict*, 4 vols. New York: N. Tibbals, 1866, 1871.

Scott, Allen M. *A New Southern Grammar of the English Language, Designed for the Use of Schools and Private Learners*. Memphis, Tenn.: Hutton and Freleigh, 1861.

The Second Confederate Speller. Nashville: Southern Methodist Publishing, 1861.

Smith, Richard M. *The Confederate Spelling Book with Reading Lessons for the Young, Adapted to the Use of Schools or for Private Instruction*. Richmond: George L. Bidgood, 1863.

[Smith, Richard McAllister]. *The Confederate First Reader: Containing Selections in Prose and Poetry; as Reading Exercises for the Young Children in the Schools and Families of the Confederate States*. Richmond: George L. Bidgood, 1864.

———. *The Confederate Primer*. 3rd ed. Richmond: George L. Bidgood, 1863.

[Smith, Roswell Chamberlain]. *Louisiana English Grammar*. Shreveport: Southwestern, 1865.

Smith, Sarah Towne. *Our Village in War-Time*. New York: American Tract Society, 1864.

Smythe, Charles W. *Our Own Elementary Grammar, Intermediate Between the Primary and High School Grammars, and Especially Adapted to the Wants of the Common Schools*. Greensboro, N.C.: Sterling, Campbell and Albright; Richmond: W. Hargrave White; Columbia, S.C.: Townsend and North, 1863.

————. *Primary Grammar for the Use of Beginners*. Greensborough, N.C.: Sterling and Campbell; Richmond: W. Hargrave White; Charleston: M'Carter and Dawson, 1861.

Sterling, Richard. *Our Own Second Reader: For the Use of Schools and Families*. Greensboro, N.C.: Sterling, Campbell and Albright; Richmond: W. Hargrave White, 1862.

The Story of a Mayflower; Printed for the Benefit of the Loyal People of East Tennessee. Boston: Wright and Potter, 1864.

Taylor, J. C. R. *The Southern Primer, or the Child's First Book*. Charleston: A. E. Miller, 1864.

Thayer, William Makepeace. *A Youth's History of the Rebellion*. 4 vols. Boston: Walker, Fuller, 1864–65.

The Tract Primer. Petersburg: Evangelical Tract Society, 1864.

Trowbridge, J. T. *Frank Manly, the Drummer Boy: A Story of the War*. Boston: William F. Gill, 1876.

————. *The Three Scouts*. Boston: Tilton, 1865.

Uncle Buddy's Gift Book for the Holidays, Containing a Variety of Tales, Translations, Poetry, Chronology, Games, Anecdotes, Conundrums, &c., &c. Augusta: Blome and Tehan, 1863.

Uncle William. *The Boys and Girls Stories of the War*. Richmond: West and Johnson, n.d.

The Union ABC. Boston: Degen, Estes, 1864.

The Virginia Primer. Richmond: J. R. Keiningham, 1864.

Walton, G. A. *A Written Arithmetic, for Common and Higher Schools*. Boston: Brewer and Tileston, 1865.

Warren, J. Thomas. *Old Peggy Boggs; or, The Old Dominion Inside Out: A Tale of the Great Rebellion*. New York: Beadle and Adams, 1865.

Whitney, Mrs. A. D. T. *Boys at Chequasset; or, "A Little Leaven."* Boston: Houghton Mifflin, 1862.

Willett, Edward. *Kate Sharp; or, The Two Conscripts*. New York: Beadle and Adams, 1865. Reprint, New York: Frank Starr, 1877.

————. *The Loyal Specter; or, The True Hearts of Atlanta*. New York: Beadle and Adams, 1865. Reprint, New York: Frank Starr, 1876.

————. *True Blue; or, The Writing in Cipher*. New York: Beadle and Adams, 1865. Reprint, New York: Frank Starr, 1876.

————. *The Vicksburg Spy; or, Found and Lost: A Story of the Siege and*

Fall of the Great Rebel Stronghold. New York: Beadle and Adams, 1864. Reprint, New York: Frank Starr, 1877.

Willson, Marcus. *Willson's Primary Speller: A Simple and Progressive Course of Lessons in Spelling with Reading and Dictation Exercises, and the Elements of Oral and Written Compositions.* New York: Harper and Brothers, 1863.

PUBLISHED PRIMARY SOURCES

Adams, John Quincy. *An Old Boy Remembers.* Boston: Ruth Hill, 1935.

Addams, Jane. *Twenty Years at Hull-House, with Autobiographical Notes.* New York: Macmillan, 1929.

"After the War: Everything & Everybody *en militaire.*" *Harper's New Monthly Magazine,* April 1862, 717 (cartoon).

Allan, Elizabeth Preston, ed. *The Life and Letters of Margaret Junkin Preston.* Boston: Houghton Mifflin, 1903.

Allan, Elizabeth Randolph Preston. *A March Past: Reminiscences of Elizabeth Randolph Preston Allan.* Richmond: Dietz, 1938.

Alleman, Mrs. Tillie. *At Gettysburg, or What a Girl Saw and Heard of the Battle.* New York: W. Lake Borland, 1889.

Ames, Mary. *From a New England Woman's Diary in Dixie in 1865.* New York: Negro Universities Press, 1969.

Anderson, John Q., ed. *Brokenburn: The Journal of Kate Stone, 1861–1868.* Baton Rouge: Louisiana State University Press, 1955.

Andrews, Eliza Frances. *The War-Time Journal of a Georgia Girl.* Edited by Spencer Bidwell King Jr. Macon, Ga.: Ardivan Press, 1960.

Andrews, Rufus. *"Kiss Each Other For Me": The Civil War Letters of Rufus Andrews, 1861–1863.* Iron Mountain, Mich.: Mid-Peninsula Library Cooperative, 1979.

An Appeal to the Patriotic and Humane Citizens of the Nation. [Washington, D.C., ca. 1865].

Armstrong, William H., ed. *Gerty's Papa's Civil War.* New York: Pilgrim Press, 1984.

Ashby, Newton B. *The Ashbys in Iowa.* N.p., 1925.

Ashby, Thomas A. *The Valley Campaigns: Being the Reminiscences of a Non-Combatant While between the Lines in the Shenandoah Valley during the War of the States.* New York: Neale, 1914.

Athearn, Robert G., ed. *Soldier in the West: The Civil War Letters of Alfred Lacey Hough.* Philadelphia: University of Pennsylvania Press, 1957.

Barr, Amelia E. *All the Days of My Life: An Autobiography.* New York: Appleton, 1913.

Barton, Michael, ed. "The Civil War Letters of Captain Andrew Lewis and His Daughter." *Western Pennsylvania Historical Magazine* 60 (October 1977): 371–90.

Basler, Roy P., ed. *The Collected Works of Abraham Lincoln.* 9 vols. New Brunswick, N.J.: Rutgers University Press, 1953.

Beard, Daniel Carter. *Hardly a Man Is Now Alive: The Autobiography of Dan Beard.* New York: Doubleday, Doran, 1939.

Beauchamp, Virginia Walcott, ed. *A Private War: Letters and Diaries of Madge Preston, 1862–1867.* New Brunswick, N.J. Rutgers University Press, 1987.

Beaumont, Mrs. B. *Twelve Years of My Life: An Autobiography.* Philadelphia: T. B. Peterson and Bros. 1887.

Berlin, Ira, et al., eds. *Freedom: A Documentary History of Emancipation, 1861–1867.* Ser. 1, *The Wartime Genesis of Free Labor.* 3 vols. New York: Cambridge University Press, 1990.

————. *Freedom: A Documentary History of Emancipation, 1861–1867.* Ser. 1, vol. 1, *The Destruction of Slavery.* New York: Cambridge University Press, 1985.

————. *Freedom: A Documentary History of Emancipation, 1861–1867.* Ser. 2, *The Black Military Experience.* New York: Cambridge University Press, 1982.

Blassingame, John W., ed. *Slave Testimony: Two Centuries of Letters, Speeches, Interviews, and Autobiographies.* Baton Rouge: Louisiana State University Press, 1977.

Blegen, Theodore C., ed. *The Civil War Letters of Colonel H. C. Heg.* Northfield, Minn.: Norwegian-American Historical Association, 1936.

Bolsterli, Margaret Jones, ed. *A Remembrance of Eden: Harriet Bailey Bullock Daniel's Memories of a Frontier Plantation in Arkansas, 1849–1872.* Fayetteville: University of Arkansas Press, 1993.

Botume, Elizabeth Hyde. *First Days amongst the Contrabands.* Boston: Lee and Shepard, 1893; New York: Arno Press, 1968.

Brace, Charles Loring. *The Dangerous Classes of New York and Twenty Years' Work among Them.* 3rd ed. New York: Wynkoop and Hallenbeck, 1880. Reprint, Montclair, N.J.: Patterson-Smith, 1967.

Bremner, Robert H., ed. *Children and Youth in America: A Documentary History.* Vol. 1, *1600–1865.* Cambridge, Mass.: Harvard University Press, 1970.

Brooks, Walter. *A Child and a Boy.* New York: Brentano's, 1915.

Brown, Norman D., ed. *Journey to Pleasant Hill: The Civil War Letters of Captain Elijah P. Petty, Walker's Division, C.S.A.* San Antonio: University of Texas Institute of Texan Cultures, 1982.

Bruce, William George. *I Was Born in America: Memoirs of William George Bruce.* Milwaukee: Bruce, 1937.

Buchanan, Sophia. "Letters to the Front: A Distaff View of the Civil War." Edited by George M. Blackburn. *Michigan History* 49 (March 1965): 53–67.

Buck, William P., ed. *Sad Earth, Sweet Heaven: The Diary of Lucy Rebecca Buck during the War between the States.* Birmingham, Ala.: Cornerstone, 1973.

Bulger, J. W. *Memoirs and Historical Jottings.* Davenport, Iowa: n.p., 1939.

Burr, Virginia Ingraham, ed. *The Secret Eye: The Journal of Ella Gertrude Clanton Thomas, 1848–1889.* Chapel Hill: University of North Carolina Press, 1990.

Burt, Stephen Smith. *Recollections and Reflections Chiefly of My Boyhood.* New York: S. S. Smith, 1912.

Burton, Annie L. *Memories of Childhood's Slavery Days.* Boston: Ross, 1909.

Byrne, Frank L., and Jean P. Soman, eds. *Your True Marcus: The Civil War Letters of a Jewish Colonel.* Kent, Ohio: Kent State University Press, 1985.

Campbell, Edward D. C., Jr., ed. " 'Strangers and Pilgrims': The Diary of Margaret Tilloston Kemble Nourse." *Virginia Magazine of History and Biography* 91 (October 1983): 440–508.

Cantley, Mrs. H. K. "Little Folks in War Times." *Philadelphia Weekly Times,* October 4, 1884.

Cash, William M., and Lucy Somerville Howorth, eds. *My Dear Nellie: The Civil War Letters of William L. Nugent to Eleanor Smith Nugent.* Jackson: University Press of Mississippi, 1977.

Cattell, Edward James. *Fighting Through.* Philadelphia: Dunlap, 1936.

Chadwick, Mrs. W. D. "Civil War Days in Huntsville: A Diary by Mrs. W. D. Chadwick." *Alabama Historical Quarterly* 9 (Summer 1947): 199–331.

Chancellor, Sue M. "Personal Recollections of the Battle of Chancellorsville." *Register of the Kentucky Historical Society* 66 (April 1968): 137–46.

Chatterton, Fenimore. *Yesterday's Wyoming: The Intimate Memoirs of Fenimore Chatterton, Territorial Citizen, Governor, and Statesman.* Aurora, Colo.: Powder River Publishers, 1957.

Choate, Anne Hyde, and Helen Ferris, eds. *Juliette Low and the Girl Scouts: The Story of an American Woman, 1860–1927.* Garden City, N.Y.: Doubleday, Doran, 1928.

City of Charleston Yearbook. Charleston, 1885.

Clark, Olynthus B., ed. *Downing's Civil War Diary.* Des Moines: Historical Department of Iowa, 1916.

Clary, Anna. *Reminiscences of Anna Clary.* Los Angeles: Adcraft, 1937.

Clift, G. Glenn, ed. *The Private War of Lizzie Hardin.* Frankfort: Kentucky Historical Society, 1963.

Clinkscales, John George. *On the Old Plantation: Reminiscences of His Childhood.* Spartanburg, S.C.: Band and White, 1916.

Coleman, Kenneth, ed. *Athens, 1861–1865: As Seen through Letters in the University of Georgia Libraries.* Athens: University of Georgia Press, 1969.

Connor, Seymour V., ed. *Dear America: Some Letters of Orange Cicero and Mary America (Akin) Connor,* Austin: Jenkins, 1971.

Cooley, Mortimer E. *Scientific Blacksmith*. New York: American Society of
Mechanical Engineers, 1947.
Corbett, Elizabeth Frances. *Out At the Soldiers' Home: A Memory Book*.
New York: Appleton-Century, 1941.
Cox, Florence Marie Ankeny, ed. *Kiss Josey For Me!* Santa Ana, Calif.:
Friis-Pioneer Press, 1974.
Craig, N. N. *Thrills, 1861 to 1887*. Oakland: N. N. Craig, 1931.
Crawford, William Ayers. "A Sabine Guard: The Civil War Letters of Col.
William Ayers Crawford, CSA, 1861–1865." *Arkansas Historical
Quarterly* 31 (Winter 1972): 328–55.
Cunningham, Mary E., ed. "The Background of an American (Being the
True Chronicle of a Boy of Twelve)." *New York History* 27 (January,
July 1946): 76–87, 213–23.
Cuomo, Mario, and Harold Holzer, eds. *Lincoln on Democracy*. New York:
HarperCollins, 1990.
Cutrer, Thomas W., ed. " 'An Experience in Soldier's Life': The Civil War
Letters of Volney Ellis, Adjutant, Twelfth Texas Infantry, Walker's
Texas Division, C.S.A." *Military History of the Southwest* 22 (Fall
1992): 109–72.
Cuttino, George Peddy, ed. *Saddle Bag and Spinning Wheel: Being the Civil
War Letters of George W. Peddy, M.D., and His Wife Kate Featherston
Peddy*. Macon, Ga.: Mercer University Press, 1981.
Damkoehler, Ernst. *From Wisconsin to Andersonville, 1862–1864*. N.p.,
1961.
Danbom, David B. " 'Dear Companion': Civil War Letters of a Story
County Farmer." *Annals of Iowa*, 3rd ser., 47 (Fall 1984): 537–43.
Daniel, Lizzie Cary. *Confederate Scrap-Book*. Richmond: J. L. Hill, 1893.
Davidson, Josephine M. *Josie M. Davidson, Her Life and Work*.
Prestonburg, Ky.: A. J. Davidson, 1922.
Davis, Varina Howell. *Jefferson Davis: A Memoir by His Wife*. New York:
Bedford, 1890.
Deland, Margaret Wade Campbell. *If This Be I, As I Suppose It Be*. New
York: Appleton-Century, 1936.
De Long, H. W. *Boyhood Reminiscences*. Dansville, N.Y.: F. A. Owen, 1913.
"Diary of John Magill Steele and Sarah Eliza Steele." In *Diaries, Letters,
and Recollections of the War between the States*. Winchester, Va.:
Winchester–Frederick County Historical Society, 1955.
Dillon, William P., ed. "The Civil War Letters of Enos Barret Lewis, 101st
Ohio Volunteer Infantry." *Northwest Ohio Quarterly* 57 (Spring 1985):
51–63; (Summer 1985): 83–100.
Dimond, E. Grey, and Herman Hattaway, eds. *Letters from Forest Place:
A Plantation Family's Correspondence, 1846–1881*. Jackson: University
Press of Mississippi, 1993.
Donaghey, George W. *Autobiography of George W. Donaghey, Governor of
Arkansas, 1909–1913*. Benton, Ark.: L. B. White, 1939.

Douglas, Henry Kyd. *I Rode with Stonewall.* St. Simons Island, Ga.: Mockingbird Books, 1974.

Drew, John. *My Years on the Stage.* New York: Dutton, 1922.

Drury, Marion Richardson. *Reminiscences of Early Days in Iowa.* Toledo, Iowa: Toledo Chronicle Press, 1931.

Dyer, Thomas, ed. *To Raise Myself a Little: The Diaries and Letters of Jennie, a Georgia Teacher, 1851-1886.* Athens: University of Georgia Press, 1982.

Eagleton, Ethie. "Stray Thoughts." Edited by Elvie Eagleton Skipper and Ruth Gove. *East Tennessee Historical Society Publications* 40 (1968): 128-37; 41 (1969): 116-28.

Eddy, T. M. *The Patriotism of Illinois: A Record of the Civil and Military History of the State in the War for the Union.* Chicago: Clarke, 1865.

Egan, Maurice F. *Recollections of a Happy Life.* New York: George H. Doran, 1924.

Elliott, Mrs. A. M., ed. *The Garden of Memories: Stories of the Civil War.* Camden, Ark.: H. L. Grimstead Chapter, United Daughters of the Confederacy, n.d.

Eppes, Susan Bradford. *Through Some Eventful Years.* Macon, Ga.: J. W. Burke, 1926.

Fatout, Paul, ed. *Letters of a Civil War Surgeon.* West Lafayette, Ind.: Purdue Research Foundation, 1961.

Ferguson, Herbert L., ed. "Letters of John W. Duncan." *Arkansas Historical Quarterly* 9 (Winter 1950): 298-312.

Filipovic, Zlata. *Zlata's Diary: A Child's Life in Sarajevo.* Translated by Christina Pribichevich-Zoric. New York: Viking, 1994.

Fleet, Betsy, and John D. P. Fuller, eds. *Green Mount: A Virginia Plantation Family during the Civil War: Being the Journal of Benjamin Robert Fleet and Letters of His Family.* Lexington: University Press of Kentucky, 1962.

Flint, Charles R. *Memories of an Active Life.* New York: Putnam's, 1923.

Folmar, John Kent, ed. *From That Terrible Field: Civil War Letters of James M. Williams, Twenty-first Alabama Infantry Volunteers.* University: University of Alabama Press, 1981.

Foy, Eddie. *Clowning through Life.* New York: Dutton, 1928.

"The Freedmen at Port Royal." *Atlantic Monthly,* September 1863, 291-315.

Gallagher, Gary W., ed. *Fighting for the Confederacy: The Personal Recollections of General Edward Porter Alexander.* Chapel Hill: University of North Carolina Press, 1989.

Gannett, Michael R., ed. "Twelve Letters from Altoona, June–July 1863." *Pennsylvania History* 46 (January 1980): 38-56.

Garland, Hamlin. *Main-Travelled Roads.* New York: Harper and Brothers, 1899.

Geary, Patrick J., ed. *Celine: Remembering Louisiana, 1850-1871.* Athens: University of Georgia Press, 1987.

Geer, Theodore. *Fifty Years in Oregon*. New York: Neale, 1911.

Gilder, Jeannette Leonard. *Autobiography of a Tomboy*. New York: Doubleday, Page, 1904.

Glover, Robert W., ed. "War Letters of a Texas Conscript in Arkansas." *Arkansas Historical Quarterly* 20 (Winter 1961): 355–87.

Goldman, Eric F., ed. "Young John Bach McMaster: A Boyhood in New York City." *New York History* 20 (October 1939): 316–24.

Goodell, Robert C., and P. A. M. Taylor, eds. "A German Immigrant in the Union Army: Selected Letters of Valentin Bechler." *Journal of American Studies* 4 (February 1971): 145–62.

Goodrich, Frank B. *The Tribute Book: A Record of the Munificence, Self-Sacrifice, and Patriotism of the American People during the War for the Union*. New York: Derby and Miller, 1865.

Grant, Jesse R. *In the Days of My Father General Grant*. New York: Harper and Brothers, 1925.

Grant, Robert. *Fourscore*. Boston: Houghton Mifflin, 1934.

Gregory, Addie Hibbard. *A Great-Grandmother Remembers*. Chicago: Kroch, 1940.

Grierson, Francis. *The Valley of Shadows: Recollections of the Lincoln Country, 1858–63*. Boston: Houghton Mifflin, 1909.

Griffin, Doris C., comp. *The Civil War Letters of John McKitrick to his Wife Sophia*. Lincoln: University of Nebraska Press, 1982.

Griffith, Lucille, ed. *Yours till Death: Civil War Letters of John W. Cotton*. University: University of Alabama Press, 1951.

Gwin, Minrose C., ed. *A Woman's Civil War: A Diary, with Reminiscences of the War, from March 1862*. Madison: University of Wisconsin Press, 1992.

Hall, Isaac, and Mary Hall. "The Human Side of War: Letters between a Bienville Parish Civil War Soldier and His Wife." Edited by Garnie W. McGinty. *North Louisiana Historical Association Journal* 13, no. 2–3 (1982): 59–81.

Hammock, Henry, ed. *Letters to Amanda from Sergeant Major Marion Hill Fitzpatrick, Company K, 45th Georgia Regiment, Thomas's Brigade, Wilcox Division, Hill's Corps, CSA, to his wife Amanda Olive Elizabeth White Fitzpatrick, 1862–1865*. Culloden, Ga.: Mansel Hammock, 1976.

Hank, Minnie. *Memoirs of a Singer*. London: A. M. Philpot, 1925.

Hardin, John Wesley. *The Life of John Wesley Hardin, as Written by Himself*. Norman: University of Oklahoma Press, 1961.

Harris, Lucien M. *Random Recollections of Seventy-Nine Years*. New York: n.p., 1937.

Hassler, William W., ed. *The General to His Lady: The Civil War Letters of William Dorsey Pender to Fanny Pender*. Chapel Hill: University of North Carolina Press, 1965.

Hatley, Joe M., and Linda B. Huffman, eds. *Letters of William F. Wagner, Confederate Soldier*. Wendell, N.C.: Broadfoot's Bookmark, 1983.

Hewins, Caroline M. *A Mid-Century Child and Her Books*. New York: Macmillan, 1926.

Higginson, Thomas Wentworth. *Army Life in a Black Regiment*. Boston: Fields, Osgood, 1870. Reprint, New York: Norton, 1984.

Hilen, Andrew. "Charley Longfellow Goes to War." *Harvard Library Bulletin* 14 (Winter 1960): 59–81; (Spring 1960): 283–303.

Hill, James Langdon. *My First Years as a Boy*. Andover, Mass.: Andover Press, 1927.

Hodges, Ellen E., and Stephen Kerber, eds. "Children of Honor: Letters of Winston and Octavia Stephens, 1861–1862." *Florida Historical Quarterly* 56 (July 1977): 45–74.

———. " 'Rogues and Black Hearted Scamps': Civil War Letters of Winston and Octavia Stephens, 1862–1863." *Florida Historical Quarterly* 57 (July 1978): 54–82.

Holland, Rupert Saragent, ed. *Letters and Diary of Laura M. Towne: Written from the Sea Islands of South Carolina, 1862–1864*. Cambridge, Mass.: Riverside Press, 1912. Reprint, New York: Negro Universities Press, 1969.

Holmes, Charlotte R., ed. *The Burckmyer Letters, March, 1863–June, 1865*. Columbia, S.C.: State Co., 1926.

Hopkins, Anson Smith. *Reminiscences of an Octogenarian*. New Haven: Tuttle, Morehouse, and Taylor, 1937.

Hopper, De Wolfe. *Once a Clown, Always a Clown*. Boston: Little, Brown, 1927.

Hudder, Jean Ann, ed. *Dear Wife: Captain Joseph Adams' Letters to His Wife Eliza Ann, 1861–1864*. N.p., 1985.

Hunt, Frances. "The Last Days of Richmond." *Civil War Times Illustrated* 12 (February 1974): 20–22.

Ingram, Henry L., comp. *Civil War Letters of George W. and Martha F. Ingram, 1861–1865*. College Station: Texas A&M University Press, 1973.

Jackson, Benjamin Franklin. *So Mourns the Dove: Letters of a Confederate Infantryman and His Family*. New York: Exposition Press, 1965.

Jackson, Harry F., and Thomas F. O'Donnell, eds. *Back Home in Oneida: Hermon Clarke and His Letters*. Syracuse: Syracuse University Press, 1965.

Jackson, Mary Anna. *Memoirs of Stonewall Jackson*. Louisville: Prentice Press, 1895.

Jaquette, Henrietta Stratton, ed. *South after Gettysburg: Letters of Cornelia Hancock, 1863–1868*. New York: Thomas Y. Crowell, 1937.

Johnson, Ella Hicks. *Granny Remembers*. Macon, Ga.: J. W. Burke, 1928.

Johnston, Mary Frances Hosea, comp. *Letters to Lucinda, 1862–1864*. Huntsville, Ala.: Mrs. J. H. Johnston, 1985.

Jordin, John Franklin. *Memories*. Gallatin, Mo.: North Missourian Press, 1904.

Kallir, Otto, ed. *Grandma Moses: My Life's History*. New York: Harper and Brothers, 1946.

Kellogg, John Azor. *Capture and Escape: A Narrative of Army and Prison Life*. Madison: Wisconsin History Commission, 1908.

Kemper, Mary Robinson. "Civil War Reminiscences at Danville Female Academy." Edited by Mary Lee Kemper. *Missouri Historical Review* 62 (April 1968): 314–20.

King, Grace Elizabeth. *Memories of a Southern Woman of Letters*. New York: Macmillan, 1932.

King, Spencer B., Jr., ed. *Ebb Tide: As Seen through the Diary of Josephine Clay Habersham, 1863*. Athens: University of Georgia Press, 1958.

———. *Rebel Lawyer: Letters of Theodorick W. Montfort, 1861–1862*. Athens: University of Georgia Press, 1965.

Kingsbury, Alice Eliza. *In Old Waterbury: The Memoirs of Alice E. Kingsbury*. Waterbury, Conn.: Mattatuck Historical Society, 1942.

Klaas, Helen, ed. *Portrait of Elnathan Keeler, a Union Soldier*. Wappingers Falls, N.Y.: Goldlief Reproductions, 1977.

Klein, Frederick S., ed. *Just South of Gettysburg: Carroll County, Maryland, in the Civil War*. Westminster, Md.: Newman, 1963.

Kremenak, Ben, ed. "Escape from Atlanta: The Huntington Memoir." *Civil War History* 11 (June 1965): 160–77.

Krenkel, John, ed. *Serving the Republic: Richard Yates, Illinois Governor and Congressman, Son of Richard Yates, Civil War Governor, an Autobiography*. Danville, Ill.: Interstate Publishers, 1968.

Laas, Virginia Jeans, ed. *Wartime Washington: The Civil War Letters of Elizabeth Blair Lee*. Urbana: University of Illinois Press, 1991.

Lane, Mills, ed. *"Dear Mother: Don't grieve about me. If I get killed, I'll only be dead." Letters from Georgia Soldiers in the Civil War*. Savannah: Library of Georgia, 1990.

Lawrence, F. Lee, and Robert W. Glover, eds. "A Smith County Confederate Writes Home: Letters of Z. H. Crow." *Chronicles of Smith County, Texas* 4 (Fall 1965): 11–14.

Laylander, Orange J. *Chronicles of a Contented Man*. Chicago: Kroch, 1928.

Lee, Cazenove G. "McClellan's Troops on Seminary Hill." *Alexandria History* 3 (1981): 16–20.

Lenroot, Clara Clough. *Long, Long Ago*. Appleton, Wis.: Badger Printing, 1929.

Levstik, Frank B., ed. "A Journey among the Contrabands: The Diary of Walter Totten Carpenter." *Indiana Magazine of History* 73 (September 1977): 204–22.

"Life on the Sea Islands." *Atlantic Monthly*, May 1864, 587–96.

"The 'Little Yank Girl' Saw War and Wrote of It." In *The Civil War and the Battles of Corinth and Shiloh*, edited by Beulah May Price, 2, 15. Corinth, Miss.: Daily Corinthian, 1961.

Lodge, Henry Cabot. *Early Memories*. London: Constable, 1913.

Longacre, Edward G., ed. "Letters from Little Rock of Captain James M.

Bowles, 112th United States Colored Troops." *Arkansas Historical Quarterly* 40 (Autumn 1981): 235–48.

Loughborough, Mary. *My Cave Life in Vicksburg*. New York: Appleton, 1864.

Love, Jennie. "War as a Girl Saw It: Chambersburg, Pennsylvania, during the Invasion of Lee and Ewell into Pennsylvania." *National Tribune*, May 12, 1910.

Lunt, Dolly Sumner. *A Woman's Wartime Journal*. New York: Century, 1918.

MacCorkle, William A. *Recollections of Fifty Years of West Virginia*. New York: Putnam's, 1928.

McCreary, Albertus. "Gettysburg: A Boy's Experience of the Battle." *McClure's Magazine*, July 1909, 243–53.

McCune, Julie, ed. *Mary Austin Wallace: Her Diary, 1862. A Michigan Soldier's Wife Runs Their Farm*. Lansing: Michigan Civil War Centennial Observance Commission, 1963.

Mackin, Sister Aloysius, ed. "Wartime Scenes from Convent Windows: St. Cecilia, 1860 through 1865." *Tennessee Historical Quarterly* 39 (Winter 1980): 401–22.

Mackintosh, Robert Harley, Jr., ed. *"Dear Martha . . .": The Confederate War Letters of a South Carolina Soldier, Alexander Faulkner Fewell*. Columbia, S.C.: R. L. Bryan, 1976.

McLachlan, James, ed. "The Civil War Diary of Joseph H. Coit." *Maryland Historical Magazine* 60 (September 1965): 245–60.

McLaughlin, Florence C., ed. " 'Dear Sister Jennie—Dear Brother Jacob': The Correspondence between a Northern Soldier and His Sister in Mechanicsburg, Pennsylvania, 1861–1864." *Western Pennsylvania Historical Magazine* 60 (April 1977), 109–43; (July 1977), 204–40.

Macon, Emma Cassandra Riley. *Reminiscences of the Civil War*. Cedar Rapids, Iowa: Torch Press, 1911.

Magee, Harvey White. *The Story of My Life*. Albany, N.Y.: Boyd, 1926.

Marmion, Annie P. *Under Fire: An Experience in the Civil War*. Edited by William Vincent Marmion Jr. N.p., 1959.

Marshall, Thomas R. *Recollections of Thomas R. Marshall, Vice President and Hoosier Philosopher: A Hoosier Salad*. Indianapolis: Bobbs-Merrill, 1925.

Martin, Florence Ashmore Cowles Hamlett, ed. *Courageous Journey: The Civil War Journal of Laetitia Lafon Ashmore Nutt*. Miami: E. A. Seemann, 1975.

Martin, Josephine W., ed. *"Dear Sister": Letters Written on Hilton Head Island, 1867*. Beaufort, S.C.: Beaufort Book Co., 1977.

Martin, Robert Hugh. *A Boy of Old Shenandoah*. Edited by Carolyn Martin Rutherford. Parsons, W.Va.: McClain, 1977.

Matthews, Jeremiah H. *Reminiscence of a Life-Time Experience*. Nashville: by the author, 1924.

Mattox, Henry. "Chronicle of a Mississippi Soldier." *Journal of Mississippi History* 52 (August 1990): 199–214.

Mayberry, Virginia, and Dawn E. Bakken, eds. "The Civil War Home Front: Diary of a Young Girl, 1862–1863." *Indiana Magazine of History* 87 (March 1991): 24–78.

Merritt, Lucius Manlius. *Kiss the Children for Father: Letters from a Prisoner at Fort Pickens.* Compiled by Merritt L. Nickinson. Pensacola, Fla.: Pensacola Historical Society, 1975.

Miers, Earl Schenck, ed. *A Rebel War Clerk's Diary.* New York: Sagamore Press, 1958. Reprint, Baton Rouge: Louisiana State University Press, 1993.

————. *When the World Ended: The Diary of Emma Le Conte.* New York: Oxford University Press, 1957.

Miller, Andrew James. *Old School Days: A Memoir of Boyhood.* New York: Abbey Press, 1900.

Miller, Mary Esther. *An East Hampton Childhood.* East Hampton, N.Y.: Starr Press, 1938.

Mills, George, ed. "The Sharp Family Civil War Letters." *Annals of Iowa,* 3rd ser., 34 (January 1959): 481–532.

Moneyhon, Carl, ed. "Life in Confederate Arkansas: The Diary of Virginia Davis Gray, 1863–1866." *Arkansas Historical Quarterly* 42 (Spring 1983): 47–85, 134–69.

Mott, D. C. *Fifty Years in Iowa.* Marengo, Iowa: Marengo Republican, n.d.

Moulton, Arthur Wheelock. *A Memoir of Augustine Heard Armory.* Salem, Mass.: Newcomb and Gauss, 1909.

Myers, Robert Manson, ed. *The Children of Pride.* Abridged ed. New Haven: Yale University Press, 1984.

Nagel, Charles. *A Boy's Civil War Story.* St. Louis: Eden, 1934.

Neely, Ann Eliza Sterling. *Just Me: An Autobiography.* Philadelphia: Dorrance, 1949.

Norris, George W. *Fighting Liberal: The Autobiography of George W. Norris.* New York: Macmillan, 1946.

Nott, Charles C. *Sketches of the War: A Series of Letters to the North Moore Street School of New York.* 4th ed. New York: Anson D. F. Randolph, 1865.

O'Connor, Elizabeth Paschal. *I Myself.* New York: Putnam's, 1914.

"On the Pond." *Harper's New Monthly Magazine,* February 1863, 429 (cartoon).

Our Women in the War: The Lives They Lived, the Deaths They Died. Charleston: News and Courier Book Presses, 1885.

Parmelee, Alice Maury, ed. *The Confederate Diary of Betty Herndon Maury, 1861–1863.* Washington, D.C.: privately printed, 1938.

Parsons, William T., and Mary Shuler Heimberger, eds. "Schuler Family Correspondence." *Pennsylvania Folklife* 29 (Spring 1980): 98–113.

Partin, Robert, ed. "The Wartime Experiences of Margaret McCalla:

Confederate Refugee from East Tennessee." *Tennessee Historical Quarterly* 24 (Spring 1965): 39–53.

Paxton, John Gallatin, ed. *The Civil War Letters of General Frank "Bull" Paxton, CSA, a Lieutenant of Lee & Jackson*. Hillsboro, Tex.: Hill Junior College Press, 1978.

Peacock, Jane Bonner, ed. "A Wartime Story: The Davidson Letters, 1862–1865." *Atlanta Historical Bulletin* 19, no. 1 (1975): 8–121.

Pearson, Elizabeth Ware, ed. *Letters from Port Royal, 1862–1868*. Boston: W. B. Clarke, 1906. Reprint, New York: Arno Press, 1969.

Phifer, Louisa Jane. "Letters from an Illinois Farm, 1864–1865." Edited by Carol Benson Pye. *Journal of the Illinois State Historical Society* 66 (Winter 1973): 387–403.

Powderly, Terence V. *The Path I Trod: The Autobiography of Terence V. Powderly*. New York: Columbia University Press, 1940.

Preston, Margaret Junkin. *The Life and Letters of Margaret Junkin Preston*. Boston: Houghton Mifflin, 1903.

Pyle, Howard. "When I Was a Little Boy." *Woman's Home Companion*, April 1912, 5, 103.

Racine, Philip N., ed. "Emily Lyles Harris: A Piedmont Farmer during the Civil War." *South Atlantic Quarterly* 79 (Autumn 1980): 386–97.

Rawick, George P., ed. *The American Slave: A Composite Autobiography*. 19 vols. Westport, Conn.: Greenwood, 1972–74; supplement, ser. 1, 12 vols., 1978; supplement, ser. 2, 10 vols., 1979.

Read, Opie. *I Remember*. New York: R. R. Smith, 1930.

Reese, Lizette Woodworth. *A Victorian Village: Reminiscences of Other Days*. New York: Farrar and Rinehart, 1929.

Reid-Green, Marcia, ed. *Letters Home: Henry Matrau of the Iron Brigade*. Lincoln: University of Nebraska Press, 1993.

Reinsberg, Mark, ed. "A Bucktail Voice: Civil War Correspondence of Pvt. Cordello Collins." *Western Pennsylvania Historical Magazine* 48 (July 1965): 235–48.

Reynolds, Donald E., ed. "A Mississippian in Lee's Army: The Letters of Leander Huckaby." *Journal of Mississippi History* 36 (February 1974): 53–68; (May 1974): 165–78; (August 1974): 273–88.

Reynolds, Nathaniel M. "The Civil War Letters of Nathaniel M. Reynolds." Edited by James Barnett. *Lincoln Herald* 65 (Winter 1963): 199–213.

Richards, Caroline Cowles. *Village Life in America, 1852–1872, Including the Period of the American Civil War, as Told in the Diary of a Schoolgirl*. Edited by Margaret E. Sangster. New York: Holt, 1913.

Robertson, George F. *A Small Boy's Recollections of the Civil War*. Clover, S.C.: G. F. Robertson, 1932.

Robertson, James I., Jr., ed. *A Confederate Girl's Diary*. Bloomington: Indiana University Press, 1960.

Robertson, Orrin W. "The Background of an American." Ed. Mary E.

Cunningham. *New York History* 27 (January, April 1946): 76–87, 213–23.

Rogers, Mrs. M. A. "An Iowa Woman in Wartime." *Annals of Iowa* 35 (Winter 1961): 523–48; (Spring 1961): 594–615; 36 (Summer 1961): 16–44.

Roosevelt, Theodore. *An Autobiography.* New York: Scribner, 1919.

Ross, Elizabeth W. *A Road of Remembrance.* Cincinnati: Powell and White, 1923.

Rowntree, Henry. "Freedmen at Davis Bend, April 1864." Edited by James T. Currie. *Journal of Mississippi History* 46 (May 1984): 120–29.

Rozier, John, ed. *The Granite Farm Letters: The Civil War Correspondence of Edgeworth and Sallie Bird.* Athens: University of Georgia Press, 1988.

Sanders, Samuel D. "Civil War Letters of Dr. Samuel D. Sanders." *South Carolina Historical Magazine* 65 (July 1964): 129–44; (October 1964): 218–32.

Saunders, Ellen Virginia. "War-Time Journal of a 'Little Rebel.'" *Confederate Veteran* 27 (1919): 451–52; 28 (1920): 11–12.

Schartz, Gerald, ed. *A Woman Doctor's Civil War: Esther Hill Hawks' Diary.* Columbia: University of South Carolina Press, 1984.

Scott, Robert Garth, ed. *Fallen Leaves: The Civil War Letters of Major Henry Livermore Abbott.* Kent, Ohio: Kent State University Press, 1991.

Sessions, Ruth H. *Sixty-Odd: A Personal History.* Brattleboro, Vt.: Stephen Daye, 1936.

Shaw, Anna Howard. *The Story of a Pioneer.* New York: Harper and Brothers, 1915.

Silber, Nina, and Mary Beth Sievans, eds. *Yankee Correspondence: Civil War Letters between New England Soldiers and the Home Front.* Charlottesville: University Press of Virginia, 1996.

Simon, John Y., ed. *The Personal Memoirs of Julia Dent Grant.* New York: Putnam's, 1975.

Skelly, Daniel Alexander. *A Boy's Experiences during the Battle of Gettysburg.* Gettysburg, Pa.: n.p., 1932.

Skinner, Henrietta Dana. *An Echo from Parnassus: Being Childhood Memories of Longfellow and His Friends.* New York: Sears, 1928.

Skinner, Otis. *Footlights and Spotlights: Recollections of My Life on the Stage.* Indianapolis: Bobbs-Merrill, 1924.

Smith, Barbara A., comp. *The Civil War Letters of Col. Elijah H. C. Cavins, 14th Indiana.* Owensboro, Ky.: Cook-McDowell, 1981.

Smith, Gerald J., ed. "Reminiscences of the Civil War by J. W. Frederick." *Georgia Historical Quarterly* 59, supplement (1975): 154–59.

Sousa, John Philip. *Marching Along: Recollections of Men, Women, and Music.* Boston: Hale, Cushman and Flint, 1928.

Starbuck, Mary Eliza. *My House and I: A Chronicle of Nantucket.* Boston: Houghton Mifflin, 1929.

Steele, Samuel A. *The Sunny Road: Home Life in Dixie during the War*. Memphis, Tenn.: n.p., [1924].

Strang, Ellen. "Diary of a Young Girl: Grundy County to Correctionville, 1862." Edited by Lida L. Greene. *Annals of Iowa*, 3rd ser., 36 (Fall 1962): 437–57.

Straus, Oscar. *Under Four Administrations, from Cleveland to Taft*. Boston: Houghton, 1922.

Sturtevant, Arnold H., ed. *Josiah Volunteered: A Collection of Diaries, Letters, and Photographs of Josiah H. Sturtevant, His Wife, Helen, and His Four Children*. Farmington, Maine: Knowlton and McLeary, 1977.

Sullivan, James W. *Boyhood Memories of the Civil War, 1861–1865: Invasion of Carlisle*. Carlisle, Pa.: Hamilton Library Association, 1933.

Swank, Walbrook D., ed. *Confederate Letters and Diaries, 1861–1865*. Shippensburg, Pa.: White Mane, 1988.

Swint, Henry L., ed. *Dear Ones at Home: Letters from Contraband Camps*. Nashville: Vanderbilt University Press, 1966.

Tapert, Annette, ed. *The Brothers' War: Civil War Letters to Their Loved Ones from the Blue and Gray*. New York: Vintage, 1989.

Tarbell, Ida M. *All in the Day's Work: An Autobiography*. New York: Macmillan, 1939.

Thompson, Michael Andrew, ed. *Dear Eliza . . . : The Letters of Mitchell Andrew Thompson, May 1862–August 1864*. Ames, Iowa: Carter Press, 1976.

Towers, Frank, ed. "Military Waif: A Sidelight on the Baltimore Riot of 19 April 1861." *Maryland Historical Magazine* 89 (Winter 1994): 427–46.

Truss, John W. "Civil War Letters from Parsons' Texas Cavalry Brigade." Edited by Johnette Highsmith Ray. *Southwestern Historical Quarterly* 69 (October 1965): 210–23.

Turner, Charles W., ed. "General David Hunter's Sack of Lexington, Virginia, June 10–14, 1864: An Account by Rose Page Pendleton." *Virginia Magazine of History and Biography* 83 (April 1975): 173–83.

Uhler, Margaret Anderson, ed. "Civil War Letters of Major General James Patton Anderson." *Florida Historical Quarterly* 56 (October 1977): 150–75.

Vandiver, Frank E., ed. "Letters from the Confederate Medical Service in Texas, 1861–1865." *Southwestern Historical Quarterly* 55 (January 1952): 378–93; (April 1952): 459–74.

Vincent, Elizabeth Kipp. *In the Days of Lincoln: Girlhood Recollections and Personal Reminiscences of Life in Washington during the Civil War*. Gardena, Calif.: Spanish American Institute Press, 1924.

Ward, Evelyn Douglas. *The Children of Bladensfield*. New York: Viking, 1978.

"War Diary of a Union Woman in the South," edited by G. W. Cable. In *Famous Adventures and Prison Escapes of the Civil War*, 1–82. New York: Century, 1904.

Washington, Booker T. *Up from Slavery: An Autobiography*. New York: Doubleday, Page, 1901. Reprint, Garden City, N.Y.: Doubleday, 1963.

Watson, Thomas E. *Bethany: A Story of the Old South*. New York: Appleton, 1910.

Welling, Richard. *As the Twig Is Bent*. New York: Putnam's, 1942.

Wells, Carol, ed. *War, Reconstruction, and Redemption on Red River: The Memoirs of Dosia Williams Moore*. Ruston, La.: McGinty, 1990.

Wells, Rolla. *Episodes of My Life*. St. Louis: Rolla Wells, 1933.

Welton, J. Michael, ed. *"My Heart Is So Rebellious": The Caldwell Letters, 1861–1865*. Warrenton, Va.: Fauguier National Bank, 1991.

Wenzel, Carol N., ed. "Freedmen's Farm Letters of Samuel and Louisa Mallory to 'our absent but ever remembered boy' in McHenry County, Illinois." *Journal of the Illinois State Historical Society* 73 (Autumn 1980): 162–76.

West, John. *A Texan in Search of a Fight*. Waco, Tex.: J. S. Hill, 1901.

Wharton, Mary E., and Ellen F. Williams, eds. *Peach Leather and Rebel Gray: Bluegrass Life and the War, 1860–1865*. Lexington, Ky.: Helicon, 1986.

Wiggins, Sarah Woolfolk. *The Journals of Josiah Gorgas, 1857–1878*. Tuscaloosa: University of Alabama Press, 1995.

Wilder, Laura Ingalls. *Little House in the Big Woods*. New York: Harper and Brothers, 1932. Reprint, New York: HarperCollins, 1971.

Wiley, Bell I., ed. *"This Infernal War": The Confederate Letters of Sgt. Edwin H. Fay*. Austin: University of Texas Press, 1958.

Wilkins, B. H. *"War Boy": A True Story of the Civil War and Re-Construction Days*. Tullahoma, Tenn.: Wilson Brothers, 1990.

Williams, Frederick D., ed. *The Wild Life of the Army: Civil War Letters of James A. Garfield*. East Lansing: Michigan State University Press, 1964.

Wright, Mrs. D. Giraud. *A Southern Girl in '61: The Wartime Memories of a Confederate Senator's Daughter*. New York: Doubleday, Page, 1905.

Young, Joseph Willis. *The Personal Letters of Captain Joseph Willis Young: 97th Regiment, Indiana Volunteers, 4th Division, 15th A.C., Army of the United States, Civil War*. Bloomington, Ind.: Monroe County Historical Society, 1974.

Zink, Steven D., ed. " 'if I was thare I could tel you A good bit more': The Civil War Letters of Private Jackson Davis." *Indiana Magazine of History* 78 (March 1982): 35–58.

SECONDARY SOURCES

Abbott, Edith. "The Civil War and the Crime Wave of 1865–1870." *Social Service Review* 1 (June 1927): 212–34.

Adams, David Wallace, and Victor Edmonds. "Making Your Move: The Educational Significance of the American Board Game, 1832–1904." *History of Education Quarterly* 17 (Winter 1977): 359–84.

Adler, Norman, and Charles Harrington, eds. *The Learning of Political Behavior*. Glenview, Ill.: Scott, Foresman, 1970.

Arksey, Laura, Nancy Pries, and Mencia Reed. *American Diaries*. Vol. 2, *Diaries Written from 1845 to 1980*. Detroit: Gale Research, 1987.

Ash, Stephen V. *When the Yankees Came: Conflict and Chaos in the Occupied South, 1861–1865*. Chapel Hill: University of North Carolina Press, 1995.

Ayers, Edward L. *The Promise of the New South: Life after Reconstruction*. New York: Oxford University Press, 1992.

Bailey, Fred Arthur. "Free Speech and the 'Lost Cause' in Texas: A Study of Social Control in the New South." *Southwestern Historical Quarterly* 97 (January 1994): 453–78.

———. "The Textbooks of the 'Lost Cause': Censorship and the Creation of Southern State Histories." *Georgia Historical Quarterly* 75 (Fall 1991): 507–33.

Bardaglio, Peter W. "The Children of Jubilee: African American Childhood in Wartime." In *Divided Houses: Gender and the Civil War*, edited by Catherine Clinton and Nina Silber, 213–29. New York: Oxford University Press, 1992.

Barenholtz, Bernard, and Inez McClintock. *American Antique Toys, 1830–1900*. New York: Abrams, 1980.

Beattie, Betsy. "Migrants and Millworkers: The French Canadian Population of Burlington and Colchester, 1860–1870." *Vermont History* 60 (Spring 1992): 95–117.

Becker, Carl M. " 'Disloyalty' and the Dayton Public Schools." *Civil War History* 11 (March 1965): 58–68.

Bellamy, Edward. *The Blindman's World and Other Stories*. Boston: Houghton Mifflin, 1898.

Berlinsky, Ellen B., and Henry B. Biller. *Parental Death and Psychological Development*. Lexington, Mass.: Lexington Books, 1982.

Bernstein, Iver. *The New York City Draft Riots: Their Significance for American Society and Politics in the Age of the Civil War*. New York: Oxford University Press, 1990.

Berry, Mary Frances. *The Politics of Parenthood: Child Care, Women's Rights, and the Myth of the Good Mother*. New York: Viking, 1993.

Bigelow, Martha Mitchell. "Vicksburg: Experiment in Freedom." *Journal of Mississippi History* 26 (February–November 1964): 28–44.

Billman, Carol. "McGuffey's Readers and Alger's Fiction: The Gospel of Virtue According to Popular Children's Literature." *Journal of Popular Culture* 11 (Winter 1977): 614–19.

Black, Robert L. *The Cincinnati Orphan Asylum*. Cincinnati: Robert L. Black, 1952.

Blair, William A. "Barbarians at Fredericksburg's Gate: The Impact of the Union Army on Civilians." In *The Fredericksburg Campaign: Decision on the Rappahannock*, edited by Gary W. Gallagher, 142–70. Chapel Hill: University of North Carolina Press, 1995.

Blanchard, Paula. *Sarah Orne Jewett: Her World and Her Work*. Reading, Mass.: Maddison-Wesley, 1994.

Blassingame, John W. *The Slave Community: Plantation Life in the Antebellum South*. 2nd ed. New York: Oxford University Press, 1979.

Bleyer, Herman. "Milwaukee's Civil War Newsboys." *Milwaukee History* 14 (Summer 1991): 70–72.

Blight, David W. " 'What Will Peace among the Whites Bring?': Reunion and Race in the Struggle over the Memory of the Civil War in American Culture." *Massachusetts Review* 34 (Autumn 1993): 393–410.

Bloom, Robert L. " 'We Never Expected a Battle': The Civilians at Gettysburg, 1863." *Pennsylvania History* 55 (October 1988): 161–200.

Bloomfield, Maxwell. "Wartime Drama: The Theater in Washington, 1861–1865." *Maryland Historical Magazine* 64 (Winter 1969): 342–411.

Blum, John Morton, ed. *Yesterday's Children: An Anthology Compiled from the Pages of Our Young Folks, 1865–1873*. Boston: Houghton Mifflin, 1959.

Bodman, Frank. "War Conditions and the Mental Health of the Child." *British Medical Journal* 12 (October 4, 1941): 486–88.

Bogen, Hyman. *The Luckiest Orphans: A History of the Hebrew Orphan Asylum of New York*. Urbana: University of Illinois Press, 1992.

Bohannon, Keith. "Cadets, Drillmasters, Draft Dodgers, and Soldiers: The Georgia Military Institute during the Civil War." *Georgia Historical Quarterly* 79 (Spring 1995): 5–29.

Boles, John B. "Jacob Abbott and the Rollo Books: New England Culture for Children." *Journal of Popular Culture* 6 (Spring 1972): 507–28.

Borchert, James. *Alley Life in Washington: Family, Community, Religion, and Folklife in the City, 1850–1970*. Urbana: University of Illinois Press, 1980.

Bosile, Leon. " 'Soiled Dresses Were Better Than Soiled Modesty': Decency and Delinquency in Columbus, Georgia, 1864–1865." *Lincoln Herald* 83 (Spring 1981): 575–78.

Bowman, Sylvia E. *The Year 2000: A Critical Biography of Edward Bellamy*. New York: Bookman Associates, 1958.

Boylan, Anne M. *Sunday School: The Formation of an American Institution, 1790–1880*. New Haven: Yale University Press, 1988.

Brady, Patricia. "Trials and Tribulations: American Missionary Association Teachers and Black Education in Occupied New Orleans, 1862–1864." *Louisiana History* 31 (Winter 1990): 5–20.

Branch, E. Douglas. *The Sentimental Years, 1836–1860*. New York: Appleton, 1934. Reprint, New York: Hill and Wang, 1965.

Bremner, Robert H. *The Public Good: Philanthropy and Welfare in the Civil War Era*. New York: Knopf, 1980.

Brenzel, Barbara M. *Daughters of the State: A Social Portrait of the First Reform School for Girls in North America, 1856–1905*. Cambridge, Mass.: MIT Press, 1983.

Brockett, O. G., and Lenyth Brockett. "Civil War Theater: Contemporary Treatments." *Civil War History* 1 (September 1955): 229–50.

Brown, Richard D. *Modernization: The Transformation of American Life, 1600–1865.* New York: Hill and Wang, 1976.

Bruce, Dickson D., Jr. *Archibald Grimké: Portrait of a Black Independent.* Baton Rouge: Louisiana State University Press, 1993.

———. "Play, Work, and Ethics in the Old South." *Southern Folklore Quarterly* 40 (1977): 33–51.

Buck, Paul H. *The Road to Reunion, 1865–1900.* New York: Vintage, 1937.

Burnett, John, ed. *Destiny Obscure: Autobiographies of Childhood, Education, and Family from the 1820s to the 1920s.* London: Penguin, 1982.

Bush, Robert, ed. *Grace King: A Southern Destiny.* Baton Rouge: Louisiana State University Press, 1983.

———. *Grace King of New Orleans: A Selection of Her Writings.* Baton Rouge: Louisiana State University Press, 1973.

———. "Will N. Harben's Northern Georgia Fiction." *Mississippi Quarterly* 20 (1967): 103–17.

Butchart, Ronald E. *Northern Schools, Southern Blacks, and Reconstruction: Freedmen's Education, 1862–1875.* Westport, Conn.: Greenwood, 1980.

Bynum, Hartwell T. "Sherman's Expulsion of the Roswell Women." *Georgia Historical Quarterly* 54 (Summer 1970): 169–82.

Bynum, Victoria E. *Unruly Women: The Politics of Social and Sexual Control in the Old South.* Chapel Hill: University of North Carolina Press, 1992.

Cairns, Ed. *Caught in Crossfire: Children and the Northern Ireland Conflict.* Belfast: Appletree; Syracuse: Syracuse University Press, 1987.

Caldwell, B. M., and H. N. Riccinti, eds. *Review of Child Development Research III: Child Development and Social Policy.* Chicago: University of Chicago Press, 1973.

Calvert, Karin. *Children in the House: The Material Culture of Early Childhood, 1600–1900.* Boston: Northeastern University Press, 1992.

Campbell, Randolph B. *An Empire for Slavery: The Peculiar Institution in Texas, 1821–1865.* Baton Rouge: Louisiana State University Press, 1989.

Capers, Gerald. "Confederates and Yankees in Occupied New Orleans, 1862–1865." *Journal of Southern History* 30 (November 1964): 405–26.

Caplan, Frank, and Theresa Caplan. *The Power of Play.* New York: Anchor, 1974.

Carnes, Mark, and Clyde Griffin, eds. *Meaning for Manhood: Constructions of Masculinity in Victorian America.* Chicago: University of Chicago Press, 1990.

Carpenter, Charles. *History of American Schoolbooks.* Philadelphia: University of Pennsylvania Press, 1963.

Cashin, Joan F. *Our Common Affairs: Texts from Women in the Old South.* Baltimore: Johns Hopkins University Press, 1996.

Cawelti, John G. *Apostles of the Self-Made Man*. Chicago: University of Chicago Press, 1965.

Censer, Jane Turner. *North Carolina Planters and Their Children, 1800–1860*. Baton Rouge: Louisiana State University Press, 1984.

Cimprich, John. *Slavery's End in Tennessee, 1861–1865*. University: University of Alabama Press, 1985.

Clausen, Christopher. "Some Confederate Ideas about Education." *Mississippi Quarterly* 30 (Spring 1977): 235–48.

Clement, Priscilla Ferguson. "Children and Charity: Orphanages in New Orleans, 1817–1914." *Louisiana History* 27 (Fall 1986): 337–52.

Click, Patricia C. *The Spirit of the Times: Amusements in Nineteenth-Century Baltimore, Norfolk, and Richmond*. Charlottesville: University Press of Virginia, 1989.

Clinton, Catherine. *Tara Revisited: Women, War, and the Plantation Legend*. New York: Abbeville, 1995.

Cogan, Frances. *All-American Girl: The Ideal of Real Womanhood in Mid-Nineteenth-Century America*. Athens: University of Georgia Press, 1989.

Cohen, William. *At Freedom's Edge: Black Mobility and the Southern White Quest for Racial Control, 1861–1915*. Baton Rouge: Louisiana State University Press, 1991.

Cole, Gerald L. *Civil War Eyewitnesses: An Annotated Bibliography of Books and Articles, 1955–1986*. Columbia: University of South Carolina Press, 1988.

Coles, Robert. *The Political Life of Children*. Boston: Atlantic Monthly Press, 1986.

Connell, R. W. *The Child's Construction of Politics*. Melbourne: Melbourne University Press, 1970.

Connerton, Paul. *How Societies Remember*. Cambridge: Cambridge University Press, 1989.

Cook, Raymond Allen. *Fire from the Flint: The Amazing Careers of Thomas Dixon*. Winston-Salem, N.C.: John F. Blair, 1968.

Cooper, John Milton, Jr. *Walter Hines Page: The Southerner as American, 1855–1918*. Chapel Hill: University of North Carolina Press, 1977.

———. *The Warrior and the Priest: Woodrow Wilson and Theodore Roosevelt*. Cambridge, Mass.: Harvard University Press, 1983.

"The Cost of a Bombing Error in Vietnam." *Life*, June 23, 1972, 4–5.

Cotner, Robert C. *James Stephen Hogg: A Biography*. Austin: University of Texas Press, 1959.

Cott, Nancy F. "Notes toward an Interpretation of Antebellum Childrearing." *Psychohistory Review* 6 (1978): 4–20.

Crandell, John C. "Patriotism and Humanitarian Reform in Children's Literature, 1825–1860." *American Quarterly* 21 (Spring 1969): 3–22.

Cremin, Lawrence. *American Education: The National Experience, 1783–1876*. New York: Harper, 1980.

Crume, John B. "Children's Magazines, 1826–1857." *Journal of Popular Culture* 6 (Spring 1973): 698–707.
Crunden, Robert M. *Ministers of Reform: The Progressives' Achievement in American Civilization, 1889–1920.* New York: BasicBooks, 1982.
Csikszentmihaly, Mihaly, and Reed Larson. *Being Adolescent: Conflict and Growth in the Teenage Years.* New York: BasicBooks, 1984.
Culpepper, Marilyn Mayer. *Trials and Triumphs: Women of the American Civil War.* East Lansing: Michigan State University Press, 1991.
Current-Garcia, Eugene. *O. Henry.* New York: Twayne, 1965.
Dalton, Kathleen. "Theodore Roosevelt and the Idea of War." *Theodore Roosevelt Association Journal* 7 (Fall 1981): 6–12.
Daniels, Elizabeth. "The Children of Gettysburg." *American Heritage* 40 (May–June 1989): 97–107.
Darling, Richard L. *The Rise of Children's Book Reviewing in America, 1865–1881.* New York: R. W. Bowker, 1968.
Davey, Thomas. *A Generation Divided: German Children and the Berlin Wall.* Durham, N.C.: Duke University Press, 1987.
Davis, Charles T., and Henry Louis Gates Jr., eds. *The Slave's Narrative.* New York: Oxford University Press, 1985.
Davis, Glenn. *Childhood and History in America.* New York: Psychohistory Press, 1976.
Davis, O. L., Jr. "The Educational Association of the C.S.A." *Civil War History* 10 (March 1964): 67–79.
Davis, Stephen. " 'A Very Barbarous Mode of Carrying On War': Sherman's Artillery Bombardment of Atlanta, July 20–August 24, 1864." *Georgia Historical Quarterly* 79 (Spring 1995): 57–90.
Davis, Susan G. *Parades and Power: Street Theatre in Nineteenth-Century Philadelphia.* Philadelphia: Temple University Press, 1986.
Davis, William C., ed. *Image of War.* 6 vols. New York: Doubleday, 1981–84.
Dean, Eric T., Jr. " 'We Will All Be Lost and Destroyed': Post-Traumatic Stress Disorder and the Civil War." *Civil War History* 37 (June 1991): 138–53.
De Boer, Clara Merritt. *His Truth Is Marching On: African Americans Who Taught the Freedmen for the American Missionary Association, 1861–1877.* New York: Garland, 1995.
Degler, Carl. *At Odds: Women and the Family in America from the Revolution to the Present.* New York: Oxford University Press, 1980.
Demos, John. *Past, Present, and Personal: The Family and the Life Course in American History.* New York: Oxford University Press, 1986.
Dennis, Lee. *Warman's Antique American Games, 1840–1940.* Elkins Park, Pa.: Warman, 1986.
Diffley, Kathleen. *Where My Heart Is Turning Ever: Civil War Stories and Constitutional Reform, 1861–1876.* Athens: University of Georgia Press, 1992.
Dodge, Cole P., and Magne Raundalen, eds. *Reaching Children in War:*

Sudan, Uganda, and Mozambique. Bergen, Norway: Sigma Forlag;
Uppsala, Sweden: Scandinavian Institute of African Studies, 1991.
————. *War, Violence, and Children in Uganda.* Oslo: Norwegian
University Press, 1987.
Dondero, George A. "Why Lincoln Wore a Beard." *Journal of the Illinois
State Historical Society* 24 (July 1931): 321–32.
Downs, Susan Whitelaw, and Michael W. Sherraden. "The Orphan
Asylum in the Nineteenth Century." *Social Service Review* 57 (June
1987): 272–90.
Doyle, Elisabeth Joan. "Nurseries of Treason: Schools in Occupied New
Orleans." *Journal of Southern History* 26 (May 1960): 161–79.
Duncan, Richard R. "The Impact of the Civil War on Education in
Maryland." *Maryland Historical Magazine* 61 (March 1966): 37–52.
Dye, Nancy Schrom, and Daniel Blake Smith. "Mother Love and Infant
Death, 1750–1920." *Journal of American History* 73 (September 1986):
329–53.
Earle, Edward W., ed. *Points of View: The Stereograph in America, a
Cultural History.* Rochester, N.Y.: Visual Studies Workshop, 1979.
Earls, F. "The Impact of Family Stress on the Behavior Adjustment of
Preschool Children." *Massachusetts Journal of Community Health* 1
(Fall/Winter 1980): 7–11.
Easton, David, and Jack Dennis. *Children in the Political System: Origins
of Political Legitimacy.* New York: McGraw-Hill, 1969.
Egan, Susanna. " 'Self'-Conscious History: American Autobiography after
the Civil War." In *American Autobiography: Retrospect and Prospect,*
edited by Paul John Eakin, 70–94. Madison: University of Wisconsin
Press, 1991.
Eisen, George. *Children and Play in the Holocaust: Games among the
Shadows.* Amherst: University of Massachusetts Press, 1988.
Ellis, James M. *Why People Play.* Englewood Cliffs, N.J.: Prentice-Hall,
1973.
Elson, Ruth Miller. *Guardians of Tradition: American Schoolbooks of the
Nineteenth Century.* Lincoln: University of Nebraska Press, 1964.
England, J. Merton. "The Democratic Faith in American Schoolbooks,
1783–1860." *American Quarterly* 15 (Summer 1963): 191–99.
Engs, Robert Francis. *Freedom's First Generation: Black Hampton,
Virginia, 1861–1890.* Philadelphia: University of Pennsylvania Press,
1979.
Escott, Paul D. " 'The Cry of the Sufferers': The Problem of Welfare in the
Confederacy." *Civil War History* 23 (September 1977): 228–40.
Faust, Drew Gilpin. *Mothers of Invention: Women of the Slaveholding
South in the American Civil War.* Chapel Hill: University of North
Carolina Press, 1996.
Fellman, Michael. *Inside War: The Guerilla Conflict in Missouri during the
American Civil War.* New York: Oxford University Press, 1989.
Fen, Sing-Nan. "Notes on the Education of Negroes at Norfolk and

Portsmouth, Virginia, during the Civil War." *Phylon* 28 (Summer 1967): 197–208.

Ferrell, Charles Clifton. " 'The Daughter of the Confederacy': Her Life, Character, and Writings." *Publications of the Mississippi Historical Society* 2 (1899): 69–84.

Fink, Arthur E. "Changing Philosophies and Practices in North Carolina Orphanages." *North Carolina Historical Review* 48 (October 1971): 333–58.

Finkelstein, Barbara. "Pedagogy as Intrusion: Teaching Values in Popular Primary Schools in Nineteenth-Century America." *History of Childhood Quarterly* 2 (Winter 1975): 349–78.

Fisher, Marcella C. "The Orphan's Friend: Charles Collins Townsend and the Orphans' Home of Industry." *Palimpsest* 60 (November/December 1979): 184–96.

Foner, Eric. *Reconstruction: America's Unfinished Revolution, 1863–1877.* New York: Harper and Row, 1988.

Forrester, Rebel C. *Glory and Tears: Obion County, Tennessee, 1860–1870.* Union City, Tenn.: H. A. Lanzer, 1966.

Foster, Gaines M. *Ghosts of the Confederacy: Defeat, the Lost Cause, and the Emergence of the New South.* New York: Oxford University Press, 1987.

———. "The Limitations of Federal Health Care for Freedmen." *Journal of Southern History* 48 (August 1982): 349–72.

Fraser, M. *Children in Conflict.* New York: BasicBooks, 1973.

Frederickson, George. *The Inner Civil War: Northern Intellectuals and the Crisis of the Union.* New York: Harper and Row, 1965.

Furgurson, Ernest B. *Chancellorsville, 1863: The Souls of the Brave.* New York: Knopf, 1992.

Gallarno, George. "How Iowa Cared for Orphans of Her Soldiers of the Civil War." *Annals of Iowa,* 3rd ser., 15 (January 1926): 163–93.

Gallman, J. Matthew. *Mastering Wartime: A Social History of Philadelphia during the Civil War.* Cambridge: Cambridge University Press, 1990.

Garbarino, James, Kathleen Koztelny, and Nancy Dubrow. *No Place to Be a Child: Growing Up in a War Zone.* Lexington, Mass.: Lexington Books, 1991.

Garbarino, James, Nancy Dubrow, Kathleen Koztelny, and Carole Pardo. *Children in Danger: Coping with the Consequences of Community Violence.* San Francisco: Jossey-Bass, 1992.

Gardner, George. "Child Behavior in Nation at War." *Mental Hygiene* 27 (July 1943): 353–69.

Gardner, George E., and Harvey Spencer. "Reactions of Children with Fathers and Brothers in the Armed Forces." *American Journal of Orthopsychiatry* 14 (January 1944): 36–43.

Garmezy, Norman. "Stress-Resistant Children: The Search for Protective Factors." In *Recent Research in Developmental Psychopathology,* edited by J. E. Stevenson, 220–26. Oxford: Pergamon, 1985.

Garmezy, Norman, and Michael Rutter, eds. *Stress, Coping, and Development in Children*. New York: McGraw-Hill, 1983.
Gatewood, Willard B. *Aristocrats of Color: The Black Elite, 1880–1920*. Bloomington: Indiana University Press, 1990.
Gerteis, Louis. *From Contraband to Freedman: Federal Policy toward Southern Blacks, 1861–1865*. Westport, Conn.: Greenwood, 1973.
Gesell, Arnold, and Frances L. Ilg. *The Child from Five to Ten*. New York: Harper and Brothers, 1946.
Ginzberg, Lori D. *Women and the Work of Benevolence: Morality, Politics, and Class in Nineteenth-Century United States*. New Haven: Yale University Press, 1990.
Gittens, Joan. *Poor Relations: The Children of the State in Illinois, 1818–1990*. Urbana: University of Illinois Press, 1994.
Glatthaar, Joseph T. *Forged in Battle: The Civil War Alliance of Black Soldiers and White Officers*. New York: Free Press, 1990.
———. *The March to the Sea and Beyond: Sherman's Troops in the Savannah and Carolinas Campaigns*. New York: New York University Press, 1985.
Gloster, Hugh M. "Charles W. Chesnutt: Pioneer in the Fiction of Negro Life." *Phylon* 2 (Spring 1941): 57–65.
Golay, Michael. *To Gettysburg and Beyond: The Parallel Lives of Joshua Lawrence Chamberlain and Edward Porter Alexander*. New York: Crown, 1994.
Goodman, Mary Ellen. *The Culture of Childhood: Child's-Eye Views of Society and Culture*. New York: Teachers College Press, 1970.
Gordon, Beverly. "A Furor of Benevolence." *Chicago History* 15 (Winter 1986–87): 48–65.
Gould, Lewis L. "Party Conflicts: Republicans versus Democrats, 1877–1901." In *The Gilded Age: Essays on the Origins of Modern America*, edited by Charles W. Calhoun, 215–34. Wilmington, Del.: Scholarly Resources, 1996.
Graham, Hugh Davis, and Ted Robert Gurr, eds. *Violence in America*. Rev. ed. Beverly Hills: Sage, 1979.
Graham, Paul C., comp. *History of the Indiana Soldiers' and Sailors' Orphans' Home, 1865–1904*. Knightstown, Ind.: Home Journal, 1905.
Greenstein, Fred I. *Children and Politics*. New Haven: Yale University Press, 1965.
Grimsley, Mark. *The Hard Hand of War: Union Military Policy toward Southern Civilians, 1861–1865*. Cambridge: Cambridge University Press, 1995.
Griswold, Robert L. *Fatherhood in America: A History*. New York: BasicBooks, 1993.
Gross, Theodore L. *Thomas Nelson Page*. New York: Twayne, 1967.
Grossberg, Michael. *Governing the Hearth: Law and the Family in Nineteenth-Century America*. Chapel Hill: University of North Carolina Press, 1985.

Grudzinska-Gross, Irena, and Jan Tomasz Gross. *Through Children's Eyes: The Soviet Occupation of Poland, the Deportation, 1939-1941.* Stanford: Hoover Institution Press, 1981.

Gumpert, Gustav. "Tad Lincoln and Gus Gumpert." *Journal of the Illinois State Historical Society* 48 (Spring 1955): 41-44.

Halls, W. D. *The Youth of Vichy France.* Oxford: Clarendon, 1981.

Hampsten, Elizabeth. *Read This Only to Yourself: The Private Writings of Midwestern Women, 1880-1915.* Bloomington: Indiana University Press, 1982.

Harbison, J. J., ed. *Children of the Troubles: Children in Northern Ireland.* Belfast: Straumillis College Learning Resources Unit, 1983.

Harbison, J. J. M., and J. I. Harbison. *A Society under Stress: Children and Young People in Northern Ireland.* Somerset: Open Books, 1980.

Harbison, Joan, ed. *Growing Up in Northern Ireland.* Belfast: Straumillis College, 1989.

Harlan, Louis R. *Booker T. Washington: The Making of a Black Leader, 1856-1901.* New York: Oxford University Press, 1972.

Harper, Keith. "The Louisville Baptist Orphan's Home: The Early Years." *Register of the Kentucky Historical Society* 90 (Summer 1992): 236-55.

Harris, Elizabeth. *The Boy and His Press.* Washington, D.C.: Smithsonian Institution Press, 1992.

Harris, William C. "The East Tennessee Relief Movement of 1864-1865." *Tennessee Historical Quarterly* 48 (Summer 1989): 86-96.

Harrsch, Patricia G. " 'This Noble Monument': The Story of the Soldiers' Orphans' Home." *Wisconsin Magazine of History* 76 (Winter 1992-93): 83-120.

Hartmann, Susan M. *The Home Front and Beyond: American Women in the 1940s.* Boston: Twayne, 1982.

Havighurst, Robert J., Walter H. Eaton, John W. Baughman, and Ernest W. Burgess. *The American Veteran Back Home: A Study of Veteran Readjustment.* New York: Longmans, Green, 1951.

Hawes, Joseph M. *Children in Urban Society: Juvenile Delinquency in Nineteenth-Century America.* New York: Oxford University Press, 1971.

Hawes, Joseph M., and Elizabeth I. Nybakken, eds. *American Families: A Research Guide and Historical Handbook.* New York: Greenwood, 1991.

Hearn, Chester G. *Six Years of Hell: Harpers Ferry during the Civil War.* Baton Rouge: Louisiana State University Press, 1996.

Heiges, George L. "The Mount Joy Soldier's Orphan School." *Papers of the Lancaster County Historical Society* 48 (1944): 109-31.

Heininger, Mary Lynn Stevens, et al. *A Century of Childhood, 1820-1920.* Rochester, N.Y.: Margaret Woodbury Strong Museum, 1984.

Helis, Thomas W. "Of Generals and Jurists: The Judicial System of New Orleans under Union Occupation, May 1862-April 1865." *Louisiana History* 29 (Spring 1988): 143-62.

Hendin, Herbert, and Ann Pollinger Haas. *Wounds of War: The*

Psychological Aftermath of Combat in Vietnam. New York: BasicBooks, 1984.

Hendrick, Burton J. *The Training of an American: The Earlier Life and Letters of Walter H. Page, 1855–1913.* Boston: Houghton Mifflin, 1928.

Herron, R. E., and Brian Sutton-Smith, eds. *Child's Play.* New York: John Wiley and Sons, 1971.

Hess, Earl J. *Liberty, Virtue, and Progress: Northerners and Their War for the Union.* New York: New York University Press, 1988.

Hess, Robert D., and Judith V. Torney. *The Development of Political Attitudes in Children.* Chicago: Aldine, 1967.

Higginson, Thomas Wentworth. "Children's Books of the Year." *North American Review* 102 (January–April 1866): 236–49.

History of the Confederate Memorial Associations of the South. New Orleans: Graham Press, 1904.

Hitt, Michael D. *Charged with Treason: Ordeal of 400 Mill Workers during Military Operations in Roswell, Georgia, 1864–1865.* Monroe, N.Y.: Library Research Associates, 1992.

Hoehling, A. A. *Vicksburg: Forty-seven Days of Siege.* Englewood Cliffs, N.J.: Prentice-Hall, 1969.

Hoffert, Sylvia D. *Private Matters: American Attitudes toward Childbearing and Infant Nurture in the Urban North, 1800–1860.* Urbana: University of Illinois Press, 1989.

Holliday, Joseph E. "Relief for Soldiers' Families in Ohio during the Civil War." *Ohio History* 71 (July 1962): 97–112.

Holmes, William F. *The White Chief: James Kimble Vardaman.* Baton Rouge: Louisiana State University Press, 1970.

Holoran, Peter C. *Boston's Wayward Children: Social Services for Homeless Children, 1830–1930.* Rutherford, N.J.: Fairleigh Dickinson University Press, 1989.

Holt, Marilyn Irvin. *The Orphan Trains: Placing Out in America.* Lincoln: University of Nebraska Press, 1992.

Horner, Harlan Hoyt. *Life and Work of Andrew Sloan Draper.* Urbana: University of Illinois Press, 1934.

Hornsby, Alton, Jr. "The Freedmen's Bureau Schools in Texas, 1865–1870." *Southwestern Historical Quarterly* 76 (April 1973): 397–417.

Hughes, Edward W., and William C. McCracken. *History of the Ohio Soldiers' and Sailors' Orphan Home.* Xenia, Ohio: Association of Ex-Pupils, 1963.

Humphrey, James H., ed. *Stress in Childhood.* New York: AMS Press, 1984.

Ichilov, Orit. *Political Socialization, Citizenship Education, and Democracy.* New York: Teachers College Press, 1990.

Inglis, Ruth. *The Children's War: Evacuation, 1939–1945.* London: William Collins Sons, 1989.

Inscoe, John C. "The Confederate Home Front Sanitized: Joel Chandler Harris' *On the Plantation* and Sectional Reconciliation." *Georgia Historical Quarterly* 76 (Fall 1992): 652–74.

Irwin-Zarecka, Iwona. *Frames of Remembrance: The Dynamics of Collective Memory*. New Brunswick, N.J.: Tranaction Publishers, 1994.

Jacoby, George. *Catholic Child Care in Nineteenth-Century New York*. Washington, D.C.: Catholic University of America Press, 1941.

Jenkins, Harold F. *Two Points of View: A History of the Parlor Stereoscope*. Elmira, N.Y.: World in Color Productions, 1957.

Jewett, Sarah Orne. *A Native of Winby and Other Tales*. Boston: Houghton Mifflin, 1893.

Jimerson, Randall C. *The Private Civil War: Popular Thought during the Sectional Conflict*. Baton Rouge: Louisiana State University Press, 1988.

Johannsen, Albert. *The House of Beadle and Adams and Its Dime and Nickel Novels: The Story of a Vanished Literature*. Vol. 1. Norman: University of Oklahoma Press, 1950.

Johnson, Peter Leo. *Daughters of Charity in Milwaukee, 1846–1946*. Milwaukee: Daughters or Charity, 1946.

Jones, Newton B. "The Charleston Orphan House, 1860–1876." *South Carolina Historical Magazine* 62 (October 1961): 206–14.

Kaestle, Carl F. *Pillars of the Republic: Common Schools and American Society, 1780–1860*. New York: Hill and Wang, 1983.

Kasson, John F. *Rudeness and Civility: Manners in Nineteenth-Century Urban America*. New York: Hill and Wang, 1990.

Katz, Michael B. *The Irony of Early School Reform: Educational Innovation in Mid-Nineteenth-Century Massachusetts*. Cambridge, Mass.: Harvard University Press, 1968.

Kelly, R. Gordon, ed. *Children's Periodicals of the United States*. Westport, Conn.: Greenwood, 1984.

———. *Mother Was a Lady: Self and Society in Selected American Children's Periodicals, 1865–1890*. Westport, Conn.: Greenwood, 1974.

Kelton, Anne. "A Boy Needs a Man." *Parents' Magazine*, April 1943, 31, 96.

Kennedy, David. *Over Here: The First World War and American Society*. New York: Oxford University Press, 1980.

Kennett, Lee. *Marching through Georgia: The Story of Soldiers and Civilians during Sherman's Campaign*. New York: HarperCollins, 1995.

Kett, Joseph F. "Growing Up in Rural New England, 1800–1840." In *Anonymous Americans: Explorations in Nineteenth-Century Social History*, edited by Tamara K. Hareven, 1–16. Englewood Cliffs, N.J.: Prentice-Hall, 1971.

———. *Rites of Passage: Adolescence in America, 1790 to the Present*. New York: BasicBooks, 1977.

Kiefer, Monica Mary. *American Children through Their Books, 1700–1835*. Philadelphia: University of Pennsylvania Press, 1948.

Kimmel, Michael. *Manhood in America: A Cultural History*. New York: Free Press, 1996.

King, Wilma. *Stolen Childhood: Slave Youth in Nineteenth-Century America*. Bloomington: Indiana University Press, 1995.

Knight, Grant C. *James Lane Allen and the Genteel Tradition*. Chapel Hill: University of North Carolina Press, 1935.

Kotre, John. *White Gloves: How We Create Ourselves through Memory*. New York: Free Press, 1995.

Kousser, J. Morgan. *The Shaping of Southern Politics: Suffrage Restriction and the Establishment of the One-Party South, 1880–1910*. New Haven: Yale University Press, 1974.

Kuhn, Anne C. *The Mother's Role in Childhood Education: New England Concepts, 1830–1860*. New Haven: Yale University Press, 1947.

Lack, Paul D. "Law and Disorder in Confederate Atlanta." *Georgia Historical Quarterly* 66 (Summer 1982): 171–95.

Lahad, Mooli, and Afra Ayalon. "Preserving Children's Mental Health under Threat of War." In *Children and Death*, edited by Danai Papadatou and Costas Papadatou, 65–76. New York: Hemisphere, 1991.

Langmeier, J., and Z. Matejcek. *Psychological Deprivation in Childhood*. New York: Halsted Press, 1975.

Leloudis, James L. *Schooling the New South: Pedagogy, Self, and Society in North Carolina, 1880–1920*. Chapel Hill: University of North Carolina Press, 1996.

Levine, Lawrence W. *Black Culture, Black Consciousness: Afro-American Folk Thought from Slavery to Freedom*. New York: Oxford University Press, 1977.

Levy, George. *To Die in Chicago: Confederate Prisoners at Camp Douglas, 1862–1865*. Evanston, Ill.: Evanston Pub. Co., 1994.

Levy, Joseph. *Play Behavior*. New York: John Wiley and Sons, 1978.

Lifton, Robert Jay. *Home from the War: Vietnam Veterans, Neither Victims nor Executioners*. New York: BasicBooks, 1973.

Linderman, Gerald F. *Embattled Courage: The Experience of Combat in the American Civil War*. New York: Free Press, 1987.

———. *The Mirror of War: American Society and the Spanish-American War*. Ann Arbor: University of Michigan Press, 1974.

Litwack, Leon F. *Been in the Storm So Long: The Aftermath of Slavery*. New York: Vintage, 1980.

Lively, Robert A. *Fiction Fights the Civil War: An Unfinished Chapter in the Literary History of the American People*. Chapel Hill: University of North Carolina Press, 1957.

Lord, Francis A., and Arthur Wise. *Bands and Drummer Boys of the Civil War*. New York: Yoseloff, 1966.

Lowenthal, David. *The Past Is a Foreign Country*. Cambridge: Cambridge University Press, 1985.

Lowry, Thomas P. *The Story the Soldiers Wouldn't Tell: Sex in the Civil War*. Mechanicsburg, Pa.: Stackpole, 1994.

Lyftogt, Kenneth L. *From Blue Mills to Columbia: Cedar Falls and the Civil War*. Ames: Iowa State University Press, 1993.

Lystad, Mary, ed. *Violence in the Home: Interdisciplinary Perspectives*. New York: Brunner/Mazel, 1986.

Mabee, Carleton. "Charity in Travail: Two Orphan Asylums for Blacks." *New York History* 55 (January 1974): 55–77.

McAlexander, Hubert Horton. *The Prodigal Daughter: A Biography of Sherwood Bonner*. Baton Rouge: Louisiana State University Press, 1981.

McCardell, John. *The Idea of a Southern Nation: Southern Nationalists and Southern Nationalism, 1830–1860*. New York: Norton, 1979.

McCausland, Clare L. *Children of Circumstances: A History of the First 125 Years (1849–1974) of the Chicago Child Care Society*. Chicago: Chicago Child Care Society, 1976.

McClintock, Megan J. "Civil War Pensions and the Reconstruction of Union Families." *Journal of American History* 83 (September 1996): 456–80.

McClinton, Katharine Morrison. *Antiques of American Childhood*. New York: Clarkson N. Potter, 1970.

MacLeod, Anne Scott. *A Moral Tale: Children's Fiction and American Culture, 1820–1860*. Hamden, Conn.: Archon, 1975.

McMillen, Sally G. "Antebellum Southern Fathers and the Health Care of Children." *Journal of Southern History* 60 (August 1994): 513–32.

———. *Motherhood in the Old South: Pregnancy, Childbirth, and Infant Rearing*. Baton Rouge: Louisiana State University, 1990.

McPherson, James M. *The Abolitionist Legacy: From Reconstruction to the NAACP*. Princeton: Princeton University Press, 1975.

———. *For Cause and Comrades: Why Men Fought in the Civil War*. New York: Oxford University Press, 1997.

———. *Ordeal by Fire: The Civil War and Reconstruction*. 2nd ed. New York: McGraw-Hill, 1992.

———. *What They Fought For, 1861–1865*. Baton Rouge: Louisiana State University Press, 1994.

Marsh, John L. "Drama and Spectacle by the Yard: The Panorama in America." *Journal of Popular Culture* 10 (Winter 1976): 581–92.

Marstine, Janet. "Panoramas and the Cyclorama in Pittsburgh: The Beginning and the End of a Unique Entertainment Genre." *Western Pennsylvania Historical Magazine* 69 (January 1986): 21–36.

Marten, James. "The Making of a Carpetbagger: George S. Denison and the South, 1854–1866." *Louisiana History* 34 (Spring 1993): 133–60.

———. *Texas Divided: Loyalty and Dissent in the Lone Star State, 1856–1874*. Lexington: University Press of Kentucky, 1990.

———. " 'What Is to Become of the Negro?': White Reaction to Emancipation in Texas." *Mid-America* 73 (April–July 1991): 115–34.

"Massacre of the Innocents." *Nation*, February 4, 1991, 114.

Massey, Mary Elizabeth. *Refugee Life in the Confederacy*. Baton Rouge: Louisiana State University Press, 1964.

Medrich, Elliott A., Judith Roizen, Victory Rubin, and Stuart Buckely. *The Serious Business of Growing Up: A Study of Children's Lives outside School*. Berkeley: University of California Press, 1982.

Meigs, Cornelia, Anne Thaxter Eaton, Elizabeth Nesbitt, and Ruth Hill

Viguers. *A Critical History of Children's Literature*. Rev. ed. New York: Macmillan, 1969.

Menendez, Albert J. *Civil War Novels: An Annotated Bibliography*. New York: Garland, 1986.

Mennel, Robert M. *Thorns and Thistles: Juvenile Delinquents in the United States, 1825–1940*. Hanover, N.H.: University Press of New England, 1973.

Mergen, Bernard. *Play and Playthings: A Reference Guide*. Westport, Conn.: Greenwood, 1982.

Merrill, Francis E. *Social Problems on the Home Front: A Study of War-time Influences*. New York: Harper and Brothers, 1948.

Messner, William F. "Black Education in Louisiana, 1863–1865." *Civil War History* 22 (March 1976): 41–59.

Meyer, Howard N. *Colonel of the Black Regiment: The Life of Thomas Wentworth Higginson*. New York: Norton, 1967.

Milgram, Norman A., ed. *Stress and Anxiety*. Vol. 8. Washington, D.C.: Hemisphere, 1982.

Miller, Francis T., ed. *The Photographic History of the Civil War*. 10 vols. New York: Review of Reviews, 1911. Reprint, Yoseloff, 1957.

Minnich, Harvey. *William Holmes McGuffey and His Readers*. New York: American Book, 1936.

Mintz, Steven. *A Prison of Expectations: The Family in Victorian Culture*. New York: New York University Press, 1983.

Mitchell, Reid. *Civil War Soldiers: Their Expectations and Their Experiences*. New York: Viking, 1988.

—————. *The Vacant Chair: The Northern Soldier Leaves Home*. New York: Oxford University Press, 1993.

Mitterauer, Michael. *A History of Youth*. Oxford: Blackwell, 1992.

Mohr, Clarence L. *On the Threshold of Freedom: Masters and Slaves in Civil War Georgia*. Athens: University of Georgia Press, 1986.

Moorhead, James H. *American Apocalypse: Yankee Protestants and the Civil War, 1860–1869*. New Haven: Yale University Press, 1978.

Moran, Gerald F., and Maris A. Vinovskis. *Religion, Family, and the Life Course: Explorations in the Social History of Early America*. Ann Arbor: University of Michigan Press, 1992.

Morris, Robert C. *Reading, 'Riting, and Reconstruction: The Education of Freedmen in the South, 1861–1870*. Chicago: University of Chicago Press, 1981.

Morton, Marian J. "Homes for Poverty's Children: Cleveland's Orphanages, 1851–1933." *Ohio History* 98 (Winter–Spring 1989): 5–22.

Murphy, Jim. *The Boys' War: Confederate and Union Soldiers Talk about the Civil War*. New York: Clarion, 1990.

Myers, Robert M. *Reluctant Expatriate: The Life of Harold Frederic*. Westport, Conn.: Greenwood, 1995.

Nardinelli, Clark. *Child Labor and the Industrial Revolution*. Bloomington: Indiana University Press, 1990.

Nasaw, David. *Children of the City: At Work and at Play.* New York: Oxford University Press, 1985.

Neely, Mark E., Jr., and Harold Holzer. *Mine Eyes Have Seen the Glory: The Civil War in Art.* New York: Orion, 1993.

Nietz, John A. *Old Textbooks.* Pittsburgh: University of Pittsburgh Press, 1961.

Nixon, Raymond B. *Henry W. Grady, Spokesman of the New South.* New York: Knopf, 1943.

Norse, Clifford C. "School Life of Amanda Worthington of Washington County, 1857–1862." *Journal of Mississippi History* 34 (May 1972): 107–17.

"On the Battle Field, in the Hospital, in the Parlor, at the Fair." *Iowa Heritage Illustrated* 77 (Spring 1996): 24.

Overton, Marion F. "Wintertime in Old Brooklyn." *Long Island Forum* 11 (February 1948): 23–37.

Page, Roswell. *Thomas Nelson Page: A Memoir of a Virginian Gentleman.* New York: Charles Scribner's Sons, 1923.

Paludan, Phillip Shaw. *"A People's Contest": The Union and Civil War, 1861–1865.* New York: Harper and Row, 1988.

Parke, Ross D., and Peter N. Stearns. "Fathers and Child Rearing." In *Children in Time and Place: Developmental and Historical Insights,* edited by Glen H. Elder Jr., John Modell, and Ross D. Parke, 147–70. Cambridge: Cambridge University Press, 1993.

Parrish, T. Michael, and Robert W. Willingham Jr. *Confederate Imprints: A Bibliography of Southern Publications from Secession to Surrender.* Austin: Jenkins, 1984.

Paul, James Laughery. *Pennsylvania's Soldiers' Orphan Schools.* Philadelphia: Claxton and Remson, 1876.

Peterson, Merrill D. *Lincoln in American Memory.* New York: Oxford University Press, 1994.

Piaget, Jean. *Play, Dreams, and Imitation in Childhood.* New York: Norton, 1962.

Pickering, Sam. "A Boy's Own War." *New England Quarterly* 48 (September 1975): 362–77.

"Picture of the Week." *Life,* October 4, 1937, 102.

Piehler, G. Kurt. *Remembering War the American Way.* Washington, D.C.: Smithsonian Institution Press, 1995.

Pierce, S. W. "The Iowa Home for Soldiers' Orphans." In *Proceedings of the Sixth National Conference of Charities and Corrections.* New York, 1879.

Platt, Anthony. *The Child Savers: The Invention of Delinquency.* 2nd ed. Chicago: University of Chicago Press, 1977.

Pollock, Linda A. *Forgotten Children: Parent-Child Relations from 1500 to 1900.* Cambridge: Cambridge University Press, 1983.

Poppenheim, Mary B., et al. *The History of the United Daughters of the Confederacy.* Richmond: Garrett and Massie, 1938.

Pressly, Thomas J. *Americans Interpret Their Civil War*. Princeton:
Princeton University Press, 1954. Reprint, New York: Free Press, 1965.

Preston, Ralph C. "What Children Think of War Play." *Parents' Magazine*,
March 1943, 21, 79.

Price, Kenneth M., and Susan Belasco Smith. *Periodical Literature in
Nineteenth-Century America*. Charlottesville: University Press of
Virginia, 1995.

Proctor, Samuel. *Napoleon Bonaparte Broward: Florida's Fighting
Democrat*. Gainesville: University of Florida Press, 1950.

Pulley, Raymond H. *Old Virginia Restored: An Interpretation of the
Progressive Impulse, 1870–1930*. Charlottesville: University Press of
Virginia, 1968.

Punamaki, R. L. "Childhood in the Shadow of War: A Psychological Study
on Attitudes and Emotional Life of Israeli and Palestinian Children."
Current Research on Peace and Violence 5 (1982): 26–41.

Quinlaven, Mary E. "Race Relations in the Antebellum Children's
Literature of Jacob Abbott." *Journal of Popular Culture* 16 (Summer
1982): 27–36.

Quinn, Camilla A. "Soldiers on Our Streets: The Effects of a Civil War
Military Camp on the Springfield Community." *Illinois Historical
Journal* 86 (Winter 1993): 245–56.

Rable, George C. *But There Was No Peace: The Role of Violence in the
Politics of Reconstruction*. Athens: University of Georgia Press, 1984.

———. *Civil Wars: Women and the Crisis of Southern Nationalism*.
Urbana: University of Illinois Press, 1989.

———. *The Confederate Republic: A Revolution against Politics*. Chapel
Hill: University of North Carolina Press, 1994.

Randall, Ruth Painter. *Lincoln's Sons*. Boston: Little, Brown, 1955.

Rantman, Arthur L. "Children's Play in Wartime." *Mental Hygiene* 27
(October 1943): 549–53.

Rawlings, Kevin. *We Were Marching on Christmas Day: A History and
Chronicle of Christmas during the Civil War*. Baltimore: Toomey, 1995.

Reaver, J. Russell, ed. "Letters of Joel C. Blake." *Apalachee* 5 (1957–62):
5–25.

Richardson, Joe M. "The American Missionary Association and Black
Education in Civil War Missouri." *Missouri Historical Review* 69 (July
1975): 433–48.

———. *Christian Reconstruction: The American Missionary Association
and Southern Blacks, 1861–1890*. Athens: University of Georgia Press,
1986.

Richter, Wendy. "The Impact of the Civil War on Hot Springs, Arkansas."
Arkansas Historical Quarterly 43 (Summer 1984): 125–42.

Robbins, Peggy. "Jim Limber and the Davises." *Civil War Times
Illustrated* 17 (November 1978): 22–27.

Robinson, Charles M., III. *The Court-Martial of Lieutenant Henry
Flipper*. El Paso: University of Texas, 1994.

Robinson, Norborne T. N., III. "Blind Tom, Musical Prodigy." *Georgia Historical Quarterly* 51 (September 1967): 336–58.
Rockefeller, Steven C. *John Dewey: Religious Faith and Democratic Humanitarianism.* New York: Columbia University Press, 1991.
Rodgers, Daniel T. "Socializing Middle-Class Children: Institutions, Fables, and Work Values in Nineteenth-Century America." *Journal of Social History* 3 (Spring 1980): 354–67.
Roller, Bert. *Children in American Poetry, 1610–1900.* Nashville: George Peabody College for Teachers, 1930.
Romanofsky, Peter. "Saving the Lives of the City's Foundlings: The Joint Committee and New York City Child Care Methods, 1860–1907." *New-York Historical Society Quarterly* 61 (January/April 1977): 49–68.
Rose, Anne C. *Victorian America and the Civil War.* Cambridge: Cambridge University Press, 1992.
Rose, Willie Lee. *Rehearsal for Reconstruction: The Port Royal Experiment.* New York: Vintage, 1967.
Rosenblatt, Roger. *Children of War.* Garden City, N.Y.: Anchor/Doubleday, 1983.
Rosenburg, R. B. *Living Monuments: Confederate Soldiers' Homes in the New South.* Chapel Hill: University of North Carolina Press, 1993.
Rossie, Alice S., Jerome Kagan, and Tamara K. Hareven, eds. *The Family.* New York: Norton, 1977.
Roth, Francis Xavier. *History of St. Vincent's Orphan Asylum, Tacony, Philadelphia: A Memoir of Its Diamond Jubilee, 1855–1933.* Philadelphia: n.p., 1934.
Rowland, Elizabeth McL. Gould. *Story of the Girls' High School of Portland, Maine, 1850–1863.* Lee, Maine: Press of the Valley Gleaner, 1897.
Ryan, Mary P. *Cradle of the Middle Class: The Family in Oneida County, New York, 1790–1865.* New York: Cambridge University Press, 1981.
———. *The Empire of the Mother: American Writing about Domesticity, 1830–1860.* New York: Haworth, 1982.
Schorsch, Anita. *Images of Childhood: An Illustrated Social History.* Pittstown, N.J.: Main Street Press, 1979.
Schultz, Stanley K. *The Culture Factory: Boston Public Schools, 1789–1860.* New York: Oxford University Press, 1973.
Schwartz, David C., and Sandra Kenyon Schwartz, eds. *New Directions in Political Socialization.* New York: Free Press, 1975.
Scott, Rebecca. "The Battle over the Child: Child Apprenticeship and the Freedmen's Bureau in North Carolina." *Prologue* 10 (Summer 1978): 100–113.
Seyerstad, Per. *Kate Chopin: A Critical Biography.* Baton Rouge: Louisiana State University Press, 1969.
Sigel, Roberta S., and Marilyn B. Hoskin. *The Political Involvement of Adolescents.* New Brunswick, N.J.: Rutgers University Press, 1981.

Silverthorne, Elizabeth. *Sarah Orne Jewett: A Writer's Life*. Woodstock, N.Y.: Overlook Press, 1993.

Simkins, Francis Butler. *Pitchfork Ben Tillman, South Carolinian*. Baton Rouge: Louisiana State University Press, 1944.

Small, Sandra E. "The Yankee Schoolmarm in Freedmen's Schools: An Analysis of Attitudes." *Journal of Southern History* 45 (August 1979): 381–402.

Speierl, Charles F. "Civil War Veterans and Patriotism in New Jersey Schools." *New Jersey History* 110 (Fall/Winter 1993): 41–55.

Stampp, Kenneth. *And the War Came: The North and the Secession Crisis, 1860–1861*. Baton Rouge: Louisiana State University Press, 1950.

Stearns, Peter N., and Timothy Haggerty. "The Role of Fear: Transitions in American Emotional Standards for Children, 1850–1950." *American Historical Review* 96 (February 1991): 63–94.

Stevenson, Louise L. *The Victorian Homefront: American Thought and Culture, 1860–1880*. New York: Twayne, 1991.

Stolz, Lois Meek, et al. *Father Relations of War-Born Children: The Effect of Postwar Adjustment of Fathers on the Behavior and Personality of First Children Born While the Fathers Were at War*. New York: Greenwood, 1968.

Sutherland, Daniel E. *The Expansion of Everyday Life, 1860–1876*. New York: Harper and Row, 1989.

———. *Seasons of War: The Ordeal of a Confederate Community, 1861–1865*. New York: Free Press, 1995.

Sutton, John R. *Stubborn Children: Controlling Delinquency in the United States, 1640–1981*. Berkeley: University of California Press, 1988.

Taylor, Helen. *Gender, Race, and Region in the Writings of Grace King, Ruth McEnery Stuart, and Kate Chopin*. Baton Rouge: Louisiana State University Press, 1989.

Theodore, Terry. "The Confederate Theatre in the Deep South." *Lincoln Herald* 77 (Summer 1975): 102–14.

———. "The Confederate Theatre: Richmond, Theatre Capital of the Confederacy." *Lincoln Herald* 77 (Fall 1975): 158–67.

———. "The Confederate Theatre: Theatre Personalities and Practices during the Confederacy." *Lincoln Herald* 76 (Winter 1974): 187–95.

———. "The Confederate Theatre: The Confederate Drama." *Lincoln Herald* 77 (Spring 1975): 33–41.

Thomas, Emory M. *The Confederate Nation: 1861–1865*. New York: Harper and Row, 1979.

Thompson, W. Fletcher, Jr. *The Image of War: The Pictorial Reporting of the American Civil War*. New York: Yoseloff, 1961.

Thompson, William Y. "Sanitary Fairs of the Civil War." *Civil War History* 4 (March 1958): 51–67.

Thornbough, Emma Lou. *T. Thomas Fortune, Militant Journalist*. Chicago: University of Chicago Press, 1972.

Tolley, Howard. *Children and War: Political Socialization to International Conflict.* New York: Teachers College Press, 1973.

Trelease, Allen W. *White Terror: The Ku Klux Klan Conspiracy and Southern Reconstruction.* New York: Harper and Row, 1971.

Trulock, Alice Rains. *In the Hands of Providence: Joshua L. Chamberlain and the American Civil War.* Chapel Hill: University of North Carolina Press, 1992.

"Turbulent Times in Shelbyville County, 1861–1865." *Indiana History Bulletin* 38 (May 1961): 75–93.

Tuttle, William M., Jr. *"Daddy's Gone to War": The Second World War in the Lives of America's Children.* New York: Oxford University Press, 1993.

Underwood, Betsy Swint. "War Seen through a Teen-Ager's Eyes." *Tennessee Historical Quarterly* 20 (June 1961): 177–87.

Veder, Robin. " 'Julia, Daughter of Stonewall': Julia Thomas Jackson." *Virginia Cavalcade* 46 (Summer 1996): 4–19.

Vinovskis, Maris A. "Schooling and Poor Children in Nineteenth-Century America." *American Behavioral Scientist* 35 (January/February 1991): 313–31.

Walker, Cam. "Corinth: The Story of a Contraband Camp." *Civil War History* 20 (March 1974): 5–22.

Warde, Mary Jane. "Now the Wolfe Has Come: The Civilian Civil War in the Indian Territory." *Chronicles of Oklahoma* 71 (Spring 1993): 64–87.

Washburn, Charles G. *Life of John W. Weeks.* Boston: Houghton Mifflin, 1928.

Wass, Hannelore, and Charles A. Corr, eds. *Childhood and Death.* Washington, D.C.: Hemisphere, 1984.

Webber, Thomas L. *Deep Like the Rivers: Education in the Slave Quarter Community, 1831–1865.* New York: Norton, 1978.

Weis, Robert K. "To Please and Instruct the Children." *Essex Institute Historical Collections* 123 (1987): 117–49.

West, Elliott. *Growing Up with the Country: Childhood on the Far-Western Frontier.* Albuquerque: University of New Mexico Press, 1989.

West, Elliott, and Paula Petrik, eds. *Small Worlds: Children and Adolescents in America, 1850–1950.* Lawrence: University Press of Kansas, 1992.

Westall, Robert, comp. *Children of the Blitz: Memories of Wartime Childhood.* New York: Viking, 1985.

Westerhoff, John H., III. *McGuffey and His Readers: Piety, Morality, and Education in Nineteenth-Century America.* Nashville: Abingdon, 1978.

White, Deborah Gray. *Ar'n't I a Woman? Female Slaves in the Plantation South.* New York: Norton, 1985.

Whitton, Blair. *American Clockwork Toys, 1862–1900.* Exton, Pa.: Schiffer, 1981.

———. *Paper Toys of the World.* Cumberland, Md.: Hobby House Press, 1986.

Wiebe, Robert H. *The Search for Order, 1877–1920.* New York: Hill and Wang, 1967.

Wiggins, Sarah Woolfolk. "Josiah Gorgas, a Victorian Father." *Civil War History* 32 (September 1986): 229–46.

Wiggins, William H., Jr. *O Freedom! Afro-American Emancipation Celebrations.* Knoxville: University of Tennessee Press, 1987.

Wiggins, William H., Jr., and Douglas De Natale, eds. *Jubilation! African-American Celebrations in the Southeast.* Columbia: McKissick Museum, University of South Carolina, 1993.

Wiley, Bell I. *The Life of Billy Yank: The Common Soldier of the Union.* Indianapolis: Bobbs-Merrill, 1952. Reprint, Baton Rouge: Louisiana State University Press, 1971.

———. *The Life of Johnny Reb: The Common Soldier of the Confederacy.* Indianapolis: Bobbs-Merrill, 1943. Reprint, Baton Rouge: Louisiana State University Press, 1970.

———. *Southern Negroes, 1861–1865.* New York: Rinehart, 1938.

Wilkinson, Norman B. "The Brandywine Home Front during the Civil War." Pt. 2, "1862." *Delaware History* 10 (April 1963): 197–234.

Willard, Charlotte. "Panoramas, the First 'Movies.' " *Art in America* 47 (1959): 65–69.

Williams, Anne D. *Jigsaw Puzzles: An Illustrated History and Price Guide.* Radnor, Pa.: Wallace-Homestead, 1990.

Williams, R. Hal. *Years of Decision: American Politics in the 1890s.* New York: John Wiley and Sons, 1978.

Williamson, Joel. *The Crucible of Race: Black-White Relations in the American South since Emancipation.* New York: Oxford University Press, 1984.

Wilson, Charles Reagan. *Baptized in Blood: The Religion of the Lost Cause, 1865–1920.* Athens: University of Georgia Press, 1980.

Wilson, Edmund. *Patriotic Gore: Studies in the Literature of the American Civil War.* New York: Oxford University Press, 1962.

Wilson, John Scott. "Race and Manners for Southern Girls and Boys: 'The Miss Minerva' Books and Race Relations in a Southern Children's Series." *Journal of American Culture* 17 (Fall 1994): 69–74.

Wilson, Woodrow. *Division and Reunion, 1829–1909.* New York: Longman's, 1909.

Winn, Marie. *Children without Childhood.* New York: Pantheon, 1981.

Wolf, Anna W. M. *Our Children Face War.* Boston: Houghton Mifflin, 1942.

Wolfenstein, Martha, and Gilbert Kliman. *Children and the Death of a President: Multi-Disciplinary Studies.* Graden City, N.Y.: Doubleday, 1965.

Woodward, C. Vann. *Tom Watson: Agrarian Rebel.* New York: Rinehart, 1938.

Wyatt-Brown, Bertram. *Southern Honor: Ethics and Behavior in the Old South.* New York: Oxford University Press, 1982.

Youcha, Geraldine. *Minding the Children: Child Care in America from Colonial Times to the Present.* New York: Scribner, 1995.

Yundt, Thomas M. *A History of the Bethany Orphans Home of the Reformed Church in the United States.* Reading, Pa.: Daniel Miller, 1888.

Zeitlin, Richard H. *Old Abe the War Eagle: A True Story of the Civil War and Reconstruction.* Madison: State Historical Society of Wisconsin, 1986.

Zelizer, Viviana A. *Pricing the Priceless Child: The Changing Social Value of Children.* New York: BasicBooks, 1985.

Zeringer, Lillian. "The Brandywine Home Front during the Civil War, Part III: 1863." *Delaware History* 11 (October 1964): 111–48.

————. "The Brandywine Home Front during the Civil War, Part IV: 1864–1865." *Delaware History* 11 (October 1965): 301–29.

————. *The History of Poydras Home.* New Orleans: n.p., 1977.

UNPUBLISHED DISSERTATIONS, THESES, AND PAPERS

Anders, Steven E. "History of Child Welfare in Cincinnati, 1790–1930." Ph.D. diss., Miami University of Ohio, 1981.

Bardaglio, Peter W. "On the Border: Children and the Politics of War in Maryland, 1861–1865." Paper presented at the annual meeting of the Organization of American Historians, Chicago, March 1996.

Bellows, Barbara Lawrence. "Tempering the Wind: The Southern Response to Urban Poverty, 1850–1865." Ph.D. diss. University of South Carolina, 1983.

Berman, Robert Franklin. "The Naive Child and the Competent Child: American Literature for Children and the American Culture, 1830–1930." Ph.D. diss., Harvard University, 1978.

Dulberger, Judith Ann. "Refuge or Repressor: The Role of the Orphan Asylum in the Lives of Poor Children and Their Families in Late Nineteenth-Century America." Ph.D. diss., Carnegie-Mellon University, 1988.

Ferry, Henry Justin. "Francis James Grimké: Portrait of a Black Puritan." Ph.D. diss., Yale University, 1970.

Gardner, Sarah Elizabeth. " 'Blood and Irony': Southern Women's Narratives of the Civil War, 1861–1915." Ph.D. diss., Emory University, 1996.

Glade, Mary Elizabeth. "The Boy Gangs of Richmond: A Juvenile Search for Manhood after the Civil War." Paper presented at the annual meeting of the Organization of American Historians, Chicago, March 1996.

Gold, O. David. "The Soldiers' Orphans' Schools of Pennsylvania, 1864–1889." Ph.D. diss., University of Maryland, 1971.

Hedgbeth, Llewellyn H. "Extant American Panoramas: Moving

Entertainments of the Nineteenth Century." Ph.D. diss., New York University, 1977.

Helpker, Wilma. "An Analysis of Child-Rearing Literature from 1860 to 1890." Ph.D. diss., University of Nebraska, 1976.

Kennerly, Sarah Law. "Confederate Juvenile Imprints: Children's Books and Periodicals Published in the Confederate States of America, 1861–1865." Ph.D. diss., University of Michigan, 1956.

Kirk, Robert William. "Hey Kids! The Mobilization of American Children in the Second World War." Ph.D. diss., University of California, Davis, 1991.

Krug, Donna Rebecca Donde. "The Folks Back Home: The Confederate Homefront during the Civil War." Ph.D. diss., University of California, Irvine, 1990.

Leffler, John J. "From the Shadows into the Sun: Americans in the Spanish-American War." Ph.D. diss., University of Texas, Austin, 1991.

MacCann, Donnarae, C. "The White Supremacy Myth in Juvenile Books about Blacks, 1830–1900." Ph.D. diss., University of Iowa, 1988.

McGlone, Robert Elno. "Suffer the Children: The Emergence of Modern Middle Class Family Life in America, 1820–1870." Ph.D. diss., University of California, Los Angeles, 1971.

Pflieger, Patricia Ann. "A Visit to Merry's Museum; or, Social Values in a Nineteenth-Century American Periodical for Children." Ph.D. diss., University of Minnesota, 1987.

Pope, Christie Farnham. "Preparation for Pedestals: North Carolina Antebellum Female Seminaries." Ph.D. diss., University of Chicago, 1977.

Rotundo, E. Anthony. "Manhood in America: The Northern Middle Class, 1770–1920." Ph.D. diss., Brandeis University, 1981.

Schuller, M. Viatora. "A History of Catholic Orphan Homes in the United States from 1727 to 1884." Ph.D. diss., Loyola University of Chicago, 1954.

Stone, Jane Clement. "The Evolution of Civil War Novels for Children." Ph.D. diss., Ohio State University, 1990.

Walters, Thomas Jean. "Music of the Great Sanitary Fairs: Culture and Charity in the American Civil War." Ph.D. diss., University of Pittsburgh, 1989.

Wickman, Richard Carl. "An Evaluation of the Employment of Panoramic Scenery in the Nineteenth-Century Theatre." Ph.D. diss., Ohio State University, 1961.

Index

Fremaux, Celine, 107, 160–61, 170, 207
Fremaux, Leon, 107
Frémont, John C., and Jessie Benton, 183
Friend, Jane, 193, 207
Front Royal, Va., 142
Frosts, William Goodell, 238
Fuller, Elizabeth, 112
Furness, Marion Ramsey, 155

Gaillard, Franklin, 88
Gallatin, Tenn., 155
Games, war-related, 16
Gangs, boy, in Confederacy, 163
Gannett, William C., 281 (n. 65)
Garfield, James, 76, 94
Garland, Hamlin, 204–6
Garland, Richard, 204–6
Garrison, Francis J., 237
Garrison, William Lloyd, 237
Georgia Military Institute, 166
Georgia Relief and Hospital Association, 229
Gettysburg, Pa., 215–16
Gettysburg, battle of, 105–6, 111, 125
Gilder, Jeannette, 114, 162, 163
Girls' High School (Portland, Maine), 284 (n. 7)
Goodnow, James, and sons, 89–92, 95
Gordon, Krilla, 77
Grady, Henry, 220
Grand Army of the Republic, 206, 212, 213, 217, 220, 299 (n. 44)
Grand Review, 191 (ill.)
Grant, Fred, 154
Grant, Jesse, 103, 154
Grant, Julia Dent, 161
Grant, Nellie, 117, 183 (ill.)
Grant, Ulysses S., 154, 234
Gray, Nelly, 139
Green, Rosa, 128
Green, Sarah Anne, 137
Gregory, Addie Hibbard, 117–18

Grenada, Mo., 178
Grimké, Archibald, 201
Grimké, Francis, 176, 199, 201
Grimké, Sara and Angelina, 199
Grosport, N.C., 136
Gulf War, 1

Hagerstown, Md., 156
Hall, James, 84, 92
Hampton, Jestin, 94
Hampton, Thomas B., 94
Hampton, Wade, 232
Hampton, Va., 132
Hampton Institute, 135–36
Harben, Will N., 225
Hardin, John Wesley, 166, 194, 198
Harpers Ferry, Va., 101
Harper's Weekly, 11, 14
Harris, David Golightly, 171
Harris, Joel Chandler, 224–25
Harris, William D., 136
Harrisburg, Pa., 125, 216
Haskins, Nannie, 157
Hawks, Alice, 118–19
Hawthorne, Sally, 171
Hayes, Rutherford B., 213
Heffelfinger, Jacob, 74, 85
Heg, Hans, 81, 116
Helena, Ark., 130, 196
Hewins, Caroline M., 180
Higginson, Thomas Wentworth, 49–50, 74–75
Highgate, Edmonia, 136
Hilby, Hattie, 172
Hillsboro (North Carolina) Military Academy, 166
Hitchcock, Henry, 82
Hogg, James Steven, 230
Holmes, Oliver Wendell, Jr., 189
Holocaust, 1, 159
Honor, as motivation for military service, 82
Hope and Glory, 1
Hough, Alfred Lacy, 76
Houston, Tex., 198
Howard, O. O., 215

Howard University, 200, 238
Huckaby, Leander, 99
Hull, Lucy, 124
Humiston, Amos, 215
Huntington, Henry, 170

Institute of Reward for Orphans of
    Patriots, 14–15
Ireland, 159

Jackson, Andrew, 229
Jackson, Julia, 78, 218–19
Jackson, Thomas "Stonewall," 8,
    52, 59, 75, 218–19
Jacobs, Harriet, 65
Jewett, Sarah Orne, 222–23
Johnny Tremain, 1
Johnson, Alice, 136
Johnson, Andrew, 130
Johnson, Anna, 175
Johnson, Jane, 202
Johnson, Mary Ellen, 195
Jones, Mrs. F. C., 114
Jones, Hugh N., 85
Jones, John B., 121, 156
Jones, Joshua, 68
Junior Confederate Memorial Asso-
    ciation, 218
Junior Hollywood Memorial Asso-
    ciation, 218

Keeler, Jane, 174
Kimmel, Michael, 240–41
King, Grace, 141, 146–47, 225–26
King, Margaret, 77, 97
King, Philander, 77
Kingsbury, Willie, 164, 181
Knickerbocker, The, 98
Ku Klux Klan, 198–99, 200, 217

Lakin, C. J., 85
Lamb, Matilda, 81
Lanier, Eliza Ann, 109
League of Nations, 236
Le Conte, Emma, 114, 178, 207
Le Conte, Joseph, 114

Lee, Robert E., 108, 110, 125, 253
    (n. 8)
Lenroot, Clara, 177, 208
Leslie, Mandy, 139
Levi, Keeler, 174
Lewis, Thomas, 138
Lexington, Va., 144, 148
Libby Prison, 108, 177, 204
Lifton, Robert Jay, 144
Limber, Jim, 125–26, 175–76
Lincoln, Abraham, 5, 14, 58, 103,
    117, 149, 152, 157, 158, 202, 203,
    218, 219, 229; assassination of,
    118, 189, 208–11
Lincoln, Tad, 103, 161–62
Lincoln, Willie, 161–62
Lincoln University, 199
Lindsley, Margaret Lawrence, 121
Literature: children's, 19, 31–52;
    prewar, 23–24; African Ameri-
    cans in, 24, 33, 36, 37, 42–45,
    52; patriotism in, 34, 36–37;
    description of soldiers' experi-
    ences in, 34–35; drummer boys
    in, 35–36; children's relation-
    ships with soldiers in, 37; chil-
    dren's increased responsibilities
    during war in, 38–39; war as
    moral test in, 39–40; description
    of South in, 40–41; southern
    Unionists in, 41–42, 255 (n. 20);
    children's philanthropy in,
    42–43; boys as heroes of, 45–46;
    girls as heroes of, 46–47; in
    South, 50–52, 257 (n. 38);
    alphabets, 51–52, 257 (n. 39);
    postwar, 187–88; by adult chil-
    dren of war, 222–27
Little American, 254 (n. 15)
Little Corporal, The, 66
Little Fork Rangers (boys' com-
    pany), 160
Little Pilgrim, The, 42–43, 45
Little Women, 70–71
Livingston, Ala., 217
Lodge, Henry Cabot, 190, 235–37

Longfellow, Charlie, 117
Longfellow, Henry Wadsworth, 117, 209
Lord, Mrs. W. W., 109
Lost Cause, 218–20, 224–26, 228, 236–37, 238
Loughborough, Mary A., 109
Louisville, Ky., 123, 211
L'Ouverture, Toussaint, 65, 154
Low, Juliette, 142
Lucas, Mary Jane, 124
Lynching, 199, 231, 232, 233, 238–39

McClellan, George B., 154, 234
McClendon, Charlie, 139
MacCorkle, William A., 116, 170
McCreary, Albertus, 106, 111
McCurdy, Charles, 105
MacDonald, Cornelia, 104–5
McDonald, W. N., 219–20
McEnery, Ruth, 225–26
McGuffey's Readers, 142
McIver, George Wilcox, 222
McKinley, William, 237
McLeague, Eliza, 157
McMaster, John Bach, 107
McMurtrey, M. A., 92
Macon, Ga., 122, 160
Magazines: for children, 31–32, 33–44; in South, 50–51; for African Americans, 61–66; postwar, 190–92
Manhood, models of, 240–41
Manuals, child-rearing, 19
Marianna, Fla., 200
Marietta, battle of, 84
Marmion, Annie P., 101
Marshall, C. K., 15
Marshall, Thomas R., 233
Martin, Robert, 121, 185
Massachusetts State Industrial School for Girls, 169
Maury, Nannie Belle, 165
Meacham, J. G., 86
Memminger, Christopher, 12, 172

Memorial Bazaar, 192
Memorial Day, 203, 216
Memory, of Civil War children, 26–28, 101–2, 188–90, 192–94, 201–2, 204–39
Memphis, Tenn., 130, 198
Meridian, Miss., 136
Merrimack, USS, 81
Mexico, 124
Michaux, Jacob, 107–8
Miller, Andrew, 155
Milwaukee, Wis., 211, 234
Minor, Eddy, 74
Mixon, Liza, 138
Mobile, Ala., 111, 168, 196, 262 (n. 72)
Monroe County, Miss., 198
Montfort, Theodore, 88, 171
Montgomery County, Tenn., 217
Moore, Mrs. M. B., 57, 59
Moore, Martha, 152–53, 194
Moran, Dennis, 256 (n. 28)
Moravians, 124
Morong, A. B., 117
Morrison, Phoebe, 115
Mothers, 21–22, 165; correspondence with husbands, 69–70, 76–78; responses to war-time conditions, 111–16
Mott, D. C., 208
Murfree, Mary Noailles (Charles Egbert Craddock), 224
Murfreesboro, Tenn., 9, 129
Myriopticon, The, 187

Nagel, Charles, 124
Nantucket, Mass., 119
Nashville, Tenn., 122, 131, 153, 168
Natchez, Miss., 122, 130, 157
National Association for the Advancement of Colored People, 201, 238
National Homestead (Gettysburg), 215, 216–17
National Soldiers' and Sailors' Orphans' Home, 211

Rable, George C., 69
Raleigh, N.C., 124
Ramsey, Margaret Lawrence, 153
Randolph-Macon College, 228
Read, Opie, 103, 106–7, 141–42, 153
Reagan, John, 230
Reconstruction, 188
Republican Party, 6–7, 153, 155,
    193, 198, 200, 216, 220, 223, 234,
    235–37
Revere, Lucretia, 192
Revere, Paul, 192
Rhodes, James Ford, 220
Rice, John H., 54
Rice, Spotswood, 92
Richardson, Caroline, 137
Richmond, Va., 107–8, 125–26, 133,
    139, 141, 144, 155, 163, 164, 168,
    172, 178, 192, 218
Rigger, Charlie, 139
Riley, Norman, 68
Robertson, Anna, 208
Robertson, George F., 192–93
Rock Island, Ill., 181
Rockland, Del., 150–51
Rogers, Frank, 173–74
Rogers, Mrs. M. A., 253 (n. 9), 268
    (n. 24)
Roosevelt, Theodore, 190, 200,
    233–34, 237, 241
Rose, Anne, 194
Rosedale Seminary, 125
Ross, Elizabeth W., 180
Ross, Minnie, 138
Ruffin, Edmund, 149
Rutherfordton, N.C., 163

St. Anthony's Orphanage, 153
St. Cecilia Academy, 124
St. Landry Parish, La., 198
St. Louis, Mo., 176, 183, 211, 226
Sanitary Fairs, 11, 19–20, 117, 118,
    180–83
Santa Claus, 120–22
Schoolbooks: antebellum, 23–24,
    52–53; Confederate, 32–33,

52–59; Union, 59–61; for Afri-
    can Americans, 61–66; postwar,
    219–20, 301 (n. 57)
Schools, 23, 219–20; in South,
    13–14, 53–54, 124; for African
    Americans, 132–36, 151–52, 196–
    97, 198; patriotism in, 150–54;
    fund-raising by, 181–82
Sea Islands, S.C., 129, 132, 133, 134,
    151
Secession, 41, 58–59, 149
Second World War, 1, 29–30, 159,
    206, 251 (n. 34), 286 (n. 24), 291
    (n. 54)
Segregation, 238, 240
Sessions, Ruth Huntington, 3,
    167–68
Sewell, Alfred L., 184–85
Shanghai, China, 1
Sharp, Helen, 72
Shaw, Anna Howard, 167, 174,
    207–8
Shaw, Robert Gould, 235
Shelter for Orphans of Colored Sol-
    diers and Friendless Colored
    Children, 212
Sheppard, Louisa, 170
Sherman, William T., 122, 140, 142,
    199, 234
Sherman, Tex., 219
Shippery, Eliza, 141
Sivley, Jane, 96
Sivley, Willie, 96
Sixth Massachusetts Regiment, 164
Skinner, Charlie, 164, 165–66
Skipworth Landing, Ark., 132
Slaughter, Billy, 201–2
Smith, Edward Parmelee, 35, 85
Soldiers, 6, 116; historiography of,
    1, 243 (n. 2); and African Ameri-
    cans, 10; on children as motiva-
    tion for fighting, 11–12; dreams
    of, 68–69; as fathers, 68–100;
    worries about families' health,
    72–74, 94; African American sol-
    diers, 74–75; encounters with

other children, 74–75; fear of being forgotten, 75–76; sending home presents, 79–80; military service as duty to family, 81–83; descriptions of war in letters to children, 83–86; advice to children, 87–93, 99; advice to wives, 93–95; brothers' advice to siblings, 95–97; fear of death, 97; and African American children, 136–41; and white children, 141–45, 165–66; as veterans, 190, 204–7

Soldiers' Orphans' Homes, 211–17

Sons of Confederate Veterans, 217–18

Sousa, John Philip, 117

South Carolina, 198

Southern Boys' and Girls' Monthly, 192

South Mountain, battle of, 154

Spalding, Genie, 115

Spanish-American War, 234, 305–6 (n. 93)

Spartanburg, S.C., 202

Spartanburg (S.C.) Methodist Sunday School Relief Society, 178–79

Spencer, Lilly Martin, 12

Spiegel, Marcus, 12, 81, 85, 116

Stanley, Sara G., 136

Starbuck, Mary Eliza, 119, 204, 209

Stationery, war-related, 17

Stearns, Nellie, 135

Stebbins, Laura W., 84–85

Steele, John and Sarah, 119–20

Steele, Samuel A., 149, 297–98 (n. 37)

Stein, Gertrude, 186

Stem, Leander, 78

Stephens, Winston, 69

Stimson, William R., 86

Stokes, William, 69, 76

Stone, Emma, 161

Stone, Jimmy, 123

Stone, Johnny, 123

Stone, Kate, 123, 166

Stone, Walter, 166

Stonewall Jackson Institute, 219

Stratton, Charles, 151

Student and Schoolmate, The, 33, 40–41

Sturtevant, Helen, 77

Sturtevant, Josiah, 77

Sublett, Emmie, 141

Sullivan, James, 105, 154

Sumner, Charles, 235

Sunday schools, 197

Tama County, Iowa, 164

Tarbell, Ida, 208

Taylor, Zachary, 229

Tennessee, 183

Tenth United States Cavalry, 200

Texas, 124, 128, 134, 195, 197

Thirkield, Wilbur P., 238

Thomas, Ella Gertrude Clanton, 121

Thompson, Corry, 72

Thompson, Mitchell, 72

Tillman, Benjamin, 232–33, 239

Towne, Laura, 134, 135, 151–52

Trowbridge, J. T., 35, 40, 41–42

Troy Female Seminary, 118

Tuskegee Institute, 238

Twenty-fifth United States Colored Troops, 139

Twenty-first United States Colored Troops, 196

Tyler, Jane, 172

Tyler, Tex., 123

Union Home School for the Children of Volunteers, 15

Union League, 153

United Confederate Veterans, 217–18

United Daughters of the Confederacy, 217–19, 221

United States Christian Commission, 35

United States Sanitary Commission, 5, 6, 36–37, 38, 180–85, 215; Northwestern Branch, 181
Utica, N.Y., 223

Valentine, Andrew, 79
Vallandigham, Clement, 149, 153
Vardaman, James K., 231, 239
Vaughan, James Archer, 155–56
Vicksburg, Miss., 103, 109, 115, 123, 128–29, 144–45, 166
Vietnam War, 1, 5, 144, 206
Vincent, Elizabeth Kipp, 117

Wallace, William, 108
Walton, William, 81
Ward, B. F., 231
Ward, Evelyn, 160, 221
Ward, William, 160
Wardwell, Ernest, 164
Warrenton, Va., 155
"War Spirit at Home," 12
Washington, Booker T., 126, 127, 174, 195, 201, 203, 241
Washington, D.C., 131
Washington Arsenal, 173
Watson, Tom, 231–32, 235, 239
Watson, William, 84
Wells, Rolla, 117
Wesleyan Female College, 160
West, John, 75, 86
West Point, 199
Whatley, Nannie, 79, 94
Whatley, William, 79, 94
Wheatley, Phillis, 65
Wheeler, Joseph, 138, 140, 161

White, Cyrus, 136
Wideawakes, 193
Wiebe, Robert, 240
Wilder, Laura Ingalls, 204
Wilderness, battle of the, 36, 88, 116
Wiley, Bell I., 69–70
Wiley, Calvin Henderson, 13, 41
Wilkins, B. H., 163, 193
Williams, Dosia, 142–43
Williams, John Sharp, 230
Williamson, Alice, 155
Williamson, Joel, 238–39
Williamson, Sarah Cook, 118
Wilson, Amos, 136
Wilson, Edmund, 302–3 (n. 66)
Wilson, Woodrow, 229–30, 233, 234
Winfree, Sally, 172
Woman's Soldiers' Aid Society of Northern Ohio, 181
Women, during Civil War: historiography of, 1, 243–44 (n. 3)
Woodward, Delia White, 142
Woodworth, Lizette, 149, 208, 209
Works Progress Administration, interviews with former slaves, 27–28, 252 (n. 39)
Wright, Mrs. D. Giraud, 221
"Writing to Father," 80
Wytheville, Va., 163

Yates, Richard, Jr., 101
Yonkers, N.Y., 162
York County, S.C., 198
Young, Joseph, 72, 83, 88